W9-ABM-237

Latin poetry in verse translat

3 0301 00034815 7

1958

LATIN POETRY

IN VERSE TRANSLATION

Riverside Editions

RIVERSIDE EDITIONS

UNDER THE GENERAL EDITORSHIP OF

Gordon N. Ray

LATIN POETRY

IN VERSE TRANSLATION

From the Beginnings to the Renaissance

EDITED BY

L. R. Lind

UNIVERSITY OF KANSAS

HOUGHTON MIFFLIN COMPANY

BOSTON · The Riverside Press Cambridge

LIBRARY
College of St. Francis
JOLIET, ILL.

COPYRIGHT ©, 1957, BY L. R. LIND

ALL RIGHTS RESERVED

The Riverside Press

CAMBRIDGE, MASSACHUSETTS

PRINTED IN THE U.S.A.

———————

ACKNOWLEDGMENTS AND COPYRIGHT NOTICES

AN ANTHOLOGY is always the work of other people: the anthologist merely recognizes the need for a collection and organizes the effort which brings it together in a book. This one represents eight years of assembling contributions and carrying on a far-flung correspondence, part of which has resulted in the production of many hitherto unpublished items. I should like to express my deep appreciation for kind assistance of various sorts freely and willingly given me by many friends, colleagues, and correspondents here and abroad. I wish to single out for special mention Mr. Eugene Magner, of the Lockwood Memorial Library, The University of Buffalo, for his prolonged and untiring efforts to unearth material from that remarkable collection of poetry; James Laughlin for reading the manuscript in its earlier stages and making many valuable critical judgments as well as obtaining contributions; Gilbert Highet, Hubert Creekmore, Rolfe Humphries, and Kenneth Rexroth for expert advice and contributions; Richmond Lattimore, Ray West, Jr., and R. W. Stallman for putting me in touch with translators and books; C. K. Hyder and John E. Hankins for several useful suggestions and to the latter for a contribution; Dudley Fitts and C. M. Bowra for helpful letters; Peter Russell, editor of Nine, who arranged a number of excellent contributions; Frances Fletcher for her contributions and for her courage in taking up my challenge to translate all of Propertius; Miss Nellie Barnes for showing me J. S. Blake-Reed's translations of Horace; Prof. T. O. Mabbott for bringing Edgar Allan Poe's translation to my attention; G. S. Fraser for his cooperation and permission to use his printed and unprinted translations; and Very Reverend Martin C. D'Arcy, S.J., for allowing me to reprint Gerard Manley Hopkins' recently discovered versions; the staff of the University of Kansas Library for patient assistance of a most important kind, including inter-library loan; to many contributors whose offerings I could not

871.08
L744

include, my regrets, and hearty thanks, as well as to a number of well-wishers who wrote me during the book's progress; and to my wife for constant assistance and encouragement: she has earned a dedication.

For hitherto unpublished contributions I wish to thank Leonard Albert, Don Cameron Allen, my old friend and colleague, Richard A. Bell, the British publisher, Robert A. Brooks, Myron H. Broomell, Zechariah Chafee, Jr., Albert Cook, Hubert Creekmore, J. V. Cunningham, Robert Fitzgerald, Frances Fletcher, Mary Grant, Anne Greet, John G. Hawthorne, Barbara J. Hodge, Asa M. Hughes, Rolfe Humphries, Geoffrey Johnson, Robie Macauley, John Angus Macnab, W. Taylor McLeod, W. K. Newton, John Frederick Nims, The Reverend William J. Philbin, Ezra Pound, Robert R. Schnorr, Muriel Spark, and Louis Zukofsky.

Acknowledgments are also due the following copyright proprietors for permission to reprint translations; I wish also to thank the translators who have given a similar permission.

Richard Aldington, for his versions from the Renaissance Humanists from *Medallions,* Chatto and Windus, London, 1930.

Lucius Beebe for his version of Horace printed in "The Conning Tower" of *The New York World.*

G. Bell and Sons Ltd., London, for Sir Richard Jebb's Catullus 34 from *Translations* by R. C. Jebb, H. Jackson, and W. E. Currey.

Walter J. Black, for Horace's Satire I, 8 from *Selected Poems of Horace* by George F. Whicher, Classics Club, copyright 1947 by Walter J. Black; reprinted by permission of Walter J. Black, Inc., Roslyn, N. Y.

Lady Blackett, for versions by the late Sir Basil Blackett.

The Clarendon Press, Oxford, for Robert Bridges' version of Vergil, *Aeneid* VI, from *Ibant Obscuri, an experiment in the classical hexameter,* 1916, also published in *Poems in Classical Prosody;* and for selections from Martial first published in *Greece and Rome.*

The Cleaners' Press, Galveston, Texas, for Basil Bunting's lines from Lucretius, Book I, from his *Poems: 1950.*

Constable and Co., Ltd., London, for versions from medieval Latin by Helen Waddell, *Mediaeval Latin Lyrics,* 1929.

Andrew Dakers Ltd., London, for selections from Ausonius, Avianus, and Carmina Burana by Jack Lindsay from *Song of a Falling World: Culture during the Break-up of the Roman Empire,* 1947.

The Devin-Adair Company, New York, for selections from Ennius and Horace by John Wight, and from Horace by Richard Eberhart and Gardner Taplin, from the anthology by Richard Eberhart and Selden Rodman, *War and the Poet,* 1945.

Elkin Mathews and Marrot Ltd., London, for selections from Naevius, Lucretius, Vergil, Horace, Tibullus, and Sulpicia II by Jack Lindsay from *I Am a Roman,* 1934, and a translation from St. Columban by Jack Lindsay in *Medieval Latin Poets,* 1934.

28026

Arthur Cole, Esq., literary executor of the late Sir Stephen Gaselee, for a version by the latter.

Horace Gregory, and Grove Press-Evergreen Books, New York, for four translations from *The Poems of Catullus,* translated by Horace Gregory, copyright 1956.

Haldeman-Julius, Girard, Kansas, for Miriam Allen deFord's version of Juvenal, Satire III, from *Rome as Viewed by Tacitus and Juvenal,* Little Blue Books No. 899 (1925).

The Harvil Press and Editions Poetry, London, for G. S. Fraser's Epode XV of Horace from his book, *The Traveller Has Regrets,* 1948.

William Heinemann Ltd., London, for selections from Lord Dunsany, *The Odes of Horace,* 1947.

Gilbert Highet for permission to print selections from Plautus and from Publilius Syrus from his *Roman Drama in Translation: Illustrative Material for Comparative Literature 252,* Columbia University, mimeograph.

Henry Holt and Company, Inc., New York, for Horace's Ode IV, 7 from *Collected Poems* by A. E. Housman; copyright, 1940, by Henry Holt and Company, Inc.; by permission of the publishers.

The editors of *The Hudson Review,* for Robert Fitzgerald's Catullus 101 and Horace, Ode I, 25, copyright by Robert Fitzgerald, 1955; for Joseph Bennett's version of Horace, Ode I, 5, copyright by Joseph Bennett, 1951; and for Vergil's Eclogue I by John Thompson, Jr., reprinted from *The Hudson Review,* Vol. VII, No. 3, Autumn 1954, copyright 1954 by The Hudson Review, Inc.

Alfred A. Knopf, Inc., New York, for the translation of Hadrian's "Address to His Soul," reprinted from *Collected Poems of Elinor Wylie,* by permission of Alfred A. Knopf, Inc., copyright 1932 by Alfred A. Knopf, Inc.; and for Gilbert Highet's translations from Horace, Odes I,5, I,33, I,38, and III,13, reprinted from *Poets in a Landscape* by Gilbert Highet, by permission of Alfred A. Knopf, Inc., copyright 1957 by Gilbert Highet.

F. L. Lucas, for selections from the Carmina Epigraphica from his *Authors Dead and Living,* Chatto and Windus, London, 1926.

Martin Secker and Warburg Ltd., London, for Arthur Symons' translations of Catullus from his *Collected Works* and from *Catullus: Chiefly Concerning Lesbia,* 1924.

New Directions, New York and Norfolk, Connecticut, for Vergil's Eclogue IV, by James Laughlin, copyright 1939 by J. Laughlin, reprinted by permission of New Directions; for Vergil's Georgic I from *In the Rose of Time* by Robert Fitzgerald, copyright 1956 by Robert Fitzgerald, reprinted by permission of New Directions; for Petronius I–VIII reprinted from *The Signature of All Things* by Kenneth Rexroth, all rights reserved; for selections from Abelard and from Sulpicius Lupercus Servasius, Jr., from *The Phoenix and the Tortoise* by Kenneth Rexroth, copyright 1945 by New Directions, reprinted by permission of New Directions; and for selections from *The Goliard*

Poets by George F. Whicher, copyright 1949 by George F. Whicher, reprinted by permission of New Directions.

The New Mexico Quarterly Review for J. V. Cunningham's Decimus Laberius from Vol. 16 (1946) and the "Confession of Bishop Golias" from Vol. 15 (1945).

The editor of *The Nineteenth Century and After,* London, for H. W. Household's Catullus 96.

Oxford University Press, New York, for Vergil's Eclogue III from *Short Is the Time* by C. Day Lewis; © 1940, 1943 by Oxford University Press, Inc.; reprinted by permission.

Oxford University Press, London, for Ode I,22 from Sir William Marris' translation of *The Odes of Horace;* and for Gerard Manley Hopkins' translation of the "Rhythmus ad SS. Sacramentum" of St. Thomas Aquinas, from *Poems of Gerard Manley Hopkins.*

The Phoenix Press, London, and *Translation,* until recently published by Neville Braybrooke and Elizabeth King, for selections by M. H. Tattersall from Catullus, Edmund Blunden from Horace, and G. S. Fraser from Horace.

Random House, Inc., New York, for "Solvitur Acris Hiems" (Horace, Ode I,4) translated by Louis MacNeice in *Poems 1925–1940* by Louis MacNeice, copyright 1937, 1939, 1940 by Louis MacNeice. Reprinted by permission of Random House, Inc., and of Faber and Faber Limited, London.

The Rarity Press, New York, for selections from Petronius by Jack Lindsay in *The Complete Works of Gaius Petronius,* 1932.

Routledge and Kegan Paul Ltd., London, for selections from Plautus from F. A. Wright, *Three Roman Poets,* 1938; for selections from Johannes Secundus from F. A. Wright, *The Love Poems of Johannes Secundus,* 1930; and for translations from Lucretius, Catullus, Horace (Ode II,11), Ovid, Propertius, Lucan, and Juvenal by Gilbert Highet.

Peter Russell, editor of *Nine,* London, for permission to reprint George Santayana's and G. S. Fraser's versions from Tibullus, from *Nine,* No. 2, Winter 1949–50.

Charles Scribner's Sons, New York, for a selection from Petronius from *Selected Poems* by John Peale Bishop, copyright 1941 by John Peale Bishop and reprinted by permission of Charles Scribner's Sons; for "The Vigil of Venus" from *Poems 1922–1947* by Allen Tate, copyright 1947 by Charles Scribner's Sons and reprinted by their permission; for selections reprinted from *The Aeneid of Virgil: A Verse Translation* by Rolfe Humphries, copyright 1951 by Charles Scribner's Sons, used by permission of the publishers; for E. A. Robinson's version of Horace, Ode I,11, from *Children of the Night,* 1897; and for two versions of Martial by L. R. Lind from Hubert Creekmore, ed., *A Little Treasury of World Poetry,* 1952.

Sheed and Ward, Inc., New York, for three selections from *Horace: A Portrait* by Alfred Noyes, copyright 1947, Sheed and Ward, Inc., New York.

The Society of Authors, London, as the Literary Representative of the Trustees of the Estate of the late A. E. Housman, and Messrs. Jonathan Cape Ltd., publishers of A. E. Housman's *Collected Poems*, for a version of Horace's Ode IV,7.

The Sylvan Press, London, for a selection from Catullus by Jack Lindsay in *The Complete Poems of Catullus*, 1948.

The University of Chicago Press, for a selection from Paul the Deacon by Howard Mumford Jones from P. S. Allen, *Medieval Latin Lyrics*, 1931.

The University of Illinois Press, for permission to reprint my version of Hildebert of Le Mans, Seneca's Epitaph, from my edition of Reginald of Canterbury, *Vita Sancti Malchi*, 1942.

The University of Kansas City Review, for John E. Hankins' version of Ovid's *Metamorphoses*, in the volumes for 1934–35, and for Howard Mumford Jones' translation of "Dies Irae," 1934.

The University of North Carolina Press, for selections from Claudian, Octavianus, Ausonius, and Alcuin, translated by H. M. Jones, from P. S. Allen, *The Romanesque Lyric*, 1928.

A. P. Watt and Son, London; Martin Secker and Warburg Ltd., London; and Mrs. James Elroy Flecker; for two translations from Catullus in *The Collected Poems of James Elroy Flecker*, 1916.

Whitehead Morris, of Alexandria, Egypt, and Mr. J. S. Blake-Reed, Judge of the Mixed Court of Appeal, for selections from Mr. Blake-Reed's *More Odes of Horace Rendered into English*, 1944.

FOR ELENA

"Dulce razón de la jornada"

CONTENTS

OVID

INTRODUCTION

by L. R. Lind

THE WORLD OF THE LATIN POETS, especially those of the Augustan Age and of the first century after Christ, is perhaps closer to us today than it has been for more than fifty years. At least it is now possible to find translations of these poets which make Ezra Pound's remark about the great Elizabethan translators almost a prophecy: "A great age of literature is perhaps always a great age of translations; or follows it." If ours is an age of criticism and of poet-critics, it is also one of translation. Pound, Eliot, and some of their followers have demonstrated an amazing combination of skills in poetry, criticism, and translation. Their threefold talents seem to have come into ideal conjunction in our time and to be rooted in new standards of discrimination and taste.

The affinity of the modern poets for the Latins is one, first, of feeling, of a kinship both personal and social. Catullus and Lucretius, the first really great Latin poets after Plautus and Terence from whom we have complete works, lived in a society of decay and political reaction. Their protest against things as they were has, at this far end of time, its diminished echo in the poetry of England and America in the nineteen-thirties, and there is in it the same appeal to a private world, the same frustration and despair. The Latin poets after them lived in a more stable society but one which had lost its freedom. The personal tensions and struggles of Vergil, Horace, Ovid, and Propertius were resolved at last into harmonies with their world which made their poetry possible, as poetry became possible in spite of their disillusions to the poets of World War II. Since 1914 the poets of Europe and America have lived in a world threatened by totalitarianism also, although one far more sinister than that of the Augustan rule in the time of Christ. The Latin poets of the Silver Age after Nero and down to Hadrian lived too under conditions of chronic apprehension and fear toward the tyrant Domitian.

The modern translators have, of course, found more than a vague but unmistakable similarity of environment to justify their tastes in Latin poetry. Pound, here as elsewhere the pioneer, discovered in Propertius a special sense of life congenial with his own and invented not only the language but the mood in which to convey that sense of life. After him Horace Gregory rendered Catullus in somewhat the same idiom: there followed the translators presented in this volume, each with his differing affection and capacity for the Latin poets as well as the hard, sharp, clear phrases needed to translate them for our generation.

A second bond between the poets has been technique. It is not altogether a historical accident that the Latin poets have made so decisive an appeal to the modern poets. Some of the same qualities occur in the work of both Latins and moderns: a serious restraint of language, an economy and bareness of image and metaphor, a skillful use of rhetoric. Latin poetry is an unusually fruitful and instructive series of technical achievements. In fitting the Latin language to Greek meters, Lucretius, Catullus, and Horace created a group of poems unparalleled for their influence upon the history of literary technique. To say that their work, with that of Vergil, Ovid, Propertius, and Tibullus, served as the foundation for medieval and Renaissance poetry — epic, lyric, pastoral, epigram, and elegy — is a truism which bears repetition. It is in eighteenth-century English, nineteenth-century French and German, and in twentieth-century British and American verse that the poetry of the Romans, by a miracle of interpenetration and absorption, refreshed and stimulated the poets of the vernacular tongues. We are the heirs of the Roman poets in ways which criticism is only now revealing: one of them is in the renewed emphasis upon a scrupulous respect for the *craft* of poetry as distinguished from the *urge* to write it.

This is not to say, however, that such a specialized craftsmanship is in every sense an inheritance direct from the Latins. It is easy enough to insist upon our debt in the traditional themes and genres; more subtle relationships often escape us. Whatever the classical attitude may be, I am convinced that it is more than a matter of demonstrable influences, traditional material, or verbal echoes. It is a parallel phenomenon which, although altered in detail, appears in later ages as a set of similar ideals in art. For all that may be said of the technique of both modern and Latin poets is true also of the Symbolists, who have exerted a greater influence upon the moderns than the Latin poets have.

The chief characteristic of Symbolist poetry is a tendency toward "pure" poetry, relatively free from ideas as such and from romantic inspiration or subjectivity. It is written slowly, deliberately, with a disciplined choice of words and great attention to rhythms and associations. The Symbolist poem shows a high percentage of nouns and sometimes a lack of internal unity which can be traced to a habit of writing without methodical progression, in blocks or units fitted together later (Valéry, Rilke). What the Symbolists did was to pursue much the same procedure as Horace and Vergil pursued, following Catullus and the Alexandrian Greek Neoterics, the modern poets of their day. Donatus says Vergil wrote in blocks or sections out of chronological order and licked his poems into shape as a bear licks its cubs. The Alexandrians and the Latins made the poem a work of art, elaborating form often to the disadvantage of content. The Symbolists produced even less than Horace or Vergil; they felt the full distinction between *ars* (technique) and *ingenium* (natural talent). While the Latins in spite of their deliberation and practice of objectivity felt themselves as *vates,* divinely inspired bards, the Symbolists, with Mallarmé as their high priest, insisted that supreme knowledge could be attained through the practice of the craft of poetry. The Latin poets might have agreed with Valéry when he said, "Enthusiasm is not an artist's state of mind" or with Eliot's dictum, "Poetry is not a turning loose of emotion, but an escape from emotion; it is not the expression of personality but an escape from personality." They might even have concurred in Mallarmé's assertion, "It is not with ideas that one makes verses but with words." I should add in all fairness, and to avoid overstating a case which I admit cannot be completely proved, that the Latins, with their different conception of the moral life, would probably not have accepted Baudelaire's flatly declared dogma: "Many people imagine that the purpose of poetry is some sort of instruction. Poetry . . . has no other end but itself. No poem will be so great, so noble, so truly worthy of the name as that which is written simply for the sake of writing a poem."

Other links between the Latin poets and the Symbolists have suggested themselves; Ernst Howald made a tentative statement about them in his little essay, *Das Wesen der lateinischen Dichtung (The Nature of Latin Poetry)* (Zurich, 1948). Vergil uses symbols in recurring themes, as one may see in R. W. Cruttwell's *Virgil's Mind at Work* (Oxford, 1946), a book of amazing if not always convincing detail. Horace, although not profuse in metaphor, uses familiar figures and quasi-correspondences which recall Baudelaire's famous sonnet, "Correspondances." There is even a hint of Symbolist synaesthesia, the confusion of one bodily sense with another or the representation of one sense by means of another, in Vergil, *Aeneid* XII. 591, *ater odor* (black smell) . . . *murmure caeco* (blind murmur) and in Horace, Odes I, 12, 3 (*iocosa . . . imago,* jocose image, the echo). The lack of external unity in some of Horace's lyrics is a Symbolist trait, and "O fons Bandusiae" (O fountain of Bandusia), with its central theme of the repulsive bloodying of crystal waters, is in the same vein as Baudelaire's "A Carrion" or Rimbaud's "Venus Anadyomene" in its deliberate mingling of horror and beauty.

This is not the place to speak of the deep classical influences, including the irony of Petronius, upon the poetry of John Peale Bishop; of the shadow cast by Vergil on the poems of Allen Tate, Robert Lowell, and Rolfe Humphries, who have translated, respectively, the *Vigil of Venus,* an elegy of Propertius, and both Vergil's *Aeneid* and Ovid's *Metamorphoses;* or of the growing number of "re-creations" in the tone of Pound's *Personae* which have been bringing classical themes and myths to the little magazines; all this must be thoroughly discussed in a history, not yet written, of classical influences upon modern poetry. It is sufficient comfort for those who love them that the Latin poets now suffer few judgments of caprice or ignorance such as that of Hermann Hesse, to whom the temperature of Roman antiquity was always "somewhat cool" and from whose list of favorite books the names of Catullus and Propertius are missing; or of Heinrich Heine, who spoke of the Latin language as one "for military commands, governmental reports, usurers' judgments, a lapidary speech for the flinty Roman folk." Robert Fitzgerald's fine poem, "Latium," now sums up the worthiest feelings of the moderns toward Roman antiquity: and it is clear that no great literature is more complex or varied than the Latin. From Plautus to the Middle Ages, Latin writers show a wealth of mood and talent, of subtle invention and artistic development, and a series of highly individual and often incredibly sensitive personalities, a warmth, color, and depth, which defy a superficial analysis. It is not possible, of course, in a brief essay to reveal fully the separate and quite different claims to our attention of these poets; but I have sought to indicate the great variety of sophistication, and similarity in modes of thought, which the Latin and the modern poets share.

Greek poetry begins magnificently with Homer, with two complete great epics. The beginnings of Latin poetry are almost a reluctant afterthought and must be salvaged from the quotations of grammarians, orators, and other unpoetic people. These beginnings are painful and often harsh. It is as though Ennius, Naevius, and the other early poets were feeling their way in the darkness. And a sort of darkness it is: an atmosphere hostile to literature which seems to allow chiefly derivative patriotic and moralistic verse, plays or epics on mythological themes adapted from the Greek, a rude sententious joke or two. The early original Roman verse is liturgical or magical, fit only for practical purposes.

Plautus bursts upon the reader with a great gust of laughter, although it is easy to see that even he is an arrant borrower. Terence, too, more pensive and decorous, is not an original writer. Behind these writers looms the Roman rise to power and luxury in the Mediterranean; they cater to a vulgar world of social parasites who were pleased with a slapstick humor that reveals themselves more than it does the authors.

Catullus and Lucretius, with a freshness which is like rain in a desert, are the first to strike out on new paths, to exhibit their own personality, and to set a new standard of art for the Romans. The measure of their individuality is the measure of their greatness; with them begins the Roman poetry which is meaningful to the modern age. For the first time we find psychological depths and obscure tensions in Roman poetry. And after these poets we come, almost abruptly, to the Augustans.

Here at last are the "moderns" among the Romans, with a polished and versatile technique adapted for the most serious purposes: to tell the story of Rome's greatness without mere banal patriotism or to analyze personal emotions without triviality. Building upon an enriched tradition of form and theme inherited from the Greeks and shaped for the Latin language by the earlier Romans, the Augustans keep the old myths, re-work them, and make new ones. Vergil is the greatest of them. From pastoral to didactic to epic is the course of his fascinating progress — from studied simplicity which conceals its real elaboration to a profound and complex work of art before which the hackneyed question of Roman originality becomes idle and pointless. Lucretius may have been his master as a philosopher, as he is surely Vergil's most important single source of inspiration; but only Vergil knew how to turn history, myth, and philosophy into a sustained masterpiece. This is all the more true because Vergil undertook a subject in the *Aeneid* made all the more difficult by its hero, who by his very nature was destined to bear the full symbolism of Roman responsible government on its way to world empire. Aeneas is not Achilles; but the loss to us in the dramatic appeal of his character is made up by the intensity of Dido's — surely one of the half-dozen most poignantly attractive women in all Western literature. In Vergil there appears most evidently an aspect of technique which brings him close to the author of "The Waste Land." Long ago, Richard Heinze in the best book yet written on Vergil's methods (*Virgils Epische Technik*) showed how Vergil, like many a modern poet from Coleridge on, re-combined and integrated elements from hundreds of earlier poems, Latin and Greek, to form his epic. No Latin poem can prove to the modern critic more effectively than the *Aeneid* how similar are the methods of great poets and their use of traditional material. The growing present-day preoccupation of the critic with myths and psychological imagery will also find a fertile subject in Vergil's work. Perhaps one of the best illustrations of this phase of his poetry is the fusion of both history and myth into one unbroken perspective in Allen Tate's "Aeneas at Washington"; for Tate, whose poetry appears to be influenced elsewhere also by Vergil, has done what Vergil did in his long epic: he has made the myth contemporary and integral with the present.

The other great Augustans are far different men from Vergil. Where he is clairvoyant and visionary, their view of life is less mystical, more limited and personal; they are also less "national." I do not mean to say that Horace does not have his moments of elevation and absorption in an idea; the Roman Odes (the first six of the third book) are lofty and serious. But, except for occasional glimpses, especially in the fourth book of Propertius' elegies, the patriotic seer is not part of their temperaments. With them, the decline of strict social responsibility at Rome is heavily underlined. While they indulge their private fancies and amours the Roman state recedes from their thoughts into its majestic past; each of these poets in turn, Horace, Ovid (except in his most shameful adulatory passages), Propertius, and Tibullus renounce the high themes of national glory, protest that they cannot write patriotic epic, and retreat into a world of curious anxieties where their energies are spent upon love and learning. Like Marcel Proust's hero, Swann, or Italo Svevo, Proust's Italian imitator, their lives become a continuous analysis of their own weaknesses, jealousy, and despair.

Ovid deserves more attention than he is likely to receive in a brief introduction. As the years wear away, more and more men of letters and plain ordinary readers rise up and call him blessed. His astounding production in all its brilliant variety might have made a half-dozen poets famous if each of them had written only a small part of it. His wonderful imagination and his excellent rhetoric, always leisurely, never boresome, are combined in some of the world's most delightful verses to form a rich body of poetic lore which nourished the writers of the Middle Ages and Elizabethan England as well as those of the Continent as no other single poet has. Genial, urbane, witty, and charming, no praise is too high for him; the debt of Chaucer and Shakespeare alone to him is enough to place him among the greatest literary figures. In the *Metamorphoses*, which have not yet been properly analyzed for their careful structure, he is master of the iridescent, ever-fading aspect of reality; his pictures of miraculous change are like a good Walt Disney feature, but with even more delicacy and finesse. In the *Amores* and the *Art of Love* his wit is wickedly keen and his sensuous feeling for the erotic overwhelming. His skill in transitions, motivation, characterization, and general con-

struction is so good that it escapes casual notice. It is in a double
sense that we must read the opening lines of the *Art of Love:*

> If anyone among this people does not know the art of love,
> Let him read this poem and, having learned from it, let him love.

Propertius, for all his stature, is unknown to those who cannot read
Latin because there has never been an adequate English verse translation of his elegies. Pound's "Homage to Propertius" is not, and was
never intended to be, a translation. Yet for all its oddity (and it is
made of as much Pound as of Propertius) it gives us the temperament
of the poet in the chief elements of its neurotic complexity. Mingled
with his frank sexual passion there is also an irony of objective self-
analysis matched among later poets in a few lyrics of Petronius.
Propertius and the other elegiac poets dissect their emotions like the
characters of Racine and with much the same clear consciousness of
inevitable disaster. Their erotic experience is fused with elaborate
myths as if they felt that only through the great symbols could their
private sufferings be sublimated and even justified: the tragedy of
unsuccessful love is made noble in the framework of the Greek tales.

The elegiac poets are highly conscious of themselves as men of
letters. To the traditional elegiac motives of love and myth they
added the motives of literature and, in small part, national pride.
They are acutely aware of their inheritance from the Alexandrian
Greeks and salute them at every opportunity: unlike the moderns,
these poets eagerly acknowledge their sources.

What is the Roman conception of purpose in poetry? Among the
differences between Latin and modern poetry is the ancient adherence
to a tradition of utilitarianism. Strange as it may seem to us, Latin
poetry was generally not written for its own sake or for what we
consider its legitimate aesthetic values alone. It was used to express
the facts of some branch of learning or information: genealogy,
astronomy, physical science, agricultural lore, mythology, history, and
moral teaching are represented in the extant texts. The Latin epic
and epyllion (or short epic), the counterparts of the modern novel
and short story, were used in great variety for the historic-patriotic
epic (Vergil's *Aeneid*), mythological epic (Ovid's *Metamorphoses*),
didactic-scientific-philosophic epic (Lucretius' *De Rerum Natura*),
amatory-didactic epic (Ovid's *Art of Love*), and agricultural epic or
epyllion (Vergil's *Georgics*). The Romans made no fetish of originality; indeed, Lucretius boasted he was the first to borrow his
philosophy from a Greek, Horace that he imitated the Greek lyric
meters. Vergil too used Theocritus, Hesiod, and Homer to help him

create the *Eclogues,* the *Georgics,* and the *Aeneid.* Imitation was a convention the Greeks themselves had employed and had elevated into a literary dogma which existed in actual practice in some form or other until the time of Winckelmann and Goethe, in the eighteenth century.

The elevation of form over content is a natural result of the Roman theory of imitation, set forth most conveniently in Horace's *Art of Poetry.* To us, idea is more important than form; we thus fall into a formlessness from which a new school of critics is trying to rescue us. The limitations of his art and of his material forced the Roman to a mastery of both.

Roman literary form was the expression of an attitude toward life which we describe rather vaguely by such words as classicism, restraint, balance, moderation, judgment. The extravagant and fantastic are generally reduced to a minimum in Roman literature. The great concentration of the poet upon the unifying form and purpose of his work does not give way until the age of Lucan and his melodramatization of the epic. Classicism was not proof against the disquietude of soul produced by the intermittent tyrannies of the Emperors, the loss of liberty, and the precarious existence of the writer and thinker in post-Augustan days.

This disquietude was reflected in the poetry of the Silver Age, especially in Lucan, Petronius, Martial, and Juvenal. The so-called Silver Age of Latin literature has long been considered inferior, in some unexplained manner, to the, again so-called, Golden Age of the Augustans. The Silver Age is indeed different from the Golden, but only in degree and in its peculiar emphases. There are in it the same tendencies toward subjective analysis exaggerated by the conditions of life into fierce resentment and hatred, into a mocking and bitter resignation where only savage humor preserves the poet from madness, into a lurid sensationalism which strains for its effects by concentration on horror and violence for their own sakes. Or there is a subtle and urbane irony so deep that one is appalled by the clarity of perception which sees in humanity little else than greed, lust, cruelty, and injustice.

All this is to say that the Silver Latins develop to the point of distortion the old Roman emphasis upon moralism and satire. It is a pity that so little Roman satire (the literary type of which Quintilian said, "Satire at least is entirely our own") has been adequately translated, for in it appears much of the true originality of mind in Roman literature. Martial and Juvenal experienced the indignities of poverty, while Lucan and Petronius were forced by Nero to commit suicide. All of them made their enemies by the simplest method: telling the truth. It is *saeva indignatio,* fierce indignation, which inspired these poets, their violent revulsion against shams and injustices. Much of Ezra Pound's writing has had much the same tone and purpose, the same invigorating denunciation of ignorance and stupidity, the same moral passion. Their poetry is full of epigrams in the wry, dry fashion of Pound's "Mauberley," with which contemporary English and American poetry may be said to begin:

> war useful to many; the name of virtue will be given to vicious rascality; the victorious cause pleased the gods, but the cause of the conquered was pleasing to Cato (Lucan); righteousness is praised and freezes to death; it's difficult *not* to write satire; what shall I do at Rome? I don't know how to lie; unhappy poverty has nothing harsher than this: it makes men ridiculous; but who will guard the guards? (Juvenal); glory comes late to one's ashes; let there be patrons, Flaccus, and Vergils won't be lacking; no one hurries up fast enough to live; you will always have only the riches you have given away; cash comes to no one but the rich (Martial); fear first made gods in the world (Petronius).

The Romans did not write for children. Almost all extant Latin literature is adult and mature in theme, content, and form. It embraces a wide sweep of civilized, sophisticated, and at times decadent attitudes and individual minds. The worldly humor of Plautus and Terence, the rugged moralism of Cato, the austere and profound scepticism of Lucretius, the bitter passion of Catullus, the pensive gravity of Vergil, the sharp political analysis of Cicero are beyond the grasp of children.

What we read today of classical Latin literature is written in a language whose syntax and grammar are formidable. That language bristles with strange proper names, mythological figures, rhetorical devices, and curious allusions of every sort. By centuries of use, by passage into the colorless diction of clerks, lawyers, priests, and professors it has become hard for us to uncover the original fresh metaphor of Latin, the strong flavor it once drew from the soldier's camp and the merchant's table, the earthy quality of a language of farmers and fighters.

Not only the language but the mental processes of the people who once wrote and spoke it seem at this distance rigid and inflexible. A tolerably comprehensive description of the typical Roman would give us a personality remarkable for its stubborn conservatism, its concentration upon warfare, power, and law, its respect for birth and family. To the Roman, race and clan meant more to the preservation of the state than did the individual; the gifts and talents of the Roman were his to use only for the common good.

The Roman tradition, nevertheless, has no unity, no single period in which it was better than at any other, at least down to the early Empire. It is the result of a long evolution reaching from Rome's earliest beginnings to the time of Tacitus. The interpretation of this tradition is not primarily a matter of method or of facts transmitted but the comprehension of its many divergences from modern conceptions of historical, aesthetic, moral, and political thought.

Among the significant differences between Roman civilization and modern life is the basically rhetorical nature of Roman politics, education, and literature. An understanding of this condition leads to the understanding of other phenomena: the Roman theory of imitation in art and literature; the elevation of form over content; and the fact that much of the best writing of the Augustan Age was part of a program of social reform.

Joined with rhetoric in Latin culture is the Roman belief in knowledge as a basis for action. Training in rhetoric was planned to make efficient rulers and military leaders, lawyers and legates, as well as men of letters. Beneath the carefully evolved styles of the Latin writers often lay some practical purpose, usually educational. They attempted to apply new techniques or points of view to the traditional material of literature drawn from mythology, history, and social life.

The doctrine of *decorum* (fitness, propriety) was practiced by the Romans in both literature and ethics. In adopting it from the Greek literary theorists the Romans showed their intellectual satisfaction with the principle of moderation from which the doctrine arose. This principle was employed in oratory as well, in the search for balance in structure and the harmony of style with subject.

Vergil in his first and fourth Eclogues, Horace in the fourteenth Ode of the first book, herald the arrival of a leader and the establishment of an age of peace which seems only the transposition to a universal plane of the artistic striving for harmony and balance. The great Altar of Peace with its stately procession and its scenes from religious life is the most exquisite visible testimony to such an age. The Roman peace provided the atmosphere in which a moral regeneration was possible, inspired by a nationalism which was one of Rome's deepest sources of strength. The *De Re Rustica* of Varro, the *History* of Livy, the *Georgics* of Vergil, the *Secular Hymn* of Horace are some of the literary contributions to this imperial theme; above them all stands the national epic, the *Aeneid*. Sculpture, architecture, administration contributed to the re-establishment of moral ideals and the glorification of Augustus in a program thus described by Hermann Fraenkel in his excellent *Ovid: a Poet Between Two Worlds* (1945):

At the time of Augustus, a powerful movement was under way

which tried to reverse the development of civilization and to revive the ideals and virtues of the past. The reformers wanted the people of Rome once more to become a nation of modest and laborious farmers, brave and strenuous soldiers, and exemplary statesmen. Private life was to be governed again by the old, stern standards; the religion of the forefathers was to be restored; and the taste in art, language, and literature was to orient itself toward models from former times. The age was certainly not ignorant of its own decadence; in fact, for a long time writers had been lamenting that the political and economic expansion of the Empire had brought in its train a steady decline in morality, discipline, and firmness of character. Augustus was the chief exponent of the reformatory tendencies, and he promoted them with all the powerful means at his disposal, including legislation. This grandiose scheme did not reach the masses or stir them to self-improvement; the necessary economic reforms under which such a regeneration could have been possible were not made. The upper classes ignored the legislation directed toward them and continued those practices of divorce and childlessness which had given Augustus so much concern.

Only the writers and artists came forward to give life and breath to the new vision of Roman culture. In a generation more brilliant than any other in the ancient world since the time of Pericles they produced the great books and sculptures of the Augustan Age, embodying in their prose and verse and carvings the ideals of a higher life. With the steadily increasing despotism and degeneracy of the emperors down to Nero, any chance of success the program might have had faded away forever.

The contributions of Rome to later civilization are numerous and not to be summed up adequately in a short space. Rome preserved Greek culture from its barbarous enemies; her ancient peace maintained other native cultures until the Middle Ages, under Christianity and the national states of Europe, could continue to protect them. Roman law became the sheltering matrix for much later law; her political organization was copied, among other features of Roman life, by the Holy Roman Empire and by the Catholic Church of Rome. Her Stoic ethics deeply influenced Christianity by way of Cicero and the Church Fathers. Her language was the foundation of the Romance languages and provided a grammatical model for other languages; her alphabet became universal in western Europe outside Russia. Her roads, bridges, public and private buildings are still a testimony to the vision and skill of her architects and engineers; her roads were, in fact, the best in the world until the nineteenth century.

Roman commercial methods, coinage, handwriting and shorthand, weights, measures, calendar, science, and military medicine were only a few of the models that Europe was to follow. Her capacity for purposeful action and cooperation were not transmitted so fully to some of the later peoples, nor were certain other admirable traits of Roman character. Her great ideas — *pietas, virtus, humanitas,* and many more — passed into the thought and language of the people who knew her hand through the centuries.

It is in literature, however, that Rome's force is felt today perhaps more strongly than in the other ways in which she influenced posterity. This influence began with the close of classical antiquity somewhere between the sixth and the ninth centuries and has continued to our time. The literary types, imagery, figures of speech were Roman; the liberal arts of the university curriculum, the entire fabric of medieval rhetoric were Roman. The Roman Muses inspired the poets of the Middle Ages in the new forms they created — the hymn, the sequence, the modus or prosa, and the new types of verse-forms with their intricate variations.

Medieval Latin poetry in the twelfth century stands beside Medieval French poetry, which in turn influenced the early poetry of Spain. Italian poetry does not begin until the thirteenth century and is oriented by the Provençal poets until Dante, who was the first Italian to use the Latin inheritance in a thorough and conscious manner.

Juvenal is the last of the great Roman poets. With his gloomy and violent outbursts against folly, greed, and injustice, the lights of Roman poetry in the classical age begin to dwindle and to give way to a series of lesser luminaries. Every age has need of good satire; it is a pity his poems have never been adequately translated even by that other great satirist, Dryden. Juvenal's contemporary allusions and personal references are lost upon a modern audience, but some way should be devised to bring him over into English without the use of too many footnotes: to turn his personalities into their contemporary equivalents would be tempting, but libelous. His genius for epigram, for vivid observation, for accurate, merciless logic, his highly original style and his overpowering anger make him a challenging figure even today.

The other poets of his age, Petronius and Martial, are slighter both in production and in earnest passion. Seneca, the single playwright of that age, is not so much an important talent as an important influence and a poet whom the Elizabethans felt to be almost one of themselves. It is still the Elizabethan poets who have translated him best, although perhaps to our taste in a manner somewhat fantastical. His sense of melodrama is akin to that of Lucan and peculiarly Roman in its love of bloodcurdling themes and situations. After him come the quieter Statius and the poets of the Latin Anthology with their frequent flashes of genuine poetry in a minor key.

Of the one hundred forty-four important Latin writers from the beginnings down to the early Middle Ages, sixty-four have lost the majority of their works, forty-three have survived with most of their writings, and thirty-seven have come down to us with practically all they produced. Roman literary history falls into several chronological divisions. The first, from about 500 B.C. to 240 B.C., contains the formation of the Latin language from its various native, Greek, and Etruscan components and the growth to power of Rome in the Italian peninsula. We cannot say much that is dependable fact about this largely pre-literary period when not even inscriptions are available beyond the sixth century Praenestine fibula, on which is written in archaic Latin the words "Manius made me for Numerius." With the year 240 begins Latin literature as we know it, in the works of Livius Andronicus (see the first headnote of this anthology), Naevius, Ennius, Plautus, and Terence. The loss of most of the writing from this second period is discouraging indeed for anyone who wishes to form a comprehensive view of Roman literature. It is the age of creative invention and great activity which may be compared to the Elizabethan Age in English literature. In it arose epic, drama, and satire; the Roman literary personality gained confidence for ample expression, formed literary schools and circles of patrons, produced some of the finest Latin works. During the course of the first Christian centuries many of these works were lost forever except for the fragments rescued by grammarians and other extant authors who quoted these early writers; the Silver Age imitated this period by going back to its types and vocabulary, preferring Ennius to later writers. The third period opens around 70 B.C., when Cicero had well begun his activity as an orator and Lucretius, Catullus and his group of poets were at their height of production. Again serious losses are recorded, especially in lyric and epic poetry. The Augustan or Golden Age, generally regarded as the finest of all, begins around 50 B.C. with the publication of Caesar's *Commentaries on the Gallic War*. In rapid succession Livy, Horace, Vergil, Ovid, and the elegiac poets join the illustrious procession of Roman authors.

The Golden Age ends with the death of Augustus in A.D. 14 at the age of seventy-seven, after forty-five years of peaceful rule. Thenceforward to the death of Marcus Aurelius (himself a writer of philosophy) in A.D. 180 extends the Silver Age of Lucan, Suetonius, Petronius, Martial, Juvenal, the two Senecas and Plinys, Tacitus, Quintilian, and Apuleius. After 180 begin those centuries which were a kind of interim period neither wholly classical nor wholly medieval. The Middle Ages themselves — at least a thousand years of enormous literary production — begin, according to various estimates, in the first half of the fourth century and extend into the thirteenth or fourteenth, although Ludwig Traube, the famous medievalist, preferred to begin the Middle Ages with the sixth century in his course of lectures on medieval literature.

Within these centuries Western civilization was saved or renewed by a series of at least three renaissances, all of them springing from Latin literature. The first is the Carolingian, based at the court of Charlemagne in the ninth century and nourished in part by British and Irish scholarship. The second is distinguished by the rise of the universities and of Latin studies in scholastic philosophy, literary criticism, and by the development of secular Latin lyric poetry in the twelfth century. The third renaissance in the thirteenth century brings into the world Italian and then European humanism, the last great upsurge of Latin culture until modern times. All three rebirths of learning and art drew their primary sustenance and inspiration from classical Latin literature.

No people's history, viewed across this tremendous expanse of time, through twenty-four and a half centuries, reveals more fully than that of ancient Rome the impact of a highly individualized national character upon its environment. There is no later parallel closer or more significant today than the historical experience of the American people which, like the Roman, grew from humble origins to the status of a world power, with all the responsibilities and international commitments which that power implies. This fact should remind us again that the story of Rome has much to tell us at a time when the study of Classical Greco-Roman culture has been pushed to the periphery of our educational curriculum.

The Middle Ages are a monumental and immensely fruitful period for Latin poetry. Much of it clings to older themes, forms, and methods but gropes toward the poetry of another age and of other tongues historically close to the Roman. There is in it an often elegiac longing for the past, a flight from reality that resembles the pastoralism of the ancients, and a good deal of elaborate pedantry. Yet a fresh note of vigorous sensuality more delicate than that of the Priapic poems of the Latin Anthology is sounded in the *Pervigilium Veneris*. It is as though in this work of some unidentified poet a new breath of life, a new kinship with nature, had begun to enjoy a springtime the Romans had not known. At the beginning of the

Middle Ages this delightful poem heralds the spring songs of the *Carmina Burana*, those simple and spontaneous poems of the wandering European students written and sung nine hundred years later. Between these landmarks the structure of medieval poetry arises, with its often inextricably mingled Christian and pagan elements. Medieval Latin poetry reached the people in a way that Roman poetry, by reason of its social limitations, could not reach them. No class differences could bar the way to hymns, poems of nature, and the amazing expressions of the medieval personality in verse. Even Abelard, the scholar, can touch the simple soul with his poems, and the great hymns are essentially folk-poetry of the noblest kind even though written by the most austere of churchmen.

Personalities are sometimes difficult to discern, however, in the vast collections of medieval poetry. Ausonius (c. A.D. 310–394), the mellow spirit who enjoys his well-earned luxury in the pleasantest parts of France; Claudian (fl. A.D. 400) who harks back again and again to the ancients but gives his classically inspired poems a new and somehow original flavor; Prudentius, the first great Christian poet; Hugo Primas; the Archpoet of Cologne; and Walter of Chatillon: strong and highly individual personalities whose mark is plain in all their lines — these are among the greater figures of their time. But it is often from an anonymous snatch of verse, mutilated and dog-eared in the manuscript, that the reader gathers his most lasting impressions of the medieval poet, as Rolfe Humphries has from "Vidi viridi Phyllida," an echo and nothing more from one stirring springtime morning of the Medieval past.

More than a thousand years of poetic production in the Latin language could not fail to provide many examples to challenge the translator, from the *Pervigilium Veneris*, that strange and passionate hymn to nature, down to the neo-Latin verses of Herbert and Crashaw in the seventeenth century. In many respects the later Latins have fared better than some earlier poets; the anonymous writers of the *Carmina Burana* and of the familiar hymns have fared quite well indeed. It is gratifying to be able to exhibit the amazing continuity of Latin poetry almost to our own time. It is in the later periods, in fact, that some of the best color and flavor, the richness, sweep, and variety of this poetry can be seen: in the fading classicism of Ausonius and Claudian, with their special and personal charm; in the great religious outbursts of the hymns by Ambrose, Prudentius, Venantius Fortunatus, St. Peter Damian, Bernard of Clairvaux, and Thomas of Celano; in the deep pessimism of Boethius or Bernard of Morlas; in the pulsing happiness and springtime animal vigor of the *Cambridge Songs* and the *Carmina Burana;* in the cynicism and wit of Hugo Primas and the

Archpoet; and in the exquisite if often decadent grace of the Renaissance lyricists. This is a panorama of poetry which might be even wider were there more translations to choose.

When I began this collection I knew only a few translations by modern poets, by Hopkins, Housman, Robinson, MacNeice, which I had copied into the flyleaves of my Latin texts and offered occasionally to students as private diversions. The pleasure these gave and the possibility that a more complete anthology might be put together led me to make a long search through many books and magazines and to enlist the generous assistance of friends and colleagues on two continents. However excellent are most of the poems printed here, it has been difficult to offer more than a glimpse of some poets: one selects from what is available or from what may be coaxed out of competent translators. Were it possible to assemble a corps of good modern poets who had sufficient Latin, the complete and almost perfect anthology of Latin poetry in translation could be made; yet I hope that a respectable approximation to that ideal is represented by this book.

Catullus and Horace are the most frequently translated of the Latin lyric poets; they are thus represented by more poems than can be found for other Latin poets in translation and in a greater variety of mood and method. My contributors supplied me with many versions of these two poets, and I was obliged to accept only those translations which seemed to be the very best among a number of versions of the same poem. Many of the translations were sent in by way of brief invitations printed in some of the little magazines; I am grateful to the editor of the *London Times Literary Supplement* for publishing an appeal which opened a precious vein of contributions from Great Britain. I am deeply indebted to many a contributor here and abroad who thus learned of my undertaking and gave generously toward it.

Two principles, beyond the subjective enthusiasms or prejudices with which all anthologists are equipped, have guided me in making this collection. First, I have collected all the translations, published or unpublished and for which permission to print was given, which impressed me with their quality as English poems; many of these were made by the poets and literarily sensitive scholars of the present day. I did not wish to make a book heavy with sadly dated versions by Dryden, Creech, or Conington, good as these may have been for their time. Second, wherever I could I selected those poems which as far as my ear could tell provided an unusually good refitting of the original meters to the English language. It is unfortunate that classical meters cannot be rendered in English with anything more than approximate accuracy; but I felt that the few which have been so reproduced should not be rejected simply because large statements are current to the effect that the feat is impossible. Further, I think it is absurd to allow uninstructed readers to form the impression that Catullus, for example, wrote in English ballad measures or Horace in pentameter quatrains, if a few sincere attempts to fit even one of the nineteen meters Horace used or of the dozen displayed by Catullus could be placed on exhibition. The honest feat, provided it is good English, must be respected, and the insight it can give into the nature of Latin prosody is too precious to be neglected. The notes contain references to original sources, together with brief explanations of mythological and historical allusions.

I have made no fetish of modern translations. The older versions by Crashaw, Lovelace, Jonson, or Marvell are also included wherever they seemed not too quaint for modern taste. I can claim that the first readable verse translations of Propertius are printed here, together with many unprinted and first-rate translations from many other poets. I think I have rescued Catullus from the sentimentalists and Horace from those who insist on being maudlin in their translations. The collection of verse-translations of Vergil's *Eclogues* is beyond question the best yet assembled. Sulpicia is here presented for the first time and more than adequately; so are Tibullus and Persius, one of the most difficult of Latin writers, in the first good poetic versions made. Certain poets previously untranslated such as Decimus Laberius, Publilius Syrus, the Latin Anthologists, and a few minor ones are introduced in their first appearance. The collection of Martial's epigrams is for its size the most adequate in skill and faithfulness I have seen.

I hope the book will appeal both to a wide and non-academic public as well as to students. If the classics must, more and more, be studied in translation, we should study them in the best translations available. Whether, of course, any substitute for the genuine, however excellent, can continue to nourish our imaginations and enrich our lives is a question still beyond solving. Perhaps the best service a book like this can perform is to send the reader back to the texts of the Latin poets themselves, to renew his lapsed acquaintance with them or to begin the study of Latin in order to find out for himself what the poets are *actually* saying.

The Early Roman Writers

❨ Roman literature begins with an inscription upon a safety pin, the famous Praenestine fibula. It develops through a series of relatively unliterary texts which include folk charms, epitaphs, liturgies, legal documents, and the first Western European law code, the Twelve Tables, to a more authentic beginning in a translation of Homer's *Odyssey* into Latin by Livius Andronicus (240 B.C.). Although the handbooks call him the father of Roman literature, there is good reason to believe that Appius Claudius Caecus, the blind old censor of 312 B.C. and the predecessor of Livius by more than seventy years in his activity as a writer of brief epigrams, is the first man known to have written Latin verse. Neither Appius nor Livius, however, was regarded by the Romans themselves as the founder of their literature in the true sense. If any one deserved that title it was "pater Ennius."

❨ Quintus Ennius (239–169 B.C.), of Rudiae in Calabria, comes later than both Livius and Naevius (270–c. 201 B.C.) but was the most prolific, versatile, and attractive of the early Latin writers. He was also a soldier, a teacher, and a linguist of parts, speaking Greek, Oscan, and Latin. In one of his fragments (edited and translated by E. H. Warmington, *Remains of Old Latin*, I, Loeb Classical Library, 1935, p. 80) he has given us a self-portrait, although he wrote about another man: ". . . a learned, trusty, winsome man and a fine talker, content with his own, happy and shrewd; one who spoke the right thing at the right time, and obliging; of few words; keeping many old-time ways of which a bygone age long buried is the maker, and manners old and new; keeping also to the modes of many a one of our elders, and the laws too of gods and men; one who could prudently speak out hearsay or keep it to himself." This is a picture of the best type of old Roman, all the more valuable and convincing because it appears in the very period at which Roman character was probably more admirable than it later became. The fundamental honesty and religious rectitude of that character, its tact, conservatism, prudence, and obedience to law; its ability to accept necessary change, and even the grim humor and the laconic quality of Roman speech are among its chief traits.

❨ There is a certain poetic and historic fitness not entirely accidental in the fact that Ennius has left us some of the most famous lines in all Latin literature, lines which sum up briefly much of the Roman view of life in his age. A noticeable felicity in the poetry of Ennius, more characteristic, it is true, of the pithy, sonorous *Annals* than of the melodramatic bits of his tragedies, appeals not only to modern readers

1

but appealed with striking force to later Latin writers. His influence was powerful upon Cicero, Lucretius, and Vergil. He is the solitary Latin writer to inspire Lucretius in the *De Rerum Natura;* even Silius Italicus, almost at the end of Latin literary history, was deeply under his spell. The loss of Ennius' poems (little more than 1,100 lines survive) is undoubtedly the greatest single blow sustained by classical Latin literature besides the lost books of Livy; its magnitude can be adequately measured by the echoes from his poetry which ring through later Latin writing.

❨ Perhaps the most famous of his lines is also one of the most distinctively Roman:

> On manners and on men of olden time
> Stands firm the Roman State.

More than any single expression in Latin literature this line conveys the conviction that morality was the foundation of Roman greatness and power. This is a theme which recurs in some context or other throughout later Roman literature.

❨ We possess only 565 lines of the *Annals*, the chief work of Ennius. The poem was an epic describing Roman history from the sack of Troy to within two years of Ennius' death; he omitted the account of the First Punic War because Naevius, an elder contemporary, had already written it. Such a vast subject must have given Ennius ample opportunity to tell why the Romans were successful in the wars they undertook; even the fragments we have give us numerous glimpses of his patriotic views on Roman prowess. To him

> Brave are the Romans as the sky's profound

and to them, as men of fortitude, fortune was granted. As victors they would not, however, claim victory unless the conquered one confessed defeat. The Romans were incorruptible: of Manius Curius Dentatus, Ennius wrote "whom none could overcome with iron or gold." Ennius, as if foreseeing the age of Sallust, warned the Romans not to ruin the state through greedy hope. Discipline must be kept in the army. Great glory was the soldier's reward, alive or dead. Fortune is fickle and hard to win, a frequent thought with Ennius. Courage, honesty, self-control, manful deeds in war — the virtues of a new and virile people groping their way slowly toward empire — these merit the praise of Ennius.

❨ In his plays it is not always possible to tell whether he is translating Euripides, for example, or composing in his own right. The fragments of the plays yield little to our purpose; yet what Ennius causes Priam to say at one point in "The Ransom of Hector" is worthy of a true poet and one of the best of the Romans:

> A better thing than bravery is justice;

The Roman too is heard in the words expressed by Phoenix in the play of that name:

> The man who bears himself both pure and staunch —
> That is true liberty.

Ennius begins the literary tradition which scrupulously joined Rome's moral and martial greatness, heavily underlining the dependence of the latter upon the former. The tradition runs with varying emphasis and subtlety through the work of Livy and Sallust, Cicero, Horace, and Vergil. Augustus made a vain attempt to revive it in national life; after him the tradition became a memory which died mournfully away in the enigmatic phrases of Tacitus. The fortunes of that tradition are in themselves an important chapter in Roman spiritual history.

❨ Gnaeus Naevius, like Livius and Ennius, was a playwright who followed the normal Roman practice of borrowing plots and scenes from one or more Greek plays at a time. He created the historical drama at Rome and composed the *Bellum Punicum,* an epic on the First Punic War written in saturnian verse (six-beat accentual, the earliest Roman form later submerged by the dactylic hexameter, to reappear only in early medieval accentual verse). It was published possibly around 204 B.C., when Ennius came to Rome. In it Naevius connected Roman history with Troy; he made Romulus, the first Roman king, a grandson of Aeneas, vastly shortening the generations Vergil was to place between the two heroes. In comedy Naevius did so well that a critic's list of the ten best comic poets recorded by Aulus Gellius in the second century A.D. gives him third place. The fragments of some shorter poems show a sprightly vigor and an imagination which could nourish itself upon folk dances and rural customs. As a writer of lampoons — brief, biting couplets that named names and could wound savagely — he brought imprisonment upon himself at the hands of the powerful Metellus clan. His tragedies use the material of the Trojan saga, thus returning to the same theme as his epic poem. He was the first sharp critic of politicians and of public fakes and fools. He was original, courageous, independent, an arresting and bracing figure worthy to stand with Ennius among the pioneers.

❨ Marcus Pacuvius (220–c. 130 B.C.), the nephew of Ennius, is the single important name in early Roman tragedy except for Lucius Accius (170–c. 86 B.C), his junior by fifty years. We cannot say much about Roman tragedy because we have no complete example; the tragedies of Seneca were written to be read, not acted. Lucilius made fun of Pacuvius' style. Cicero praises him for his ability to convey feeling and character; Varro admired his overflowing abundance of language, shown, for instance, in his description of the Greek fleet caught in a storm on its way to Troy. Quintilian, an excellent critic, looked upon him and Accius as the greatest Roman tragic poets in their dignity of thought, weight of diction, and the powerful presence of their characters. It is certain that the Romans preferred and encouraged comedy, epic, and satire more than tragedy; yet tragedy continued to be written and acted after Pacuvius and Accius, at least among small groups of intellectuals, down to Cicero's day. It is beyond doubt that their plays represent a major loss to Latin literature.

❡ Roman satire is described by Quintilian in the following sentence: "Satire at any rate is completely our own." This sounds defensive, as indeed it was. Greek literature had been drawn upon in every department of Roman literature so heavily that the Roman critics treasured any evidence of originality among Roman writers. Horace boasted a bit self-consciously that he was the first to transfer Greek lyric meters into Latin; but he could not have written as he did without Greek models. Propertius says, in Frances Fletcher's graceful translation of Elegy III, 1,

> I am the first, priestlike, to appear from a clear spring,
> Uniting with Greek music the mysteries of Italy.

Clearly he is thinking here of Roman pre-eminence in elegy. There is, in fact, much reason to believe that in this type of poetry the Romans did improve considerably upon their Greek models.

❡ But satire was for them truly unique, despite all the possible Greek sources that modern scholars have brought forward to invalidate their claims. Gaius Lucilius (c. 180–103 B.C.) is a very great name in Roman satire, which he seems to have written almost exclusively. He came from Suessa Aurunca in Campania, the modern Sezze, and, like many Roman authors, of a well-to-do family. His niece became the mother of Pompey the Great. As a member of the cultured circle whose chief was the younger Scipio Aemilianus Africanus Minor, friend of Laelius in Cicero's essay *On Friendship,* Lucilius found the protection and admiration every writer craves and requires. New ideas arising from the Gracchan period of social unrest (133–122 B.C.) took shape in his thirty books of satires, of which about 1,300 lines remain, written in several meters from which the hexameter finally won out in later satire over elegiacs and trochaic or iambic meters. Gilbert Highet describes satire as "a piece of verse, or prose mingled with verse, intended to improve society by mocking its anomalies, and marked by spontaneity, topicality, ironic wit, indecent humor, colloquial language, frequent use of dialogue, constant intrusion of the author's personality, and incessant variety of tone and style." This extremely inclusive definition sums up that Roman talent for discursive social criticism which took form in the drama, anecdote, fable, and epigram as well as in satire, a talent that shaped their political organization, gave release to tensions between classes, sharpened more prosaic wits, and gave to their social life that informal charm we see in Catullus, in the letters of Cicero and Pliny, and in the later Stoic society of Tacitus, when Roman liberty had died and only the gifts of gentlemanly behavior could make life tolerable for the educated Roman. Lucilius was the father of Western satire, and across the centuries his spirit is still felt wherever a keen, disgusted mind holds up the folly and weakness of human kind to the ridicule they deserve. ❫

Ennius

From the ANNALES

Like a shower of rain
The weapons on the tribune:

They pierce his shield.
The boss is ringing with spears;
From his helmet glances a shrill sound!

Not one of all the adversaries
Can cut down his body
With the gleaming sword.

Always he shatters or strikes
Down the abundant spears.
Sweat bathes his whole body;

He labors greatly
He cannot breathe.

John Wight

Naevius

HIS OWN EPITAPH

If it were right that goddesses for men should weep,
Then would our native Muses weep for Naevius dead,
For now their poet's locked in soundless Lethe's keep,
Rome has forgotten Latin's grave majestic tread.

Geoffrey Johnson

THE GIRL FROM TARENTUM

She wanders like a shuttlecock, from side to side she flutters.
She makes a lover with a wink, with every word she utters.
She's welcomed by the younger folk, and flirtingly she stands,
then sits and rouses someone else, toes wriggling, squeezing hands.
She blows a kiss, she gazes round, she turns and shows her ring,
to one she tips the sign of love, with one she stops to sing.

Jack Lindsay

Pacuvius

HIS OWN EPITAPH

Young man, despite your hurry, mark this little stone's
Appeal to look, then ponder what the phrases tell:
Marcus Pacuvius, poet, here has stretched his bones.
I did not wish to leave you uninformed. Farewell.

Geoffrey Johnson

Lucilius

THE MARKET PLACE

Now from reveille till dark, on work-days, holidays,
Lords and commons alike, the whole of the populace
Toss and swirl in the Forum, conceding to nobody foothold,
Burning with one and the same desire of passionate cunning,
Cheating where craft can conceal, fencing with falsehoods,
Vying with smoothest words to show how moral their make-up,
Setting their traps, as though each man were the foe of his fellow.

Geoffrey Johnson

Plautus

❪ Titus Maccius Plautus (c. 254–184 B.C.), of Sarsina in Umbria, is the most brilliant and prolific of the Roman comic playwrights. He is not often a great artist, but he knew how to extract the greatest amount of laughter from his situations. He comes between Naevius and Ennius and must have profited from their witty writings; at least they prepared the proper climate for his plays, presented probably betwen 206 and 191 B.C. We have twenty plays of Plautus and fragments of another; he wrote at least forty-eight. Those we have show a wide variety in theme and handling. His models were Greek, but his handling peculiarly Roman in many details. His special gift is a rollicking, breathless, slapdash momentum of laughter which runs the gamut of comedy from burlesque to pantomime. Mistaken identities, deceptions of many kinds, the use of varied types — reckless young men in trouble over girls or money, stingy fathers, braggart soldiers, parasites who complicate the plot, tricky slaves, white-slavers who hold the heroines in their power — these form the basis of his plays. Obscenity, slapstick, word-plays, and humorous insults are features of his style; short songs give a lyrical quality to parts of the plays. A skillful use of several meters, each adapted to the emotion of the particular situation, lends a sophisticated sparkle to his Latin, in which amazing word-coinages are another ingredient. His plays were imitated by dozens of later playwrights in Europe, especially in Renaissance Italy and England. Shakespeare borrowed *The Menaechmi* for his *Comedy of Errors,* complicating its mistaken identities by using two pairs of twins instead of one. Molière adapted the *Aulularia* for his *Miser* and the *Amphitryon* for his own play of that name. The most recent adaptations of Plautus are Jean Giraudoux's *Amphitryon 38* (so named because it is the 38th adaptation of that delightful play); the Rodgers and Hart musical, *The Boys from Syracuse* (again *The Menaechmi* by way of the *Comedy of Errors*); and the Cole Porter musical comedy, *Out of This World,* straight out of *Amphitryon.* Modern vaudeville begins with Plautus, and his spirit still inspires it where it has found an amazing re-birth — on television. ❫

MOSTELLARIA 84–117

I often have pondered and puzzled and wondered;
I've racked all the brains I possess

7

To gather some clues that a fellow might use
If he wishes that riddle to guess —
"What does Man most resemble?" I think you'll agree
He is like a new house, if you listen to me.

When a house is complete, finished off trim and neat,
Then the builder is praised, and each man
Would have just such another, that house's twin brother,
Constructed upon the same plan.
But if good-for-naught untidy slackers move in
The fine house is soon spoiled and its troubles begin.

When a storm sweeps away tiles and gutters one day
Things are left and the rain finds an entry.
It rots all the walls and the timber work falls
And the house goes to ruin. These gentry
Won't trouble to spend a few pence of their own,
But wait until neglect brings the whole building down.

F. A. Wright

CURCULIO 95–110

To my nose there came a whiff,
 Wine, old wine;
In the darkness just a sniff,
 Scent divine:
Darling Bacchus, art thou near?
Quick, and to thy love appear.
We are of one age, my dear:
 Wine, old wine.

In my grave of thee I'll dream,
 Wine, old wine;
Other perfumes rancid seem
 Matched with thine:
"Peau d'Espagne" or "New Mown Hay,"
"Attared Roses," "Giroflée,"
Nothing equals thy bouquet,
 Wine, old wine.

Now my nose has had its fill,
 Wine, old wine:
But my throat desires thee still,
 Bacchus mine.

No, no! Help me, and the lot'll
Vanish down my parching throttle.
I will drink the whole damn bottle,
    Wine, old wine.

F. A. Wright

CASINA 217–227

There's nothing in the world like love,
    So delicate and savory.
The sweetest flower has not such power:
    It is so full and flavory.
I wonder why cooks do not try
    To use it as a spice.
        A tiny trickle
        Our tongues would tickle:
    It is so very nice.

If there's love in the dish, be it meat, game or fish,
        on all palates 'twill work like a spell,
But your salt will not taste, and your sugar you'll waste,
        if you don't have some love in as well.
It makes gall into honey; sad faces look sunny;
        a puritan turns to a rake.
And that this is its way is not merely hearsay:
        from myself I example can take.

For ever since I've been in love,
    By Gad, I have blossomed out.
Each barber's shop is on the hop
    Whenever I'm about.
The choicest scent they me present —
    I do not count the cost —
        To please my dear.
        And I've no fear
    My labor will be lost.

F. A. Wright

CURCULIO 147–149

Bolt and bar, bolt and bar,
    Listen to my greeting.

You my trusty comrades are,
You I am entreating.
Hearken to a lover's plea;
Let my lady come to me.

F. A. Wright

TRUCULENTUS 565–575

These courtesans are like the sea,
All that is brought to them they take;
But though the current flows in free
No difference will it make.
Whatever enters, that they hold,
Whether it water be or gold.

That hussy with her wanton ways
Has bled my luckless master dry,
He has seen the last of happy days
Faced now by beggary.
Gold, honor, friends, they all have gone,
And soon he will be left alone.

F. A. Wright

ASINARIA 215–226

This trade of mine, dear boy,
Is like the methods fowlers oft employ.
They choose a place and scatter first the grain,
For you must spend ere you can hope to gain.
The birds become familiar with the spot,
And eat, and eat — until he gets the lot.
And so with me. My lodgings will be found
To take the place of fowlers' trapping ground.
Girls are my bait, and beds are my decoys;
The birds I angle for are you bright boys.
Soft words and pleasant greetings make you tame,
Kisses and whispers and love's lightsome game.
A milk-white breast — you see the smoothness of it
And gently touch: that touch will bring me profit.
Two rosy lips — you long a kiss to get
And take it: taken yourself without a net.
That is the way. You ought to know the rule,
Who were so long a pupil in my school.

F. A. Wright

AMPHITRYO 218–247

Then the armies came out,
And we both marched about
With our ranks close arrayed
And our standards displayed,
While the generals twain
In the midst of the plain
Met together for compact of battle.
Whichever should yield,
They agreed, on that field
Should surrender their lives,
And their altars and wives,
And their city and land
To the conquering band —
And then came the bugle's quick rattle.

The soldiers around
With their shouts shook the ground
As their general prayed
And his vows to Jove made.
Then each man did his best,
In the battle close pressed,
And fought might and main without stopping.
As the foeman advances,
We shiver his lances;
The heavens ring loud
O'er the clamorous crowd,
With a vapor beneath
From our hot panting breath;
And on every side dead men were dropping.
At last they were beat;
But they did not retreat.
Not a man in their host
Would abandon his post.
In heaps they were slain,
But their line they maintain
Unbroken, though fierce we attacked them.
When my lord saw that sight
He cried, "Wheel from the right."
Our horsemen obeyed
And a gallant charge made,
Swooping down with a shout,
Till the foe fled in rout —
So Justice prevailed: and we whacked them.

F. A. Wright

MILES GLORIOSUS 287–363

Pyrgopolinices, Artotrogus

Py. See that upon my shield the sheen is brighter
than the sun's rays in weather fine and dry,
so that in time of need, when battle's joined,
it dazzle and blind the enemy's vanguard.
And my poor sword deserves some consolation
so that it may not droop or grow despairing
in its desire to mash the foe to mincemeat.
Now where is Artotrogus?

Art. Here, by the hero
valiant and fortunate and princely handsome,
the warrior — Mars himself dares not to speak
or to assimilate his deeds to yours!

Py. Was't he I saved in the field of Weevilsburg
where Bombochampion von Furioschki,
Neptune's grandson, was generalissimo?

Art. I well remember — he with golden armor
whose regiments you scattered with your breath
as the wind scatters leaves, or a brush plaster.

Py. Tush, it was nothing.

Art. No, it was nothing indeed,
compared with other deeds (you never did;   (*aside*)
if anyone here knows a greater liar,
more full of braggadocio than this man here,
I swear I'll give myself to him as a slave!
there's only one thing — I adore his sandwiches!)

Py. Where are you?

Art. Here! Take the Indian elephant
whose arm you shattered with one blow of your fist.

Py. His arm?

Art. No, no, I meant to say his leg.

Py. I swung without aiming.

Art. If you really had
put out your full strength, through the hide and flesh
and through the bones your arm would have transpierced.

Py. No more of that.

Art. It's scarcely worth my while
for you to tell me, since I know your prowess.
(My stomach makes this trouble — I must hear   (*aside*)
with my ears, to keep my teeth from teething,
and must confirm each single lie he tells.)

Periplecomenus, Palaestrio

Per. Think, and I'll retire a little over here.
Just look at him,
how he stands with beetling brows, worrying and wondering!
There he's knocking on his chest, calling wisdom out of doors.
Now, he turns away. He leans with his left hand on his left leg;
with the fingers of his right hand, look, he's figuring, and hitting
his right thigh, hitting it hard — he finds the planning difficult.
He snaps his fingers; he's in trouble; shifting here and shifting there.
Now look how he shakes his head — that last idea didn't suit him;
when he brings his plan to light, it won't be raw but nicely cooked.
Look, he's building! he's put up a pillar underneath his chin.
Ugh, I tell you, I don't like that kind of building, not a bit;
for I have heard about a foreign poet with a pillared face,
who has two guards that lie and watch and weigh him down by day
and night.
Hurrah! he strikes an attitude, a knavish slavish comic pose:
he'll never rest until he finishes whatever job he has begun.
I think he's got it. Go on! action! keep awake! don't think of sleep!
would you rather lie awake all striped and streaky from your strokes?
It's you I'm talking to, bestir yourself at once, Palaestrio.
Watch, I say, wake up, I say, it's daylight here, I say.
                                                          Pal. Yes, yes.
   Per. The enemy besets your rear and threatens you. Come, make a
      plan;
bring up reinforcements quickly, hurry, there's no time to lose.
Make a forced march, swing your forces round over a mountain pass,
catch the foe between your pincers, bring relief to our own men,
cut hostile communications, keep your own open and free
to bring up food and all supplies to you and to your regiments
safely and securely: this is urgent and imperative.
Think, divine, devise, supply a swift and subtle strategy,
so that what was seen be unseen, what was done here be undone.
Vast the plans this fellow makes, vast his great fortifications.

Sceledrus, Palaestrio

   Scel. Just by chance I happened to look in next door through our
      neighbors'
skylight: there I saw our Philocomasium in the arms of some young
      man,
kissing him!
                  Pal. Oh, oh, Sceledrus, what a skeleton in the cupboard!
   Scel. Yes, I saw it.
                  Pal. Who did? You did?

Scel. I did, with my own two eyes.

Pal. Nonsense, man, it's most unlikely, and you never saw it.

Scel. Do I look as if I'm blind and bleary?

Pal. Better ask the oculist. Just the same, if you are prudent, you won't wag that tale around — you're creating dreadful danger for your legs and for your head.

Scel. What will happen to me I don't know: but I know what I saw. What is more, she's still next door there.

Pal. Wow, isn't she at home?

Scel. Go and see, go in yourself. I do not ask to be believed.

Pal. Right, I shall. (*exit*)

Scel. And I'll wait here — and lay a little ambuscade, to catch our little heifer coming back from pasture to the byre . . .

(*re-enter Palaestrio*)

Pal. O Sceledrus, O Sceledrus, you're the biggest scoundrel living and most certain to be damned and tortured horribly!

Scel. What's wrong?

Pal. Go on, get your eyes extracted, you see things that aren't there.

Scel. How not there?

Pal. I wouldn't give a rotten leek for your life.

Scel. Why, what's wrong?

Pal. You're asking me what's wrong?

Scel. Of course I am.

Pal. Why don't you take that talkative tongue of yours and get it amputated?

Scel. Why should I do that?

Pal. Because Philocomasium is in our house, though you said you saw her next door making love to someone else . . .

Scel. I can see and think for myself, I trust myself most of all; nobody can tell me that she isn't in the house next door. I shall block its doors to catch her if she tries to sneak across.

Pal. (Now I've got him, now I'll blast him out of his Maginot line.) Shall I force you to admit that you are quite cock-eyed?

Scel. Just try . . .

Pal. All right, if the girl's at home here, if I bring her out our door, do you not deserve a thrashing?

Scel. A hearty one.

Pal. Well, watch *that* door, so that she doesn't slip across from it in secret to our house.

Scel. Certainly I'll do that.

Pal. Right. I'll bring her here in front of you . . .

(*exit and re-enter with Philocomasium*)

Pal. Hey, Sceledrus!

Scel. I'm busy now. But I've got ears, say what you will.
  Pal. That's the attitude I think you'll die in at the city-gate,
with your hands outstretched upon a gibbet-cross.

                        Scel. Oh, really? Why?
  Pal. Look to your left. Who is that woman?

                  Scel. Heavenly gods above protect me,
that's the master's mistress!

            Pal. Yes, that's what she looks like to me.
On you go then when you're ready —

                  Scel. To do what?
                      Pal. Why, to kill yourself.

874–890

Acroteleutium, Periplecomenus

Pe. Acroteleutium, I told you all our plan within,
and you too, Milphidippa. If you do not fully grasp
the tricks and all the technique, you must learn it all again;
but if you do, we'll talk of other more important things.
  Ac. Dear sir, it would be folly and insanity for me
to enter someone else's business, offering my help.
if I couldn't be a cunning worker and a cheat.
  Pe. Still, I should remind you.

                  Ac. Surely everybody knows
how much good it does to remind a courtesan!
Why, as soon as my ears sipped a morsel of your speech,
I myself could tell you how to whittle down the soldier.
  Pe. Yet no one's wise enough alone. I've often seen a man
overrun the zone of reason, only later finding it.
  Ac. But if a woman does a cruel and malicious thing,
her memory's immortal, everlasting to remember.
While if she must do any fine and faithful job,
suddenly she can't remember anything at all!

Gilbert Highet

MERCATOR 40–84

As soon as I passed out of my first youth,
I fell in love here with a courtesan.
My money fled to her, unknown to father.
The churlish slavemonger who was her owner
gouged and grasped for himself whatever he could.

My father then reproached me night and day,
explained that slavemongers were treacherous,
swelling their own fortunes at his expense.
Sometimes he'd shout this; and sometimes he'd mutter
that he'd disown me and deny his son,
that he'd go through the city warning people
not to trust me if I tried to borrow.
Love, he said, brought many men to ruin.
I was extravagant and criminal,
he said; I ought to go, and leave his house,
since the good property which he himself
amassed by toil and labor was most foully
wasted by me, under the power of love.
He had brought me up (he said) just to disgrace him,
He'd rather see me dead than lost to honor.
After he grew up beyond his own first youth,
he never wasted time on love and leisure
(he said); he was not even his own master,
but was controlled by his own father's orders:
engaged in long and dirty work upon the farm,
he came to town at four-year intervals
and even then, if he saw a skirt in passing,
his father rushed him straight back to the farm.
And there (said he) he worked harder than all
the servants, since his father used to say
"You plow and harrow, sow and reap for yourself:
at last this work will bring you happiness."
After his father's life had left his body,
he sold the farm, and with the money purchased
a freight-ship of three hundred barrels' burden,
and carried goods to every port and harbor
until he made his present capital.
He said I'd do that, if I were right-minded.
So when I realised he hated me,
and scorned me, though I should have made him love me,
I hardened my heart to all my love and lust,
and told him, if he asked, I'd go to sea,
and cast away my love, obeying him.

Gilbert Highet

Lucretius

❡ For a relatively unphilosophical people, Titus Lucretius Carus (c. 99–55 B.C.) is a unique contribution from the Romans. Little known in his own time, probably the victim of an officially inspired conspiracy of silence hostile to Epicureanism, he nevertheless won his way to lasting fame with his only book, *De Rerum Natura* (On the Nature of Things), perhaps written between 69 and 60 B.C. Borrowing from a large prose work on nature by the Greek Epicurus (341–270 B.C.), who had in turn borrowed from Democritus and Leucippus, Lucretius wrote in this glowing, magnificent poem the most complete analysis of the atomic composition of matter ever made until modern science revived atomism and led the way through nuclear physics to the atom bomb.

❡ The purpose of Lucretius in writing on materialistic theories was to dispel fear of Nature, of the gods, and of death; hence his description of the causes of natural phenomena leads to the loftiest of ethical conclusions. The principles of conservation of matter and energy, the constitution of the universe from atoms and void, the postulation of infinite worlds, the emphasis on the mortality of the soul, and the evidence of the senses as the sole guide to certain knowledge are fundamental to Lucretius' treatment of physics, cosmology, psychology, sociology, optics, mechanics, anthropology, linguistics, meteorology, and theology. He is in certain respects the first of psychiatrists. His ethical doctrines, diffused throughout the six books of the poem and concentrated in no one place, are the fruits of his physics and logic. These include the salvation of man through the use of his own brains, the abandonment of fears which fact and reason show to be groundless, the injunction to be happy, to use the world and its goods well, to be a good friend, the conquest of nature by understanding her laws, the placing of responsibility for man's actions on man alone and not on supernatural agencies, and the removal of the reward-motive for living through the attainment of Epicurean tranquillity. The civil wars and dictatorships, the cowardly materialism and superstition of his own troubled times, made Lucretius a moral teacher, for the pedagogical devices of his poem are numerous and obvious. The Four-fold Cure of Epicurus,

> In God there is nothing to fear,
> In Death there is nothing to feel;
> What is good is easily won,
> What is ill is easily borne.

is still valid for those whose intelligence and will, guided by the poetry of Lucretius, can achieve such a high goal: the liberation of man in the true sense.

❴ Jerome, a saint of the Catholic Church, gives us the single biographical reference to this strange man, but it is completely untrustworthy and to be regarded merely as the first in the centuries-long series of ignorant attacks upon Epicureanism. The character of Lucretius is to be deduced from his poem. He was a tortured intellectual who sought salvation in philosophy, but like Socrates could not be content with salvation for himself alone. The purpose of his thought was a social reform that was to begin in the heart of the individual, haunted by fear of death and cowed by dictatorship. His social ideals are worthy to be placed beside those of the greatest reformers; his intense faith in life, in love as the generative force of the universe, and in the physical foundations of existence makes him a modern among moderns. In addition he is the finest thinker the Romans produced. ❵

ON THE NATURE OF THINGS

I, 1–24

Darling of Gods and Men, beneath the gliding stars
you fill rich earth and buoyant sea with your presence
for every living thing achieves its life through you,
rises and sees the sun. For you the sky is clear,
the tempests still. Deft earth scatters her gentle flowers,
the level ocean laughs, the softened heavens glow
with generous light for you. In the first days of spring
when the untrammelled all-renewing southwind blows
the birds exult in you and herald your coming.
Then the shy cattle leap and swim the brooks for love.
Everywhere, through all seas, mountains and waterfalls,
love caresses all hearts and kindles all creatures
to overmastering lust and ordained renewals.
Therefore, since you alone control the sum of things
and nothing without you comes forth into the light
and nothing beautiful or glorious can be
without you, Alma Venus! trim my poetry
with your grace: and give peace to write and read and think.

Basil Bunting

I, 1014–1051

THE CREATION OF THE INFINITE UNIVERSE; HOW IT IS MAINTAINED

Nor sea, nor land, nor heaven's lucid stretch
nor mortal men, nor the Gods' own holy forms
could stay the quickest portion of an hour;
because dissolved, and freed from its close tie,
all matter's store goes stirring through the void,
or rather never could have closed compact
in solid things, since, scattered, never could
have driven together in a partless whole.
For surely not by plan the first of things
ordered or placed themselves by intellect
determined on the motions each described;
but being many and in many ways,
throughout the universe pushed on by blows,
explore all motions, every kind of form,
at last display themselves in such a cast
as now the universe is found to show.

And this preserved through markless stretch of time,
once shaped in genial motion for the whole,
impels the rivers with broad waves to feed
the hungry seas; the earth by moist sun-heat
renews its fruit, and breathing things spring forth.
And all the gliding fires of heaven do live.
But this would never be unless supplies
of matter from the infinite rose up,
from which, in season, they replace their loss.
For in the manner of a beast that starves,
its body wasting and dissolved away,
so all things ought, as soon as by some chance,
turned from their course, the reinforcements cease.
Nor can the force without on every side
conserve the whole of things which have been joined.
By constant blows it can delay some part
until another comes to fill the sum.
Yet sometimes to rebound they are impelled,
leaving the atoms time and space for flight,
and able to secede from their strict tie.
Again, and yet again, I say they must
rise up profusely: and that force itself
can be delivered in a constant stream,
so matter must on every side exist.

Robie M. Macauley

II, 1–61

From the Shore of Life

Soothing it is, when over mighty seas
winds churn the waters, to behold from shore
another tossed in trouble; not because
to see men harassed is a genuine joy,
but that to mark what evils you escape
is comfort in itself. This also soothes,
to watch the far-flung legions vie in war,
massed on the plain, yourself exempt from peril;
but bliss's very essence is to have
a calm inviolable stronghold, reared
on wise men's love and teaching, whence you may
look down and watch unshepherded mankind
wandering and seeking for the path of life,
these vying with their wits, and those with rank,
and all alike, through days and nights, with zeal
unparalleled, endeavoring to emerge
pinnacled on power, with riches at their feet.

O wretched minds of men, O blinded souls,
in what a darkness, what imperilled ways
your dribble of life is spent. When will you see
that Nature cries aloud for nothing more
than that the body should escape from pain,
the mind take pleasure in delightful sense,
enwalled from worries and the fear of death?
Therefore we see that for the body's ease
few wants are truly needs, save anodynes.

It's true you may voluptuously encouch
a man, who finds this welcome as a change,
but Nature neither asks it, nor complains
if golden youthful statues through the house,
their right hands clasping lamps of sleepless fire,
are lacking to illume the night's carousals,
nor if the mansion lacks the sheen of gold
and shine of silver, or no lyres resound
from panelled crossbeams round the gilded roof.
For just as well, when sprawled on velvet grass
in random groups beside a river-shore
under a tall tree's branches, men will sun
and sleek their bodies at a farthing's cost,
and most of all, if heaven and season smile
together, and sprinkle the verdurous floor with flowers.
For no whit swifter do hot fevers flee

from your frail person, if you shake and toss
on richly broidered silks and glowing purples
than if you must lie low in peasant homespun.
Wherefore since untold treasures, lofty birth,
and glory of princes profit not at all
the body, it follows we must think the mind
likewise can reap no profit from them.
                    Say,
perchance you see your legions swarm along
the field of Mars in mime of sternest war
with vast reserves and solid power of horse
as proudly armored as their spirit's proud;
or, say, you see your navy crowding sail
or far deploying, then if by such pomps
all superstitious terrors are not driven
in headlong panic from your mind; if dread
of Death is not swept clean from you thereby,
leaving a care-free heart, what profits power?
    But if we see these pomps are laughable
sham subterfuges; if indeed, though men
are dogged by fears and cares, they do not fear
the rattle of arms, the weapon's wanton edge,
but boldly mingle with great kings, the lords
of temporal might, undaunted by the gleam
of gold or flawless glow of purple robes,
why do you doubt this independent power
is Reason's rare prerogative, most rare
because our life's one travail through the dark?
For just as children in the dead of night
cower, and dread whatever fancy shapes,
so we at whiles in open daylight fear
shapes no more to be feared than bogey-men
that children, panting at the masks of gloom,
imagine bearing down. Wherefore not rays
of sunlight, nor the shining shafts of day,
but Nature's law, her calm of countenance
must drive these glooms and terrors from the soul.

Geoffrey Johnson

III, 59–93

On Human Ambitions

The blinding lust for honors, money-greeds,
which force unhappy men to pass the bounds

of justice and conspire in whispering crimes
and day and night to sweat with conquering strain
to reach the height of power: these sores of life
are largely festered by the fear of death.
For always filthy scorn and pinching want
are seen as foes to life's secure delight,
a loitering before the gates of death.

So men who're driven by a lying dread,
seek ever to escape, to run and hide.
They use the civic broils as source of wealth
and heap their coins like corpses that they heap.
They triumph daily in a brother's death,
and hate and fear the happy meals of kin.
Then often, through these plagues of fear, they rot
with envy. There's a man who's hedged with power;
all eyes are on him shining in his state;
these others mourn their wallowing glooms and dirt.

And some will die to gain a statued name.
Sometimes the fear of death will bring a man
to hate the sunlight fostering his life
till, grieving, he will toss his life away,
forgetting that his cares are fear of death,
the fear that weakens decency and snaps
our friendships, gnawing duty at its roots.
Yes, often men betray their homes, their loves,
in seeking to escape the shrine of hell.

Like children trembling in the blinded dark
and fearing every noise, we sit and dread
the face of light, and all our fears are vain
like things the child has fancied in the dark.
This fear, this darkness of the mind, we break
not by the sun, the glittering shafts of day,
but by perception of the natural truth.

Jack Lindsay

IV, 1053–1148

THE SICKNESS WHICH IS LOVE

So then the lover, wounded by Venus' darts
(Be it a boy with womanish limbs who sends them

Or be they sped from a woman's radiant limbs),
Pursues what wounds him, eager to unite
With it and cast his seed within its body;
For his desire dumbly foretells the pleasure.
This pleasure, then, is Venus; love is named
Cupido, the Desire, from that Desire
Whence flows the first delicious drop of love
Into men's hearts, and cold care afterwards.
For when the lover loses his beloved,
Her image still remains, her name still sounds
Sweet in his ears. Avoid these images
And shun the food of love! Distract your mind!
Cast your collected seed in any body
And do not harbor it by loving one
And one alone — that brings unfailing sorrow.
The ulcer lives, and feeds, and grows malignant,
The anguish rises to a flood of madness,
Unless you strike elsewhere, to erase the wound
And cure it while yet fresh, roaming abroad
After a commoner Venus, or transfer
Elsewhere the motions and desires of your heart.
But Venus is not barren to the loveless —
Rather she bears them blessings without pain.
Pleasure is purer for the healthy man
Than for the lovesick — all a lover's ardors
Wander and waver in possession,
He cannot tell what pleasure first to enjoy . . .
    From lovely faces and fair colored flesh
Nothing comes which the body may enjoy,
But flimsy little images, hopeless hopes
Which the wind often seizes and carries away.
As thirsty men, trying to drink in their sleep,
Can find no water to quench their burning limbs,
But struggle for imaginary water
In vain, and thirst among torrential streams,
So Venus dupes lovers with images:
They cannot satisfy themselves with gazing
Nor rub some satisfaction from these limbs
Though they caress and handle the whole body . . .
Moreover strength is lost, the labor wastes them;
Moreover all their life is enslaved to another.
Their wealth becomes carpets from Babylon,
Duty falls ill and reputation totters.
But soft luxurious shoes laugh on her feet;
Enormous emeralds, glittering green,

Are set in gold; raiment of ocean-purple
Is worn constantly, drenched with Venus's sweat.
A father leaves estates honestly earned,
And they become turbans and tires and coifs,
Sweeping silks, and Oriental robes.
Feasts are prepared, costly, luxurious,
Gaming and wine, perfumes and crowns and garlands —
But all in vain. From the wellspring of joy
Rises a bitterness among the flowers —
Because the heart sees truth and gnaws itself
For living slothfully in dens of vice;
Because a lady casts a doubtful word
Which hits and festers in the burning soul;
Or else because her glances are too free
And stolen smiles linger upon her face.
    These are the evils of a prosperous love.
In adverse love they come in multitudes
Past counting, to be caught even with closed eyes.
Better to watch beforehand, as I teach,
Beware, and be not drawn into the trap.
For to avoid the gins and nets of Venus
Is not so hard as breaking them when caught,
And struggling free from closely knotted meshes.

Gilbert Highet

V, 925–987

THE LIFE OF PRIMITIVE MAN

But the men of the steppes were tougher then by far, naturally,
Since the tough earth bore them
Built on a huge and massive frame and strong-set bone,
Slung with corded sinews through the flesh, not lightly
To be crippled by heat or cold or unproved food or any
Paroxysm of body. A ranging
Life they led while the sun wheeled countless decades through
The heavens, rovers in the style of the killer animals, for then
No one was a hardy steersman of the beak-nosed plough, or knew
To harry the fields with iron or plant young shrubs in the earth,
Or lop with billhooks the dead branches from tall trees. What sun
And rain coaxed out and earth threw up unaided was windfall
Enough to delight their hearts. Among acorn-dropping oaks mostly
They refreshed their bodies; and the wild tree-strawberry
Which is yet to be found ripening

In wintertime with scarlet freckle then tangled the hillsides
In more succulent and teeming plenty; and much rough fodder besides
The budding freshness of earth forced, more than enough for the
Wretched creatures. Burns and rills beckoned them to slake
Their thirst as nowadays a tumbling of waters from the heights
    summons
From far and wide the thirsty troops of animals with its clear gurgle.
In their rovings too they'd overrun the well-known woodland haunts
Of the nymphs, where they knew the trickling rivulets welled, washing
The pebblestones in their fussing,
The wet and glistering stones, and seeping through bright mosses,
Spilled in places to wander
Out to the plains. As yet they couldn't tame fire for their needs,
Or knew to use pelts and clothe their bodies with hides of beasts,
But would hug the glades and hill-caves and forests, and in the
    brushwood
Bury their unkempt limbs when driven to flee the lashings
Of wind and rain. Neither were they up to having an eye to
The common good, or availing themselves of any prevalent customs
Or laws; but what luck threw into any man's hand as booty
That he would hurry off with, schooled to live for himself
And thrive by his own device.
Sexual appetite brought couples to the woods together delightedly,
For either desire persuaded the woman, or the headstrong haste
And impetuous rut of the man; or she was wheedled with wide eyes by
    a bribe
Of acorns or a handful of wild berries or choice pears.
Trusting to their incredible swiftness of hand or foot they hunted
    down
The animals of the woods with showers of stones and ponderous clubs,
And many they would get the better of, but a few they shunned in
Hidey-holes. Like bristly boars they would hurl their forester
Limbs on the ground, naked as they were, night's prisoners,
Pulling leaves and branches over them: they didn't howl after daylight
And shriek for sunrise,
Rushing terror-stricken over the steppes through the folds of night,
But silent, sleep-drowned, they waited until the sun
With glowing torch had hurled
Light through the heavens. From their boyhood they had been the
    constant
Familiars of the alternate winking of dusk and dawn, so that never
Could they raise the hand in wonder at the miracle, or have any
    lurking
Fear that the sun might be dragged down and perpetual night grip
    earth

28026

LIBRARY
College of St. Francis
JOLIET, ILL.

For ever and ever. But this was their worry rather, that hordes of killer
Animals made sleep fatal to the wretches, and startled from their homes
When a foaming boar turned up or a roaring lion, they would put
As much ground as possible between them and their rocky tents, leaving
Their leaf-strewn lairs to their ruffian guests in their terror in the still hours . . .

W. Taylor McLeod

LIBRARY

College of ...

3 2 7 0 2 6

Catullus

❮ Gaius Valerius Catullus (c. 84–54 B.C.) and Horace are the chief Roman lyric poets, sole survivors of a large company whose names we know and little else. Catullus is the more profound and passionate, the more direct, appealing, and human of the two. His Celtic race, his early life at Verona, his association with the greatest and the vilest men and women in Roman society gave him his material — these, and a long, desperate, finally broken-off love affair with an enchanting, although notorious, married woman whom he called Lesbia. She was in real life named Clodia, the wife of Metellus Celer, governor of Cisalpine Gaul in 62 B.C.

❮ The 116 poems of Catullus, apparently all he ever wrote, are divided into lyric epigrams, elegiacs, and short epyllia or idyllic epics. They reflect the intimate interests, revulsions, and passions of this Roman lover, dilettante, man-about-town, amateur public servant, and political lampoonist. One-third of these poems contain enough obscenity to make them unreadable even in our frank age in any literal translation. No "complete" version of his poems is really complete; Jack Lindsay in Britain and Horace Gregory in America perhaps come closest to catching the sensuous, humorous, amorous, and jealous nature of Catullus. The most simple and poignant romance, pure as crystal, gives way in the next poem to savage coarseness. The courage to attack Caesar changes to abject self-pity over some momentary rejection by Lesbia. Caught in a hopeless love, he at last struggled through to some measure of objectivity and serenity. His deep friendships shine through the delightful epithalamia. His graceful learning is revealed in a number of poems inspired by the Alexandrian Greeks, especially in the *Lock of Berenice,* the second in a series of such poems which extends from Callimachus to Pope. But above the despair and loneliness of a man with many friends and enemies there ring the tones of a master artist who saw reality and turned it into great poetry, not mere cynicism. Sappho and Shelley, Robert Burns and Edgar Allan Poe are his special companions, different as these lyric poets were.

❮ Catullus pioneered in the complex task of adjusting the Latin language to Greek meters, but he does not boast of his successes. He wrote of his life as simply as he could, in its swiftly changing moods of glorious elation, dejection, pathos, and hatred. Although he wore his heart on his sleeve he was never silly. In the elegy to his dead brother he could easily have become maudlin; it is, on the contrary, the most dignified and at the same time touching memorial poem

27

ever written. He handles his meters with incredible skill, especially in that haunting evocation of orgiastic hypnotism, the *Attis,* which Sellar called the most original of his poems, or in that wonderful piece of wit (No. 17) about the stupid old man of Cologna. No one ever wrote quite like him in Latin literature before or since his time; his genius is perhaps the hardest to explain among all the Roman poets. He has appealed to writers as far apart as Tennyson and Ezra Pound, who saw in him something that fascinated each in its own way: perhaps it was the frank, ingenuous wit of a man who could make of beauty and of sadness a poem to touch any heart.]❭

1

For whom this pretty pamphlet, polished new
With pumice-stone? Cornelius, for you:
For you were never unprepared to deem
My simple verses worthy of esteem,
Though you yourself — who else in Rome so bold? —
In volumes three have labored to unfold
A "Universal History of Man" —
Dear Jove! a learned and laborious plan!

Wherefore to you, my friend, I dedicate
This so indifferent bookling; yet I pray,
Poor as it is — O goddess of my fate,
Let it outlive the writer's transient day!

James Elroy Flecker

2

Sparrow, my mistress' pet
With whom she often frolics
When she, my radiant one,
Has a mind for play,
Holding you upon her knee
She gives you her finger-tip
And provokes you to peck sharply.
It is, as I think, that you
May be a solace to her grief
When the fever of love is over;
Ah, little sparrow, might I
But play with you as she
And unburden the cares of my heart!

. . . . .

These to me are tidings
Such as the golden apple
Brought to the swift maiden,
Loosing her girdle which too long
Had guarded her celibacy.

W. K. Newton

4

Proud is Phasellus here, my friends, to tell
That once she was the swiftest craft afloat:
No vessel, were she winged with blade or sail,
Could ever pass my boat.
Phasellus shunned to shun grim Adria's shore,
Or Cyclades, or Rhodes the wide renowned,
Or Bosphorus, where Thracian waters roar,
Or Pontus' eddying sound.
It was in Pontus once, unwrought, she stood,
And conversed, sighing, with her sister trees,
Amastris born, or where Cytorus' wood
Answers the mountain breeze.
Pontic Amastris, boxwood-clad Cytorus!
You, says Phasellus, are her closest kin:
Yours were the forests where she stood inglorious:
The waters yours wherein
She dipped her virgin blades; and from your strand
She bore her master through the cringing straits,
Nought caring were the wind on either hand,
Or whether kindly fates
Filled both the straining sheets. Never a prayer
For her was offered to the gods of haven,
Till last she left the sea, hither to fare,
And to be lightly laven
By the cool ripple of the clear lagoon.

This too is past; at length she is allowed
Long slumber through her life's long afternoon,
To Castor and the twin of Castor vowed.

James Elroy Flecker

5

Let us live, O my Lesbia, and go on loving!
As for gabble of graybeards, stern, reproving,

Mark them down to a cent for all their scorning!
Suns may set and for them is sure returning;
We, when once in the west our flames diminish,
Fade forever in night no dawn shall banish.
Give me kisses: a thousand, then a hundred,
Then more thousands, and then another hundred!
Keep on kissing until with thousands taken
We lose count and the number may not reckon,
And no evil voyeur may note and number
All these kisses his lustful eyes remember.

Asa M. Hughes

8

Miserable Catullus, stop being foolish
And admit it's over,
The sun shone on you those days
When your girl had you
When you gave it to her
    like nobody else ever will.
Everywhere together then, always **at it**
And you liked it and she can't say
    she didn't.
Yes, those days glowed.
Now she doesn't want it: why
    should you, washed out,
Want to? Don't trail her,
Don't eat yourself up alive,
Show some spunk, stand up
    and take it.
So long, girl. Catullus
    can take it.
He won't bother you, he won't
    be bothered:
But you'll be, nights.
What do you want to live for?
Whom will you see?
Who'll say you're pretty?
Who'll give it to you now?
Whose name will you have?
Kiss what guy? bite whose
    lips?
Come on, Catullus, you can
    take it.

Louis Zukofsky

10

Varus took me to call upon his sweetheart
(He'd encountered me idling in the Forum) —
Meretricious, but as she first impressed me,
Not devoid of her charms and frank attractions.
Scarcely were we received before she started
Firing questions in my direction, such as
What Bithynia looked like now, and how it
Got along, and had I made money out there.
I replied but the truth, that neither natives,
Governors, or their aides had any reason
To come out and behave like wealthy dandies —
More especially since the present praetor
Was a bear who ignored his aides completely.
"Oh, but certainly," someone said, "you found there
What is known as the country's native product —
Men to carry your litter." I, then, thinking
I would seem to the girl a bit more lucky,
Said, "Oh well, I — I didn't fare so badly —
Though the province has gone to rack and ruin —
That I couldn't obtain eight strong-backed fellows."
Frankly, though, I had neither here nor elsewhere
Anyone who could shoulder an old, broken
Bedstead easily (*litter*ally speaking).
Then this wanton and impudent young baggage
Chimed in, "Please, that's a sweet Catullus, lend me
Them; tomorrow I'm visiting Serapis."
"Wait a minute," I stammered, "you've confused me.
When I said for a moment that I had — I
Don't know what I was thinking. My companion,
Gaius — Cinna, I mean — they're his; *he* bought them.
Really, whether they're his or mine, what matter?
I can use them as much as though I'd bought them,
But the point is that you deserve a gagging
If you can't let a man imagine freely."

Myron H. Broomell

11

Furius and Aurelius, Catullus's comrades,
Whether he penetrate the ultimate Indies,
Where the rolling surf on the shores of Morning
    Beats and again beats,

Or in the land of Bedouin, the soft Arabs,
Or Parthians, the ungentlemanly archers,
Or where the Nile with seven similar streamlets
    Colors the clear sea;
Or if he cross the loftier Alpine passes
And view the monuments of almighty Caesar —
The Rhine, and France, and even those remotest
    Shuddersome British —
Friends, prepared for all of these, whatever
Province the celestial ones may wish me,
Take a little bulletin to my girl friend,
    Brief but not dulcet:
Let her live and thrive with her fornicators,
Of whom she hugs three hundred in an evening,
With no true love for any, leaving them broken-
    Winded the same way.
She need not look, as once she did, for my love.
By her own fault it died, like a tumbling flower
At the field's edge, after the passing harrow
    Clipped it and left it.

Robert Fitzgerald

14

If I did not love you more than my very eyes,
My dear friend Calvus, I should hate you, for this
Gift, with the kind of hatred Vatinius inspires.
What did I do — what did I say —
That you should lay me low with these poetasters?
May the gods curse the hangers-on
Who sent you this sacrilegious collection!
But if, as I suspect, this rare new gift
Is a prize handed you by the pedagogue Sulla,
Why, then, I am delighted, not angry
Because your studies have borne fruit.
Great gods! It's a horrible and impious book
You sent your Catullus, that he should
Perish, no doubt, on the very next day
After the Saturnalia, of all days the best!
But you'll not succeed in your plot, villain:
For with the break of day I'll run
To the booksellers, collect from their shelves
Caesii, Aquini, Suffenus, and all
The other poisonous trash — and
With these tortures, I shall repay you.

Meantime, O very bad poets, goodbye!
From whatever place you brought
Your wretched lines, get you gone thither:
Bad poets, lumber of this age!

Frances Fletcher

17

Colonia, you wish to have a long bridge built, I hear,
To stage your games. The present bridge is ricketty and queer.
You want to dance about and skip; but if you do, you fear

A kick will send the piles and beams upon the mud below.
I hope you get a splendid bridge, one fit to hold your Show.

Then all the Salisubsilian Rites you want can gambol there,
And only one condition I'll exact for my best prayer —
That I may laugh my loudest at the whole absurd affair.

O, there's a fellow-citizen I'd like to witness slung
Head-over-heels from off your bridge to disappear among
The greenest holes of sludging bog and stinking quags of dung.

The man's a dolt: with no more sense or gumption he's possessed
Than any two-year baby whom its father rocks to rest.
He's married to a lovely girl just blossoming her best.

A girl more delicate than any tender-stepping kid,
A girl that like ripe clustering grapes from robbers should be hid.
And yet he lets her gad about and does just what he's bid.

He doesn't blink an eye but squats at home contentedly.
A log, which some Ligurian's chopped to earth, could never be
More doggedly oblivious of the world around than he.

An alder-log, snug in its ditch, would see as much about
As all the ways of wives and men are guessed-at by this lout.
If he exists or doesn't, he's not sure, I have no doubt.

This is the man that I want flung amid the bridge's muck;
For he might leave his stupid mind behind, if he had luck,
Like iron shoes that from a mule the mud will sometimes suck.

Jack Lindsay

22

This Suffenus, Varus, with whom you are acquainted,
Is a charming person: fluent, too, and worldly.
In the quantity of his poems, he outstrips all others.
He has, I believe, completed ten thousand or more —
And not, as is usual, written down on mere scraps:
No, he must have paper imperial, fresh rolls,
Fresh bosses, red leather ribbons, parchments —
Everything lead-ruled and pumice-polished.
When you read his verses, and then glance back at him,
This fine cultured Suffenus takes on the appearance of
Some goatherd or digger of ditches: so ludicrously he changes.
How explain? He who, a moment ago, was the image of a mirth-
Provoking anecdotist, or something more expert (if it exists),
Becomes, when he puts his hand to poetry,
More inept than inept rusticity. Yet
He is never so happy as when writing verses;
He charms and admires himself so much!
We all, indeed, err in the same direction. There is no one
In whom you may not recognize, in some aspect, Suffenus.
Each has a private self-deception to support: but we do not see
The hind-part of the sack on our own shoulder.

Frances Fletcher

23

Furius, you've no slaves, no box to hold your money,
For you have no money,
No spiders (and no walls where spiders live), no hearth, nor
  fire —
Father, you have, step-mother, whose teeth grown sharp with
  hunger
Split stones. O what a cheerful time you have with them —
  your father,
His wooden wife. All's well and it's no wonder:
You still digest what food may come your way: no falling
House to fear (no home) to be destroyed by fire, wind, or rain, or
Thieves, no poison will end your lives. Ill fortune cannot perfect
  your ruin.
Your bodies now are dry as old bones, and more so, if it's likely
One can be; heat of sun and winter's cold, starvation
Will help you. Why here's prosperity!
You cannot sweat, saliva

Shall not drip from your lips, you have no phlegm and therefore
No running nose. You're clean; your buttocks are
As clean and pure as salt is;
Your bowels refuse to move more than ten times a year and
Whatever you discharge is dry and sanitary.
Why beg the gods for more, my Furius, remember
One hundred coins (pure gold) are nothing —
When you're happy.

Horace Gregory

26

This villa is raked of winds from fore and aft,
All Boreas' sons in bluster and yet more
Against it is this TWO HUNDRED THOUSAND sesterces,
All out against it, oh my God:

some draft.

Ezra Pound

31

O my little almost island, little island Sirmio,
This brave eye, this green-bright jewel set in Neptune's fair estate
Of lucid waters and broad seas.
And it's good to look upon you; even now I can't believe
That the plains lie far behind me, weary Thrace and Bithynia.
You are still secure my own.
After many months of travel, nothing's better than to rest
Relaxed and careless; sleep is heaven in our own beloved bed.
Here's enough reward for exile, and long roads through foreign lands;
Now, my Sirmio, greet your master, make these waves bring laughter up
Till the Lydian lakes re-echo all the laughter in my home.

Horace Gregory

34

Diana guardeth our estate,
Girls and boys immaculate;
Boys and maidens pure of stain,
Be Diana our refrain.

O Latonia, pledge of love
Glorious to most glorious Jove,

Near the Delian olive-tree
Latona gave thy life to thee.

That thou should'st be for ever queen
Of mountains and of forests green;
Of every deep glen's mystery;
Of all streams and their melody.

Women in travail ask their peace
From thee, our Lady of Release:
Thou art the Watcher of the Ways:
Thou art the Moon with borrowed rays:

And, as thy full or waning tide
Marks how the monthly seasons glide,
Thou, Goddess, sendest wealth of store
To bless the farmer's thrifty floor.

Whatever name delights thine ear,
By that name be thou hallowed here;
And, as of old, be good to us,
The lineage of Romulus.

Sir Richard Jebb

42

Come to me, my poems, all my far-flung armies
Marching out in time with eleven bitter syllables,
Some filthy, naked whore has seized upon my papers,
Walked away with them and now she won't return them.
Hound her down, my boys — and who is she?
              I'll tell you:
She's that female beast that walks about the streets here
Proud of herself and bold (not even with the grace of
A human animal) laughing with her tongue out
Like a Gallic bitch.
              O my boys, surround her,
Chant your claim against her:
              "Dirty little bitch,
              Give us back our poems,
              Give us back our poems."
What? She doesn't hear? Then louder:
              "Lousy bloody whore,
              bitch littered in a
              brothel — "

But even these sweet names can never make you blush now
(Blushing never was a special trait of bitches);
Still she's quite unmoved, and we must change our tactics,
Say to her:
"O beautiful sweet untarnished virgin."

Horace Gregory

43

Madame, whose nose is not of the smallest, greetings!
Your foot is not shapely, either; nor have you black eyes.
Your fingers are too short; your mouth is over-moist;
And your speech has no elegance in it.
Greetings, mistress of the ruined Formianus!
You are celebrated in the provinces for beauty?
Our Lesbia is compared with you?
O stupid and undiscerning age!

Frances Fletcher

45

Septimius held his Acme close,
Close to his heart, saying "My dearest,
Unless I love you desperately,
Constantly, always, for ever, more than
The fondest lover in all the world,
May I be dropped in the African desert
To face a green-eyed lioness!"
Love had been slow before, but now
Sneezed on the right to show his favor.
  Now Acme turned her head softly,
  Kissing her lover's drunken eyes,
  With crimson lips kissing them,
  Saying "My darling Septimillus,
  Now let us worship Love for ever,
  The God who has kindled a stronger and keener
  Love-flame within my gentle heart."
Love had been slow before, but now
Sneezed on the right to show his favor.
  And now their God is favorable,
  Now they are both in love and beloved.
  Septimius holds his Acme dearer
  Than all the wealth of the furthest Indies.

Acme loves Septimius
Faithfully, gaily, deliciously.
Who ever saw a happier pair?
Where is a kindlier God of love?

Gilbert Highet

46

Now Spring brings back the tepid breeze,
Now Winter's raging gale is still
Beneath the West Wind's soothing breath.
And now, Catullus, you have left
The Phrygian fields, the fertile land
Of hot Nicaea disappears.
To Asia's famous cities we
Shall sail, and now our anxious hearts
Are eager for new wandering,
And now our steps are firm and joyful.

Dear band of comrades, fare you well,
Who long ago left home together
Return by many a different road.

L. R. Lind

51

He is changed to a god who looks on her,
Godlike he shines when he's seated beside her,
Immortal joy to gaze and hear the fall of
    Her sweet laughter.
All of my senses are lost and confounded;
Lesbia rises before me and trembling
I sink into earth and swift dissolution
    Seizes my body.
Limbs are pierced with fire and the heavy tongue fails,
Ears resound with noise of distant storms shaking
This earth, eyes gaze on stars that fall forever
    Into deep midnight.

. . . .

This languid madness destroys you, Catullus,
Long day and night shall be desolate, broken,
As long ago ancient kings and rich cities
    Fell into ruin.

Horace Gregory

55 and 58 *b*

Do please show me, if it's not too much trouble,
Where is your hidingplace.
I have looked for you in the lesser Campus,
In the Circus, at all the bookstores,
And in great Jupiter's holy temple.
I waylaid every female:
On no face did I see a guilty look.
You, you, I kept paging thus:
"Naughty girls, I want my Camerius!"
And one of them, revealing her nudity, said:
"He's hidden here, see, between my pink breasts."
To keep up with you has become a labor of Hercules.
Not if I were metamorphosed into the bronze guardian of Crete;
Not if I soared on the wings of Pegasus;
Or became Ladas or pinioned Perseus;
Or sped like the swift snowy team of Rhesus —
Not even then could I overtake you.
Add to these whatever gods go feather-footed and winged;
At the same time demand the wind's speed;
And give me the use of them all, Camerius:
Still my very bones would cry out with weariness,
And I should perish from excessive debility
While I tried, my friend, to discover your whereabouts.
Thus arrogantly you deny yourself?
Tell me where you are to be found. Publish it
Boldly. Confide in me. Trust the light of day.
You are held captive by milkwhite girls?
Persisting in this tightlipped silence,
You recklessly destroy love's blossoming:
Venus delights in a generous discourse.
But, if you will, put a lock on your palate:
Only let me share in your affection.

Frances Fletcher

61

You who dwell upon Helicon,
You the son of Urania,
Who snatch for her husband the tender girl,
O Hyménaean Hymen,
O Hymen Hymenaéan!

Bind your temples with marjoram,
With the flower that smells so sweet,
Take your torch and, delighted, come
Here with slippers upon your feet,
Yellow slippers on white feet.

Roused up now for the happy day,
Singing loudly the marriage hymns,
Singing the songs with a silvery voice,
Strike the ground with your feet and shake
The pine torch high in your handclasp.

For Vinia now to Manlius,
Just as Venus, Idalian one,
Came to Paris, the Phrygian judge,
She a chaste and a spotless girl
Comes well-omened in marriage.

Like the myrtle of Asia, bright,
Shining forth with its flowery twigs,
Which the tree-nymphs who play with it
There in the wood-land of Lydia
Nourish with the dewdrops.

Therefore come, make your entrance now,
Leave the village of Thespiae,
Leave the Aonian caves and cliffs
Which the nymph with her fountain chills,
Aganippe, the cold one,

And call the mistress unto her home,
She who wishes to see her man,
Fasten her heart in the bonds of love
Like the tough ivy that here and there
Wanders winding the tree trunk.

You too, maidens still virginal,
You for whom such a day is near,
Lift the chorus and sing with me,
"O Hyménaean Hymen,
O Hymen Hymenaéan!"

So more willingly when he hears
Us who call him to carry out
His task, the union of men and girls,

So the leader of honored love
Will come and join them in loving.

Who among all the gods is sought
More by eager lovers than he?
Whom of immortals do mortal men
Worship more? O </sup>Hyménaean,
O Hymen Hymenaéan!

You the trembling father calls
For his daughters, and virgins loose
For you the girdle that binds their breast;
Fearfully eager the bridegroom tries
To catch the sound of your music.

You yourself to the man's fierce hands
Give the shy little blooming girl,
Taking her from her mother's lap,
O Hyménaean Hymen,
O Hymen Hymenaéan!

Venus is helpless without your aid
To take her pleasure and still retain
Her name untarnished, but when you nod
Your head, she's happy. Who dares compare
Anyone else to this god?

There is no house that without you can
Bring offspring forth, not a father who
Can prolong his stock; but he can when you
Are willing. Who is it that dares compare
Anyone else to this god?

Whatever land lacks your sacred rites,
It cannot give to the border-watch
Soldiers as guard; but it can when you
Are willing. Who is it that dares compare
Anyone else to this god?

Open the doorway, open wide,
The virgin is here. Don't you see the torches shaking their shining hair about?

(four lines are missing)

Slow is ingenuous modesty:
Yet she hears him more than our call,
And weeps because she must marry.

Stop your weeping. Not for you, Au-
runculeia, the danger falls
Lest any woman more beautiful
Should see the brilliant day arrive,
Rising out of the Ocean.

So in a garden of varied bloom
Owned by a wealthy master, there
The blue-veined iris is wont to stand.
But you are delaying, the day goes by:
Bring her forth, the new bride-girl.

Bring her forth, the new bride-girl, if
Now you are ready, and listen to
Our words. See how the torches shine;
They're shaking their golden hair about.
Bring her forth, the new bride-girl.

Yours is a man who's not given to
Evil adulterous carryings-on,
Seeking a filthy, disgraceful life;
He's not a man who will wish to rest
Apart from your tender bosom.

Not he; but like the slow vine that climbs
Around the trees that it grows beside,
So will he twine in your warm embrace.
But hurry, the day is going by:
Bring her forth, the new bride-girl.

O bridal bed that for everyone
                    (*three lines are missing*)
Feet of the bed made of ivory,

What joys for your master are coming now,
What joys in the vanishing hours of night,
What joys in the middle of noon-day sleep!
But hurry, the day is going by:
Bring her forth, the new bride-girl.

Lift the torches on high, my boys;
I see her coming, all dressed in flame.
Come, sing all in a harmony,
"Io Hymen Hymenaee io,
Io Hymen Hymenaee!"

Let no longer in silence lie
The bawdy shouts of our pleasantry,
Let not the master's boy-friend deny
Nuts for the children to throw; he hears
His love is shunned by the master.

Give nuts to the children, you concubine;
Long enough you have lived at ease
And played with nuts like a child. You may
Now be slave to Talasio.
Boy-friend favorite, give nuts.

The foremen's wives on the farm for you
Were low and mean, yesterday, today:
Now let the hair-dresser shave your face.
Wretched boy-friend, ah, give nuts.

Perfumed bride-groom, they'll curse you for
Leaving the delicate boys alone.
But leave them, for all their grief, alone.
O Hymen Hymenaee io,
O Hymen Hymenaee!

We know the pleasures you give yourself
Are secret from others; no husband can
Enjoy this sort of a secret life.
O Hymen Hymenaee io,
O Hymen Hymenaee!

Bride-girl, whatever your husband wants,
Give it to him, and don't be coy:
Don't let him seek for it somewhere else.
O Hymen Hymenaee io,
O Hymen Hymenaee!

Look, how powerful just for you,
How prosperous too is your master's house.
Let it serve you forever now,
O Hymen Hymenaee io,
O Hymen Hymenaee!

Till age grown feeble and silver-haired,
Shaking its palsy-stricken brow,
Nods yes to all and to everything.
O Hymen Hymenaee io,
O Hymen Hymenaee!

Lift, and may the omen be good,
Over the threshold your golden feet,
Enter the polished gateway here,
O Hymen Hymenaee io,
O Hymen Hymenaee!

Look, how lonely upon his couch
Your husband lies in the Tyrian bed!
With his whole being he longs for you.
O Hymen Hymenaee io,
O Hymen Hymenaee!

For him no less than it burns for you
Love burns inside of his inmost heart.
For him it burns more secretly.
O Hymen Hymenaee io,
O Hymen Hymenaee!

Bride-boy escort who brings the bride,
Loose her soft little lovely arm.
Now let her come to her husband's bed.
O Hymen Hymenaee io,
O Hymen Hymenaee!

O good women, the wives of men
Honored and aged, bestow her well;
Place the girl in the bridal room.
O Hymen Hymenaee io,
O Hymen Hymenaee!

Now you may come to her, married man:
Your wife is here in your bedroom now,
Blushing, bright, with a flowering face
Like the snow white feverfew
And the flame-colored poppy.

But, husband, (so may the gods be kind)
You're no less beautiful now than she.
You're a handsome man; nor did Venus fail
To care for you too. But the day goes by:
Carry on, do not tarry.

Not for long have you dragged your feet;
Now you're coming. Let Venus be

Good to you, help you, since openly
That which you wish is a love that's good,
A love that need not be hidden.

Let him number the seashore sands
Of Africa, and the shining stars,
Let him number them all before,
Who wishes to count your joys of love,
Joys in their many thousands.

Play as long as you like, and soon
Give us children. It does not suit
So ancient a name to long remain
Barren of offspring, but from the same
Stock always to bring children.

I wish to see a small Torquatus
Stretching his little hands toward me
Out of his mother's lap, to see
Him sweetly smiling at his papa,
His baby mouth falling open.

Let him be like his father too,
Let him be easily known to all
Even to those who aren't family friends,
And let him prove with his little face
His mother's pure chastity.

May such high praise for his mother rise
To honor the family fame and name
As once for Telemachus from the best
Of mothers, an honor that is unique,
From Penelope lasted.

Close the doors of the bridal room,
Maidens; now we have sung enough.
Married folks, live long and well,
Making the most of your dear delight
While you are young and still able.

L. R. Lind

63

Across the roaring ocean, with heart and with eye of flame,
To the Phrygian forest Attis in an eager frenzy came:

And he leapt from his lofty vessel, and he stood in the groves of pine
That circled round with shadows Cybele's mystic shrine:
And there in a frantic fury, as one whose sense has flown,
He robbed himself of his manhood with an edge of sharpened stone.
But as soon as he felt his body bereft of its manly worth,
And saw the red blood trickle on the virgin soil of earth,
With his blanched and womanish fingers a timbrel he gan to smite
(A timbrel, a shawm, Cybele, thine, mother, O thine the rite!),
And he beat the hollow ox-hide with a furious feminine hand,
As he cried in trembling accents to the listening Gallic band:

"Arise, away, ye Gallae! to Cybele's lofty grove!
Together away, ye straylings of our Lady of Dindyma's drove!
Who have sought with me, like exiles, a far and a foreign home:
Who have borne with me the buffets of the sea and the fleeting foam:
Who have followed me, your leader, through the savage storms of
    night:
Who have robbed your frames of manhood in dainty love's despite.
Make glad the soul of our Lady with the rapid mazy dance.
Away with slothful loitering. Together arise, advance
To Cybele's Phrygian forest, to the Goddess's Phrygian home,
Where ring the clanging cymbals, where echoes the bellowing drum,
Where slow the Phrygian minstrel on his reed drones deep and dread,
Where the Maenad tosses wildly her ivy-encinctured head,
Where the mystic rites of the Goddess with piercing shrieks they
    greet,
Where our Lady's vagrant votaries together are wont to meet —
Thither must we betake us with triply-twinkling feet."

And thus to his eager comrades the unsexed Attis cries,
In a sudden shriek the chorus with quivering tongue replies:
The hollow timbrel bellows, the tinkling cymbals ring.
Up Ida's slopes the Gallae with feverish footsteps spring.
At their head goes frantic, panting, as one whose senses rove,
With his timbrel, fragile Attis, their guide through the glimmering
    grove,
Like a heifer that shuns, unbroken, the yoke's unaccustomed weight:
And with hurrying feet impetuous the Gallae follow straight.
So, when Cybele's precinct they reached in the inmost wood,
With over-travail wearied they slept without taste of food.
On their eyelids easy Slumber with gliding languor crept,
And their spirit's fanatic ecstasy went from them as they slept.
But when golden-visaged Phoebus with radiant eyes again
Surveyed the fleecy aether, solid land, and roaring main,
And with mettlesome chargers scattered the murky shades of night,

Then Attis swift awakened, and Sleep fled fast from his sight.
(In her bosom divine Pasithea received the trembling sprite.)
So, roused from gentle slumber and of feverish frenzy freed,
As soon as Attis pondered in heart on his passionate deed,
And with mind undimmed bethought him where he stood and how
    unmanned,
Seething in soul he hurried back to the seaward strand;
And he gazed on the waste of waters, and the tears brimmed full in
    his eye;
And he thus bespake his fatherland with a plaintive, womanish cry:

"O fatherland that bore me! O fatherland my home!
In an evil hour I left thee on the boundless deep to roam.
As a slave who flees his master I fled from thy nursing breast,
To dwell in the desolate forest upon Ida's rugged crest:
To lurk in the snows of Ida, by the wild beast's frozen lair:
To haunt the lonely thickets in the icy upper air.
O where dost thou lie, my fatherland, in the ocean's broad expanse?
For my very eyeball hungers upon thee to turn its glance.
While my soul for a little moment is free from its frenzied trance.
Shall *I* from my home be hurried to this grove so far away?
So far from my goods and my country, from my kith and my kin shall
    I stray?
From the games and the crowded market, from the course and the
    wrestling-plain?
Ah, hapless, hapless Attis, thou must mourn it again and again.
For what form or fashion is there, what sex that I have not known?
I was a child and a stripling, a youth, and a man full grown:
I was the flower of the athletes, the pride of the wrestlers' zone.
My gates were thronged with comrades, my threshold warm with feet;
My home was fair encircled with flowery garlands sweet,
When I rose from my couch at sunrise the smiling day to greet.
Shall *I* be our Lady's bondmaid? a slave at Cybele's hand?
Shall *I* be a sexless Maenad, a minion, a thing unmanned?
Shall I dwell on the icy ridges under Ida's chilly blast?
Shall I pass my days in the shadows that the Phrygian summits cast,
With the stag that haunts the forest, with the boar that roams the
    glade?
Even now my soul repents me: even now is my fury stayed."

From the rosy lips of Attis such plaint forth issuing flowed,
And straight the rebellious message rose up to the Gods' abode.
From the brawny neck of her lion Cybele loosed the yoke,
And, goading on his fury, to the savage beast she spoke:
"Up, up!" she cried; "dash onward! Drive back with a panic fear,

Drive back to the lonely wilderness the wretch who lingers here!
Who dares to flee so lightly from the doom that I impose!
Lash, lash thy side in anger with thine own impetuous blows!
Let the din of thy savage bellowing roar loud on the startled plain,
And thick on thy tawny shoulders shake fierce thy shaggy mane!"

So threatening spoke Cybele and loosed from his neck the yoke;
And the brute, himself inciting, with a roar through the thicket broke:
And lashed his side in anger, and he rushed to the hoary main
Till he found the fragile Attis by the shore of the watery plain:
Then he gave one bound. But Attis fled back to the grove aghast.
There all the days of his lifetime as Cybele's thrall he passed.

Goddess! mighty Goddess! Cybele! who rulest Dindyma's height,
Far from my home, O Lady, let thy maddening wrath alight!
Upon others rain thy frenzy! Upon others wreak thy might!

Grant Allen

68 a

Burdened as you are with misfortune and sorrow,
You nevertheless send me a tearful letter, Manlius,
In behalf of a man shipwrecked but saved from death by water.
This man, to whom holy Venus permits no restful sleep
In his lonely bed, and to whose apprehensive mind
The soft poetry of our older writers brings no delight —
This man you ask me to help, to restore to life.
I am grateful that, as a mark of your friendship,
You call on me to provide gifts of Venus and the Muses.
But, Manlius, I must tell you of my own difficulties,
Lest you feel I shirk the office of host.
I am myself contending with stormy fortune. Understand this,
So you'll not again seek divine gifts from indigence.
When I first put on the white toga of manhood
And youth, in flower, was one long May festival, I wrote,
For diversion, a number of verses: I am not a stranger to
The goddess who gives suffering a taste of bittersweet.
But mourning for my brother's death has made me
Indifferent to my art. O my brother! O sorrow!
You took with you into death, O my brother,
Whatever amenities life held. My whole house lies buried with you.
All those pleasures which you nurtured, living,
Have perished with you.
I have put out of my mind, as a tribute to death,
All thought of poetry; all enchantments of the heart and spirit.

And so, when you write: "To be at Verona, Catullus,
Discredits you. All the gilded youth look
To that bed, deserted by you, for a transforming warmth" —
Well, Manlius, that is my misfortune; not my disgrace.
You understand, then, why I do not send gifts
Despondency has deprived me of: I cannot.

I live at Rome. And so it happens that I have
Few writers with me. Rome is my home;
My seat; the background of my life. Only one small
Box of books, from many, follows me here.
I should not wish you to think me ungracious;
Nor, in the conditions, ungenerous, in not showering you
With an abundance of everything you seek.
Possessing such wealth, I would have offered it unasked.

Frances Fletcher

69

That no fair woman will, wonder not why,
Clap (Rufus) under thine her tender thigh;
Not a silk gown shall once melt one of them,
Nor the delights of a transparent gemme.
A scurvy story kills thee, which doth tell
That in thine armpits a fierce goat doth dwell.
Him they all fear full of an ugly stinch,
Nor's 't fit he should lye with a handsome wench;
Wherefore this Noses's cursed plague first crush,
Or cease to wonder why they fly you thus.

Richard Lovelace

70

My woman says she wants no other lover
    than me, not even Jupiter himself.
She says so. What a woman says to an eager sweetheart
    write on the wind, write on the rushing waves.

Gilbert Highet

72

In the old days, Lesbia, you said Catullus alone
Had your favor; you would rather have me than Jove.

I loved you then as the man in the street loves his girl;
And as a father loves his sons and sons-in-law.
Now I understand you. And if love burns in me more fiercely
You have become, even so, an object of levity, rather; of vice.
How, you ask, is this possible? Because an injury like yours to me
Compels a lover to love more — but with less consideration.

Frances Fletcher

76

If, to one who remembers his past beneficences,
There is satisfaction in thinking himself a man of integrity:
One who has not violated faith; nor, in the name of religion,
Falsely persuaded, in any covenant, his fellow mortals:
Then many joys, Catullus, have been prepared for you,
For years to come, by this thankless love.
All that a human being can say or do, for his neighbor's dignity,
You, Catullus, have said and done.
Yet this generosity was lost on the nature entrusted with it:
Why then torture yourself further?
Why not be resolute, withdraw altogether,
And cease to suffer since the gods are unwilling?

It is difficult to slough off a love of long standing:
Difficult: yet by hook or crook you must do it.
It's the only way out— this is your superhuman task —
This you have to do, be it possible or impossible.
O gods, if you know mercy; if ever you brought
Last-minute help to those in the grasp of death —
Then mark me in my wretchedness. And if I have lived honestly,
Tear out of me this disease, this horror!
Inertia, coiling itself in my very veins,
Has drained from me every spark of animation.
I no longer ask that she love me in return:
Nor, what is impossible, that she live in decency.
I ask only for health: release from this sickness; this venom.
I have been reverent, O gods. Hear me, then, now!

Frances Fletcher

83

Her husband present, Lesbia lashes me with words:
  An exquisite delight to that fatuous man.

Mule, you sense nothing. If, ignoring me, she held her tongue,
She would be normal. By hectoring and abusing me,
She proves she still remembers and — more sharply to the point —
Is furious. She wants me, that is: and so she raves.

Frances Fletcher

84

Sir 'Arry, though lately created a knight,
Is unable to order his "h's" aright.
He expounds the wise views of "a man of haffairs"
Or explains " 'ow 'e 'ates haristocracy's hairs."
(To his mother, née 'Awkins, he owes, I expect,
This unpleasant, invincible vocal defect.)
His victims had looked for a respite at least
While Sir 'Arry is occupied "doin' the Heast."
But alas for our hopes! You've not heard the news? What?
Sir 'Arry finds "Hindia 'ellishly 'ot."

Anonymous

85

"At once I hate and love as well."
— "In heaven's name, Catullus, how?"
— "God knows! And yet I feel it now
Here in my heart: the whole of hell."

M. H. Tattersall

86

Quintia is beautiful, many will tell you: to me
She is white, she is straight, she is tall: to all this I agree,
But does this make her beautiful? Though she be found without fault,
Can you find in the whole of her body the least pinch of salt?
But Lesbia is beautiful: hers is the secret alone
To steal from all beauty its beauty, and make it her own.

Arthur Symons

92

Lesbia swears at me continually; she's never quiet
    About me; damned if I don't think she's in love with me.

The proof? Because we are even: I swear at her in the same way
   Day after day, but damned if I'm not in love with her.

L. R. Lind

96

If ever aching heart can speed across the years
      Its word of love;
         Or, Calvus, if our tears
For friend or heart's beloved may pierce the gloom,
         And move
      Its load of sadness from the silent tomb;
   Why then, to know your faithful love for her,
         Shall surely stir
      Quintilia's heart to joy; she will forget
Grief that death came so soon because you love her yet.

H. W. Household

101

By strangers' coasts and waters, many days at sea,
   I came here for the rites of your unworlding,
Bringing for you, the dead, these last gifts of the living,
   And my words — vain sounds for the man of dust.
            Alas, my brother,
You have been taken from me. You have been taken from me,
   By cold Chance turned a shadow, and my pain.

Here are the foods of the old ceremony, appointed
   Long ago for the starvelings under earth:
Take them; your brother's tears have made them wet; and take
   Into eternity my hail and my farewell.

Robert Fitzgerald

107

If a wished-for thing and a thing past hoping for
Should come to a man, will he welcome it not the more?
Therefore to me more welcome it is than gold
That Lesbia brings me back my desire of old,
My desire past hoping for, her own self, back.
O mark the day with white in the almanac!
What happier man is alive, or what can bring
To a man, whoever he be, a more wished-for thing?

Arthur Symons

Furius Bibaculus

❨ Marcus Furius Bibaculus, a contemporary of Catullus who out-lived the latter, came from Cremona and wrote an epic on Caesar's Gallic Wars; he is probably the Bibaculus mentioned by Catullus in poems 11, 23, and 26. ❩

CATO'S WAY OF LIFE

Whoever sees my friend's, my Cato's cottage,
Its peeling walls vermilion-dyed, and those
Green beds where Priapus preserves the pottage,
Must marvel on what hardy fare he rose
To be the wisest man Rome ever knew.
A half-pound loaf a day, three heads of kale
A day, and then a bunch of grapes or two
Under the same tiled roof, sufficed for him
Now gazing, almost, on life's furthest rim.

Geoffrey Johnson

Decimus Laberius

❴ Roman drama dwindled away to the mime and finally the pantomime in the age of Cicero and Caesar. The mime, also borrowed from
Greece, seems to have been a sort of vaudeville skit in which figures
of the day were ridiculed and mimicked. As Duff says, "its travesties
of life and personages became in time more literary and more varied,
if no less indecent. By gesticulations, grimaces, imitations of man,
beast, or bird, and the roughest buffoonery, it guaranteed laughter."
We have the titles of forty-four plays by Decimus Laberius (c. 105–43
B.C.), and the extant fragments show a picturesque humor and a colloquial touch fitting for this type of play.
❴ The mime could be a wry performance when its criticism of society
or individuals backfired upon the author, as happened to Laberius in
45 B.C. when he was about sixty years old. Macrobius says (*Saturnalia,* II, 7) that Julius Caesar forced Laberius, a bitter critic of the
dictator, to act in his own mime. Laberius, however, neatly turned
the tables on Caesar before the audience by uttering a two-edged
recantation, part of which, the prologue to Necessity, is given here.
The translation is an approximation of the original meter, the iambic
senarius, or six-foot iambic. ❵

AN OLD ACTOR ADDRESSES
JULIUS CAESAR

Necessity, the impact of whose sidelong course
Many attempt to escape and only few succeed,
Whither have you thrust down, almost to his wits' ends,
Him whom flattery, whom never bribery
Could in his youth avail to shake him from his stand?
But see how easily an old man slips, and shows —
Moved by the complacency of this most excellent man —
Calm and complaisant, a submissive, fawning speech!
Yet naught to a conqueror could the gods themselves deny,
And who then would permit one man to say him nay?
I who existed sixty long years without stain,
A Roman Knight who went from his paternal gods,
Now return home a mime. And certainly today
I've lived out one more day than I should have lived.
Fortune, unrestrained in prosperity and ill,

54

Were it your pleasure with the lure and praise of letters
To shatter the very summit of my good name,
Why when I prospered, when my limbs were green with youth,
When I could satisfy an audience and such a man,
Did you not bend my suppleness and spit on me?
Now you cast me? Whither? What brought I to the stage?
The ornament of beauty, dignity of flesh,
Fire of the spirit, the music of a pleasing voice?
As twining ivy kills the stout heart of the tree,
So has senility in time's embrace destroyed me
And like a sepulchre I keep only a name.

J. V. Cunningham

Publilius Syrus

❨ Publilius the Syrian (hence Syrus), a slave who may have come from Antioch, gained his freedom through his talent as a playwright of the mime and as a composer of proverbial sayings. He was the rival of Laberius in the contest staged in 45 B.C. and was awarded the prize by Caesar. His plays were excerpted in the form of *Sententiae* in the first century A.D.; some 700 lines, chiefly iambic senarii, exist. They are part of the proverb-literature of Rome, favorite among a people whose practical wisdom is often of a sententious kind. ❩

MAXIMS

Love, or hate: a woman knows no third.

✿

Love is not driven out, but slips away.

✿

Scarcely a god can both love and be wise.

✿

To take a kindness is to sell your freedom.

✿

To die at another's will is to die twice.

✿

Good reputation is more safe than wealth.

✿

To be reconciled with foes is never safe.

✿

Danger comes quicker when it is despised.

✿

War long prepared brings rapid victory.

✿

Women know how to tell a lie by weeping.

✿

Kindness is doubled if it is but hastened.

✿

Even a single hair still casts a shadow.

＊

He whom fate cherishes becomes a fool.

＊

Dangerous he who thinks it safe to die!

＊

Poverty needs a little; greed needs all.

Gilbert Highet

Vergil

(Publius Vergilius Maro (70–19 B.C.), a farmer boy born at Andes near Mantua, is the greatest of Roman poets; his only equal in power of thought and choice of theme is Lucretius. Like that of James Joyce, Vergil's work shows a steady progression and development from the early short poems called the *Catalepton* (or, prosily, the *Appendix Vergiliana*) through the *Eclogues* and *Georgics* to his masterpiece, the *Aeneid*. The *Eclogues* are ten brief pastoral poems, set among shepherds and flocks, with the quaint artificial charm of the Alexandrian Greek poems of Theocritus, which were Vergil's models. The *Georgics*, four longer poems on crop-raising, tree-growing (the olive and vine), cattle-raising, and bee-keeping, are polished examples of a favorite literary tradition among the Romans: didactic epic, or instruction in verse. Here too he improved on his Greek model, Hesiod's *Works and Days*. Close examination of his poems such as that made by Richard Heinze in his book, *Vergil's Epic Technique* (available, unfortunately, only in German), shows how deeply dependent on a multitude of sources, both Greek and Latin, the art of Vergil was; he is a learned poet of the kind we have come to know in our own day in T. S. Eliot and Ezra Pound.

(In the *Aeneid* Vergil tells how Aeneas fled from Troy, fought the native tribes in Italy for three years and won supremacy there. Surprisingly, Rome's foundation by the remote descendants of Aeneas is not dwelt upon, although the story of Romulus and Remus would have made a fascinating episode, as it is in Livy's history. Only in "flash-forwards" does Vergil give us glimpses of Roman history, not legend, as in Book VI, where later historical characters are pointed out to Aeneas by his father Anchises. This twelve-book epic in all its dignity, passion, and sadness is a synthesis of Roman character in the person of its hero. Unlike previous epic heroes Aeneas is a man who submerges his private wishes to the needs of his people; rather, their wishes are his. He is the first true folk-leader in literature. Structurally, the *Aeneid* combines the plots of both the *Iliad* and the *Odyssey*: the attack upon a nation and the return-home of the hero, for Italy is the early homeland of the Trojans, to which they return at last. A deep love of Italy and her landscape runs through the *Aeneid* as it does through the *Georgics*.

(The tragic meeting with Dido (IV), the funeral games for Anchises (V), the descent of Aeneas into Hades (VI), the combat between Cacus and Hercules (VIII), the last decisive duel between Turnus and Aeneas (XII) are among the major episodes of the poem. It is, however, the imperial destiny of Rome as the subjugator and civilizer of the earth's peoples against the background of patient, suffering humanity that is Vergil's central theme. In spite of the blinding force of military glory the tragedy and essential pathos of human existence are never far from his hero's thoughts, nor from Vergil's. Romance, symbolism, warfare, history, folklore, and legend are woven together in this national epic of the Romans.])

COPA: THE BARMAID

O Syrian dancing-girl with the filleted hair,
who taught you to swing your flanks with that shiver and shake?
She's dancing drunk in the tavern's smoky air,
lewd wench, to the clicketing sound the castanets make.

Why stay in the dusty heat where everything withers?
Come here, lie down, and be drunk awhile, you fool.
Look! tankards, cups, bowls, roses, flutes, and zithers,
and a trellis-arbor shadowed by reeds and cool.

In a cave full of music, like Pan's own cave, you can stretch —
the kind of piping you hear 'neath the open sky.
Thin wine just drawn from a pitchy cask they'll fetch,
and, brabbling and murmuring, water goes swiftly by.

Look! there are wreaths from crocus and violets wrought,
gold melilot mixed with the rose's crimson hue.
From the virgin stream of Acheloïs are brought
lilies in willow-baskets — and all for you.

Look! little cheeses drying in baskets of rush,
and plums that come to their sweetness in autumn weather;
chestnuts, and apples with red that is pleasantly lush.
Look! fine Ceres and Love and Bacchus together.

Look! reddened blackberries, grapes in placid clusters,
sea-green cucumbers hanging from tendrils of shade.
Look! the arbor-god — with his willow-hook he blusters,
but even his terrible middle won't make us afraid.

Hither O wanderer. The little ass sweats, and he faints.
The dear little ass is Vesta's own darling. So spare.
The crickets are splitting the thickets with shrilling complaints,
The lizard is lurking cool in a bramble-lair.

Be wise and drench out the heat with wine in a glass
Or a crystal cup, if that's how you like your wine.
Lie tired in the vine-shade and let the summer hours pass,
And round your nodding head let the roses twine.

Yes, reap the kisses from someone mouth-open, kindly.
Death to the fellows whose questioning eyebrows frowned!
Why keep your wreaths for the ashes huddled blindly?
See your life and not your tombstone with roses crowned.

To hell with the future! Bring wine and the dice-box here.
"I'm coming, so kiss," says Death, and pinches my ear.

Jack Lindsay

ECLOGUE I

Meliboeus, Tityrus

M. You to your beech tree, Tityrus, withdraw
  And whistle at the Tree Muse through a straw.
  I leave my sweet fields, leave my country. This
  Is exile, Tityrus. But loaf in the shade!
  Pipe until the woods learn what you've played
  And echo with your *Amarillis-illis.*

T. Oh Meliboeus, a god gave us this peace.
  I'll stain his altar with a bloody fleece
  And call him *God* a hundred times. You see
  My flocks graze by his grace; his grace lets me
  Play what I feel like playing on this straw.

M. I feel no envy, but a sort of awe:
  There's trouble all around you. See, I go
  Dragging with pain to drive my goats. This doe,
  Tityrus, I can scarcely drag along.
  Here in the hazel thicket she was wrung
  In labor till she dropped her kids, those twins,
  The hope of all the flock, on naked flint.
  When heaven blasts the oaks to make them signs
  I know bad luck is what that lightning augurs,
  But my left-handed wits passed me no hint.
  Well, tell me, Tityrus — this god of yours?

T. Meliboeus, I thought the place called Rome
  Was like our little city here at home

Where we shepherds drive our weaned Spring lambs.
Pups are just like dogs, kids like their dams,
Small things are much like big ones: so I said.
The others since this one reared up her head
Are topped the way a cypress tops a weed-bed.

M. You saw Rome; tell me your great reason why.

T. Freedom came late to me. She let me lie
In dullness, never looked, till the dull years
Had taught my beard to grow white for the shears.
Then she came and looked me in the eye.
And Amarillis had me. She let go,
That other, Galatea. Well, you know
How Galatea bitched me. All it meant
Was slavery. I couldn't save a cent.
I'd take my best pressed cheese, tear from my fold
My lambs, the innocents! slaughtered and sold!
And walk home wondering where the money went.

M. Amarillis, you were gloomy at prayer,
You let the apples rot and didn't care —
I never guessed why. Tityrus had left.
How our pines, springs, orchards howled, bereft!

T. What could I do? Stay home and be a slave,
Leave home and lose whatever my gods gave —
Here, Meliboeus, here I saw that youth
Our altars burn for every year twelve days,
Who took my questions, gave me my first truth:
"Feed your cows, boys; breed bulls; keep the old ways."

M. Lucky old man! Your country still is yours.
And big enough for you, this field of rocks
And muddy rushes — so the swamp assures
Your breeding ewes from pest-rid neighbor flocks
And all temptation of strange nourishment.
Lucky old man, here with the streams you know,
The sacred springs, withdraw to the cool shade.
Here let Hybla's bees in your neighbor's willow
Hedge sipping, forever humming, persuade
You gently, "Go to sleep." Under the high
Rock there the woodsman sings a song to the sky
While your pet pigeons utter squawks of content
And doves still in the airy elm lament.

T. And so trembling deer shall graze in the air,
The seas shall strand their fishes on a bone-
Dry coast, and each gone past the other's frontier
Shall Gaul drink Tigris, Parthian drink Saône
Before my heart loses his countenance.

M. But we must go. Some to reach the torrents
Of Crete's Oaxes, some to the Ukraine,
The thirsty Africans, and some where Britain
Floats cut off entirely from the world.
Ah, years to come, will I ever see again
My country, years and years from now, my old
Shack and its sod roof; will I ever come
To stare at a couple of corn stalks, once my kingdom?
Will some damned soldier hold this land I've ploughed,
Foreigners reap these crops? So we are bowed
And broken by disorder. Is this my harvest?
Now, Meliboeus, dress your vine rows, graft
Your pears. Let's go, my goats. I'll never rest
Again beneath some cave's eave while you drift
Away on the distant crags, browsing and slow;
I'll sing no songs; come, my goats, where no
Alfalfa flowers bloom, no bitter willow.

T. Well, you might have stayed and made your bed
On green boughs here with me tonight. Chestnuts
And apples all are ripe, the cheese is salted.
Look, the smoke is rising from those huts.
See where the shadows of the mountains spread.

John Thompson, Jr.

ECLOGUE II

Burning with love, the shepherd Corydon,
(Alexis was his love, his master's pride),
Often, for comforting, would haunt alone
Dense shadowy beeches on the mountain-side;
There, underneath their branches spreading wide,
Knowing not what to hope for, he would sing
These artless songs to woods and mountains listening:

"Cruel Alexis, do you scorn my song?
Have you no pity? Then you bid me die!

The flocks seek shade and coolness, and along
The sheltering hedge the bright green lizards lie,
And Thestylis a savory feast near by
Prepares for heat-worn reapers; I, alone,
Trace and retrace your steps under the burning sun

In vineyards shrill with grasshoppers. Ah, why
Such suffering? Were it not best to bear
Proud Amaryllis' changeful tyranny,
Menalcas' whims, though he is dark, you, fair?
In trusting to pale beauty, youth, beware!
White privet falls unheeded; the deep hue
Of velvet hyacinths is ever sought anew.

You scorn me then, and do not seek to know
What flocks I have, what mountain-pastures sweet
My thousand lambs stray over, how in snow
Their white milk fails not, nor in summer's heat;
You do not know my songs! As long ago
Amphion sang under the Attic sky
When calling home his cattle, so sing I.

Nor am I so unsightly. On the strand
When peaceful to the winds lay all the sea,
I saw my image: gladly I would withstand
Daphnis as rival, and you judging me,
If images speak truth. Come, then, and be
Sharer of my poor homestead — pierce the hind,
Or with green switch urge on the goats that lag behind,

And we will rival Pan in singing. Pan,
Friend of the shepherds' flocks, was first to blow
On wax-joined reeds, and teach the song to man.
Your chafed lip would not fret you, could you show
The skill that raised Amyntas' envy so!
I've a pipe, too, of hemlock stalks uneven
Damoetas, dying, gave — its hollow reeds are seven.

And thus he spoke (Amyntas envying):
'It has a second master, now, in you!'
Then, too, for your own prize, two fawns I'll bring;
I found them in a rugged vale — an ewe
Their foster-mother — dappled white, the two.
Thestylis begs to have them, night and day,
And she shall take them, since you laugh my gifts away.

Come hither, youth! Nymphs in your honor bear
Baskets brimful of lilies, and, behold!
Gathering pale wall-flowers, a Naiad fair
Adds anise and narcissus, and the bold
Bright poppy-heads; the yellow marigold
She sets off with dark hyacinths, and weaves
Cassia with them, and other herbs with scented leaves.

I will myself pluck quinces with soft down,
And chestnuts, which my Amaryllis loves;
Apples and waxen plums shall win renown;
The laurel, too, which mingles, as it moves,
Sweet scents with those of neighboring myrtle groves — "

Foolish! Alexis would such gifts despise,
Nor, if you strove with gifts, would Iollas yield the prize.

What have I done but loose the South Wind's heat
Upon my flowers, in madness, and on the blue
Of my clear streams the wild boar's muddying feet?
Whom do you flee? The Gods once wandered through
Such forests — dwelt there — Trojan Paris, too!
Let Pallas seek the cities she has raised;
The woods are mine, and in my songs let woods be always praised!

After the wolf the tawny lioness
Follows — the wolf pursues the kid — the sight
Of flowering clover lures the kid — I press
Close on your steps, Alexis; the delight
Of each draws each. And now the sunset light
Lengthens the shadows; plowmen homeward move,
And yet my love still burns — for what can limit love?

Ah, Corydon! What madness seizes you?
Half-pruned upon the leafy elm, the vine
Neglected hangs! Up, idler, and pursue
The task that daily need sets forth, and twine
The river reeds with osiers smooth and fine.
You'll find, if such tasks do not solace prove,
Another fairer youth, since this one scorns your love.

Mary Grant

ECLOGUE III

Damoetas, Menalcas

D. From Jupiter the Muse begins, and Jupiter is everywhere:
   He makes the earth all fruitful to be, he doth unto my ditties give ear.

M. But I'm the man that Phoebus loves. My garden is Apollo's seat.
   I give him gifts, the bay-tree and the hyacinth do blush so sweet.

D. Now Galatea throws at me an apple, she's a wanton maid:
   Off to the sally-trees she do run, wishing I spy where to she's fled.

M. But dear Amyntas is my flame. He is my flame, and never coy:
   My little dog knows Delia well, far better doth he know that boy.

D. I have a present for my Venus, I've a present for my love,
   Since I myself did notice a spot where nesties high have builded the doves.

M. Ten golden apples did I pluck, ten golden apples a wild tree bore:
   All that I could I sent to my boy, tomorrow he shall have ten more.

D. O many times, O charming words she's spoke to me — my Galatea!
   Whisper a little part of them, you breezes, into heaven's ear!

M. Oh what avails, Amyntas dear, that after me your heart's inclined,
   If while you hunt the ravening boar, you leave me the nets to mind?

D. Send Phyllis here, send Phyllis now, Iollas, since it is my birthday:
   Until I sacrifice a heifer for the crops, you keep away!

M. Phyllis I love before the rest, and Phyllis wept when she saw me go:
   Long did she say farewell to me, farewell, farewell, my handsome beau.

D. The wolf is cruel to the sheep, and rain to cornfields that ripened be,
   Cruel the wind to orchard trees, Amaryllis' rage is cruel to me.

M. Sweet is a shower to crops, and arbute boughs to kids that weaned be,
   Sallies are sweet to breeding herds, none but Amyntas sweet to me.

D. My Muse is but a country girl, yet Pollio this girl adores:
   Fatten a heifer, Pierian maids, for him who reads the song that is yours.

M. Fatten a bull, I'd liefer say, for Pollio new songs doth write:
   Fatten a bull with venturesome horn and hooves that kick the dust about.

D. Let him who loves thee, Pollio, come thither where thy enjoyment lies:
   Let honey flow for him in streams and brambles bear the cardamum spice.

M. Let one who hates not Bavius, let him adore e'en Maevius' ditties —
 Aye, let him yoke a fox to his plough and milk he-goats that have no titties.

D. O children dear who gather flowers, who gather flowers and wild strawberries,
 Run away fast, dear children, oh run! a cold cold snake do lurk on the leaze.

M. O sheep, beware, stray not too far, and never trust the river bank:
 Look at the ram your master, O sheep, drying his fleece that still is dank.

D. Now Tityrus, keep you the kids from grazing nigh to the river brim:
 I mean to dip them all myself into the spring when it be time.

M. Now fold the flock, my shepherd boys: for if the heat turn the milk again
 As it has done these latter days, then we shall squeeze their dugs in vain.

D. Ah welladay, my little bull he peaks and pines where thick vetches grow:
 Love is the same for man or beast, 'tis death to herd and herdsman also.

M. My flock are naught but skin and bone — and 'tis not love, I tell thee true.
 An evil eye hath overlooked my pretty lambs, I know not who.

D. I have a riddle — where on earth do space of sky measure but three yard?
 Answer my riddle, and I'll say Apollo's not a greater bard.

M. I have a riddle — where on earth are flowers signed with a king's name grown?
 Answer my riddle, and I'll say that Phyllis you shall keep for your own.

C. Day Lewis

ECLOGUE IV

Muses
Muses of Sicily
Now let us sing a serious song
There are taller trees than the apple and the crouching tamarisk
If we sing of the woods, let our forest be stately

Now the last age is coming
As it was written in the Sibyl's book

The great circle of the centuries begins again
Justice, the Virgin, has returned to earth
With all of Saturn's court
A new line is sent down to us from the skies
And thou, Lucina, must smile
Smile for the birth of the boy, the blessed boy
For whom they will beat their swords into ploughshares
For whom the golden race will rise, the whole world new
Smile, pure Lucina, smile
Thine own Apollo will reign

And thou, Pollio
It is in thy term this glorious age begins
And the great months begin their march
When we shall lose all traces of the old guilt
And the world learn to forget fear
For the boy will become divine
He will see gods and heroes
And will himself be seen by them as god and hero
As he rules over a world of peace
A world made peaceful by his father's wisdom

For thee, little boy, will the earth pour forth gifts
All untilled, give thee gifts
First the wandering ivy and foxglove
Then colocasia and the laughing acanthus
Uncalled the goats will come home with their milk
No longer need the herds fear the lion
Thy cradle itself will bloom with sweet flowers
The serpent will die
The poison plant will wither
Assyrian herbs will spring up everywhere

And when thou art old enough to read of heroes
And of thy father's great deeds
Old enough to understand the meaning of courage
Then will the plain grow yellow with ripe grain
Grapes will grow on brambles
Hard old oaks drip honey

Yet still there must remain some traces of the old guilt
That lust that drives men to taunt the sea with ships
To circle cities with walls
And cut the earth with furrows
There must be another Tiphys

Another Argo carrying picked men
And there must be a war, one final war
With great Achilles storming a last Troy

But when thou hast grown strong and become a man
Then even the trader will leave the sea
His pine ship carry no more wares
And everywhere the land will yield all things that life requires
No longer need the ground endure the harrow
Nor the vine the pruning hook
The farmer can free his oxen from the yoke
Then colored cloths no longer will need lying dyes
For the ram in the field will change his own fleece
To soft purple or saffron yellow
Each grazing lamb will have a scarlet coat

> *"Onward, O glorious ages, onward"*
> *Thus sang the fatal sisters to their spindles*
> *Chanting together the unalterable Will*

Go forward, little boy, to thy great honors
Soon comes thy time
Dear child of gods from whom a Jupiter will come
See how for thee the world nods its huge head
All lands and seas and endless depths of sky
See how the earth rejoices in the age that is to be

O may my life be long enough to let me sing of thee
With strength enough to tell thy deeds
With such a theme not even Thracian Orpheus could outsing me
Not Linus either, though Apollo prompted him
Help from Calliope herself could not make Orpheus' song the best
And even Pan, with Arcady as judge
Yes Pan, would fall before me when I sang of thee

Learn, little boy, to greet thy mother with a smile
For thee she has endured nine heavy months
Learn, little boy, to smile
For if thou didst not smile
And if thy parents did not smile on thee
No god could ask thee to his table
No goddess to her bed.

James Laughlin

ECLOGUE V

DAPHNIS

Menalcas, Mopsus

Men.   Come sit where elm twig scrapes on hazel shoot
And I will sing, and you on reedy flute
Blow lightly.

Mop.   Shall we find a cave or go
Where shadows tremble in the wind? You know
For you're the elder. See, there gleam along
Our cave, the wild vine's scattered grapes.

Men.   In song
Amyntas only rivals you.

Mop.   He'd win
Though striving with Apollo.

Men.   Hush — begin
Some song of Phyllis, taunt for Codrus. I
Shall sit and rest while Tityrus drives by
The feeding goats.

Mop.   Lately on green beech bark
I scratched some words and now I'll sing them. Hark
To the tune. Then let Amyntas start to play.

Men.   As green-gray olives outshine a willow spray,
The Punic rose excels the Celtic reed,
So you surpass Amyntas. Now give heed,
Come — sit within the cave and pipe to me.

Mop.   Daphnis is dead. Now, nymphs, weep mournfully.
The hazel trees and rivers saw him die.
Daphnis is dead, and, near, his mother cries
To all the gods, the stars. No shepherd drives
His flock through field or stream. No beast will pass
To drink from icy pool or crop the grass.
Daphnis, the woods and dreaded hills have said
That the fierce lion weeps since you are dead.
You told us Asian tigers draw the god's
Swift chariot. We followed you and trod
The fields in Bacchic dance and wove soft leaves
With wands. As wild vines tangling crown the trees,
Grapes grace the vine, the bull the herd, and corn-
Sheaves glitter in the grass, so you adorned
Your comrades. Fate has seized you. Now the fields
Are empty of the rural gods. Now yields
The furrow, which we sowed with barley seed,

Unfruitful darnel. And the wild oats breed.
Where waving violets and narcissus grew
Are brambly shrubs. Here softly, shepherd, strew
The ground with leaves, the fountain, there, with shade;
He'd like it so. And when the grave is made
We'll add this: star-famed Daphnis roamed this hill
With lovely goats — he was more lovely still.

Men. Some god has blown your reed. Sweet songster, pass.
As sleep to the weary resting in the grass,
As to the thirsty summer's stream, your song
Has been to me. By Daphnis you belong
In reed and voice. Now with less skillful breath
I'll sing less mournfully our shepherd's death.

Mop. He's worth your praise. Nothing could please me more.

Men. White Daphnis wondering sees through heaven's floor
The clouds and stars. Love fills the woodland shades,
The country Pan and shepherds, dryad maids.
No wolf in ambush meditates the sheep,
No net awaits the stag. Stars hear the steep
Cliffs sing. They mourn no more but name
You god. The woodlands echo with your fame.
Two altars for you and for Phoebus two
We've placed. And I shall bring you cups of new
Milk, bowls of olives, wicker baskets filled
With wine. We'll feast you by the hearth when chilled
Or in the shade at harvest. Shrines remain
For you while men still purify the plain
And pay the nymphs their vows. While the wild pig
Haunts mountain tops, bees hum in every sprig
Of thyme, fish fill the rivers, crickets thrive
On dew, your name and honor still shall live,
And farmers offer Daphnis sacrifice,
A god like Dionysus.

Mop.   Singer, wise
In song no whispering south wind knows, no shore
With tides, nor brook that meets the valley floor
In misty falls, what gift can pay you more?

Men.   First,
This hemlock take — for many notes have burst
From it in song.

Mop.   And you this shepherd's cane.
Antigenes once asked for it in vain
Though he was worth my love. Menalcas, see
The knots and bronze crook shining beautifully.

                                        Anne Greet

ECLOGUE IX

Lycidas, Moeris

L. Whither, Moeris, your haste? By the usual road to the city?

M. Lycidas, Oh! we have struggled through, but only
To suffer this grief undreamed, that a soldier-stranger
Should grab our dear little farm and bellow to us:
"These fields are mine; uproot yourselves, you fossils."
Beaten and down, for Luck must dip full circle,
We are sending him now these kids (may they breed him
mischief!)

L. Yes, I had heard, where the hills begin to lessen
And soften down their ridge in a gentle falling
To the pool's old beech-tops torn with recent ravage,
That rhymes of your Menalcas had charmed away ruin.

M. Yes, as you heard, so rumor went; but poems,
My Lycidas, count no more when war is rampant
Than do Chaonian doves at an eagle's arrival;
And had not a left-hand crow from a hollow ilex
Warned me to dodge somehow the quarrel's renewal,
Your Moeris here would be dead, and so would Menalcas.

L. Alas, can a crime so foul occur to anyone,
All but snatching, Menalcas, with you our song-joy?
Who then would sing of the Nymphs, of Earth in blossom,
Who bower the fountains round with verdurous darkness,
Who chant the lines I overheard in silence
Lately, when you went wooing our dear Amaryllis?
"Tityrus, while I am away (not a great while) pasture
The she-goats, lead them to drink, and beware, though busy,
The he-goat's venomous jab with his near-side horn-tip."

M. But, why not the half-wrought lines he sang to Varus? —
"Only preserve to us Mantua, Mantua, neighbor
Too near to tragic Cremona, then swans in chorus
Shall waft your glory, Varus, among the immortals."

L. So may your bees avoid the Corsican yew-trees,
And your cattle, browsing in clover, swell their udders.
Begin, if your memory holds. Me also the Muses
Have made a poet; yes, poems are mine; the shepherds

Style me the seer, but I waive their flattering garlands,
For nothing I have sung so far seems worthy of Varus
Or Cinna, but mere goose-gabble jarring a swans' choir.

M. But, Lycidas, so I do, in silence pondering
In hope to remember; the poem repays recapture:
"Come hither, my Galatea; why sport in the billows?
Here is the sheeny Spring, here Earth from the river-meads
Pours many-hued flowers, the poplar's shivering whiteness
Hangs over the cave, and pliant vines weave arbors.
Come hither, and leave mad waves to their boulder-bashing."

L. What of the lines I heard you singing alone once,
Under the cloudless night? I recall the metre
But the phrases fail me: "Daphnis, why do you watch so
For the risings of ancient constellations? Look you,
The star of Caesar, the child of Venus, has risen
Whose influence gladdens the crops with abounding harvests
And mantles the sunny hills in vineyard purples.
Daphnis, graft your pears; your children's children
Shall pluck them in peace."

M.   Age robs us mortals of all things,
Even the mind. And yet I remember how often
My boyhood beguiled long summer days with singing
So many songs I forget now. Voice, too, fails now
Your poor old Moeris; death's wolfish eyes have marked him.
Yet often enough Menalcas will chant you the passage.

L. By subtle asides you torture my loving patience.
But see how soundless and boundless the plain now glimmers,
How quietly die the last wind's farewell murmurs.
From here we are now half-way, for Bianor's tombstone
Is beginning to gleam. Here, Moeris, here, where farmers
Are stripping the crowded leaves, let us sing together.
Set the kids down here; we still shall reach the city,
But if night seems to be brewing an early rainstorm,
We still may sing as we go, and lighten the journey.
To sing as we go, I will ease you of this burden.

M. Boy, urge me no more; but let us be doing what presses.
Better shall we sing verse when the Master meets us.

Geoffrey Johnson

GEORGIC I

1

Until Jove let it be, no colonist
Mastered the wild earth; no land was marked,
None parcelled out or shared; but everyone
Looked for his living in the common wold.

And Jove gave poison to the blacksnakes, and
Made the wolves ravage, made the ocean roll,
Knocked honey from the leaves, took fire away —
So man might beat out various inventions
By reasoning and art.
           First he chipped fire
Out of the veins of flint where it was hidden;
Then rivers felt his skiffs of the light alder;
Then sailors counted up the stars and named them:
Pleiades, Hyades, and the Pole Star;
Then were discovered ways to take wild things
In snares, or hunt them with the circling pack;
And how to whip a stream with casting nets,
Or draw the deep-sea fisherman's cordage up;
And then the use of steel and the shrieking saw;
Then various crafts. All things were overcome
By labor and by force of bitter need.

2

Even when your threshing floor is leveled
By the big roller, smoothed and packed by hand
With fuller's earth, so that it will not crack,
There are still nuisances. The tiny mouse
Locates his house and granary underground,
Or the blind mole tunnels his dark chamber;
The toad, too, and all the monsters of the earth,
Besides those plunderers of the grain, the weevil
And frantic ant, scared of a poor old age.

Let me speak then, too, of the farmer's weapons:
The heavy oaken plow and the plowshare,
The slowly rolling carts of Demeter,
The threshing machine, the sledge, the weighted mattock,
The withe baskets, the cheap furniture,
The harrow and the magic winnowing fan —

All that your foresight makes provision of,
If you still favor the divine countryside.

3

Moreover, like men tempted by the straits
In ships borne homeward through the blowing sea,
We too must reckon on Arcturus star,
The days of luminous Draco and the Kids.
When Libra makes the hours of sleep and daylight
Equal, dividing the world, half light, half dark,
Then drive the team, and sow the field with barley,
Even under intractable winter's rain.
But Spring is the time to sow your beans and clover,
When shining Taurus opens the year with his golden
Horns, and the Dog's averted star declines;
For greater harvests of your wheat and spelt,
Let first the Pleiades and Hyades be hid
And Ariadne's diadem go down.
The golden sun rules the great firmament
Through the twelve constellations, and the world
Is measured out in certain parts, and heaven
By five great zones is taken up entire:
One glowing with sundazzle and fierce heat;
And far away on either side the arctics,
Frozen with ice and rain, cerulean;
And, in between, two zones for sick mankind:
Through each of these a slanting path is cut
Where pass in line the zodiacal stars.

Northward the steep world rises to Scythia
And south of Libya descends, where black
Styx and the lowest of the dead look on.
In the north sky the Snake glides like a river
Winding about the Great and Little Bear —
Those stars that fear forever the touch of ocean;
Southward they say profound Night, mother of Furies,
Sits tight-lipped among the crowding shades,
Or thence Aurora draws the daylight back;
And where the East exhales the yellow morning,
Reddening evening lights her final stars.

4

As for the winter, when the freezing rains
Confine the farmer, he may employ himself

In preparations for serener seasons.
The plowman beats the plowshare on the forge,
Or makes his vats of tree-trunks hollowed out,
Brands his cattle, numbers his piles of grain,
Sharpens fence posts or pitchforks, prepares
Umbrian trellises for the slow vine.
Then you may weave the baskets of bramble twigs
Or dip your bleating flock in the clean stream.
Often the farmer loads his little mule
With olive oil or apples, and brings home
A grindstone or a block of pitch from market.

And some will stay up late beside the fire
On winter nights, whittling torches, while
The housewife runs the shuttle through the loom
And comforts the long labor with her singing;
Or at the stove she simmers the new wine,
Skimming the froth with leaves. Oh idle time!
In that hale season, all their worries past,
Farmers arrange convivialities —
As after laden ships have reached home port,
The happy sailors load the prow with garlands.
Then is the time to gather acorns and
Laurel berries and the bloodred myrtle,
To lay your traps for cranes and twist a sling
To chase the long-eared leveret and the deer,
And listen to attentive pleasantries:
When snow is deep and ice is on the rivers.

5

What of the humors and the ways of autumn?

Just when the farmer wished to reap his yellow
Fields, and thresh his grain,
I have often seen all the winds make war,
Flattening the stout crops from the very roots;
And in the black whirlwind
Carrying off the ears and the light straw.
And often mighty phalanxes of rain
Marched out of heaven, as the clouds
Rolled up from the sea the detestable tempest;
When the steep aether thundered, and the deluge
Soaked the crops, filled ditches, made the rivers
Rise and roar and seethe in their spuming beds.

The Father himself in the mid stormy night
Lets the lightnings go, at whose downstroke
Enormous earth quivers, wild things flee,
And fear abases the prone hearts of men —
As Jove splits Athos with his firebolt
Or Rhodope or the Ceraunian ridge.
The southwind wails in sheets of rain,
And under that great wind the groves
Lament, and the long breast of the shore is shaken.

If you dislike to be so caught, mark well
The moon's phases and the weather signs;
Notice where Saturn's frigid star retires,
Mercury's wanderings over heaven; and revere
Especially, the gods. Offer to Ceres
Annual sacrifice and annual worship
In the first fair weather of the spring,
So may your sheep grow fat and your vines fruitful,
Your sleep sweet and your mountains full of shade.
Let all the country folk come to adore her,
And offer her libations of milk and wine;
Conduct the sacrificial lamb three times
Around the ripe field, in processional,
With all your chorus singing out to Ceres;
And let no man lay scythe against his grain
Unless he first bind oakleaves on his head
And make his little dance, and sing to her.

6

When shall we herd the cattle to the stables?

The wind, say, rises without intermission;
The sea gets choppy and the swell increases;
The dry crash of boughs is heard on hills;
The long sound of the surf becomes a tumult;
The gusts become more frequent in the grove;
The waves begin to fight against the keels;
From far at sea the gulls fly shoreward crying;
The heron leaves his favorite marsh and soars
Over the high cloud. Then you will see
Beyond thin skimrack, shooting stars
Falling, the long pale tracks behind them
Whitening through the darkness of the night;
And you'll see straw and fallen leaves blowing.

But when it thunders in rough Boreas' quarter,
When east and west it thunders — every sailor
Furls his dripping sail.

A storm should never catch you unprepared.
Aerial cranes take flight before its rising,
The restless heifer with dilated nostrils
Sniffs the air; the squeaking hirondelle
Flits round and round the lake, and frogs
Inveterate in their mud, croak a chorale.
And too the ant, more frantic in his gallery,
Trundles his eggs out from their hiding place;
The rainbow, cloud imbiber, may be seen;
And crows go cawing from the pasture
In a harsh throng of crepitating wings;
The jeering jay gives out his yell for rain
And takes a walk by himself on the dry sand.
Stormwise, the various sea-fowl, and such birds
As grub the sweet Swan River in Asia,
May be observed dousing themselves, as if they wished —
What odd exhilaration! — to bathe themselves.

7

After a storm, clear weather and continuing
Sunny days may likewise be foretold:
By the sharp twinkle of the stars, the moon
Rising to face her brother's rays by day;
No tenuous fleeces blowing in the sky,
No halycons, sea favorites, on the shore
Stretching out their wings in tepid sunlight;
But mists go lower and lie on the fields,
The owl, observing sundown from his perch,
Modulates his meaningless melancholy.
Aloft in crystal air the sparrow hawk
Chases his prey; and as she flits aside
The fierce hawk follows screaming on the wind,
And as he swoops, she flits aside again.
With funereal contractions of the windpipe
The crows produce their caws, three at a time,
And in their high nests, pleased at I know not what,
Noise it among themselves: no doubt rejoicing
To see their little brood after the storm,
But not, I think, by reason of divine
Insight or superior grasp of things.

8

But if you carefully watch the rapid sun
And the moon following, a fair night's snare
Never deceives you as to next day's weather.
When the new moon collects a rim of light,
If that bow be obscured with a dark vapor,
Then a great tempest is in preparation;
If it be blushing like a virgin's cheek,
There will be wind; wind makes Diana blush;
If on the fourth night (most significant)
She goes pure and unclouded through the sky,
All that day and the following days will be,
For one full month, exempt from rain and wind.
The sun, too, rising and setting in the waves,
Will give you weather signs, trustworthy ones,
Whether at morning or when stars come out.
A mackerel sky over the east at sunrise
Means look out for squalls, a gale is coming,
Unfavorable to trees and plants and flocks.
Or when through denser strata the sun's rays
Break out dimly, or Aurora rises
Pale from Tithonus' crocus-colored chamber,
Alas, the vine-leaf will not shield the cluster
In the hubbub of roof-pattering bitter hail.

It will be well to notice sunset, too,
For the sun's visage then has various colors;
Bluish and dark means rain; if it be fiery
That means an East wind; if it be dappled
And mixed with red gold light, then you will see
Wind and rain in commotion everywhere.
Nobody can advise me, on that night,
To cast off hawsers and put out to sea.
But if the next day passes and the sunset
Then be clear, you need not fear the weather:
A bright Norther will sway the forest trees.

9

Last, what the late dusk brings, and whence the fair
Clouds are blown, and secrets of the Southwind
You may learn from the sun, whose prophecies
No man denies, seeing black insurrections,
Treacheries, and wars are told by him.

When Caesar died, the great sun pitied Rome,
So veiling his bright head, the godless time
Trembled in fear of everlasting night;
And then were portents given of earth and ocean,
Vile dogs upon the roads, and hideous
Strange birds, and Aetna quaking, and her fires
Bursting to overflow the Cyclops' fields
With flames whirled in the air and melted stones.
Thunder of war was heard in Germany
From south to north, shaking the granite Alps;
And a voice also through the silent groves
Piercing; and apparitions wondrous pale
Were seen in dead of night. Then cattle spoke
(O horror!), streams stood still, the earth cracked open
And tears sprang even from the temple bronze.
The Po, monarch of rivers, on his back
Spuming whole forests, raced through the lowland plains
And bore off pens and herds; and then continually
The viscera of beasts were thick with evil,
Blood trickled from the springs; tall towns at night
Reechoed to the wolf-pack's shivering howl;
And never from pure heaven have there fallen
So many fires, nor baleful comets burned.
It seemed that once again the Roman lines,
Alike in arms, would fight at Philippi;
And heaven permitted those Thessalian fields
To be enriched again with blood of ours.
Some future day, perhaps, in that country,
A farmer with his plow will turn the ground,
And find the javelins eaten thin with rust,
Or knock the empty helmets with his mattock
And wonder, digging up those ancient bones.

Paternal gods! Ancestors! Mother Vesta!
You that guard Tiber and the Palatine!
Now that that century is overthrown,
Let not this young man fail to give us peace!
Long enough beneath your rule, O Caesar,
Heaven has hated us and all those triumphs
Where justice was thrown down — so many wars,
So many kinds of wickedness! No honor
Rendered the plow, but the fields gone to ruin,
The country-folk made homeless, and their scythes
Beaten to straight swords on the blowing forge!
War from the Euphrates to Germany;

Ruptured engagements, violence of nations,
And impious Mars raging the whole world over —
As when a four-horsed chariot rears away
Plunging from the barrier, and runs wild,
Heedless of the reins or the charioteer.

Robert Fitzgerald

GEORGIC II, 475–498

My heart's desire is that the Muses fair,
The Muses dear above all else to me,
Would take me for their own and teach me all
The paths of heaven, the stars, the sun's eclipse,
The labors of the moon; why shakes the earth;
From what great force the deep seas toss and rage,
Burst through their barriers, and once more subside;
Why haste so fast the winter suns to dip
In Ocean and the nights delay so long.
But if the cold blood round my heart forbid
That I should sing the mighty works of God,
Then be the country my delight, and brooks
Which wash the valleys; let me love
Unknown to fame the hills and woods and streams.
Oh joy to be amid the fields where flow
Spercheus and Taygetus, on whose banks
The Spartan maidens leap in bacchic song!
Oh who will take me to the cool ravines
Of Haemus underneath the boughs' thick shade!
That man is happy who has understood
Life's mysteries and trampled underfoot
Terrors and fears, inexorable fate,
And the loud roar of greedy Acheron.
He too is fortunate who learns to know
The rural gods, Silvanus old and Pan,
And many a woodland nymph. He is not moved
By fasces which the fickle crowd bestow,
Or by the purple robe of regal pomp;
Nor does he view with anxious, brooding heart
Dear brothers plunged in bloody civil strife,
The Dacian marching down from Ister's shore,
The Empire, and the tottering power of Rome.

Z. Chafee, Jr.

AENEID IV, 160–194

Aeneas and Dido

                    The heaven
Darkens and thunder rolls, and rain and hail
Come down in torrents. The hunt is all for shelter,
Trojans and Tyrians and Ascanius dashing
Wherever they can; the streams pour down the mountains.
To the same cave go Dido and Aeneas,
Where Juno, as a bridesmaid, gives the signal,
And mountain nymphs wail high their incantations,
First day of death, first cause of evil. Dido
Is unconcerned with fame, with reputation,
With how it seems to others. This is marriage
For her, not hole-and-corner guilt; she covers
Her folly with this name.
                    Rumor goes flying
At once, through all the Libyan cities, Rumor
Than whom no other evil was ever swifter.
She thrives on motion and her own momentum;
Tiny at first in fear, she swells, colossal
In no time, walks on earth, but her head is hidden
Among the clouds. Her mother, Earth, was angry,
Once, at the gods, and out of spite produced her,
The Titans' youngest sister, swift of foot,
Deadly of wing, a huge and terrible monster,
With an eye below each feather in her body,
A tongue, a mouth, for every eye, and ears
Double that number; in the night she flies
Above the earth, below the sky, in shadow
Noisy and shrill; her eyes are never closed
In slumber; and by day she perches, watching
From tower or battlement, frightening great cities.
She heralds truth, and clings to lies and falsehood,
It is all the same to her. And now she was going
Happy about her business, filling people
With truth and lies: Aeneas, Trojan-born,
Has come, she says, and Dido, lovely woman,
Sees fit to mate with him, one way or another,
And now the couple wanton out the winter,
Heedless of ruling, prisoners of passion.

Rolfe Humphries

AENEID IV, 521–553

Night: and tired creatures over all the world
Were seeking slumber; the woods and the wild waters
Were quiet, and the silent stars were wheeling
Their course half over; every field was still;
The beasts of the field, the brightly colored birds,
Dwellers in lake and pool, in thorn and thicket,
Slept through the tranquil night, their sorrows over,
Their troubles soothed. But no such blessèd darkness
Closes the eyes of Dido; no repose
Comes to her anxious heart. Her pangs redouble,
Her love swells up, surging, a great tide rising
Of wrath and doubt and passion. "What do I do?
What now? Go back to my Numidian suitors,
Be scorned by those I scorned? Pursue the Trojans?
Obey their orders? They were grateful to me,
Once, I remember. But who would let them take me?
Suppose I went. They hate me now; they were always
Deceivers: is Laomedon forgotten,
Whose blood runs through their veins? What then? Attend them,
Alone, be their companion, the loud-mouthed sailors?
Or with my own armada follow after,
Wear out my sea-worn Tyrians once more
With vengeance and adventure? Better die.
Die; you deserve to; end the hurt with the sword.
It is your fault, Anna; you were sorry for me,
Won over by my tears; you put this load
Of evils on me. It was not permitted,
It seems, for me to live apart from wedlock,
A blameless life. An animal does better.
I vowed Sychaeus faith. I have been faithless."
So, through the night, she tossed in restless torment.

Rolfe Humphries

AENEID VI, 125–155

THE LOWER WORLD (THE SIBYL SPEAKS)

"Son of Anchises, born of godly lineage,
By night, by day, the portals of dark Dis
Stand open: it is easy, the descending
Down to Avernus. But to climb again,

To trace the footsteps back to the air above,
There lies the task, the toil. A few, beloved
By Jupiter, descending from the gods,
A few, in whom exalting virtue burned,
Have been permitted. Around the central woods
The black Cocytus glides, a sullen river;
But if such love is in your heart, such longing
For double crossing of the Stygian lake,
For double sight of Tartarus, learn first
What must be done. In a dark tree there hides
A bough, all golden, leaf and pliant stem,
Sacred to Proserpine. This all the grove
Protects, and shadows cover it with darkness.
Until this bough, this bloom of light, is found,
No one receives his passport to the darkness
Whose queen requires this tribute. In succession,
After the bough is plucked, another grows,
Gold-green with the same metal. Raise the eyes,
Look up, reach up the hand, and it will follow
With ease, if fate is calling; otherwise,
No power, no steel, can loose it. Furthermore,
(Alas, you do not know this!), one of your men
Lies on the shore, unburied, a pollution
To all the fleet, while you have come for counsel
Here to our threshold. Bury him with honor;
Black cattle slain in expiation for him
Must fall before you see the Stygian kingdoms,
The groves denied to living men."

Rolfe Humphries

AENEID VI, 268–751

Ibant Obscuri: Vision of Aeneas

(line for line paraphrase)

They wer' amid the shadows by night in loneliness obscure
Walking forth i' the void and vasty dominyon of Ades;
As by an uncertain moonray secretly illumin'd
One goeth in the forest, when heav'n is gloomily clouded,
And black night hath robb'd the colours and beauty from all things.

Here in Hell's very jaws, the threshold of darkening Orcus,
Have the avenging Cares laid their sleepless habitation,
Wailing Grief, pallid Infections, and heart-stricken Old-age,

Dismal Fear, unholy Famine, with low-groveling Want,
Forms of spectral horror, gaunt Toil and Death the devourer,
And Death's drowsy brother, Torpor; with whom, an inane rout,
All the Pleasures of Sin; there also the Furies in ambusht
Chamber of iron, afore whose bars wild War bloodyhanded
Raged, and mad Discord high brandished her venomous locks.

Midway of all this tract, with secular arms an immense elm
Reareth a crowd of branches, aneath whose leafy protection
Vain dreams thickly nestle, clinging unto the foliage on high:
And many strange creatures of monstrous form and features
Stable about th' entrance, Centaur and Scylla's abortion,
And hundred-handed Briareus, and Lerna's wildbeast
Roaring amain, and clothed in frightful flame the Chimaera,
Gorgons and Harpies, and Pluto's three-bodied ogre.

In terror Aeneas upheld his sword to defend him,
With ready naked point confronting their dreaded onset:
And had not the Sibyl warn'd how these lively spirits were
All incorporeal, flitting in thin maskery of form,
He had assail'd their host, and wounded vainly the void air.

Hence is a road that led them a-down to the Tartarean streams,
Where Acheron's whirlpool impetuous, into the reeky
Deep of Cokytos disgorgeth, with muddy burden.
These floods one ferryman serveth, most awful of aspect,
Of squalor infernal, Charon: all filthily unkempt
That woolly white cheek-fleece, and fiery the blood-shotten eyeballs:
On one shoulder a cloak knotted-up his nudity vaunteth.
He himself plied oar or pole, manageth tiller and sheet,
And the relics of men in his ash-grey barge ferries over;
Already old, but green to a god and hearty will age be.

Now hitherward to the bank much folk were crowding, a medley
Of men and matrons; nor did death's injury conceal
Bravespirited heroes, young maidens beauteous unwed,
And boys borne to the grave in sight of their sorrowing sires.
Countless as in the forest, at a first white frosting of autumn
Sere leaves fall to the ground; or like whenas over the ocean
Myriad birds come thickly flocking, when wintry December
Drives them afar southward for shelter upon sunnier shores,
So throng'd they; and each his watery journey demanded,
All to the further bank stretching out their arms impatient:
But the sullen boatman took now one now other at will,
While some from the river forbade he, an' drave to a distance.

Aeneas in wonder alike and deep pity then spake.
"Tell me (said he), my guide, why flock these crowds to the water?
Or what seek the spirits? or by what prejudice are these
Rudely denied, while those may upon the solemn river embark?"
T' whom then briefly again the Avernian priestess in answer:
"O Son of Anchises, heavn's true-born glorious offspring,
Deep Cokytos it is thou seest and Hell's Stygian flood,
Whose dread sanction alone Jove's oath from falsehood assureth.
These whom thou pitiedst, th' outcast and unburied are they;
That ferryman Charon; those whom his bark carries over
Are the buried; nor ever may mortal across the livid lake
Journey, or e'er upon Earth his bones lie peacefully entomb'd:
Haunting a hundred years this mournful plain they wander
Doom'd for a term, which term expired they win to deliv'rance."

Then he that harken'd stood agaze, his journey arrested,
Grieving at heart and much pitying their unmerited lot.
There miserably fellow'd in death's indignity saw he
Leucaspis with his old Lycian seachieften Orontes,
Whom together from Troy in home-coming over the waters
Wild weather o'ermastered, engulphing both shipping and men.
And lo! his helmsman, Palinurus, in eager emotion,
Who on th' Afric course, in bright star-light, with a fair wind,
Fell by slumber opprest unheedfully into the wide sea:
Whom i' the gloom when hardly he knew, now changed in affliction,
First he addrest. "What God, tell me, O Palinurus, of all gods
Pluckt you away and drown'd i' the swift wake-water abandoned?
For never erst nor in else hath kind responsive Apollo
Led me astray, but alone in this thing wholly deluded,
When he aver'd that you, to remote Ausonia steering,
Safe would arrive. Where now his truth? Is this the promis'd faith?"
But he, "Neither again did Phoebus wrongly bespeak thee,
My general, nor yet did a god in his enmity drown me:
For the tiller, wherewith I led thy fleet's navigation,
And still clung to, was in my struggling hold of it unshipt,
And came with me o'erboard. Ah! then, by ev'ry accurst sea,
Tho' in utter despair, far less mine own peril awed me
Than my thought o' the ship, what harm might hap to her, yawing
In the billows helmless, with a high wind and threatening gale.
Two nights and one day buffeted held I to the good spar
Windborne, with the current far-drifting, an' on the second morn
Saw, when a great wave raised me aloft, the Italyan highlands;
And swimming on with effort got ashore, nay already was saved,
Had not there the wrecking savages, who spied me defenceless,
Scarce clinging outwearied to a rock, half-drowned and speechless,

Beat me to death for hope of an unfound booty upon me.
Now to the wind and tidewash a sport my poor body rolleth.
Wherefore thee, by heav'n's sweet light and airiness, I pray,
By thy Sire's memories, thy hope of youthful Iulus,
Rescue me from these ills, brave master; Go to Velija,
O'er my mortality's spoil cast thou th' all-hallowing dust:
Or better, if so be the goddess, heav'n's lady-Creatress,
Show thee the way, nor surely without high favoring impulse
Mak'st thou ventur' across these floods and black Ereban lake, —
Give thy hand to me, an' o'er their watery boundary bring me
Unto the haven of all, death's home of quiet abiding."
Thus he lamented, anon spake sternly the maid of Avernus.
"Whence can such unruly desire, Palinurus, assail thee?
Wilt thou th' Eumenidan waters visit unburied? o'erpass
Hell's Stygian barrier? Charon's boat unbidden enter?
Cease to believe that fate can be by prayer averted.
Let my sooth a litel thy cruel destiny comfort.
Surely the people of all thy new-found country, determin'd
By heav'n-sent omens will achieve thy purification,
Build thee a tomb of honour with yearly solemnity ordain'd,
And dedicate for ever thy storied name to the headland."

These words lighten awhile his fear, his sadness allaying,
Nor vain was the promise his name should eternally survive.

They forthwith their journey renew, tending to the water:
Whom when th' old boatman descried silently emerging
Out o' the leafy shadows, advancing t' ward the river-shore,
Angrily gave he challenge, imperious in salutation.
"Whosoever thou be, that approachest my river all-arm'd,
Stand to announce thyself, nor further make footing onward.
Here 'tis a place of ghosts, of night and drowsy delusion:
Forbidden unto living mortals is my Stygian keel:
Truly not Alkides embarkt I cheerfully, nor took
Of Theseus or Pirithous glad custody, nay though
God-sprung were they both, warriors invincible in might:
He 'twas would sportively the guard of Tartarus enchain,
Yea and from the palace with gay contumely dragged him;
They to ravish Hell's Queen from Pluto's chamber attempted."

Then thus th' Amphrysian prophetess spake briefly in answer.
"No such doughty designs are ours, Cease thou to be moved!
Nor these sheeny weapons intend force. Cerberus unvext
Surely for us may affray the spirits with howling eternal,
And chaste Persephone enjoy her queenly seclusion.

Troian Aeneas, bravest and gentlest-hearted,
Hath left earth to behold his father in out-lying Ades.
If the image of a so great virtue doth not affect thee,
Yet this bough" — glittering she reveal'd its golden avouchment —
"Thou mayst know." Forthwith his bluster of heart was appeased:
Nor word gave he, but admiring the celestial omen,
That bright sprigg of weird for so long period unseen,
Quickly he turneth about his boat, to the margin approaching,
And the spirits, that along the gun'al benchways sat in order,
Drave he ashore, offering ready room: but when the vessel took
Ponderous Aeneas, her timbers crankily straining
Creak'd, an' a brown water came trickling through the upper seams.
Natheless both Sibyl and Hero, slow wafted across stream
Safe on th' ooze and slime's hideous desolation alighted.

Hence the triple-throated bellowings of Cerberus invade
All Hell, where opposite the arrival he lies in a vast den.
But the Sibyl, who mark'd his necklaces of stiffening snakes,
Cast him a cake, poppydrench'd with drowsiness and honey-sweeten'd.
He, rabid and distending a-hungry his triply-cavern'd jaws,
Gulp'd the proffer'd morsel; when slow he relaxt his immense bulk,
And helplessly diffused fell out-sprawl'd over the whole cave.
Aeneas fled by, and left full boldly the streamway,
That biddeth all men across but alloweth ne'er a returning.

Already now i' the air were voices heard, lamentation
And shrilly crying of infant souls by th' entry of Ades.
Babes, whom unportion'd of sweet life, unblossoming buds,
One black day carried off and chokt in dusty corruption. —
Next are they who falsely accused were wrongfully condemn'd
Unto the death: but here their lot by justice is order'd.
Inquisitor Minos, with his urn, summoning to assembly
His silent council, their deed or slander arraigneth. —
Next the sullen-hearted, who rashly with else-innocent hand
Their own life did away, for hate or weariness of light,
Imperiling their souls. How gladly, if only in Earth's air,
Would they again their toil, discomfort, and pities endure!
Fate obstructs: deep sadness now, unloveliness awful
Rings them about, and Styx with ninefold circle enarmeth. —

Not far hence they come to a land extensiv on all sides;
Weeping Plain 'tis call'd: — such name such country deserveth.
Here the lovers, whom fiery passion hath cruelly consumed,
Hide in leafy alleys and pathways bow'ry, sequester'd
By woodland myrtle, nor hath Death their sorrow ended.

Here was Phaedra to see, Procris and sad Eriphyle,
She of her unfilial deathdoing wound not ashamed,
Evadne, and Pasiphae and Laodamia,
And epicene Keneus, a woman to a man metamorphos'd,
Now by Fate converted again to her old feminine form.

'Mong these shades, her wound yet smarting ruefully, Dido
Wander'd throu' the forest-obscurity; and Aeneas
Standing anigh knew surely the dim form, though i' the darkness
Veil'd, — as when one seeth a young moon on the horizon,
Or thinketh to have seen i' the gloaming her delicate horn:
Tearfully in once-lov'd accents he lovingly addrest her.
"Unhappy! ah! too true 'twas told me, O unhappy Dido,
Dead thou wert; to the fell extreme didst thy passion ensue.
And was it I that slew thee? Alas! Smite falsity, ye heav'ns!
And Hell-fury attest me, if here any sanctity reigneth,
Unwilling, O my Queen, my step thy kingdom abandon'd.
Me the command of a god, who here my journey determines
Through Ereban darkness, through fields sown with desolation,
Drave me to wrong my heart. Nay tho' deep-pain'd to desert thee
I ne'er thought to provoke thy pain of mourning eternal.
Stay yet awhile, ev'n here unlook'd for again look upon me:
Fly me not ere the supreme words that Fate granteth us are said."

Thus he: but the spirit was raging, fiercely defiant,
Whom he approach'd with words to appease, with tears for atonement.
She to the ground downcast her eyes in fixity averted;
Nor were her features more by his pleading affected,
Than wer' a face of flint, or of ensculptur'd alabaster.
At length she started disdainful, an' angrily withdrew
Into a shady thicket: where her grief kindly Sychaeus
Sooth'd with other memories, first love and virginal embrace.
And ever Aeneas, to remorse by deep pity soften'd,
With brimming eyes pursued her queenly figure disappearing.

Thence the Sibyl to the plain's extremest boundary led him,
Where world-fam'd warriors, a lionlike company, haunted.
Here great Tydeus saw he eclips'd, and here the benighted
Phantom of Adrastus, of stalwart Parthenopaeus.
Here long mourn'd upon earth went all that prowess of Ilium
Fallen in arms; whom, when he beheld them, so many and great,
Much he bewail'd. By Thersilochus his mighty brothers stood,
Children of Antenor; here Demetrian Polyboetes,
And Idaeus, in old chariot-pose dreamily stalking.
Right and left the spirits flocking on stood crowding around him;

Nor their eyes have enough; they touch, find joy unwonted
Marching in equal step, and eager of his coming enquire.
But th' Argive leaders, and they that obey'd Agamemnon,
When they saw that Trojan in arms come striding among them,
Old terror invaded their ranks: some fled stricken, as once
They to the ships had fled for shelter; others the alarm raise,
But their thin utterance mock'd vainly the lips wide-parted.
Here too Deiphobus he espied, his fair body mangled,
Cruelly dismember'd, disfeatur'd cruelly his face,
Face and hands; and lo! shorn closely from either temple,
Gone wer' his ears, and maim'd each nostril in impious outrage.
Barely he knew him again cow'ring shamefastly an' hiding
His dire plight, and thus he his old companyon accosted.
"Noblest Deiphobus, great Teucer's intrepid offspring,
Who was it, inhuman, coveted so cruel a vengeance?
Who can hav adventur'd on thee? That last terrible night
Thou wert said to hav exceeded thy bravery, an' only
On thy faln enemies wert faln by weariness o'ercome.
Wherefor' upon the belov'd sea-shore thine empty sepulchral
Mound I erected, aloud on thy ghost tearfully calling.
Name and shield keep for thee the place; but thy body, dear friend,
Found I not, to commit to the land ere sadly I left it."

Then the son of Priam "I thought not, friend, to reproach thee:
Thou didst all to the full, ev'n my shade's service, accomplish.
'Twas that uninterdicted adultress from Lacedaemon
Drave me to doom, and planted in hell her trophy triumphant.
On that night, — how vain a security and merrymaking
Then sullied us thou know'st, yea must too keenly remember, —
When the ill-omened horse o'erleapt Troy's lofty defences,
Dragg'd in amidst our town pregnant with a burden of arm'd men.
She then, her Phrygian women in feign'd phrenzy collecting,
All with torches aflame, in wild Bacchic orgy paraded,
Flaring a signal aloft to her ambusht confederate Greeks.
I from a world of care had fled with weariful eyelids
Unto my unhappy chamber, an' lay fast lockt in oblivyon,
Sunk to the depth of rest as a child that nought will awaken.
Meanwhile that paragon helpmate had robb'd me of all arms,
E'en from aneath the pillow my blade of trust purloining; —
Then to the gate; wide flings she it op'n an' calls Menelaus.
Would not a so great service attach her faithful adorer?
Might not it extinguish the repute of her earlier illdeeds?
Brief be the tale. Menelaus arrives: in company there came
His crime-counsellor Aeolides ... So, and more also
Deal ye, O Gods, to the Greeks! an if I call justly upon you. —

But thou; what fortune hitherward, in turn prithy tell me,
Sent thee alive, whether erring upon the bewildering Ocean,
Or high-prompted of heav'n, or by Fate wearily hunted,
That to the sunless abodes and dusky demesnes thou approachest?"

Ev'n as while they thus converse it is already mid-day,
Unperceiv'd, but aloft earth's star had turn'd to declining.
And haply Aeneas his time in parley had outgone,
Had not then the Sibyl with word of warning avized him.
"Night hieth, Aeneas; in tears our journey delayeth.
See our road, that it here in twain disparteth asunder;
This to the right, skirting by th' high city-fortresses of Dis,
Endeth in Elysium, our path; but that to the leftward
Only receives their feet who wend to eternal affliction."
Deiphobus then again, "Speak not, great priestess, in anger;
I will away to refill my number among th' unfortun'd.
Thou, my champyon, adieu! Go where thy glory awaits thee!"
When these words he had spoken, he turn'd and hastily was fled.

Aeneas then look'd where leftward, under a mountain,
Outspread a wide city lay, threefold with fortresses engirt,
Lickt by a Tartarean river of live fire, the torrential
Red Phlegethon, and huge boulders his roundy bubbles be:
Right i' the front stareth the columnar gate adamantine,
Such that no battering warfare of men or immortals
E'er might shake; blank-faced to the cloud its bastion upstands.
Tisiphone thereby in a bloodspotty robe sitteth alway
Night and day guarding sleeplessly the desperat entrance.
Wherefrom an awestirring groan-cry and fierce clamour outburst,
Sharp lashes, insane yells, dragg'd chains and clanking of iron.

Aeneas drew back, his heart by his hearing affrighted:
"What manner of criminals, my guide, now tell me (he question'd),
Or what their penalties? what this great wail that ariseth?"
Answering him the divine priestess, "Brave hero of Ilium,
O'er that guilty threshold no breath of purity may come:
But Hecate, who gave me to rule i' the groves of Avernus,
Herself led me around, and taught heav'n's high retribution.
Here Cretan Rhadamanthus in unblest empery reigneth,
Secret crime to punish, — full surely he wringeth avowal
Even of all that on earth, by vain impunity harden'd
Men sinning have put away from thought till impenitent death.
On those convicted tremblers then leapeth avenging
Tisiphone with keen flesh-whips and vipery scourges,
And of her implacable sisters inviteth attendance."

— Now sudden on screeching hinges that portal accursed
Flung wide its barriers. — "In what dire custody, mark thou,
Is the threshold! guarded by how grim sentry the doorway!
More terrible than they the ravin'd insatiabl Hydra
That sitteth angry within. Know too that Tartarus itself
Dives sheer gaping aneath in gloomy profundity downward
Twice that height that a man looketh up t'ward airy Olympus.
Lowest there those children of Earth, Titanian elders,
In the abyss, where once they fell hurl'd, yet wallowing lie.
There the Aloidae saw I, th' ungainly rebel twins
Primaeval, that assay'd to devastate th' Empyraean
With huge hands, and rob from Jove his kingdom immortal.
And there Salmoneus I saw, rend'ring heavy payment,
For that he idly had mockt heav'n's fire and thunder electric;
With chariot many-yoked and torches brandishing on high
Driving among his Graian folk in Olympian Elis;
Exultant as a God he rode in blasphemy worshipt.
Fool, who th' unreckoning tempest and deadly dreaded bolt
Thought to mimic with brass and confus'd trample of horses!
But him th' Omnipotent, from amidst his cloudy pavilyon,
Blasted, an' eke his rattling car and smoky pretences
Extinguish'd at a stroke, scattering his dust to the whirlwind.
There too huge Tityos, whom Earth that gendereth all things
Once foster'd, spreadeth out o'er nine full roods his immense limbs.
On him a wild vulture with hook-beak greedily gorgeth
His liver upsprouting quick as that Hell-chicken eateth.
She diggeth and dwelleth under the vast ribs, her bloody bare neck
Lifting anon: ne'er loathes she the food, ne'er fails the renewal.
Where wer' an end their names to relate, their crimes and torments?
Some o'er whom a hanging black rock, slipping at very point of
Falling, ever threateneth: Couches luxurious invite
Softly-cushion'd to repose: Tables for banqueting outlaid
Tempt them ever-famishing: hard by them a Fury regardeth,
And should they but a hand uplift, trembling to the dainties,
She with live firebrand and direful yell springeth on them.

"Their crimes, — not to hav lov'd a brother while love was allow'd
    them;
Or to hav struck their father, or inveigled a dependent;
Or who chancing alone on wealth prey'd lustfully thereon,
Nor made share with others, no greater company than they:
Some for adultery slain; some their bright swords had offended
Drawn i' the wrong: or a master's trust with perfidy had met:
Dungeon'd their penalties they await. Look not to be answer'd
What that doom, nor th' end of these men think to determine.

Some aye roll heavy rocks, some whirl dizzy on the revolving
Spokes of a pendant wheel: sitteth and to eternity shall sit
Unfortun'd Theseus; while sad Phlegias saddeneth hell
With vain oyez to all loud crying a tardy repentance,
'Walk, O man, i' the fear of God, and learn to be righteous!'
Here another, who sold for gold his country, promoting
Her tyrant; or annull'd for a base bribe th'inviolate law.
This one had unfather'd his blood with bestial incest:
All some fearful crime had dared and vaunted achievement.
What mind could harbour the offence of such recollection,
Or lend welcoming ear to the tale of iniquity and shame,
And to the pains wherewith such deeds are justly requited?"

　　Ev'n when thus she had spok'n, the priestess dear to Apollo,
"But, ready, come let us on, perform we the order appointed!
Hast'n we (saith she), the wall forged on Cyclopian anvils
Now I see, an'th' archway in Aetna's furnace attemper'd,
Where my lore biddeth us to depose our high-privileg'd gift."

　　Then together they trace i' the drooping dimness a footpath,
Whereby, faring across, they arrive at th' arches of iron.
Aeneas stept into the porch, and duly besprinkling
His body with clear water affixt his bough to the lintel;
And, having all perform'd at length with ritual exact,
They came out on a lovely pleasance, that dream'd-of oasis,
Fortunat isle, the abode o' the blest, their fair Happy Woodland.
Here is an ampler sky, those meads ar' azur'd by a gentler
Sun than th' Earth, an' a new starworld their darkness adorneth.

　　Some were matching afoot their speed on a grassy arena,
In playful combat some wrestling upon the yellow sand,
Part in a dance-rhythm or poetry's fine phantasy engage;
While full-toga'd anear their high-priest musical Orpheus
Bade his prime sev'n tones in varied harmony discourse,
Now with finger, anon sounding with an ivory plectrum.
And here Aeneas met Teucer's fortunate offspring,
High-spirited heroes, fair-favor'd sons o' the morning,
Assarac and Ilos and Dardan founder of Ilium:
Their radiant chariots he espied rank't empty afar off,
Their spears planted afield, their horses wandering at large,
Grazing around: — as on earth their joy had been, whether armour
Or chariot had charmed them, or if 'twer good manage and care
Of the gallant warhorse, the delight liv'd here unabated:
Lo! then others, that about the meadow sat feasting in idless,
And chanting for joy a familyar paean of old earth,

By fragrant laurel o'ercanopied, where 'twixt enamel'd banks
Bountiful Eridanus glides throu' their bosky retirement.
Here were men who bled for honour, their country defending;
Priests, whose lives wer' a flame of chastity on God's altar;
Holy poets, content to await their crown of Apollo;
Discoverers, whose labour had aided life or ennobled;
Or who fair memories had left through kindly deserving.
On their brow a fillet pearl-white distinguisheth all these:
Whom the Sibyl, for they drew round, in question accosted,
And most Musaeus, who tower'd noble among them,
Center of all that sea of bright faces looking upward.
"Tell, happy souls, and thou poet and high mystic illustrious,
Where dwelleth Anchises? what home hath he? for 'tis in his quest
We hither have made journey across Hell's watery marshes."

Therto with brief parley rejoin'd that mystic of old-time.
"In no certain abode we remain: by turn the forest glade
Haunt we, lilied stream-bank, sunny mead; and o'er valley and rock
At will rove we: but if ye aright your purpose arede me,
Mount ye the hill: myself will prove how easy the pathway."
Speaking he led: and come to the upland, sheweth a fair plain
Gleaming aneath; and they, with grateful adieu, the descent made.

Now lord Anchises was down i' the green valley musing,
Where the spirits confin'd that await mortal resurrection
While diligently he mark'd, his thought had turned to his own kin,
Whose numbers he reckon'd, an' of all their progeny foretold
Their fate and fortune, their ripen'd temper an' action.
He then, when he espied Aeneas t'ward him approaching
O'er the meadow, both hands uprais'd and ran to receive him,
Tears in his eyes, while thus his voice in high passion outbrake.
"Ah, thou'rt come, thou'rt come! at length thy dearly-belov'd grace
Conquering all hath won thee the way. 'Tis allow'd to behold thee,
O my son, — yea again the familyar raptur' of our speech.
Nay, I look't for't thus, counting patiently the moments,
And ever expected; nor did fond fancy betray me.
From what lands, my son, from what life-dangering ocean
Art thou arrived? full mighty perils thy path hav opposed:
And how nearly the dark Libyan thy destiny o'erthrew!"
Then he, "Thy spirit, O my sire, 'twas thy spirit often
Sadly appearing aroused me to seek thy far habitation.
My fleet moors i' the blue Tyrrhene: all with me goeth well.
Grant me to touch thy hand as of old, and thy body embrace."
Speaking, awhile in tears his feeling mutinied, and when
For the longing contact of mortal affection, he out-held

His strong arms, the figure sustain'd them not: 'twas as empty
E'en as a windworn cloud, or a phantom of irrelevant sleep.

On the level bosom of this vale more quickly the tall trees
Grow, an' aneath quivering poplars and whispering alders
Lethe's dreamy river throu' peaceful scenery windeth.
Whereby now flitted in vast swarms many people of all lands,
As when in early summer honey-bees on a flowery pasture
Pill the blossoms, hurrying to and fro, — innumerous are they,
Revisiting the ravish'd lily cups, while all the meadow hums.

Aeneas was turn'd to the sight, and marvelling enquired,
"Say, sir, what the river that there i' the vale-bottom I see?
And who they that thickly along its bank have assembled?"

Then lord Anchises, "The spirits for whom a second life
And body are destined ar' arriving thirsty to Lethe,
And here drink th' unmindful draught from wells of oblivyon.
My heart greatly desired of this very thing to acquaint thee,
Yea, and show thee the men to be born, our glory her'after,
So to gladden thine heart where now thy voyaging endeth."
"Must it then be believ'd, my sire, that a soul which attaineth
Elysium will again submit to her old body-burden?
Is this well? what hap can awake such dire longing in them?"
"I will tell thee, O son, nor keep thy wonder awaiting."
Answereth Anchises, and all expoundeth in order.
"Know first that the heavens, and th' Earth, and space fluid or void,
Night's pallid orb, day's Sun, and all his starry coaevals,
Are by one spirit inly quickened, and, mingling in each part,
Mind informs the matter, nature's complexity ruling.
Thence the living creatures, man, brute, and ev'ry feather'd fowl,
And what breedeth in Ocean aneath her surface of argent:
Their seed knoweth a fiery vigour, 'tis of airy divine birth,
In so far as unimpeded by an alien evil,
Nor dull'd by the body's framework condemn'd to corruption.
Hence the desires and vain tremblings that assail them, unable
Darkly prison'd to arise to celestial exaltation;
Nor when death summoneth them anon earth-life to relinquish,
Can they in all discard their stain, nor wholly away with
Mortality's plague-spots. It must be that, O, many wild graffs
Deeply at heart engrain'd have rooted strangely upon them:
Wherefore must suffering purge them, yea, Justice atone them
With penalties heavy as their guilt: some purify exposed
Hung to the viewless winds, or others long watery searchings
Cleanse i' the ocean-salt, some bathe in fiery renewal:

Each cometh unto his own retribution, — if after in ample
Elysium we attain, but a few, to the fair Happy Woodland,
Yet slow time still worketh on us to remove the defilement,
Till it hath eaten away the acquir'd dross, leaving again free
That first fiery vigour, the celestial virtue of our life.
All whom here thou seest, hav accomplished purification:
Unto the stream of Lethe a god their company calleth,
That forgetful of old failure, pain and disappointment,
They may again into earthly bodies with glad courage enter."

  . . . .

Twin be the gates o' the house of sleep: as fable opineth
One is of horn, and thence for a true dream outlet is easy:
Fair the other, shining perfected of ivory carven;
But false are the visions that thereby find passage upward.
Soon then as Anchises had spok'n, he led the Sibyl forth
And his son, and both dismiss't from the ivory portal.

Robert Bridges

AENEID VII, 803–817

CAMILLA

And last of all
Camilla rode, leading her troops on horseback,
Her columns bright with bronze, a soldieress,
A woman whose hands were never trained to weaving,
To the use of wool, to basketry, a girl
As tough in war as any, in speed afoot
Swifter than wind. She could go flying over
The tips of the ears of the wheat, and never bruise them,
So light her way, she could run on the lift of the wave,
Dry-shod; and they came from the houses and fields to wonder,
To gaze at her going, young men, and matrons thronging,
Wide-eyed and with parted lips, at the glory of royal crimson
Over her shoulders' smoothness, the clasp of the gold
In her hair, and the way she carried the Lycian quiver,
The heft of the pastoral myrtle, the wand with the spear-point.

Rolfe Humphries

AENEID VIII, 313–336

AENEAS AT THE SITE OF ROME

King Evander

Began the story: — "Native Nymphs and Fauns
Dwelt in these woodlands once, and a race of men
Sprung from the trunks of trees, or rugged oak,
Men primitive and rude, with little culture:
They had no knowledge of ploughing, none of harvest;
The fruits of the wild trees, the spoils of hunting,
Gave them their nourishment. Then Saturn came here,
Fleeing Jove's arms, an exile from his kingdom.
He organized this race, unruly, scattered
Through the high mountains, gave them law and order.
He gave the place a name; Latium, he called it,
Since once he lay there safely, hiding in shelter.
Under his rule there came those golden ages
That people tell of, all the nations dwelling
In amity and peace. But little by little
A worse age came, lack-luster in its color,
And the madness of war, and the evil greed of having.
Then came the Ausonian bands, Sicanian peoples,
And the land of Saturn took on other names,
And the kings came, and the fierce giant Thybris
For whom we named our river; we forgot
Its older title, Albula. Here I came
An exile from my country; over the seas,
Driven by fate and fortune, which no man
Can cope with or escape. The nymph Carmentis,
My mother, led me here with solemn warnings
Under Apollo's guidance."

Rolfe Humphries

Horace

❰ Quintus Horatius Flaccus (65–8 B.C., born at Venusia) is one of the world's best-loved poets. Of his poems (the *Satires, Epodes, Odes, Epistles,* and *Secular Hymn,* written between 35 and 13 B.C.), the *Odes* — on many themes, including politics, religion, friendship, gallantry, and national greatness — have always attracted readers with their finished lyric art, their beautifully expressed if rarely profound ideas, and the sophisticated, many-sided charm of Horace's mind. He wrote much about himself and his circle; practically every one of the 104 *Odes* is addressed to a friend. The sixteen women to whom he wrote poems do not alter the fact that he was a cautious bachelor whose melancholy Epicureanism concealed a lack of genuine passion.

❰ The *Satires* and *Epistles* — discourses dealing with self-justification, personal or literary, and true *saturae* in the moral sense — make fun of social nuisances, love of money, philosophic sects, the discontented, gluttons, the excesses of lust, and of dissolute women. The *Epistles,* his latest work, emphasize the values and pleasures of philosophy. They also contain much good advice for writers, as in the famous *Art of Poetry.* The *Epodes,* among his earliest poems, contain some violent attacks upon certain obscure people. The *Secular Hymn* is a formal commissioned poem in sapphics for the celebration of Rome's birthday, 19 B.C.; the inscription which records its performance is in the Terme museum at Rome. Horace's gift for memorable phrases is well known; his skill in handling nineteen different Greek meters entitled him to boast that he had in his poetry "erected a monument more lasting than bronze." ❱

ODES

I, 1

O Maecenas, of kings boasting your ancestry:
O my bulwark benign, glory of my poor name:
Some men live for the hour when on their chariot wheels,
Glowing, grazing the goals, dust of Olympia clings —
When as lords of the earth near to the gods they soar,
Borne in triumph aloft by the ennobling palm.

This man's only delight is the inconstant crowd
When their favor confers triple-ranked offices.

That one's joy is the wheat heaped in his granary —
All that Africa yields, swept from her threshing-floors.

All great Attalus' wealth though you should offer him,
Never, leaving the hoe, leaving th' ancestral field,
Would that prosperous man, daring the rock and reef,
Plow with Cyprian bark, trembling, the southern sea.

Traders, fearing the squall, sigh for their placid homes,
While the Libyan gale shakes the Icarian sea;
Soon, though, after the storm, mending their shattered ships,
Hopes high, danger defied, eastward they sail again!

One type scorns not the cup brimming with Massic wine;
Idly stealing an hour out of the tedious day,
Now he stretches his limbs beneath the arbutus tree,
Now he dreams at the fount, source of some sacred spring.

Many thrill to the camps' trumpet and bugle calls,
Sounds prophetic of war, chilling a mother's blood.
Tenting under the stars, happy, the huntsman stays,
Mindless of his young wife, waiting beside his hearth,
Whether hunting the hind, trapped by his faithful hounds,
Or, with well-plaited net, stalking the Marsian boar.

Me, though, happier than they, branches of ivy twined,
Prize of well-tutored brows, link with the gods above!
Me cool groves of the Nymphs, light-footed Satyr-bands,
Set apart from the crowd — if neither Euterpe
Holds her pipe-notes from me, nor Polyhymnia
Fails to tune to my song strings of her Lesbian lyre.

But, Maecenas, should you rank me among the bards,
Then I'll strike with my brow, proudly, the very stars!

Leonard Albert

I, 2

Surely enough of rain and rattling showers
The Father now has dashed on every side.
His red right hand has struck the sacred towers
    And Rome is terrified,
Aye, all the Earth, lest once again comes round
That time when Pyrrha shrank at monstrous sights
And Proteus drove his shoals to pass their bound
    And view the mountain heights.

For we have seen the Tiber, thick and brown,
Flung tumbling back from the Etruscan shore,
Spreading, to harry Numa's building down
    And batter Vesta's door.
What god shall we, the People, now beseech
To prop the Empire? Ah, what vows and prayers
Will now avail the Virgin Choir to reach
    Vesta who scarcely cares?
To whom will Jove assign the cleansing task?
Augur Apollo, clouding from our gaze
Your gleaming shoulders, come, we humbly ask,
    Lead us to better ways.
Or is it Venus with her deathless smile
And Jest and Cupid flitting in her train?
Or Mars, who left his children all this while,
    Come to be kind again,
Weary with war's long sport of cruel glee,
Though well he loves the shouts, the helmet-glow,
And Moorish footmen grinning savagely
    Down at a bleeding foe.
Has Maia's son assumed a young man's frame
And left his wings of godhood in the sky?
Caesar's Avenger is the chosen name
    He bids us know him by.
O stay with us on earth. Be glad to draw
The citizens of Rome from civil strife.
Bear with our evil hearts, and let no flaw
    Too soon return your life
To heaven. No, still triumph far and wide,
Still be the Prince and Father to our need,
And do not let the Medes unpunished ride
    While you as Caesar lead.

Jack Lindsay

I, 3

Wave-born Queen of the Cyprian foam,
    Far-famed glittering twins, beautiful pilot-stars;
Thou, too, Father of winds and waves,
    Watch well over that ship, spreading her sail to-night, —

Ship now bearing away from us
    Virgil, half of my soul, over the darkening sea;
Keep her true to her trust, we pray!
    Bring him safe to his goal, yonder in Attica.

Three-fold bronze, indestructible oak,
    Armed that seaman who, first, fearing not Aquilo,
Pushed out into the roaring deep
    Past thy ship-wrecking rocks, Acroceraunia!

Vain, ah vain, was the god's behest;
    His, who sundered the lands, once, by that salt decree.
Man still follows the Titan's road,
    Storms through heaven and, now, thunders at Acheron, too.

Bearing Virgil away from us . . . .
    Ours, all ours, was the sin, sending him hence in vain,
Sin, compelling the lightning flash,
    Wrong, compelling the gods, hesitant long, to smite.

Alfred Noyes

I, 4

Winter to Spring: the west wind melts the frozen rancour,
    The windlass drags to sea the thirsty hull;
Byre is no longer welcome to beast or fire to ploughman,
    The field removes the frost-cap from his skull.

Venus of Cythera leads the dances under the hanging
    Moon and the linked line of Nymphs and Graces
Beat the ground with measured feet while the busy Fire god
    Stokes his red-hot mills in volcanic places.

Now is the time to twine the spruce and shining head with myrtle,
    Now with flowers escaped the earthy fetter,
And sacrifice to the woodland god in shady copses
    A lamb or a kid, whichever he likes better.

Equally heavy is the heel of white-faced Death on the pauper's
    Shack and the towers of kings, and O my dear
The little sum of life forbids the ravelling of lengthy
    Hopes. Night and the fabled dead are near

And the narrow house of nothing past whose lintel
    You will meet no wine like this, no boy to admire
Like Lycidas who to-day makes all young men a furnace
    And whom tomorrow girls will find a fire.

Louis MacNeice

I, 5

What slim elegant youth, drenched in effusive scent,
now sits close to your side, Pyrrha, in some recess
    rich with many a rosebloom?
    Who loves smoothing your yellow hair,
chic yet daintily plain? How many gods profaned,
what indelible vows he will lament, and oh,
    what dark hurricane-lashed seas
    he will watch with a pallid cheek!
Poor fool, golden he thinks you will for ever be,
heart-free always, he hopes, always adorable —
    yet knows not the deceitful
    offshore squalls. To a novice, you
shine too temptingly bright. Here on the temple wall
one small tablet of mine, offering up my clothes
    (all I saved from a shipwreck)
    says Thank God, that I just escaped.

Gilbert Highet

I, 5

What slim youth, moistened with liquid perfumes,
Entreats you, Pyrrha, with garland roses,
    In the charming grotto?
    For him you bind
Your flaxen hair, purely composed! Alas, how many times
Shall he of faith and changed gods weep, how many times
    The black outrageous winds, the stormy seas,
    Shall him astonish
Who now enjoys you, credulous of your gold;
Who hopes you always foot-loose and susceptible!
    He has not sailed in the treacherous winds.
    And glittering, your sea will craze
The unappeased who stand on shore. But I have vowed
My tablet to the sacred wall and hung as consecrate
    My dripping garments to the puissant One
    God-mastering the sea.

Joseph Bennett

I, 9

Look up at Mount Soracte's dazzling snow
Piling along the branches that can barely
    Withstand its weight, while piercing ice
    Impedes the river's flowing!

So, Thaliarch, let's dissolve the cold, stacking
The hearth with logs, and with a rash indulgence
 Fetch up the four-year vintage jars
  Of undiluted Sabine wine.

All else trust to the gods at whose command
Contending winds and seething seas desist
 Until the sacred cypress-tree
  And ancient ash no longer quake.

Then cast aside this contemplation of
The future, reckoning the random day's
 Advantage, youngster, nor despise
  The sweets of love and festival.

While boyhood yet forestalls cantankerous age,
Now is the time appropriate to whispered
 Seductive twilight messages
  In city court and empty lot;

Now too the time for secret pleasantries
With a girl-friend mocking from her corner ambush,
 The time to steal a token from
  Her arm or half-protesting finger.

          Muriel Spark

I, 11

I pray you not, Leuconoë, to pore
With unpermitted eyes on what may be
Appointed by the gods for you and me,
Nor on Chaldaean figures any more.
'T were infinitely better to implore
The present only: — whether Jove decree
More winters yet to come, or whether he
Make even this, whose hard, wave-eaten shore
Shatters the Tuscan seas to-day, the last —
Be wise withal, and rack your wine, nor fill
Your bosom with large hopes; for while I sing,
The envious close of time is narrowing; —
So seize the day, or ever it be past,
And let the morrow come for what it will.

       Edwin Arlington Robinson

I, 13

When you to Telephus devote,
    O Lydia, your choicest phrases,
And either Telephus' white throat
    Or wax-like arms excite your praises,
Bah! my disgusted anger surges
Like waves which stormy Notus urges.

Then I am blinded by my wrath,
    And quite unstable my complexion;
While on my cheek a tear-stained path
    Shows how I mourn your changed affection.
For when to me you're ever lost
I burn, a lingering holocaust.

I burn to think how, mad with wine,
    That boy in drunken rage may mar
With blows those gleaming arms of thine,
    Or leave upon thy lips a scar.
Ah! who could that fair mouth abuse
Which Venus will all sweets endues!

O thrice and four times blessèd they
    Whose life no evil quarrel knows,
But calm and peaceful day by day
    Glides as a quiet river flows;
Whom an unbroken bond holds ever
Until the last sad day shall sever.

George F. Whicher

I, 18

Plant no tree, O my friend,
    sooner than plant,
        here in the kindly soil,
Sacred vines round the walls
    of Tivoli,
        founded by Catilus.
Men who won't touch a drop
    get from the gods
        nothing but evil days;
Cares that gnaw at the heart,
    wine scatters them,
        no other thing than wine.

Who prates of poverty
 or army-life,
  after a glass or two?
Who sings not then of thee,
 Goddess of Love,
  of Father Bacchus then?
But let no one abuse
 Bacchus's gifts,
  gifts that can loosen tongues.
We are warned by the fight
 of the Centaurs
  fought to the bitter end
Once with the Lapithae,
 after the wine;
  and by the cruel fate
Of those Thracians whom he,
 god of orgies,
  punished so heavily.
Man in passion can see
 between right and wrong
  only a narrow line
Set by lustful desires.
 O shining one,
  wearing the fox's pelt,
Not if thou willest not
 shall I bestir
  thee, and in haste bring out
Thy rich treasures, that lie
 buried in leaves,
  hid from the light of day.
Check now Cybele's horn
 and savage drums,
  whereupon follows close
Blind Self-Love in her train;
 Vain Glory too,
  strutting with empty head;
False Faith follows, that sets
 in her window
  secrets for all to see.

Barbara J. Hodge

I, 21

Virgins, sing the Virgin Huntress;
 Youths, the youthful Phoebus sing;

Sing Latona, she who bore them
   Dearest to the eternal King:
Sing the heavenly maid who roves
Joyous, through the mountain groves;
She who winding waters loves;
   Let her haunts her praises ring!

Sing the vale of Peneus' river;
   Sing the Delian deity;
The shoulder glorious with its quiver;
   And the lyre of Mercury.
From our country, at our prayer —
Famine, plague, and tearful war
These, benign, shall drive afar
   To Persia's plains or Britain's sea.

Patrick Branwell Brontë

I, 22

He who is innocent and pure
   Needs not to go equipped
With spear or quiver of the Moor
   And arrows poison-tipped.

Not though he fare through Syrtes' waves,
   Cold Caucasus' expanse,
Or regions that Hydaspes laves,
   That river of romance.

I roamed beyond my farm at ease,
   I sang of Lalage,
And met unarmed among the trees
   A wolf, who fled from me.

Martial Apulia, forest-land,
   Bred never monster worse;
Nor such was weaned 'mid Juba's sand,
   The lions' thirsty nurse.

Set me on steppes, where summer air
   No leaf has ever kissed,
The zone that lies in dull despair
   Of sombre sky and mist;

Set me where flames so fierce a heat
   That there no dwellers be:
Yet will I love her — smiling sweet,
   Sweet-speaking Lalage.

W. S. Marris

I, 23

A young deer lost on the mountain
   Whimpering for its mother, frightened
     By a mere breeze in the branches —
     So skittish you are toward me.

With the little leaves blowing to shadows
   In the fresh wind of springtime, and
     Brambles clutching about her,
     Her knees and heart grow faint.

Come now! It's not as if I were a
   Lion or tiger a-prowl for you!
     It's time you forgot your mother,
     Time you went after a man.

                       Robert Fitzgerald

I, 24

Now is the hour of sorrow unreproved
And tears unchecked for one we dearly loved:
   O sad Melpomene, bring
   Your lyre and sadly sing.

And so Quintilius sleeps eternally!
When shall such gentleness and modesty
   Honor and truth and faith
   Again inherit breath?

Quintilius is dead and good men mourn,
And you, Vergil, are most of all forlorn.
   And all your prayers are vain:
   The gods give not again.

If you had sweeter notes than Orpheus played
You could not now bring blood to that pale shade:
   Not even if the trees
   Could hear your melodies.

Those whom the god has touched and driven below
Are held by power no pleas can overthrow:
   Patience alone, my friend,
   Will ease what none can mend.

                 The Rev. William J. Philbin

I, 25

The young men come less often — isn't it so? —
To rap at midnight on your fastened window;
Much less often. How do you sleep these days?

There was a time when your door gave with proficiency
On easy hinges; now it seems apter at being shut.
I do not think you hear many lovers moaning

"Lydia, how can you sleep?
"Lydia, the night is so long!
"Oh, Lydia, I'm dying for you!"

No. The time is coming when you will moan
And cry to scornful men from an alley corner
In the dark of the moon when the wind's in a passion,

With lust that would drive a mare wild
Raging in your ulcerous old viscera.
You'll be alone and burning then

To think how happy boys take their delight
In the new tender buds, the blush of myrtle,
Consigning dry leaves to the winter sea.

Robert Fitzgerald

I, 25

Less and less often now, the horny young men
Rattle your bolted shutters, and the door
That used to turn on easy hinges keeps
Faith with the threshold.

Seldom, or never, now, you hear them crying
Across your sleep, "Lydia, let me in;
The nights are long, and wasted, and your lover
Is dying for it."

Finally, never. An old woman living
Unnoticed in an alley, all alone,
You grieve for those hot rowdies, while a cold
Thracian comes brawling,

Rattling the shutter, a cold Thracian wind,
No good for you, in whom the heat that drives

Mares to the stud-horse, burns the ulcered loins
Not without anguish

That high young men go happily elsewhere
For their green ivy and dark myrtle, leaving
The withered leaves to winter's boon companion,
Chilly old Eurus.

Rolfe Humphries

I, 25

Ribald romeos less and less berattle
Your shut window with impulsive pebbles.
Sleep — who cares? — the clock around. The door hugs
    Firmly its framework
Which once, oh how promptly it popped open
Easy hinges. And so rarely heard now:
"Night after night I'm dying for you, darling,
    And you — you just lie there."
Turnabout. For insolent old lechers
You will weep soon on the lonely curbing,
While, above, the dark of the moon excites the
    Wind from the mountain.
Then, deep down, searing desire (libido
That deranges, too, old rutting horses)
In your riddled abdomen is raging
    Not without heartache
That the young boys take their solace rather
In the greener ivy, the green myrtle;
And such old winter-bitten sticks and stems they
    Figure the hell with.

John Frederick Nims

I, 27

It is a Thracian trick to brawl in wine,
    And fight with vessels dedicate to pleasure;
Bacchus will all such services decline —
    Strike up the drinking, not the martial measure!

There is no bond between the lighted feast
    And the accursed assassin's Median blade.
Such quarrels, gentlemen, should long have ceased —
    Be seated, let your turbulence be stayed.

You bid me stay and drink Falernian rare?
Then let the lad, Megillia's own brother,
The source of his sweet wound to us declare:
So let him name his sweetheart and none other!

What, you refuse? I will not drink a swallow
Until I know. Whoever is your passion,
There is no reason for such shame to follow.
An honest love has ever been your fashion.

Whatever is the manner of your fate,
Trust it to loyal ears . . . O cursed shame
That this Charybdis should have seized you straight
When you, poor youth, should have less fierce a flame!

What witchcraft now can free your pinioned arms?
What god, what mystic lore of Thessaly?
From such chimerian triple-folded charms
Winged Pegasus himself might not win free.

Lucius Beebe

I, 31

And now before the new-built shrine
    Of his Apollo, what shall be
The poet's prayer? Now while the wine
    Flows bright, what blessing more seeks he?
        Sardinia's harvests though they brim
        The granaries there are not for him.

The cattle which so take the eye
    Sleek in Calabria's sunshine, gold
And Indian ivory pass him by;
    He would not covet a freehold
        Where Liris' currents still devour
        The meadow-banks with stealthy power.

Let others as their fortune's made
    Prune the Calentan vine; let those
Whose money's in the Eastern trade
    Swallow the vintage — down it goes
        From cups of gold and nothing less:
        These are the men the gods caress.

It must be so; how else might these
    In perfect safety thrice a year

Make their Atlantic voyages?
    Meanwhile I make my dinner here
      On olives, or on endives feast,
      And mallows, which I can digest.

Son of Latona, grant me this:
    What's set before me to enjoy,
To keep my health and strength, to miss
    Nothing which rightly should employ
      One's mind, and gently reach the end
      Still calling poetry my friend.

Edmund Blunden

I, 33

Now don't overindulge grief for your lost coquette,
my poor comrade, and don't publish lugubrious
dark-blue dirges for love, endlessly asking why
    she broke faith, took a younger man.

See how Audrey — a rare beauty with clustered curls —
burns for David; and he yearns for the arrogant
Eileen; yet we shall see slavering mountain wolves
    mated with delicate fallow deer

far, far sooner than Eileen will indulge his lust.
Cruel Love always conjoins two inappropriate
hearts, minds, bodies in one pair of unbroken chains:
    Love does relish a savage joke.

I too, though a liaison with a kinder girl
was quite possible, still clung to my cruel Sue —
slum-bred woman, and wild: stormier than the waves
    wind-whipped, lashing Atlantic rocks!

Gilbert Highet

I, 38

I condemn all luxury Oriental:
bring me no fat leis of frangipani,
boy, and don't search every forgotten nook where
    lingers a late rose.
Nothing but one plain little crown of myrtle
need you weave me. Myrtle is no disgrace to

you as page-boy, nor to your master, drinking,
    shaded by vine-leaves.

Gilbert Highet

II, 1

Strife in Metellus' year first stirred,
Its grounds, its gropings, how it grew,
The share of Luck, of leading men,
Of ominous alliance,

Of arms still caked with crying blood —
Your task how like a gambler's throw! —
You trace; and, treading tricky ash,
May start on hidden embers.

Let not your haughty tragic Muse
Long leave our stage; when you complete
Our public story, then once more
Stride out in Attic buskin!

Prop at the Bar of anxious worth,
Strength of the Senate, Pollio, too,
Whom laurels crown with lasting fame
For your Dalmatian triumphs!

Even now, the angry trumpets snarl —
You burst my ears! — the clarion shrills,
Bright armor scares and dazzles both
Horsemen and rearing horses,

I seem to hear the shouting chiefs
Dusty with no ignoble dust
And all the earth beside cast down
Except dire Cato's courage!

Juno and gods of Africa,
Often rebuffed, now bring the killed
Descendants of the men who won
To soothe Jugurtha's spirit!

Where lies a soil now not made rich
With Latian blood? To impious war
Far graves are witness, and the Mede
Has heard Hesperia falling.

What pool or stream laps not the gloom
Of combat? By our Daunian deaths
What sea is not discolored, what
Coast for our blood still clamors?

Oh, not the Cean dirge once more!
Strayed Muse, desert not all delights!
With me, in some Dionean cave
Try for a happier measure!

G. S. Fraser

II, 3

Remember, Dellius, when times are bad
    Keep a calm mind, and in good times no less
    Let it be tempered against all excess
Of insolent rejoicing. Whether sad

You live, or whether upon holidays,
    Along a green lawn far secluded laid,
    Where the great pine-tree's branches join their shade
With that of the white poplars, you shall raise

Cups of the best Falernian, while there flows
    A slanting rivulet that hurries by
    With rippling waters, some day you must die.
Here bid them bring wine, unguents and the rose,

Whose flower lasts for such a little space,
    While the occasion and your youth permit,
    And the dark threads where the three sisters sit.
Your woods, your mansion, and your country place

That yellow Tiber washes you will leave.
    Aye, you will leave your riches, and an heir
    Will come to have for his enjoyment there
The wealth that you have labored to achieve.

Rich, of the line of Inachus of old,
    Or beggarly and of some mean descent,
    It matters not; beneath the firmament
Awhile you linger, then will Orcus hold

Unpitying his victim. We are all
    To one place driven; soon or late the urn
    Throws out the fatal lot for each in turn
Which sends us to the boat with no recall.

Lord Dunsany

II, 4

Xanthias Phoceus, never mind your loving
Merely a slave-girl. Long ago Achilles
Felt the same way about the slave Briseis,
  Charmed by her whiteness.

Tecmessa too stirred Telamonian Ajax
With her fair form, a captive; and Atreides
Loved in the midst of his victorious triumphs,
  Captured, a maiden.

After the slaughter of the foreign squadrons
Done by Achilles, when the death of Hector
Gave to the Greeks more easily the city
  Weary with warfare.

You know not whether the important parents
Of your blonde Phyllis would not bless your wedding;
Surely of royal blood, her grief is only
  Unjust Penates.

Think not your love from common folk was taken,
Nor yet that one so faithful as your Phyllis,
So free from greed, could ever have for mother
  One who would shame you.

Immune I sing her arms' and features' praises
And tapering calves; but banish your suspicion
Of one who sees the days of his eighth lustrum
  Rapidly ending.

       Lord Dunsany

II, 5

  Unschooled as yet the yoke to wear
  Or equal-paced the plough to pull,
  Your heifer, still too young to bear
  The ardors of the amorous bull,

  In grassy meadow delights to stray,
  Where cool the summer rillets flow,
  With the young herd to frisk and play
  Beside the streams where willows grow.

Let unripe grapes ungathered still
Hang green upon the unravished vine;
Full soon the purple autumn will
The clusters pale incarnadine.

Time speeds along in restless dance;
The years you forfeit she will gain.
And bolder as her days advance
Your Lalage will seek her swain.

More than elusive Pholoe
Or Chloris loved, her shoulders white
Shine like the moon above the sea
That silvers all the summer night.

And as amid the maidens' dance
With damask cheek and flowing curl,
Gyges deceived the keenest glance,
You question: Is she boy or girl?

J. S. Blake-Reed

II, 7

Pompeius, best of all my comrades, you and I
Often faced death when we were rebels.
Who brings you back, a citizen again,
To Italian gods and sky?

With ointment on our hair and wine
We helped along the days that used to linger.
We went through Philippi's swift rout together, too.
That little shield of mine

Was thrown away, while all around us
Courage broke and the threateners,
Chins in the dust, grovelled on
The disgraceful ground.

Me out of danger's reach the god of poets bore
Swiftly through the sustaining air;
You the boiling tides sucked back again
To fight once more.

Finally, your lengthy service ended,
Lay your weariness beneath my laurel tree.

Feast, and do not overlook the dreamy Massic
Just for you intended.

Fill up the polished cups. Whom will the Venus-throw receive
As drinking master? Who will see that crowns are made
Of parsley with the moisture still upon it
Or of myrtle leaves?

Pour ointment from the shells, and comb
It in your hair. I will drink like any toper.
For it is sweet to be a little mad
When a friend comes home.

John Wight

II, 8

If for all the promises you regard so lightly
One, *one* penalty ever held, Varina,
Should one tooth darken, even a torn toenail
    Leave you less smooth, dear,
Yes, I'd trust you. But when you avow with
"God strike me dead!" and falsify it, Lord you're
Lovelier yet as you parade! The whole male
    Populace wants you.
You swear by your poor mother's corpse and
Right away two-time; swear by every sign, by
Heaven itself, and by the very gods, those
    Durable persons.
This, I assume, amuses even Venus,
Amuses nymphs (good simple souls) and hardened
Cupid, forever honing up hot steel on
    His bloody whetstone.
What's more, all the adolescents love you;
Droves of new callers come; their predecessors
Never stamp from the house of the proud lady
    Much as they vow to.
Mothers worry for their husky youngsters;
Dads for bank-accounts; nice girls at the altar
(Poor things!) brood, for fear they'll soon be groaning
    "Where is that husband?"

John Frederick Nims

II, 11

Thoughtful Quinctius, cease to ask
What fierce Spain and the savage Goth

(Barred from us by the Adriatic)
    Threaten. Abandon forethought.
Life needs little, but graceful youth
Soon will vanish, and beauty soon;
Soon will drowsy and wrinkled age
    Deaden our wanton loves.
Even the bright blossom of spring must fade,
Even the moon's radiant face grows pale
Soon: then why with eternal thoughts
    Weary your mortal mind?
Come now, under this lofty plane
Lying carelessly, take your ease,
Rest, and garland your hair with flowers,
    Perfume yourself, and drink,
While you may — for the god expels
Gnawing care. Let a slave quench
Our too ardent vintage in cool
    Draughts from the passing brook.
Lyde, willing but coy, must come.
Bring her now, with her ivory lyre,
Neatly knotting her hair in haste
    After the Spartan mode.

                      Gilbert Highet

II, 14

Postumus, Postumus, the years glide by us,
Alas! no piety delays the wrinkles,
    Nor old age imminent,
        Nor the indomitable hand of Death.

Though thrice each day a hecatomb were offered,
Friend, thou couldst soften not the tearless Pluto,
    Encoiling Tityos vast,
        And Geryon, triple giant, with sad waves —

Waves over which we all of us must voyage,
All whosoever the fruits of earth have tasted;
    Whether that earth we ruled
        As kings, or served as drudges of its soil.

Vainly we shun Mars and the gory battle,
Vainly the Hadrian hoarse with stormy breakers,
    Vainly, each autumn's fall,
        The sicklied airs through which the south wind sails.

Still the dull-winding ooze of slow Cocytus,
The ill-famed Danaids, and to task that ends not
    Sentences, Aeolides;
        These are the sights on which we all must gaze.

Lands, home, and wife, in whom thy soul delighteth,
Left; and one tree alone of all thy woodlands,
    Loathed cypress, faithful found,
        Shall follow to the last the brief-lived lord.

The worthier heir thy Caecuban shall squander,
Bursting the hundred locks that guard its treasure,
    And wines more rare than those
        Sipped at high feast by pontiffs, dye thy floors.

Lord Lytton

II, 18

With no wrought roof of ivory and gold
    My cottage gleams;
No columned shafts from Africa uphold
    Hymettan beams.
No Attalus to me, an unknown heir,
    His wealth has left;
No noble maidens weave for me the rare
    Laconian weft.
Honor I have; of wit a kindly vein
    The gods have given;
Nor do the great my humbleness disdain;
    And I of heaven
Or high-placed friend would ask no further boon,
    My Sabine fields
Content to own, as day to day and moon
    To new moon yields.
You on the very threshold of the grave
    The marble spoils
Of Parian quarries purchase; where the wave
    At Baiae boils
Your pile-built terrace would extend the shore
    The sea to own;
Your avaricious pride uproots the poor
    Man's boundary stone.
Forth to the friendless world the rustic plods,
    Condemned to roam

With wife and children and the humble gods
    That blessed his home.
One last abode for all alike, my friend,
    Alone is sure;
The unsated grave must open at the end
    For rich and poor.
Nor would the sentinel of Orcus dire
    For any bribe
Release the sage Prometheus; Pelops' sire
    And all his tribe
In everlasting bondage still enthralled
    He holds and he
The laborer from his toil, called or uncalled,
    At last sets free.

J. S. Blake-Reed

III, 1

Tread back — and back, the lewd and lay!
Grace guard your tongues! — what never ear
Heard yet, the Muse's man, today
I bid the boys and maidens hear.

Kings herd it on their subject droves
But Jove's the herd that keeps the kings —
Jove of the Giants: simple Jove's
Mere eyebrow rocks this round of things.

Say man than man may more enclose
Of rankèd vineyards; one with claim
Of blood to our green hustings goes;
One with more conscience, cleaner fame;

One better backed comes crowding by: —
That level power whose word is Must
Dances the balls for low or high:
Her urn takes all, her deal is just.

Sinner who saw the blade that hung
Vertical home, could Sicily fare
Be managed tasty to that tongue?
Or bird with pipe, viol with air

Bring sleep round then? — sleep not afraid
Of country bidder's calls or low

Entries or banks all over shade
And Tempe with the west to blow.

Who stops his asking mood at par
The burly sea may quite forget
Nor fear the violent calendar
At Haedus-rise, Arcturus-set,

Nor hail upon the vine nor break
His heart at farming, what between
The dog-star with the fields abake
And spiting snows to choke the green.

Fish feel their waters drawing to
With our abutments: there we see
The lades discharged and laded new,
And Italy flies from Italy.

But fears, fore-motions of the mind,
Climb quits: one boards the master there
On brazèd barge and hard behind
Sits to the beast that seats him — Care.

O if there's that which Phrygian stone
And crimson wear of starry shot
Not sleek away; Falernian-grown
And oils of Shushan comfort not.

Why . . . .
. . . .
Why should I change a Sabine dale
For wealth as wide as weariness?

Gerard Manley Hopkins

III, 2

Let the youth hardened by a sharp soldier's life
Learn thoroughly to suffer cheerfully harsh injury, and
    Let him as a horseman feared because of his spear
      Harass the ferocious Parthians.

And let him lead his life under the open sky and among
Scenes of peril. As she watches him from hostile battlements,
    Let the warring tyrant's ripening daughter,
      Watched by her mother, yet sigh out,

"Alas, let not the royal bridegroom, unskilled
In conflicts, stir up the lion harsh to the touch,
    Whom bloody wrath snatches through
        The midst of slaughter."

Pleasant and fitting it is to die for one's own country.
But death tracks down the man who flies away,
    Nor does it spare the hams or cowardly backs
        Of youths unwarlike.

Martial courage, which knows nothing of disgraceful defeat,
Gleams with untarnishable honors; it neither
    Takes up nor lays down the axes
        At the breath of popular favor.

Laying open the heavens for those who do not deserve to die,
It forces its way by a course denied to common men
    And scorns with flying wing the mouldering earth
        And the common comings-together.

There is assured reward for faithful silence: I will forbid
Him who spreads to the multitude the sacred rites of mystic Ceres
    To be with me under these same beams, and to set sail
        His fragile skiff with me again.

Often the neglected Sky-Father involves
The unspotted with the defiled man. Rarely does retribution
    With halting steps abandon the wicked man,
        Even though he has the head start.

              Gardner Taplin and Richard Eberhart

III, 13

Hail, Bandusian spring, clearer than crystal pure,
fountain worthy of sweet wine and of gifts of flowers.
    Take my gift of a young kid
    whose head, swelling with early horns,
even now promises love, promises battles too —
vain forecasts: for he shall, after tomorrow's dawn,
    dye your coolness with red blood,
    he, once gayest of all the herd.
Untouched, even in the fierce hour of the blazing Dog,
unwarmed, you with your streams offer delightful cold
    to bulls tired with the heavy plow
    and to wandering herds of kine.

You too shall be among fountains of high renown,
when my song celebrates this overarching oak,
    this dark hollow of rocks whence
  leaps your chattering waterfall.

Gilbert Highet

III, 18

Faunus, fleet-foot lover of flying wood-nymphs,
Turn, on tiptoe; enter my sunlit farmland;
Look, oh gently look on my flock enfolded
    Here, with its firstlings.

Bless, and gently go. On thy boisterous feast-day,
Cyprian wine shall flow, where the chosen victim
Stains the fresh-cut turf, and thine ancient altar
    Smokes with our incense.

Goat and kid shall frisk in the flowering grasses,
Ploughmen dance! — on earth! — while the festal village
Claps its hands in time, and the unyoked oxen
    Rest where the streams flow.

There the wolf shall stray, and the flock not fear him,
There, while all the slaves of the land go singing,
Autumn beech-leaves, flying in gold and crimson,
    Fall, at thy feet, Faun.

Alfred Noyes

III, 23

If suppliant palms, upraised at the sacrifice,
Placate the gods, my field-weary Phidyle,
    At each new moon, if hard-won first-fruits
      Plead, and the darkening blood between them,

Fear, then, no more that wind out of Africa!
What need hast thou of costlier offerings?
    Far, far from here, though the axe be waiting,
      Feeds upon Alba the Pontiff's victim.

Our Lares ask — no gift of thy lowlihead!
Crown them with sprays of myrtle and rosemary!
    Their small bright statues, no less kindly,
      Cherish your hearth and your clustering vineyard.

O guiltless hands, your touch on the altar-stone
Moves all the heavens, though nothing of cost you bring,
    But crackling salt and sacred wheat-cake,
      Piously flung to the dying embers.

                     Alfred Noyes

IV, 7

The snows are fled away, leaves on the shaws
    And grasses in the mead renew their birth,
The river to the river-bed withdraws,
    And altered is the fashion of the earth.

The Nymphs and Graces three put off their fear
    And unapparelled in the woodland play.
The swift hour and the brief prime of the year
    Say to the soul, *Thou wast not born for aye.*

Thaw follows frost; hard on the heels of Spring
    Treads Summer sure to die, for hard on hers
Comes Autumn, with his apples scattering;
    Then back to wintertide, when nothing stirs.

But oh, whate'er the sky-led seasons mar,
    Moon upon moon rebuilds it with her beams:
Come *we* where Tullus and where Ancus are,
    And good Aeneas, we are dust and dreams.

Torquatus, if the gods in heaven shall add
    The morrow to the day, what tongue has told?
Feast then thy heart, for what thy heart has had
    The fingers of no heir will ever hold.

When thou descendest once the shades among,
    The stern assize and equal judgment o'er,
Not thy long lineage nor thy golden tongue,
    No, nor thy righteousness, shall friend thee more.

Night holds Hippolytus the pure of stain,
    Diana steads him nothing, he must stay;
And Theseus leaves Pirithöus in the chain
    The love of comrades cannot take away.

                    A. E. Housman

EPODE VII

Whither, curs'd rabble, do you rush? Why show
    Swords that were sheathed a while ago?
Has not on land and Neptune's waste been spilt
    Enough of Latin blood in guilt?
Not that proud Carthaginian towers should feel
    The might of Roman fire and steel,
Or that the Sacred Way should witness lamed
    With fetters Britons yet untamed,
But that the Parthian prayers should win at length
    And Rome be stabbed by her own strength.
No wolves or lions are so fiercely blind;
    They do not fight with their own kind.
Is it a madness, ravening energy,
    Or urge of sin? Come, answer me.
There is no answer. Pale and horror-eyed,
    Men shrink with misery stupefied.
I see. The old curse harries Rome again,
    Penalty for a brother slain.
The innocent blood of Remus from the earth
    Taints generations ere their birth.

Jack Lindsay

EPODE XV

It was night with the shine of the moon amid the smaller stars shining,
    And no night could be clearer,
When you (but you schemed then already to cheat the Immortals)
    You swore to me, traitress,
And tighter around me your sensuous arms were clinging
    Than ivy to ilex,
"While the wolf to the flock — or, as deadly to steersmen, Orion
    Excites winter storms,
"While in dawnlight still shiver the long golden locks of Apollo,
    This love shall be ours!"
But take care lest the day should arrive when my firmness, Neaera,
    Shall bring you misfortune,
Because if poor Flaccus has still in these veins but one drop
    Of manly blood throbbing,
He'll not suffer the strenuous nights it's your pleasure to grant
    To a lustier rival,
But will seek in his anger another girl to requite him
    With an equaller love.

You are lovely, but loyalty pardons you only the first time
    When the torture is real.
And you, sir, whoever you are, lucky dog, sir! Walk sprucely:
    Make mock of my fall:
Have fat flocks and great holdings: and over the limestone rock flow
    Your sun-dappled streams,
Let Pythagoras fail to surpass you in modish abstruseness,
    Nireus in looks . . .
Aye me! you'll weep for the love to another conceded:
    My turn to laugh!

G. S. Fraser

SATIRES I, 5

I left great Rome. Aricia offered me
a middling inn, with Heliodorus. (He
talks well in Greek.) Then Forum Appi. There
sailors and surly landlords fouled the air.
That stage we halved, being lazy: those who please
may make it one. The Appian Way for ease!
Here I, who drank the filthy water, heard
strife in my guts. Impatiently I stirred
while the others guzzled. Then the landscape blurred,
Night drew her curtains, hanging out the stars.   10

Our slaves began to abuse the answering tars.
Hubbub. "Bring to." "You're stowing hundreds." "Fool,
enough." To pay the fare and tie the mule
wasted an hour. Marsh-frogs and gnats at play
spoiled sleep. With songs of sweethearts far away
the sailor and a passenger vied, both soused
and full of brag. Tiring, the passenger drowsed
at last. The sailor tied the mule ashore
fast to a stone, lay back, and gave a snore.

Day broke. The boat was still, without a doubt,   20
till wrathfully a passenger leaped out
and with his cudgel dressed the idlers down,
both man and mule. So, late we reached the town,
Feronia, where we washed our hands and face
and dined. Then, three miles on, our crawling pace
found Anxur, gleaming white, a rocky land.
Here we'd to meet the good Maecenas and
Cocceius, legates on a great affair,
at reconciling friends an expert pair;

and here black salve I rubbed on eyes aflame   30
with travel-dust. Meanwhile Maecenas came;
Cocceius; Capito, who truly can
speak as Antonius' friend, a finished man.

We laughed past Fundi. — Praetor there, Aufidius,
the lazy scribe, would like his rank to giddy us,
his incense-pan, his gown, his purple-threads.
Then the Mamurran town. We drooped our heads:
Capito proffered food, Murena beds.

The next day dawned with pleasure, bringing us
Plotius, Varius, and Vergilius   40
at Sinuessa. Earth could never see
more candid souls or men more dear to me.
O, what a greeting as embraced we stood!
While sane, I'll count good friends my greatest good.

By the Campanian Bridge we found a village,
lodging, and wood and salt: our legal pillage.
Next, Capua. There, the mules their saddles shed.
To ball Maecenas, and the poets to bed!
Tennis ill suits sore eyes and feeble frame.

Then to Cocceius' well-stocked house we came,   50
above the Caudian Inns. Tell, Muse, I pray,
how Messius Cicirrus had a fray
with clown Sarmentus. Say what soil and father
begot them. Messius is Oscan, rather;
Sarmentus' mistress lives. Thus known to fame,
the heroes clashed.
          Sarmentus: "What's-your-name,
you look like a mad horse."
          We laughed. The foe
replied, "Get on," and wagged his noddle.
          "Ho,
it's good your horns are gone, so wild you are
without them, butting round." A dreadful scar   60
showed on the bristly brow (left side) its trace.
Then jokes on his Campanian plague, and face.
"Come, do the Cyclops Jig-trot," he was asked.
"Don't worry to be buskined, lad, or masked."

Cicirrus answered, "What about those fetters
you vowed the Lares? Though you know your letters,

your mistress owns you still." He cried in scorn,
"Why did you run away? A pound of corn
would feed you daily, you're so lank and lean."
We lounged at supper long to watch the scene.   70

Then on to Beneventum. There, to roast
some thrush, the tavern almost burned the host.
The flames crept out and found the rotten floor
and licked the kitchen-rafters with a roar,
till hungry guests and frightened servants beat
the spreading blaze and snatched the charring meat.

Apulia now revealed her famous slopes,
scorched by Atabulus, to end my hopes.
We never would have crossed, but Trivicus
received us, with a tearful smoky fuss: 80
for on the hearth were green and crackling boughs.
Here I, a fool, believed a wench's vows
and stood past midnight, waiting. Slumber came
at length, and eased me, till a gush of shame
awoke me from a dream of sudden marriage.

Two dozen miles next day, inside a carriage.
Next stop, a little town with name too queer
for verse, but soon described. They sell you dear
the vilest water, but the bread they grind
is good. Be wary: take some loaves. You'll find   90
Canusium fills its bread and springs with grit
(they say stout Diomedes founded it).
There sadly Varius left his grieving friends,
and tired we came to Rubi, what with bends
and twisting tracks, through rain that made us curse.

Next day the weather cleared, the road was worse,
right up to fishy Barium. Gnatia, sheer
upon the water, bade us laugh and jeer.
The incense melted there without a gust
of kindling flame. Let Jew Apella trust,   100
not me. I've learnt that gods are tranquil folk:
when nature swerves, we cannot blame the stroke
on peevish gods come down from depthless blue.

Brundisium ends my trip, and paper too.

Jack Lindsay

SATIRES I, 8

A fig-tree log I used to be;
The carpenter long considered these
Two things to make of useless me:
Priapus, or a stool of ease;
But finally settled on the god.
So godlike now with my right hand
I guard from thieves this bit of land,
Or fright them off with this red rod
Projecting from my ungainly groin;
A reed above my head is bound
To scare off birds that would purloin
Tidbits from this new garden ground.

In old days carcasses of slaves,
Dragged rudely from their narrow lairs
And borne by hirelings to their graves,
Here rested from their wretched lot
With all the refuse of the town.
Here among paupers you might find
The spendthrift Nomentanus, dead,
Likewise Pantolabus the clown.
A boundary pillar marked the spot:
"Frontage, three thousand feet," it read,
"Three hundred deep," with words designed
To save the burying ground from heirs.

Now property on the Esquiline
Has quite recovered from the slump:
It's healthy; people take the air
Along the sunny rampart, where
The dismal view they used to see
Was of a boneyard and a dump.
Prowlers no longer trouble me,
But once let fitful moonlight shine
When Luna bares her beauteous face,
And witches vex me worse than thieves;
They plague men's souls with drugs and spells,
And much my guardian spirit grieves
To hear their midnight songs and yells
And not to drive them from this place;
Nothing that I can threaten curbs
Their search for bones and baneful herbs.

I've seen (even I, the garden god)
The witch Canidia flitting round,
Swathed in black cloak, with feet unshod,
And shrouded in disheveled hair;
Beside her Sagana, her dam,
Piercing the air with owlish cries.
Horribly pale their faces were!
First they began to tear the ground
With talons, and a black ewe-lamb
Rent all to pieces with their teeth;
The dark blood filled the trench beneath
That ghosts might drink and make replies,
Uttering prophecies. This done
They took a puppet wrought of wool
And one of wax; the woolen one
Was larger, fashioned of a size
To daunt the weaker shape of wax,
Which like a suppliant, pitiful,
Cringed as if sentenced to the axe.
Then one witch summoned Hecate,
And one Tisiphone the dire,
While hell-hounds crept about and snakes;
The shrinking moon you now might see
Behind tall tombs hiding her fire
That such iniquities should be!

If any lying word I've said,
May crows' white droppings foul my head!
Get thief Voranus, Julius too,
And Pediatia, he who makes
Puddles, and let me be their jakes!

Would you hear more, most strange, most true?
How ghosts, when Sagana spoke, would mow
And gibber echoes sad and shrill,
And how the witches on the sly
Buried a wolf's beard in the ground
With tooth of spotted snake, and how
Fire from the waxen man blazed high,
And I was frightened fit to kill
At each ungodly sight and sound.
But quick to get revenge was I,
For bango! like a bladder burst,
Sudden my fig-wood buttock split,
Exploding in a cough reversed.

It makes me chuckle just to tell:
You should have seen them run for it!
Canidia lost the teeth she wore,
And Sagana's towering head-dress fell,
As scattering herbs and magic charms
A filthy litter from her arms,
Back into town those witches tore.

George F. Whicher

EPISTLES II, 3

The Art of Poetry

Should a painter join a human head   1(1)
And horse's neck, add limbs from every beast
And cover them with multi-colored feathers,
So that a lovely woman at the top
Ends in a black and ugly mermaid's tail,
When you saw this, my friends, wouldn't you laugh?
Believe me, Pisos, such will be a book
Where idle fancies, like a sick man's dreams,
Are fashioned without unity of head or foot.
"Poets and painters though have always had   10(9)
An equal power of daring what they like."
I know; I claim and grant this right in turn,
But not so much that savage mate with tame,
Snakes pair with birds and lambs with tigresses.
    Often, in serious works that promise much
A purple patch that flings its splendor wide
Is stitched, describing "Dian's grove and altar,"
"Swift waters wand'ring through the flow'ry fields,"
Or "Rhenish stream," or "rainbow arc of Heav'n."
Now there's no place for these. You may know how   20(19)
To paint a cypress tree; what of it, if
The man who's paid you for his portrait's shown
Swimming in desperation from a wreck?
A wine-jar is begun, but as the wheel
Is rolling round, why does a pot emerge?
To put it briefly, work at what you will,
If only it be uniform and whole.
    We poets, noble sir and worthy sons,
Are cheated most by what we think is right.
I labor to be brief and am obscure;   30(25)
I follow smoothness: fire and spirit fail;

Would one be grand, he rants, or be too safe
And fearful of a storm, he hugs the ground.
By wanting to adorn a simple theme
Too lavishly, he paints among the woods
A dolphin, or a boar between the waves.
A flight from blame brings faults, if you lack skill.
Close to Aemilius' school, far down the street,
There lives a smith who can cast fingernails
And mould a tender lock of hair in bronze;   40(33)
But he is unsuccessful in his work
Because he cannot represent a whole.
Were I to work, I would no more be he
Than go through living with a crooked nose
To match my handsome black eyes and black hair.
    You poets, take a subject in your power;
Reflect at length how much your shoulders will
Or will not bear. A theme within your range
Will not lack eloquence nor lucid form.
Form's power and its charm, if I am right,   50(42)
Will be to say now what must now be said,
Postpone and, for the time, omit the rest.
Choose this, scorn that while working on your poem.
    Be safe and sparing when you sow your words.
You will have spoken well, if some known word
By clever placing comes to life again.
Or if a new expression is required
To clarify a subject that's abstruse,
You'll have the lucky chance to fashion words
That lawyers of the old school never heard,   60(50)
And license, shyly used, will be allowed.
Words new and freshly-formed will win belief
If they are sparingly extracted from
The flowing fountain of the Greeks. Why should
Caecilius and Plautus have from Rome
What Varius and Vergil may not have?
If even I can add a word or two,
Should I be grudged it, after Cato's tongue,
And Ennius', enriched our fathers' speech
With new-made names? It was and always is   70(58)
A privilege to stamp and mint new words.
As forests change their leaves when year is out,
Dropping their first to earth, so among words
The older generation perishes
And like young men the new ones bloom and flower.
Death claims us all, and our productions too.

Though we build man-made lakes, a royal task,
To guard our navy from the Northern winds,
Or drain a marsh long barren, fit for boats,
To feed the neighboring towns and feel the weight   80 (66)
Of ploughs, or change a river's course, that harmed
Our crops, and set it in a better way,
All mortal works will die; much less the grace
And charm of words will stay alive and sure.
A rebirth often comes to words now dead,
While others, now in honor, will soon die,
If usage so decrees, for in its power
Decision, right and rule of speech reside.
     The meter to narrate unhappy wars,
The deeds of kings and leaders, Homer showed.   90 (74)
Couplets of different length were used for dirges,
Then for thanksgivings for a granted vow.
Who first composed the slender elegy
Critics dispute; the case is still in court.
And indignation armed Archilochus
With the iambic or lampooning foot;
This foot the sock and high, grand buskin took
As fit for dialogue, for action born,
For drowning out the noises of the crowd.
To lyric song the Muse apportioned praise   100 (83)
Of gods and demi-gods, the champion horse
And boxer, young men's loves and generous wine.
If I cannot or know not how to keep
The different rules and tones of poetry
Why greet me as a poet? Why should I
Be ignorant with false shame and not learn?
A comic theme rejects the tragic verse;
The banquet of Thyestes will not brook
Colloquial talk, more fit for comedy:
Let each type keep its due allotted place.   110 (92)
Yet, now and then, the comic voice is raised
And Chremes in his wrath declaims his wrongs
In mouthing phrase; while tragic heroes too,
Like Telephus or Peleus, sound their grief
In common speech as, poor and exiled both,
They throw away their paint-pots and their words
Sesquipedalian, and hope to touch
The heart of their spectators by a moan.
     That poems should be fine is not enough;
They must have charm and lead their hearer's mind   120 (100)
Which way they will. The face of man will smile

With those that smile or mourn with those that weep:
If you would make me weep, you first yourself
Must grieve; then, Telephus or Peleus, I
Shall mourn your fate; but if you speak a part
Ill-suited, I shall fall asleep or laugh.
Sad words befit a mourning face and threats
An angry one, and jests belong to sport,
Solemnity of speech to seriousness.
For Nature shapes our souls to every phase   130 (108)
Of fortune and she pleases, drives to wrath
Or bows us down with heavy grief and hurts;
Then later uses as interpreter
The tongue to let the feelings be expressed.
So if the speaker's words belie his fate
The Roman audience will raise a laugh.
It matters greatly who it is that speaks:
A god or hero, ripe old man, or youth
Still hot with vigor, or a stately dame,
Officious nurse, or merchant travelling,   140 (116)
Or farmer of a happy little plot,
Russian, Assyrian, Argive, or Theban-bred.
Follow tradition or see that you invent
Consistently; should you again portray
The famous man, Achilles, make him hot
And full of wrath, inexorable, keen,
Denying law and claiming all by force
Of arms. Medea should be wildly fierce,
Unconquered, Ino tearful, Ixion
Perfidious, Io lost, Orestes sad.   150 (124)
Or if you do put on the stage a thing
Untried and boldly dare to introduce
A novel character, it should proceed
From start to finish with consistency.
        It is not easy to say well-known things
In ways that are peculiarly your own.
You are more sensible to dramatize
The Iliad than be the first to tell
A tale unknown and never yet expressed.
A well-known theme allows for private rights,   160 (131)
If you will fly the cheap and hackneyed round
And not translate too closely, word for word,
Nor, like a common imitator, jump
Into a hole from which your shame, if not
The nature of your work, forbids escape.
Do not start as the cyclic writer did:

"Of Priam's fate I'll sing, and glorious war."
How will a boaster such as he maintain
A level worthy of this gaping phrase?
Mountains will labor: born, a silly mouse!   170(139)
Much better he who suitably begins:
    "Tell of the man, O Muse, who on Troy's fall
    Saw many towns and customs of the world."
He does not plan to give us smoke from fire
But from the smoke a light to let him show
Beautiful wonders, an Antiphates,
A Scylla, Cyclops, a Charybdis too.
He does not trace a Diomede's Return
From Meleager's death, or Trojan War
From the twin eggs, but hurries to the end,   180(147)
Taking his hearer to the midst of things
As if they were well-known and he omits
What cannot by his touch be turned to gold;
He lies so well, so mixes false with true
That start and end and middle harmonize.
    Now hear what I and what the public like.
If you would keep your audience in their seats
Until the curtain and the time for cheers,
You must observe the traits of every age
And give each changing life and year its due.   190(157)
A boy, who now can talk and walk aright,
Loves playing with his friends, gets angry soon,
Calms down as soon and changes every hour.
A beardless youth, his tutor gone at last,
Loves horses, hounds, the sunny Campus grass,
Pliant as wax to crime, to counsellors harsh,
Slow to provide for his best interests,
Extravagant, high-minded, amorous,
And quick to change the object of his love.
A man, in prime of life, foregoes these tastes,   200(166)
Seeks wealth and friendships, is ambition's slave,
And shuns what he may soon find hard to change.
Old age has many troubles; for the wretch
Still seeks, but fears and will not use his hoard;
Or else does everything in fear and cold;
He puts things off and spins his hopes out long,
Slow, greedy of the future, difficult,
Full of complaints, a praiser of the past
When he was young, a censor critical
Of all the modern generation.   210(174)
The rising tide of years brings many a joy;

The ebb removes as many. Do not give
Old roles to youth or manhood's part to boys;
Our interest is always fixed on traits
Appropriate and fitted to their age.
      A deed's reported or else done on stage.
The mind is stirred less sharply through the ear
Than if we watch with eyes, our clearest sense,
And as spectators vouch for what we see.
You will not put what should be done off-stage   220(183)
Upon the scene, but keep much out of sight
That soon an eye-witness will tell; let not
Medea's murder of her boys be shown,
Nor wicked Atreus cooking human flesh,
Nor Procne's transformation to a bird
Or Cadmus' to a snake; that kind of sight
I disbelieve and am disgusted at.
A play should have five acts, no less, no more,
To be successful and be staged again.
No god should intervene unless the knot   230(191)
Requires such liberation; and the sum
Of speaking actors should be only three.
The chorus should perform an actor's role
With strength and force; it should not interpose
Ill-fitting songs between the acts which have
No suitable relation to the plot.
Its total duty is to help the good,
Give friendly counsel, temper the irate
And cherish those who fear to do a wrong;
Let it praise modest fare, health-giving laws   240(198)
And justice, and the open gates of peace;
Let it keep secrets; ask the gods in prayer
That fortune help the poor, desert the proud.
      The accompanying flute was not, as now, of brass
And rival to the trumpet, but it gave
From its few stops a single, slender note,
Useful to help the chorus and to fill
With tune the not-yet-overcrowded seats,
Where once the people, countable, since few,
Foregathered soberly, good, honest men   250(207)
Who led god-fearing lives, till victory
Enlarged their lands and stretched their city's walls
And urged them to appease their guardian powers
By drinking early with impunity
On holidays. Then greater license came
To tunes and rhythms both. What taste would you

Expect from unskilled laborers at ease,
Low peasants mingling with the town's élite?
So to his ancient art the flautist gave
Extravagance and movement, trailed his gown,   260(214)
And roamed at random all about the stage.
So, too, the solemn lyre received new notes,
And headlong eloquence produced strange speech,
And worldly-wise, prophetic thoughts outdid
Even the sacred Delphic oracles.
   The man who strove to win the cheap goat-prize
In tragic verse, soon stripped the rustic Satyrs
And in rough sort, his dignity unharmed,
Tried on a jesting play to keep and charm
With pleasing novelties an audience   270(223)
Now drunk and lawless after sacrifice.
Yet when the Satyrs laugh and bandy jokes
And as you turn from seriousness to jest,
It would be out of taste to introduce
Heroes or gods, who were just recently
Admired in royal purple and in gold,
Crowding with filthy language to dark dives
Or grasping clouds and nonsense in the air.
And tragedy stoops not to babbling verse,
But, like a matron asked to dance en fête,   280(232)
Will shrink in shame from Satyrs' wantonness.
My friends, were I to write a Satyr-play,
I would not stick to common nouns and verbs
With no embellishment, nor would I try
To differ so much from the tragic tone
That it might well be Davus speaking there
Or brazen Pythias, a dollar richer
For having wiped old Snub-nose in the ground,
And not Silenus, Bacchus' guard and slave.
I would adopt a fiction known to all,   290(240)
That anyone might hope or dare to write,
But find his work and sweat are all in vain.
So great a power has order and good choice,
So great an honor lies in common tales.
My judgment is that woodland fauns should not
Be overcute with sentimental plaints
Nor bellow out obscenities and filth
Like guttersnipes or loiterers on the streets.
This will offend the freeborn, wealthy knights,
And though approved by those who buy and eat   300(249)
Peanuts and popcorn, it will not find grace

Among the better class nor win the prize.
        The verse-foot that is short, then long, is called
Iambus, and is quick; hence came the name
Of trimeter, which, though it had six beats,
Had every foot the same. Not long ago,
That it might slowly strike with heavier weight,
It added to its old inheritance
The steady spondee, yielding patiently,
Yet not so much as to give up the fourth   310 (257)
Or second foot, where it remained, a friend.
Yet in the famous lines of Accius
It shows up rarely and for Ennius' verse,
That tramps across the stage so heavily,
It brings the crushing and disgraceful charge
Of careless work, too quickly hammered out,
Or simply of artistic ignorance.
Not every critic sees a faulty verse
And Roman poets have been spared too much.
Should I then run amok and write unchecked?   320 (265)
Or should I think that every eye will see
My faults and so stay cautiously and safe
Within the hope of pardon? There, it seems,
I have avoided blame but earned no praise.
So turn the pages of your Greek examples
By night and in the day. Your ancestors,
It will be said, extolled the verse and wit
Of Plautus; yes, and too much tolerance,
Not to say folly, caused their admiration,
If only you and I can separate   330 (272)
Vulgarity from charm and tell by ear
Or finger how to scan a proper verse.
        The unknown Muse of tragedy, it's said,
Was found by Thespis first, who carried round
His plays for men with faces smeared with lees
To act and sing from wagons. After him
Aeschylus, who introduced the mask
And robe of honor, built a modest stage
And taught his actors to raise high their voice
And wear the buskin. These were followed by   340 (280)
Old Comedy, which earned a wealth of praise.
But soon its freedom turned to viciousness
And violence, that called for legal curbs;
A law was passed; the chorus in disgrace
Was henceforth silent, losing its right to hurt.
Nothing of these our poets left untried;

And when they dared to leave the tracks of Greece
And celebrate Italian themes, they won
Great fame in tragic and in comic dress.
In fact the power of Rome would no more rest   350 (289)
On courage and nobility of arms
Than on her native tongue, had not each one
Among her poets all too hastily
Rejected the slow labor of the file.
You, royal blood of King Pompilius,
Should blame a poem which has not been worked
For days on end, through endless alterations,
Ten times corrected by the close-cut nail.
    Democritus believed that innate skill
Brought more success than miserable art   360 (295)
And shut sane poets out of Helicon.
Hence a good number do not take the care
To cut their nails or shave their beards or bathe,
But seek out places set apart from men.
They think that they will win the name of poet
And its reward if they will never let
The barber Licinus come near their head
That triple cures for madness will not help.
Fool that I am to purge my bile in spring!
If not, none would write better poems, yet   370 (303)
Nothing is worth so much; I shall perform
The part of whetstone, which can sharpen steel
Again but cannot cut a thing itself.
Though I write nothing, still I shall impart
The function and the duty of a poet,
His sources and what trains and fashions him,
What fits him, what does not, and where the path
Of excellence and error will end up.
The spring and fountain-head of writing well
Is wisdom; the Socratic dialogues   380 (310)
Will show you matter and, the matter found,
The words will follow not unwillingly.
Who knows his duty to his land and friends
And how to love a parent, guest or brother,
The proper role of senator or judge
Or soldier sent to war, assuredly
He understands the way to represent
The fitting part for every character.
I will command the learned imitator
To take real life and manners as his guide,   390 (317)
And hence to draw a language that's alive.

Sometimes a play with brilliant passages
And well-drawn characters, though lacking grace,
Artistic skill and solid weight, will charm
More strongly, hold the people more, than lines
Devoid of substance, trifles with a tune.
    The Muses gave the Greeks their native skill
And power to speak in well-turned, rounded phrase,
The Greeks, whose only avarice was fame.
The Roman students with long reasoning   400(325)
Learn how to split an as a hundred ways.
Albinus' son shall answer: "If a twelfth
Is taken from five-twelfths, what then remains?
You used to know it once." "A third." "Correct;
You won't lose money. Add one, what d'you get?"
"A half." I ask, when once this cankerous love
Of slavish gain has dyed their hearts and minds,
Can we expect them to produce a book
Worth cedar polish and smooth cypress wood?
    The poet's aim is teaching or delight   410(333)
Or to speak both with charm and benefit.
When you instruct be brief, so that our minds
May see and learn and faithfully retain
The words that you have briefly said, for all
Superfluous words run off a brimming heart.
If you would please, let fiction follow fact,
So that your work does not demand belief
For anything it will, nor drag alive
A well-digested boy from Lamia's paunch.
The older audiences will hiss at plays   420(341)
Without a moral, while the dry-as-dust
Are passed up by the young aristocrats.
But he who mixes usefulness with charm
By teaching and delighting equally
Wins every vote. This is the book that pays
The publishers, is taken overseas
And brings its famous author lasting life.
    Yet there are faults we'd gladly overlook;
The note you strike is sometimes not the one
Your mind and hand intend; you often get   430(348)
A sharp where you desired a flat; nor will
The arrow always strike the threatened mark.
So when a work is full of shining gems
I shall not baulk at one or two dull spots
That carelessness let fall or human nature
Did not sufficiently beware against.

How so? I mean that, if a copyist
In spite of warning makes the same mistake
Incessantly, he will not be forgiven;
Or if a player never is in tune,   440(355)
He will be ridiculed; and so for me
The man who fails much is a Choerilus
Whose two or three good passages excite
A smile of wonder; but I am annoyed
Whenever Homer nods, for he is good.
Yet sleep may steal upon a lengthy work.
As pictures, so are poems; one will charm
If you stand near, another from afar;
One needs a gloomy light, another shines
In brightness, fearing not the sharpest eye;   450(364)
One pleases for a day, another will
Be sought ten times and still will please again.
　　　My older friend, although your father's voice
Guides you correctly and your thoughts are wise,
Take this remark to heart, remember it:
For certain things a mediocrity,
A bearable performance, is allowed,
And properly — for a solicitor
Or lawyer who is second-rate is lost
Before Messalla's brilliant eloquence   460(370)
Or Aulus's vast knowledge of the law,
And yet he has his value nonetheless — ;
But mediocre poets are disbarred
By men, by gods and by the bookshops too.
As at a pleasant feast discordant tunes,
Coarse perfume and Sardinian honey-meal
Offend, because we could have dined without,
So, if a poem written for our joy
Falls slightly short, it plunges to the depths.
He does not handle arms who cannot shoot;   470(379)
He does not play who fumbles with the ball,
The discus or the hoop, because he fears
The open laughter of the heavy crowd.
The man who can't write verse still does. Why not?
He's not a slave; his father too was free;
He's rated in the highest class of knights;
No stain lies on his character or birth!
But you, however, will not say or do
A thing against the grain; such is your plan
And such your judgment. Good; but if one day   480(386)
You do write something, drop it down to me

And to your father and to Maecius
To criticise; then put it in your drawer
And keep it there nine years; you can destroy
Unpublished manuscripts, but once they're sent
Out to the world, they cannot be recalled.
  When men lived wild, a spokesman of the gods,
The sacred Orpheus, scared them from their foul
And murderous ways; and so the legend says:
Ravening lions and tigers Orpheus tamed.   490(393)
Amphion too, who built the walls of Thebes,
As legend has it, *with his lyre moved stones*
And by sweet song enticed them where he would.
This was the poet's wisdom in those days:
To keep apart public and private spheres,
Religious and profane, and to prevent
Promiscuous love, make rules for married life,
Build towns and carve their laws on wooden posts.
And thus the name and honor of divine
Was given to those poets and their hymns.   500(400)
Thereafter Homer grew to fame, and next
Tyrtaeus whetted manly hearts by song
To martial deeds; then oracles were sung,
The way of life was shown, and royal favor
Was courted in Pierian strains; at last,
To crown the year's long labor in the fields,
The festivals were founded; so you see,
Apollo's song, the Muse's skillful lyre
Should cause no blush upon the cheek of man.
  Now whether art or nature is the source   510(408)
From which praiseworthy poems spring to life
Has long been asked; myself, I do not see
The worth of study where the vein is poor
Nor yet of innate skill if left untaught;
Each claims the other's aid and partnerlike
They swear alliance. For the man who aims
To win the coveted athletic crown
Has practised hard and suffered as a boy,
Sweated and shivered, kept from love and wine;
The player who is chosen to perform   520(414)
The Pythian music learnt his lesson once
And trembled at his master long ago.
But nowadays it is enough to say:
. . . "The poems that I write are wonderful;
. . . Plague take the hindmost; it's a shame for me
. . . To straggle lamely after and admit

... My ignorance of what I never learnt."
    An auctioneer attracts a crowd to buy
His bargains, and a poet rich in lands,
His money well-invested, orders men   530(420)
To flatter him for gain. If there is one
Who can present a banquet formally,
Bail out a bankrupt wastrel and release
The poor man from the law's harassing toils,
I'd be surprised if he could tell apart
A false friend from a true, for all his wealth.
So if you give or mean to give a gift,
Don't disappoint the glad recipient
With verses of your own, for he will cry:
"Good! Excellent! Well-phrased!" He'll grow all pale 540(428)
At this, drop dewy, friendly tears at that
And jump about and beat time on the ground.
For just as mourners, hired for funerals,
Behave and speak with almost greater grief
Than those who feel it deeply, so the sham
Is moved more than the real enthusiast.
It's said the rich will ply with endless cups
And rack with wine the men whose loyalty
They labor to examine to the full.
If you write poems, do not be deceived   550(436)
By minds that lurk beneath the fox's face.
If you read verses to Quintilius,
He used to say: "Correct this, if you please,
And this." Then if you said you'd vainly tried
Two or three times and couldn't better it,
He'd order you to scratch it out and send
Back to the anvil every ill-turned line.
And if you still preferred to back your faults
Rather than changing them, he'd say no more
Nor waste his time, but leave your works and you 560(443)
For you to love, unrivalled and alone.
A good and honest critic will be quick
To censure dullness, harshness to reprove,
To mark black crosses on inelegance,
To prune pretentious ornament; to bid
You clarify obscurities, to blame
All ambiguity, to note what should
Be changed: to stand in Aristarchus' place.
He will not say: "Why should I hurt my friend
Over a trifle?" For this very trifle   570(450)
Will lead to serious harm, if once a man

Is scorned and greeted inauspiciously.
    As one whom leprosy or jaundice grips
Or fit of frenzy or the angry moon,
Such is a crazy poet to the wise;
They fear to touch him, fly at his approach;
Boys tease him; fools pursue. He roams around,
Head in the clouds, regurgitating verse;
And should he, like a fowler with his eye
Intent on thrushes, stumble down a well   580 (458)
Or trapper's pit and cry out loud and long:
"Help, citizens!" there will be none to care.
But if someone does care to lend a hand
And drop a rope, "How do you know," I'd say,
"If he did not deliberately jump
And does not wish a rescue?" and I'd tell
The story of the Sicilian poet's end.
Empedocles, desiring to be thought
A god immortal, coldly hurled himself
Into the fires of Etna. Suicide   590 (465)
Should be a poet's clear prerogative.
Who saves unasked but murders whom he saves.
He's done this more than once, and if he's helped,
He still will not be human nor forget
His craving for a world-resounding death.
It is not quite apparent why he's doomed
To scribble verses; maybe he defiled
His father's ashes or disturbed a spot
Blasted by lightning with his impious foot.
He's mad, it's true; and like a bear at large,   600 (472)
Its cage's intervening barriers burst,
He scares away the witless and the wise
With biting recitations; but in truth,
When he has clawed a man, he hugs him close
And kills him with his reading, like a leech
That will not leave the skin till full of blood.

John G. Hawthorne

Ovid

[No poet except Chaucer, who borrowed much from him, has created such a golden aura of geniality or known so well how to entertain his grateful readers as Publius Ovidius Naso, born at Sulmona, 43 B.C., died at Tomi (modern Constantsa, Rumania) A.D. 18. His *Metamorphoses* are a series of about 215 accounts of miraculous transformations told from the Greek myths; they are among the world's favorite stories and have been a fertile source for many later writers. His talents in narrative are further demonstrated in the *Amores, Heroides, Fasti,* and other poems. His style is graceful, urbane, simple; it is not complicated with ideas. His good-nature is expressed in such lines as these from the *Art of Love:*

> Some may like the good old days;
> I'm satisfied to be
> Alive right now; this day and age
> Just suit me to a T.

and his facility in verse is confessed thus in the *Tristia ex Ponto* (Sad Poems Written from the Black Sea, to whose coast he was exiled):

> Song with a will in ready numbers came,
> And what I tried to write — verse was its name.

His love-affair with Corinna parallels those of Catullus with Lesbia, Tibullus with Delia, and Propertius with Cynthia. It is a prominent feature in the lives of the elegiac poets. Love, fiction, mythology, his own sorrows, and the Roman calendar of festivals are among his materials; to everything he touched he gave a mellow, fluent air that has drawn readers to him for centuries.]

METAMORPHOSES I, 1–415

THE CREATION OF THE WORLD

I am minded to sing of bodies to new forms changing;
Begin, O you gods (for you these changes have made),
Breathe on my spirit and lead my continuous song
From the birth of the world to the wonders of this my own time.

Before the creation of earth and ocean and sky,
Alike was the face of nature in all her course,

One indistinct chaos: a rough, disorderly mass
Of inharmonious atoms confusedly mixed
And lacking in all but lifeless and motionless weight.
As yet no luminous sun enlightened the world,
Nor crescent moon developed her horns once more,
Nor hung the earth in the circumambient air,
Poised by her weight, nor Amphitrite the ocean
With lengthening arms had margined the shores of the land.
And while in the world were land and water and air,
The land was unstable, the water too viscous for swimming,
The air yet unlighted; nothing retained its form,
And elements warred with each other, for in the same body
Cold things fought with the hot, the moist with dry,
The soft with the hard, the weighty with unweighty things.

At length this strife was ended by God, or by Nature,
Who tore away the land from the water and sky,
And divided the denser air from the ether of heaven.
When these were evolved and freed from the general chaos,
Assigned to their places, he bound them in concord of peace.
The fiery weightless element sprang to the height
And fixed its place in the vaulted arch of the sky.
Next in place and lightness followed the air;
The heavier earth drew the coarser elements down
And sank because of its weight; the circumfluent waters
Sank lowest of all and encompassed the shores of the world.

When he, whoever it was of the gods, had divided
The mass so arranged and reduced it to integrant portions,
First, that the earth might appear from every side
The same, he gave it the form of a mighty globe.
Then at his word the tumultuous, wind-driven waters
Encircled the earth and beat on the newly-formed shores.
Fountains and lakes he created, and stagnant marshes,
And down-flowing rivers enriching their banks with moisture,
Whose waters, though drawn from regions and climes far apart,
Meet in the sea and, released from their high-walled prison,
Range in new freedom between more distant shores.
He commanded the valleys to sink, the mountains to rise,
The plains to be leveled, the forest to burgeon with leaves;
And as in the sky two zones are set to the right
And two to the left, the fifth between being warmer,
So God in his wisdom gave to the globe a like number
And stamped earth's face with the five divisions of heaven.

Of these the centermost burns with unbearable heat;
The extremes are buried in snow; two others between
He made more temperate, mingling heat with the cold.

Above he suspended the air, more heavy than fire
In the same degree that water is lighter than earth.
There he ordained the fogs, the mists, and the clouds,
And thunder shaking the hearts of men with fear,
And lightning chilling the winds with bitter cold.
The winds are allotted the air, but not uncontrolled
By the world's creator; for, though assigned to their places,
So fiercely raged their anger and brotherly strife
That their wars endangered the very life of the world.
Then Eurus at length retired to Aurora's land
Where the Persian hills flush red in the morning light;
But where the sun sinks down to the western shores
Is Zephyrus' realm; to Scythia Boreas withdrew,
And the Seven Stars of the north; to the south came Auster,
Making his home in mists and perpetual rains.
High over all was placed the heavenly ether,
Weightless and clear, retaining no fragments of earth.

No sooner had God appointed their places to all
Than stars, long hidden beneath the primeval darkness,
Shone forth and with myriad lights bespangled the sky.
And, lest any region be lacking in animate life,
The stars and the god-like forms hold the floor of heaven,
The waves of the sea are alive with shining fishes,
The beasts inhabit the earth, the birds the air.

A master of these, a being of finer clay,
Possessed of loftier thought, was yet to appear.
Then man was born, divine in his essence, so formed
By the Maker of all, desiring a better world,
Or fashioned of soil but lately drawn from the sky,
Retaining some kindred drops of the heavenly ether.
That soil Prometheus, kneading with new-fallen rain,
Infused with life and shaped in the image of God;
And while all creatures beside look downward to earth,
For man he ordained a vision encompassing heaven,
And bade him stand up and turn his face to the stars.
Thus was the world transformed from disorderly chaos
And clothed with new life in forms before then unknown.

Golden were those early years when men, uncontrolled
By any law save their own natures, loved justice and truth.

No fear or punishment then, no savage decrees
Engraved upon tablets of brass, no suppliant multitude
Dreading the frown of its judges, of whom there were none.
Not yet were the tall pines cut from their native hills
To wander the face of ocean in search of far lands,
And mortals, home-loving, explored no shores but their own.
Not yet were fortified towns encircled with moats;
No martial trumpets or horns of crooked brass,
No swords or helmets were known; unarmed and unfearing,
All peoples in happiness lived out their measure of years.
The earth, uncut by the hoe, untilled by the plow,
Put forth her abundance to nourish the bodies of men,
Who gladly received her simple and natural fare.
Mountain strawberries they gathered, and arbutus fruit,
Cornel-cherries, and thick-hanging fruit of the thorn,
And acorns which fell from Jupiter's wide-spreading tree.
Spring was eternal, resplendent with self-sown flowers
Warmed by the tender breath of soft winds blowing.
In time the earth matured and ripened her crops,
The fields, unfallowed, grew white with the harvest of grain;
Then streams of milk and streams of nectar were flowing,
And golden honey distilled from the verdurous oak.

When Saturn was banished to dark Tartarean shades
And Jupiter ruled the world, the silver age came,
Much poorer than gold, far better than yellow brass;
For Jupiter shortened the old perpetual springtime,
Dividing the year in four seasons: winter and summer,
And changeful autumn, and all too brief a spring.
Then first the parched air glowed with unbearable heat,
And icicles formed in the chilling blasts of the north.
Then houses were built — sufficient shelter before
Were caves and thickets and twigs bound together with bark.
Then first were the seeds of grain in long furrows sown,
And oxen bowed beneath the weight of the yoke.

The third and following age was of brass, its people
More savage in nature, more readily taking up arms,
But not as yet vicious. Last came the age of hard iron.
Then instantly burst forth every species of crime,
And fled were honesty, truth, and the sense of shame;
Instead of these virtues men lived by fraud and deceit,
By stratagems, force, and the vicious longing for wealth.
They spread to the winds their sails scarce known to the sailor,
And pines which formerly stood in the lofty mountains

Now bounded exultantly over unvisited seas;
The land, as common to all as the sunlight and air,
Was henceforth surveyed and divided with boundary lines.
Nor yet sufficient to men was their natural fare,
The fruit of the earth, but they pierced far into her vitals
And brought forth mineral wealth, the root of all evil,
Which God had concealed and buried in Stygian shades.
For now injurious iron and gold more maleficent
Furnish the sinews of War, that destroys mankind
And brandishes clashing arms in his blood-stained hand.
Rapine is rampant: the guest is unsafe from his host,
The son from his father-in-law, and brother from brother.
Man wishes the death of his wife, she that of her husband,
Unfeeling stepmothers poison with ghastly wolf's-bane,
And sons, impatient, would shorten the years of their fathers.
Piety lies in defeat, and the virgin Astraea,
Last of the gods, abandons the blood-dripping earth.

And, lest high heaven be too much securer than earth,
They say that giants attempted the throne of the gods
And heaped up mountains to reach the region of stars.
Then Jove the omnipotent father, hurling his thunderbolts,
Shattered Olympus and struck down Pelion from Ossa.
When the gigantic corpses lay overwhelmed,
They say that Earth, imbrued with the blood of her sons
And fearing lest every trace of them vanish away,
Gave to the warm blood life and the bodies of men.
But this unmannerly race, like their fathers before them
Contemning the gods, were savage and eager for slaughter
And given to violence — truly the children of blood.

When father Jupiter gazed from his lofty throne,
He groaned, recalling Lycaon's hideous feast —
A deed so recent as not to be widely known —
And feeling insatiate wrath arise in his heart,
He summoned his council; nor tarried the gods whom he called.

There is a lofty road, on clear nights visible,
Which for its brightness is known as the Milky Way.
Here lies the path of the gods to the Thunderer's dwelling
And regal domain; to right and left open upon it
The wide-doored halls of the high gods thronging with guests.
Elsewhere the lesser divinities, here the most noble
Of heaven's inhabitants build their magnificent homes.
Here is the spot which, lacking in language sufficient,
I should describe as the Palace-Place of the sky.

So, when the gods in the marble chamber were seated,
Jove in his high place, holding the ivory scepter,
Thrice and again shook his head, whose terrible locks
Can move the earth, the sea, and the heavenly stars.
Then in such fashion he uttered the wrath of his heart:
"No more than now for the world's dominion I trembled
In that cataclysm when each of the serpent-foot Titans
Stretched forth his hundred hands to make captive the sky.
For, although a dangerous foe, they were easily known;
From only one race and one origin issued the war.
But now through the whole world, wherever Ocean resounds,
Mankind shall be lost! I swear it by infernal rivers
Which under the earth flow downward through Stygian glades.
I have tried all else, but rotten incurable bodies
Must yield to the sword, lest all that are sound be corrupt!
Have I not mountain and forest divinities, nymphs
And rural deities, demigods, satyrs, and fauns?
Since these are considered unworthy the honor of heaven,
Let them inhabit in peace the lands where they dwell.
Or can you believe, O gods, that their fortunes are safe
When I, who hurl the thunder, who govern you all,
Was threatened with death in the snares of savage Lycaon?"
They trembled and, eager for vengeance, demanded the man
Who dared such infamy; thus, when an impious band
Shed Caesar's blood to extinguish the Roman name,
Humanity, thunderstruck, suffered the terrible fear
Of sudden ruin, and all the earth shuddered in horror.
To you no less pleasing, Augustus, your subjects' devotion
Than this was to Jove, who quickly by voice and by gesture
Subdued the tumult till silence held the assembly.
The clamor subsided, quelled by the kingly command,
And Jupiter broke the silence once more with his words:
"He has been punished (dismiss that care from your minds),
But listen to what he has done, and what is his fate.
An evil report of the times had assailed my ears;
Hoping to prove it false, I descended from Olympus
And traveled the countries of earth in the guise of a man.
Too long it would take to tell you their measure of guilt
And where it is found; the rumor was less than the truth!
I passed through Maenala, haunt of the fiercest beasts,
Over Cyllene's top and the pine-clad slopes of Lycaeus;
Thence, as the shadows of evening lengthened to night,
I reached the unfriendly abode of Arcadia's king.
A sign of my godhood I gave, and the people before me
Began to pray; Lycaon first mocked their devotions,

Then said: 'I will try this god by infallible tests,
Whether he be an immortal; no doubt shall remain.'
He planned by night to slay me while heavy with sleep,
Suspecting no evil; such was his test of the truth!
Unsatisfied yet, he slew a Molossian hostage,
Cutting his throat to prepare a hideous feast,
And some of the limbs yet throbbing with life were boiled
In scalding water, some roasted above the flame.
When these were served up to me, with avenging thunderbolt I
Hurled down the roof on its lord and his impious house.
In terror he flies and, reaching the silent countryside,
Howls in his fear and vainly endeavors to speak;
He foams at the mouth and, mad with his craving for slaughter,
Murders the sheep and gorges himself on their blood.
His arms change to forelegs, his clothing to rough, shaggy hair,
A wolf he becomes, resembling his earlier self:
The same grey hair, the same intractable countenance,
Eyes still gleaming, the mark of the beast in his face.
One house is destroyed, but not one only deserves
Destruction; throughout the earth wild fury holds sway.
You would think men sworn to crime! Let all of them suffer
The doom which all so richly deserve! I have spoken."

Some voiced their approval of Jove and further aroused him
With cries of rage, while others nodded in silence;
Yet all were sad that the race of mortals must die,
Inquiring what was to be the future of earth,
And who would bear sweet incense unto their altars,
Or whether wild beasts would wholly inherit the land.
These matters their ruler assured them should be all his care,
And bade them repine not, since from a wonderful source
Should come a new people far different from that of old.

And now he raised his lightnings to destroy the world
But paused for fear such a fire might enkindle the sky
And burn the universe unto its uttermost pole.
For well he remembered, a time was destined to come
When ocean and earth and the beautiful palace of heaven
Should blaze, and the frame of creation be sorely beset.
Replacing the thunderbolts forged by the Cyclops' hands,
He favored a different punishment: under the waves
Of a far-flung deluge to drown the races of men.

Straightway in Aeolus' cave he imprisons the North-Wind
And all other blasts that drive out the rain-bearing clouds.

The South-Wind, loosened, flies forth on dew-dripping pinions,
Pitch-black darkness covers his terrible face,
His beard is heavy, his grey hair streaming with rain,
Clouds circle his brow, bedewed are his garments and wings.
And where his broad hand presses the overhanging mist
The thunder roars and heavy rain falls from the sky,
While Juno's many-hued rainbow-messenger, Iris,
Draws up the watery vapor to nourish the clouds.
The crops are destroyed, the hopes of the husbandman ruined,
His prayers unanswered, his long year's labor in vain.

The waters of heaven suffice not the anger of Jove,
Who asks of his sea-god brother auxiliary waves.
Then Neptune summons the rivers, who, under his roof
Assembled, are told: "I have no time to explain
Or bandy words. Put forth your mightiest efforts;
Such is your task. Break open the banks which confine you,
And give free rein to your currents' turbulent force."
The streams, thus exhorted, return and unseal their fountains
And whirl unchecked in their wild career to the sea.

When Neptune strikes the ground with his terrible trident,
The quaking earth throws wide a way for his waters.
The unleashed rivers rush into the open fields,
Overwhelming orchards and dwellings, cattle and men,
Sparing not even the sacred altars and shrines.
If anywhere stands a house resisting the torrent
Unfallen, the mounting waters soon cover its top
And hide its towers beneath the all-conquering flood.
And now no boundaries separate ocean from land;
All is a sea, a sea unmarked by a shore.

Some fly to the hills, some sit in their curving skiffs
And wield the oar where once they followed the plow;
Sailing above their meadows and waterlogged homes,
They catch fish trapped in the interlaced branches of elms.
Perhaps their anchors are lowered in grassy pastures,
Or curving keels brush over their vineyard tops;
And where the slender goats were accustomed to browse
The clumsy sea-cows now lay their bodies to rest.
The Nereids wonder at forests and cities and houses
Beneath the waves, while dolphins enter the woods
And shake the massive oaks with their threshing about.
The sheep and the wolf, the tawny lions and tigers
Are borne on the waves; the lightning-like stroke of the boar,

The agile limbs of the stag are of little avail;
The wandering bird, grown weary of long land-seeking,
Furls her wings and drops to her death in the sea.
The wild, tumultuous waters have covered the hills,
And unfamiliar waves lap the mountainous peaks;
Most living creatures are drowned, and those who survive
Are fated to die by long-drawn-out starvation.
Between the Aonian and Oetean fields
Lies Phocis, fertile of soil until that occasion
When quick-rising waters had made it a part of the sea.
There rugged Parnassus lifts twin peaks to the stars
And veils her summits in all-enveloping clouds.
Here when Deucalion (for all other mountains were covered),
Had drifted to land on a raft with Pyrrha his wife,
They worshiped the mountain divinities: Corycian nymphs
And soothsaying Themis, then the most famous of oracles.
No man was ever more loving of truth than he,
No woman more reverent toward the gods than she.
When Jupiter saw that the earth was a stagnant pool,
And that of the thousands of men only one had survived,
And that of the thousands of women only one remained,
Both innocent, both fulfilling their duties to God,
He threw back the dark rain-clouds on the wings of the North-Wind,
Showing the land to the sky and the heavens to earth.
Assuaged is the wrath of the sea, for the Father of Waters,
Replacing his three-pronged weapon, makes gentle the waves
And orders his herald to blow the resounding conch
And by that signal to call back the rivers and floods.

The sea-hued Triton, lifting above the surface
His shoulders covered with shellfish, raises his horn,
A twisted spiral broadening from the base,
A horn which, blown in the mid-most part of the ocean,
Fills with its voice all shores underlying the sun.
So, when the bearded, dew-dripping mouth of the god
Now touches the musical shell and sounds a retreat,
All regions of earth and all the waves of the sea
Hear it and know that its ordinance must be obeyed.
The sea now possesses a shore, the streams hold their channels,
The rivers subside and hill-tops begin to appear;
Dry land arises and grows with the fast falling waters
Till after long waiting the trees are uncovered to view,
Their leaves still soiled with sediment left by the flood.

The world was restored; but when Deucalion saw it

Devoid of life and felt the unbroken silence
Of desolate lands he spoke to Pyrrha with tears:
"O sister, O wife, O woman the last of your sex,
Whom family, race, and the bonds of mutual love
Have united to me, now danger more closely unites.
In all of the lands from rising to setting sun,
We two are alone; the sea has taken the rest.
Nor yet is this tenuous hold upon our life
Made certain, for still the dark clouds frighten my mind.
How should you feel, poor heart, if fate had preserved you
Alone, without me? How should you conquer your fear?
Who would then comfort your uncontrollable grief?
For I, be assured, if you had drowned in the waters,
Would follow you, wife, and rest by your side in the sea.
O that the arts of my father, the giver of life,
Enabled me too to animate bodies of clay!
But now in the two of us rests the future of man;
The gods have decreed that we live while all others die."
He spoke, and they wept; then it seemed best to invoke
Celestial power and counsel to seek from the oracle.
Quickly together they visited Cephisus' stream,
Muddily flowing once more in its usual channel.
Then, having sprinkled their garments and heads with water
And made the proper libation, they turned their steps
To the shrine of the hallowed goddess, whose walls were disfigured
With filthy moss, whose altar-fires were quenched.
Approaching the steps of the temple, they fell prostrate
To the ground and gave trembling kisses to the cold stone;
And thus they prayed: "If ever the prayers of the righteous
May soften victorious gods and avert their wrath,
O Themis most merciful, help our desolate world
And tell us what art may avail to restore our race."

The goddess is moved to utterance: "Leaving the temple,
Unloosen the clasps of your garments, cover your heads,
And throw behind you the bones of your mighty mother."
They stand in amazement; then Pyrrha, breaking the silence,
Refuses at first to obey the goddess' command
And prays with quivering lips for pardon, not daring
To rouse the maternal ghost by profaning her bones.
Meanwhile they doubtfully question the oracle's meaning,
Turning the dark words over again in their minds.
The son of Prometheus soothes with comforting speech
His wife and declares: "If I am not wholly at fault,
(For surely the oracle urges no impious deed!)

The earth is our mighty mother; the stones in her body
I think are her bones; it is these we are bidden to throw."

Though Pyrrha is moved to hope by her husband's surmise,
She dares not believe it is true — so doubtful are both
Of the heavenly meaning; but why should they scruple to try?
Descending, they cover their heads, unfasten their tunics,
And backward hurl, as directed, the stones in their path.
Then (who would believe it, except for the lore of the ancients?)
The rock begins to put off its original hardness,
To soften its texture, and slowly to alter its form.
And as in the marble rough-hewn by the sculptor's hand
The inchoate figure foreshadows the statue complete,
So these, grown milder in nature and larger in size,
Show forth in their transformation the semblance of men.
The parts that are earthy and dampened with penetrant moisture
Are changed to bodily flesh; the parts that are hard,
Unyielding and rigid, become the framework of bones;
The veins of the rock remain as the conduits of blood.
And shortly the stones, through grace of the almighty gods,
If thrown by Deucalion's hand, take the bodies of men,
If thrown by Pyrrha, likewise to women are changed.
Thus, as a race we are hard and enduring of toil,
Witnessing well the origin whence we are sprung.

John E. Hankins

METAMORPHOSES I, 463–567

APOLLO AND DAPHNE

Cupid replied to him, "Phoebus, your shafts
Transfix all things, but mine wound you yourself.
All living beings yield to your godhead, you
To me!" He spoke, and leapt on rosy wings
Up to Parnassus' dark and holy peak:
There from his deadly quiver he chose two arrows,
One shaft could bring, the other banish, love —
The first was sharp with a bright golden barb,
The other leaden-shafted, blunt, and cold.
The leaden shaft sped to the heart of Daphne,
The other pierced Apollo's inmost heart.
At once the god felt passion, and she shunned it —
Loving the hidden places of the woods,
And the spoils of captured beasts — a virgin huntress.

Bound with one ribbon, lightly flew her hair.
Shrinking from all her suitors, hating men,
She wandered lonely through the pathless forest,
Careless and ignorant of love and marriage.
Her father often said, "Daughter, you owe
A husband to yourself, grandsons to me."
She shunned the marriage-torches like a crime,
With lovely blush of kindling modesty,
And, clinging to her father with soft arms,
Said, "Grant me what Diana once obtained,
My dearest father — a life of maidenhood."
He granted it: her loveliness refused it.
For Phoebus loved her, craved to be her husband,
And hoped — for his own oracles deceived him.
As fiercely as the straw after a threshing
Blazes up, or the hedge a traveller kindles,
Leaving his torch beneath it at sunrise —
So the god's heart vanished away in fire,
Blazing with love and fed with barren hope.
He saw her hair dangling carelessly down
And cried, "Ah, were it combed and dressed!" Her eyes
Burning like stars, he saw; he saw her lips —
To see them was too little. Hands and fingers,
Arms and her naked legs he saw and praised;
And more admired what was unseen. She fled
Quicker than rapid breezes, never halting
Even when he cried, "Stop, nymph! No enemy
Pursues you here! Stay, nymph! Lambs flee from wolves,
Deer from lions, the trembling doves from eagles,
Fleeing their enemies: I am your lover.
Ah stop, in case you stumble! Or the briars
Mangle your lovely legs, and I be blamed.
These are rough deserts where you run so headlong!
Ah, flee more gently, I'll pursue more gently.
Ask your adorer's name! I am no shepherd
Or mountaineer or shaggy countryman.
Know your pursuer, rash and headlong nymph,
Then you will stay. Mine is the Delphic land,
Claros, and Tenedos, and Patara.
My father, Jupiter. I know what was,
What is, and will be. I give songs their music.
Sure is my arrow, surer than all others,
Save one, which pierced me in my careless heart.
All medicines and drugs are of my finding,
I rule all herbs, and have the name of Savior.

Alas, no herbs can remedy my love!
I that save others cannot save myself."
Still he endeavored to speak, but the quick nymph
Fled from him and disappointed pleading.
Beautiful even then — she was stripped by the wind,
Her dress whirled out and beating in the breezes
Which drove her hair up in a fan behind:
Her beauty grew as she ran. The ardent god
Grew angry when his flatteries were left;
Love spurred him, and he followed her eagerly.
As when a greyhound sees in an empty field
A hare — it runs for its life, the dog for blood —
And every moment the dog closes and snaps,
Flying behind the dog with outstretched muzzle,
The hare in doubt whether the jaws have gripped
Or whether it escapes from the eager mouth —
So the nymph fled in terror, the god in hope
Pursued, and still pursued, quickened by love,
Giving the nymph no rest, clutching her back
As she fled, and breathing on her flying hair.
Exhausted, she grew pale, and was overcome
By the hot chase. She cried to Peneus stream
"Father, bring help, if you are god of the river:
And change this beauty which has ruined me!"
At once a languor swam throughout her limbs.
A film of bark covered her tender breast,
Her hair grew into leaves, her arms to branches,
Her rapid feet sank into slow roots,
The treetop was her face, whose beauty remained.
But still the god adored her: under his hand
He felt her bosom quiver beneath the bark,
And threw his arms around the branchy limbs,
Kissing the tree — the tree shrank back from him.
He cried, "Daphne, you cannot be my wife,
But you shall be my tree. My hair, my quiver,
My lyre shall always wear your garlands, Laurel.
Attend the Latin leaders, when the triumph
Shouts through the streets or mounts the Capitol.
Faithfully guard the portals of Augustus
Before his hall, and there support the oak.
And as my youthful head is never shorn,
So always wear the beauties of your leaves."
Thus the god ended, and the new-made laurel
Nodded its branches and its leafy head.

Gilbert Highet

METAMORPHOSES II, 1–49, 103–327

The Story of Phaeton

The palace of the Sun stood, reared above
On marble columns, blazing far and wide
With flame-like rubies and all precious stones.
The roof was ivory, and the shining doors
Were finest silver, dazzling to the sight,
But far inferior to the workmanship:
For Vulcan there had carved the boundless sea,
The circled earth, and overhanging sky.
The water-gods are swimming on the wave:
Here dark-blue Triton blows his sounding shell;
And yonder many-formèd Proteus lies;
There Aegeon rests upon the backs of whales;
Here Doris and her daughters play: some swim,
Some sit on rocks and dry their sea-green hair,
And some on dolphins ride. They are not all
Of one appearance, neither differ much —
But are indeed as sisters ought to be.
The earth bears men, walled cities, forests, beasts,
And rivers, nymphs, and rural deities wild.
Above these hangs the shining firmament —
Six constellations are upon each door.

When Phoebus' son had climbed the steep ascent,
He came within his doubted parent's house,
And standing off, looked toward his father's face,
Nor nearer drew, so dazzling was the light.
Clothed in a purple vesture, Phoebus sat
High on his royal throne of green emeralds.
On either hand the equidistant Hours,
The Day, the Month, the Year, and Seasons stand.
First, young Spring stood with flowery garlands crowned;
Next, unclothed Summer ripening corn-stalks bore;
Then Autumn came with ruby grape-juice stained;
Last, icy Winter with his shaggy hair.

The Sun with his all-seeing eyes beheld
The youth, who trembling stood. "Why do you come,
O boy," he said, "to this high citadel?
You are my son, whom I cannot deny."
Then Phaeton answers, "Source of light and life

For all the world, O Phoebus, father mine,
— If I may use that word — give proofs to me
Which will assure my birth and take away
All chance of error." So spoke the trembling youth.
His father, laying down the crown of flames,
Bade him come nearer and embraced his son.
"Clymene spoke the truth about your birth;
That you may be more sure, ask what you will,
And I will give it — by the Styx I swear."

Before he finished, the impetuous boy
Asked for one day the chariot of the Sun.
His father, repenting of his oath, then spoke,
Attempting to dissuade the eager youth
From his rash purpose, but he spoke in vain.
At last he led the boy where stood on high
The chariot which its maker, Vulcan, gave.
The spokes were silver, all the rest was gold;
The yokes adorned with brilliant tourmalines
Shone far with light reflected from the Sun.
While daring Phaeton wonders at these things,
And with keen eye looks at the workmanship,
The watchful Dawn unfolds the purple doors
And opens wide the rosy rooms of day,
While Lucifer drives off the fading stars.

As Phoebus saw them fleeing to the earth,
And marked the world grow red, when the dying moon
Grew faint he called his fleeting messengers,
The Hours, and bade them yoke the restless steeds.
The goddesses in haste obeyed his word
And led the fiery horses from their stalls.
Then Phoebus rubbed the oil on Phaeton's face
That gave him power to bear the raging flames,
And placed upon his head the shining rays.
Foreseeing ill, he deeply sighed and said,
"Obey at least the counsels of your father:
Spare, boy, the whip, and often use the reins.
Of their own will the horses forward speed,
The labor is to hold them in. And next
Use not the way which stretches through five zones,
But go obliquely through the middle three.
Flee both the Southern and the Arctic poles;
Where you see chariot-tracks, there take your way.
That earth and sky may have their proper heat,

Neither bear down, nor strive to soar aloft,
Lest you should burn the dwellings of the sky,
Or else the world; safest the middle way.
But while I speak damp night has run her course
And reached her western goal; Aurora lights
The fleeing darkness with her rosy torch.
Take up the reins; or if your mind is changed,
Let me ascend and take the steeds in charge,
While you look safely on." Phaeton unmoved,
Stood in the chariot, grasped the flowing reins,
And thanked his anxious father, and said farewell.
Meanwhile the winged horses of the Sun
With neighings filled the air and kicked the bars
With savage hoofs. At last the bars were dropped,
And access given to the boundless world.
The steeds sprang out upon their westward course,
Dashed through the opposing clouds and flying on
Passed by and left behind the Southeast Wind.

Just as curved ships without their ballast roll,
And sail unsteadily the stormy sea,
So lacking its accustomed heavy weight,
The chariot bounded high and made huge leaps
From side to side and seemed an empty one.
And when the horses knew who held the reins,
They galloped on and left the beaten track.
Now Phaeton fears; he does not know the way,
Or if he does he cannot guide them there.
Then first the icy Bears were heated by the sun,
And strove in vain to touch the forbidden stream;
And then the Serpent lying near the Pole,
Sluggish with cold before and feared by none,
Began to move and raise his hissing head;
Boötes from his wagon fled in fear.
But as unhappy Phaeton from his dizzy height
Looked down upon the earth, far, far below,
His face grew pale, his knees began to shake,
And spots of darkness danced before his eyes.
Why had he ever touched his father's car,
Or cared to learn his birth, or asked a proof?
So moaned the boy as he was borne along
Just as a white-sailed ship with broken helm
Is driven onward by the north-east blast.
What should he do? Behind his back there lay
A large expanse of sky; ahead he saw

The far-off West, which he would never reach.
He knew not where to drive nor had the sense
To let the horses freely take their way,
Nor had the strength to guide the fiery steeds,
Nor knew their names to call and bid them halt.
Around him through the sky he sees with fear
Here things most wonderful, there monstrous beasts.

There is a place where Scorpion bends in
His arms and occupies a double space.
When Phaeton saw him with his threatening claws
And damp with oozing poisonous juice,
Crazy with fear the boy let fall the reins;
And as they felt them touch their backs, the steeds
Dashed forward and unhindered flew ahead
Through unknown regions, and where impulse led
They ran. They struck against the shining stars,
They rose on high and then approached the earth.
The silver Moon beholds the smoking clouds,
Wondering to see the sun below herself.
The world now catches fire; the mountains first,
Then the low hills, and last the level plains.
The ground acquires huge cracks, dries up and burns.
The grass grows white; all foliage is consumed;
The dry crops give the fuel to burn themselves.
I mourn small things! Great cities with their walls,
Whole nations turn to ashes in the fire!

Athos, Cilician Taurus, Tmolus blaze,
Oete, dry Ida, famed before for springs,
Aonian Helicon, the Muses' home,
And Haemus, not yet called Oeagrian.
Aetna burns, heated now with double fires,
Twin-peaked Parnassus, Eryx, Cynthus too,
Othrys, Rhodope soon to lose her snows.
Nor was her cold of use to Scythia;
Caucasian mountains, Ossa, Pindus burn,
Olympus great in size and majesty,
The lofty Alps and snow-capped Appenines.

Then Phaeton saw a universal blaze
And could not bear the heat and fiery air
Which burnt his face as from a furnace deep.
Worse yet, his chariot began to burn
And red-hot cinders flew, and wreaths of smoke

Obscured his boyish form. Whither to go
Or where he was, he knew not, for a cloud
Of pitch-black darkness circled him around.
The horses bore him onward at their will.

They say the blood of Ethiopians,
Drawn to the surface by the fiery heat,
Darkened their skins; then Libya's deserts came;
Then nymphs wailed for their vanished lakes and springs:
Dirce sought Boeotia, Ephyre mourned
The Pirenian waves, and Argos Amymon.
The distant rivers did not safe remain:
Don smoked amid his waves and old Peneus,
And Mysian Caicus and swift Ismenus,
And Xanthus, doomed to burn a second time.
There burns Meander in his winding course,
Yellow Lycormas, Lydian Melas too.
Then Babylonian Euphrates blazed,
Orontes, Ganges, Phasis, Thermodon,
The Danube, Spercheus. Sacred Alpheus boils,
And burning Tagus melts his golden sands;
And those melodious swans which make far-famed
The banks of Cayster perished in the stream.
Nile fled in terror to a far-off land,
And hid his sources, not discovered yet.
His seven mouths lie vacant, seven beds
Of sand without a stream. The same cause dries
Ismarian Hebrus and the Strymon's wave,
And all the western streams — Rhine, Rhone, and Po,
And Tiber, small but destined for great things.

The earth yawns open, and the light of day
Shines into Tartarus, strangest of sights,
And terrifies dark Pluto and his queen.
The sea contracts and leaves a sandy plain;
And mountains, buried beneath the waves before,
Rose and increase the scattered Cyclades.
The fishes seek the bottom of the sea,
The dolphins leap no more above the waves,
And seals float lifeless on the boiling deep.
The mermaids flee away to caverns dark,
Nereus and Doris too, the story goes.
Thrice angry Neptune tried to lift his arms
Above the sea; thrice could not bear the fire.
The goddess of the earth in deep distress

Rose from her shrunken waves a little way,
"If I deserve your kindness, and it pleases you,
Why hold you back your crashing thunderbolts,
King of the gods? And if the Fates decree
That I must die by fire, then may your fire
Destroy me, still obedient to your will.
It's hard to speak." The smoke had choked her words.
"My hair is scorched and ashes blind my eyes.
Do you reward my faithful service thus?
For I have borne the wounds of plough and hoe;
I labor all the year; I give the cattle corn
And grain to men, and incense to the gods.
Perhaps I have deserved this; but the waves
And Neptune merit nothing. Yet his sea
Grows less and ever farther from the sky.
But if we both lack power to move your heart,
Have pity on your heavens! Look around!
Both poles begin to burn, and those destroyed,
The stately mansions of the sky will fall.
Atlas himself can scarce sustain the globe.
If sea and earth should perish and the sky,
We shall return to Chaos and black Night.
Save from the fire whatever its rage has spared."
So spoke the earth; she could no further speak
Nor longer bear the flames. She sank below
The waves and sought in haste the cooler depths.

Then Zeus all-powerful calls to witness him
Who gave the chariot, and the other gods,
That if he brought no help all things must fall.
He climbs the sloping way to that high tower
Whence often he spreads the rain-clouds over the world
Or sends the thunder and the lightning's flame.
But then he had no clouds to give the earth
Or rains to pour from heaven. With a crash
He hurls the deadly bolt with strong right hand
Straight at the charioteer, depriving him
Of breath and car, and conquers fire by fire.
The maddened steeds by frantic leaps break loose;
The chariot falls to earth, and all around
Are seen its fragments scattered far and wide.
Phaeton, his hair aflame, shoots down
As from a cloudless sky a meteor falls.
He lands far from his home, near Eridanus;
The mighty river bathes his smoking face.

The western Naiads bury his remains,
And over the grave this epitaph inscribe:
"Beneath this monument rash Phaeton lies,
Who drove his father's chariot through the skies;
He died and could not win a victor's meed,
But still he perished in a daring deed."

Z. Chafee, Jr.

METAMORPHOSES IV, 55–61; 65–166

Pyramus and Thisbe

Of Pyramus and Thisbe I will sing,
He handsomest of youths while she in face
Excelled all Eastern maidens. These two dwelt
At Babylon in houses side by side.
Neighborhood caused acquaintance and first steps;
Love grew with time, and marriage would have joined
The pair, had not their fathers forbid the tie.

A slender crack had split the wall of brick
Between their homes. This crack, for years unknown,
The lovers found — for what does love not find?
Through this they interchanged soft words of love,
Perceived by none. And often as they stood
On either side the wall, they thus would speak:
"O hateful wall, to separate us two!
Oh, let us meet, or if that is too much,
Allow at least that tender kisses pass.
Yet we are not ungrateful for the gift
You give us, that we hear these loving words."
In vain they speak such prayers. They part at last
As night descends, each printing on the wall
Soft kisses which did not reach the other side.

Now speedy dawn had dimmed the fires of night,
And Phoebus' rays had dried the frosted herbs,
Just as the lovers sought the accustomed place.
Then, speaking gently, they mourned many things.
At last they planned to run away that night
And meet at Ninus' tomb outside the town
And lie concealed beneath a lofty tree,
A mulberry, nearby a fountain cool.

Pleased with their plan they parted; and the day
Moved slowly onward till it reached the sea
From which the night arose. Then through the dark
The crafty Thisbe glides, escapes her guards,
And seeks the tomb, her lovely features veiled.
She gained the tree and sat beneath its shade,
Nor feared the dark, for love had made her bold.
But look, a lioness comes to slake her thirst,
Her foaming mouth red with a bloody meal.
When Thisbe saw her coming through the moonlight,
She fled in terror to a darksome cave,
And as she ran her veil slipped to the ground.
Now when the savage beast had drunk her fill
She sought again the forest and by chance
Tore with her bloody mouth the fallen veil.
But soon the lover comes and in the sand
Beholds with fear the footprints of the beast
And looking farther finds the gory silk.

"One night two lovers shall destroy," he cried,
"She well deserved long life, but I to die:
It's I who killed you, dearest, I that bade
This meeting in a dangerous place at night,
And did not come before you. Rend my limbs,
You savage beasts, as you have mangled hers.
Yet let me not desire to die, but die."
He bore the veil of Thisbe to the tree,
And as he bathed the garment with his tears
And kissed it, said, "My blood shall stain you too."
He grasped his sword and plunged it in his breast,
Then drew the weapon from the bleeding wound.
While on the ground he lies his blood shoots high
As, when a water-pipe is slightly cracked,
The hissing water cleaves the air in spurts.
The snowy fruit, stained by the scattered spray,
Is changed to red; the root is soaked with blood
And gives the mulberry a scarlet shade.

Now Thisbe, not yet free from fear, returns
Lest she should fail her lover, and looks for him,
Eager to tell the peril she has run.
And though this is the place and this the tree,
The fruit is strange in shade, which makes her doubt.
But while she hesitates she turns and sees
A body writhing on the bloody ground.

She stepped backward and shivered like a lake
Whose surface trembles in a gentle breeze.
But when she recognized her lover dear,
She beat her breast in grief and tore her hair
And clasped the loved one and wept over his wounds,
Thus mixing tears with blood, and kissed his lips.
"O Pyramus," she cried, "what cruel fate
Has taken you from me? Pyramus, arise,
Your dearest Thisbe calls you. Pyramus,
Hear me! Lift up your prostrate countenance!"
At Thisbe's name he opened his dying eyes
And, having seen her, closed them in cold death.
Then as she saw the garment, bloody sword,
And empty ivory scabbard, thus she spoke:
"Oh, you were killed by your own hand and love,
Unhappy one. My hand is strong for this;
My love shall add a courage great as yours:
I follow you to Hades. Since I caused
Your death then your companion I will be.
Unhappy parents, both of us now ask
Not to refuse to place us in one tomb,
Whom faithful love and common death has joined.
You tree, whose boughs now hide the corpse of one
And soon shall cover two, forever hold
These signs of slaughter and this scarlet fruit —
Fit shade for grief — memorial of our fate."
She spoke and fell upon his sword, still warm.
Their prayers were heard: the fruit is scarlet now;
The ashes of the pair rest in one urn.

Z. Chafee, Jr.

METAMORPHOSES X, 243–294

Pygmalion and Galatea

Pygmalion loathed the vices given by nature
To women's hearts: he lived a lonely life,
Shunning the thought of marriage and a wife.
Meanwhile he carved the snow-white ivory
With happy skill: he gave it beauty greater
Than any woman's: then grew amorous of it.
It was a maiden's figure — and it lived
(You thought) but dared not move for modesty.
So much did art conceal itself. The sculptor

Marvelled, and loved his beautiful pretence.
Often he touched the body, wondering
If it were ivory or flesh — he would not
Affirm it ivory. He gave it kisses,
Thinking they were returned; and he embraced it,
Feeling its body yield beneath his fingers,
Fearing the limbs he pressed would show a bruise.
Sometimes he courted it with flatteries
And charming gifts: shells and rounded stones,
And little birds, and many-colored flowers,
Lilies, and painted balls, and amber tears
Dropped from the trees: he dressed it with fine clothes,
Rings on its fingers, chains about its neck,
Light pearls for earrings, pendants on its bosom.
All made it lovely: it was lovely naked.
He laid the statue on a purple couch,
Calling it partner of his bed, laying its neck
On feather pillows, just as though it felt.

The festival of Venus crowded Cyprus;
And with broad horns gilded to do her honor,
The snowy heifers fell for sacrifice,
And incense fumed her altars. Then Pygmalion
Made sacrifice and prayed, "If the gods can give
Whatever they may wish, grant me a wife"
(not venturing "my ivory girl") "like her."
The golden goddess in her seat of power
Knew what the prayer meant and showed her favor:
Her altar blazed three times, shooting aloft.

When he returned, he went to his ivory image,
Lay on its couch and kissed it. It grew warm.
He kissed again and touched the ivory breast.
The ivory softened, and its carven firmness
Sank where he pressed it, yielded like the wax
Which in the sunlight takes a thousand shapes
From moulding fingers, while use makes it useful.
Pygmalion was aghast and feared his joy,
But like a lover touched his love again.
It was a body, beating pulse and heart.
Now he believed and in an ardent prayer
Gave thanks to Venus: pressed his mouth at last
To a living mouth. The maiden felt his kiss —
She blushed and trembled: when she raised her eyes
She saw her lover and heaven's light together.

Gilbert Highet

TRISTIA III, 3, 59–88

To His Wife

I wish that my soul could perish with my body
    And not a shred escape the ravenous pyre,
For if the deathless spirit hovers heavenwards
    And what Pythagoras told is truth entire,
Then will a Roman soul with Gothic phantoms
    Forever wander, lost to barbarous ways.
But bring my bones back in a tiny coffer,
    So death shall end for good this exile's phase.
No one forbids you. Antigone, true sister,
    Buried her brother, though a king said "No."
Sprinkle my dust with spikenard's leaves and essence
    And mound it near the City's pulse and glow,
Then carve the marble headstone, boldly letter
    These lines to catch the hurrying traveller's eyes:
Here Ovid, playmate of the tender passions,
    The poet, shattered by his genius, lies;
But grudge not this brief prayer, O passing lover:
    "May Ovid's heart sleep softly, healed of sighs."
Thus for the inscription. Yet my books are nobler
    And more abiding monuments of me,
For sure as they have ruined him who reared them
    They shrine his name and fame eternally.
Yet mind you always pour the dead's libations,
    And hang the garlands which your tears suffuse,
For though the flames will roar my flesh to ashes,
    Its sorrowing dust will feel the pious dues.
More would I write you, but my voice is weary,
    My tongue worn out dictating to the quill.
Receive, then, what may be my final murmur:
    Farewell, farewell, from one who fares most ill.

Geoffrey Johnson

TRISTIA III, 10

Should any one there in Rome remember Ovid the exile,
    And without me, my name still in the city survive;
Tell him that under stars which never set in the ocean
    I am existing still, here in a barbarous land.
Fierce Sarmatians encompass me round, and the Bessi and Getae;

Names how unworthy to be sung by a genius like mine!
Yet when the air is warm, intervening Ister defends us:
    He, as he flows, repels inroads of war with his waves.
But when the dismal winter reveals its hideous aspect,
    When all earth becomes white with a marble-like frost;
And when Boreas is loosed, and the snow hurled under Arcturus,
    Then these nations, in sooth, shudder and shiver with cold.
Deep lies the snow, and neither the sun nor the rain can dissolve it;
    Boreas hardens it still, makes it forever remain.
Hence, ere the first has melted away, another succeeds it.
    And two years it is wont, in many places, to lie.
And so great is the power of the North-wind awakened, it levels
    Lofty towers with the ground, roofs uplifted bears off.
Wrapped in skins, and with trousers sewed, they contend with the
      weather,
    And their faces alone of the whole body are seen.
Often their tresses, when shaken, with pendent icicles tinkle,
    And their whitened beards shine with the gathering frost.
Wines consolidate stand, preserving the form of the vessels;
    No more draughts of wine, — pieces presented they drink.
Why should I tell you how all the rivers are frozen and solid,
    And from out of the lake frangible water is dug?
Ister, — no narrower stream than the river that bears the papyrus, —
    Which through its many mouths mingles its waves with the deep;
Ister, with hardening winds, congeals its cerulean waters,
    Under a roof of ice winding its way to the sea.
There where ships have sailed, men go on foot; and the billows,
    Solid made by the frost, hoof-beats of horses indent.
Over unwonted bridges, with water gliding beneath them,
    The Sarmatian steers drag their barbarian carts.
Scarcely shall I be believed; yet when naught is gained by a falsehood,
    Absolute credence then should to a witness be given.
I have beheld the vast Black Sea of ice all compacted,
    And a slippery crust pressing its motionless tides.
'T is not enough to have seen, I have trodden this indurate ocean;
    Dry shod passed my foot over its uppermost wave.
If thou hadst had of old such a sea as this is, Leander!
    Then thy death had not been charged as a crime to the Strait.
Nor can the curvèd dolphins uplift themselves from the water;
    All their struggles to rise merciless winter prevents;
And though Boreas sound with roar of wings in commotion,
    In the blockaded gulf never a wave will there be;
And the ships will stand hemmed in by the frost, as in marble,
    Nor will the oar have power through the stiff waters to cleave.
Fast-bound in the ice have I seen the fishes adhering,

Yet notwithstanding this some of them still were alive.
Hence, if the savage strength of omnipotent Boreas freezes
    Whether the salt-sea wave, whether the refluent stream, —
Straightway, — the Ister made level by arid blasts of the North-
    wind, —
    Comes the barbaric foe borne on his swift-footed steed;
Foe, that powerful made by his steed and his far-flying arrows,
    All the neighboring land void of inhabitants makes.
Some take flight, and none being left to defend their possessions,
    Unprotected, their goods pillage and plunder become;
Cattle and creaking carts, the little wealth of the country,
    And what riches beside indigent peasants possess.
Some as captives are driven along, their hands bound behind them,
    Looking backward in vain toward their Lares and lands.
Others, transfixed with barbèd arrows, in agony perish.
    For the swift arrow-heads all have in poison been dipped.
What they cannot carry or lead away they demolish,
    And the hostile flames burn up the innocent cots.
Even when there is peace, the fear of war is impending;
    None, with the ploughshare pressed, furrows the soil any more.
Either this region sees, or fears a foe that it sees not,
    And the sluggish land slumbers in utter neglect.
No sweet grape lies hidden here in the shade of its vine-leaves,
    No fermenting must fills and o'erflows the deep vats.
Apples the region denies; nor would Acontius have found here
    Aught upon which to write words for his mistress to read.
Naked and barren plains without leaves or trees we behold here, —
    Places, alas! unto which no happy man would repair.
Since then this mighty orb lies open so wide upon all sides,
    Has this region been found only my prison to be?

                    Henry Wadsworth Longfellow

TRISTIA III, 12

Now the zephyrs diminish the cold, and the year being ended,
    Winter Maeotian seems longer than ever before;
And the Ram that bore unsafely the burden of Helle,
    Now makes the hours of the day equal with those of the night.
Now the boys and the laughing girls the violet gather,
    Which the fields bring forth, nobody sowing the seed.
Now the meadows are blooming with flowers of various colors,
    And with untaught throats carol the garrulous birds.
Now the swallow, to shun the crime of her merciless mother,
    Under the rafters builds cradles and dear little homes;

And the blade that lay hid, covered up in the furrows of Ceres,
  Now from the tepid ground raises its delicate head.
Where there is ever a vine, the bud shoots forth from the tendrils,
  But from the Getic shore distant afar is the vine!
Where there is ever a tree, on the tree the branches are swelling,
  But from the Getic land distant afar is the tree!
Now it is holiday there in Rome, and to games in due order
  Give place the windy wars of the vociferous bar.
Now they are riding the horses; with light arms now they are playing,
  Now with the ball, and now round rolls the swift-flying hoop:
Now, when the young athlete with flowing oil is anointed,
  He in the Virgin's Fount bathes, overwearied, his limbs.
Thrives the stage; and applause, with voices at variance, thunders,
  And the Theatres three for the three Forums resound.
Four times happy is he, and times without number is happy,
  Who the city of Rome, uninterdicted, enjoys.
But all I see is the snow in the vernal sunshine dissolving,
  And the waters no more delved from the indurate lake.
Nor is the sea now frozen, nor as before o'er the Ister
  Comes the Sarmatian boor driving his stridulous cart.
Hitherward, nevertheless, some keels already are steering,
  And on this Pontic shore alien vessels will be.
Eagerly shall I run to the sailor, and, having saluted,
  Who he may be, I shall ask; wherefore and whence he hath come.
Strange indeed will it be, if he come not from regions adjacent,
  And incautious unless ploughing the neighboring sea.
Rarely a mariner over the deep from Italy passes,
  Rarely he comes to these shores, wholly of harbors devoid.
Whether he knoweth Greek, or whether in Latin he speaketh,
  Surely on this account he the more welcome will be.
Also perchance from the mouth of the Strait and the waters Propontic,
  Unto the steady South-wind, some one is spreading his sails.
Whosoever he is, the news he can faithfully tell me,
  Which may become a part and an approach to the truth.
He, I pray, may be able to tell me the triumphs of Caesar,
  Which he has heard of, and vows paid to the Latian Jove;
And that sorrowful head, Germania, thou, the rebellious,
  Under the feet, at last, of the Great Captain hast laid.
Whoso shall tell me these things, that not to have seen will afflict me,
  Forthwith unto my house welcome as guest shall he be.
Woe is me! Is the house of Ovid in Scythian lands now?
  And doth punishment now give me its place for a home?
Grant, ye gods, that Caesar make this not my house and my homestead,
  But decree it to be only the inn of my pain.

                    Henry Wadsworth Longfellow

TRISTIA IV, 6, 1–38

Time Is No Remedy

In time the peasant's bull endures the ploughshare
    And offers to the collar's curve his neck;
The horse, once fire, responds to a rein's flicker,
    And gently bears the ruthless gimmal's check.
In time the raging Carthaginian lion
    Forgets the pride with which he once was thewed,
And the Indian brute obeys his master's whimsies
    Through use and wont, and bows to servitude.
Time makes the grape to swell in trailing clusters,
    Whose globes can hardly hold the sweetness in;
Time brings the seed to harvest's hoary wisdom
    And keeps the fruit from bitterness within.
Time wears the ploughblade as it bites the furrow,
    Time softens adamant and shivers flint,
And by degrees his snow of mercy covers
    Great angers and old Sorrow's acheful print.
Under the silent glide of passing seasons
    All troubles lessen, then, except my hurt.
Twice have my long-lost homefolk threshed without me,
    And twice, bare-footed, made the vintage spurt.
Yet use, however long, brings me no patience,
    No truce to tortures of my heart and soul.
Even old bulls will often flee the collar,
    The horse, well broken, fight the bit's control;
Yet grief weighs heavier now than when it struck me,
    The blow's the same, but wider spreads the bruise;
My wrongs are worse than I at first imagined:
    The more I know my wounds, the more they ooze.
And it would help a little could I marshal
    My strength of youth, not powers that age confounds:
On tawny sands the brand-new wrestler's muscles
    Outmatch the weary winner of past rounds;
Unscathed, in glittering arms, the gladiator
    Has likelier chance than one already pinked;
The new-built ship bears well the head-on whirlwind,
    A squall dissolves the vessel age has chinked.
I too once bore what now are past endurance,
    These woes on woes the hands of years have linked.

                      Geoffrey Johnson

AMORES I, 5

In summers heate and mid-time of the day
To rest my limbes vpon a bed I lay,
One window shut, the other open stood,
Which gaue such light, as twincles in a wood,
Like twilight glimps at setting of the Sunne
Or night being past, and yet not day begunne.
Such light to shamefast maidens must be showne,
Where they may sport, and seeme to bee vnknowne.
Then came Corinna in a long loose gowne,
Her white neck hid with tresses hanging downe:
Resembling fayre Semiramis going to bed
Or Layis of a thousand wooers sped.
I snacht her gowne, being thin, the harme was small,
Yet striu'd she to be couered there withall.
And striuing thus as one that would be cast,
Betray'd her selfe, and yelded at the last.
Starke naked as she stood before mine eye,
Not one wen in her body could I spie.
What armes and shoulders did I touch and see,
How apt her breasts were to be prest by me.
How smooth a belly vnder her wast saw I?
How large a legge, and what a lustie thigh?
To leaue the rest, all lik'd me passing well,
I cling'd her naked body, downe she fell,
Iudge you the rest, being tyrde she bad me kisse,
Ioue send me more such after-noones as this.

Christopher Marlowe

AMORES I, 13

Now ore the sea from her old Loue comes she
That drawes the day from heauens cold axletree.
Aurora whither slidest thou? downe againe,
And birdes for Memnon yearely shal be slaine.
Now in her tender armes I sweetly bide,
If euer, now well lies she by my side.
The aire is cold, and sleepe is sweetest now
And birdes send forth shrill notes from euery bough:
Whither runst thou, that men, and women loue not?
Hold in thy rosy horses that they moue not.
Ere thou rise, starres teach sea-men where to saile,
But when thou commest they of their courses faile.

Poore trauailers though tierd, rise at thy sight,
And souldiours make them ready to the fight.
The painefull hinde by thee to field is sent,
Slowe Oxen early in the yoake are pent.
Thou cousenst boyes of sleepe, and doest betray them
To Pedants that with cruell lashes pay them.
Thou mak'st the surety to the Lawyer runne,
That with one word hath nigh himselfe vndone.
The Lawyer and the client hate thy view,
Both whom thou raisest vp to toyle anew.
By thy meanes women of their rest are bard,
Thou setst their labouring hands to spin and card.
All could I beare, but that the wench should rise.
Who can endure, saue him with whom none lyes?
How oft wisht I, night would not giue thee place,
Nor morning starres shunne thy vprising face.
How oft that either winde would breake thy coach,
Or steeds might fall forc'd with thick clouds approach.
Whether goest thou hatefull Nimph? Memnon the elfe
Receiu'd his cole-black colour from thy selfe.
Say that thy loue with Cephalus were not knowne,
Then thinkest thou thy loose life is not showne?
Would Tithon might but talke of thee a while,
Not one in heauen should be more base and vile.
Thou leauest his bed, because hee's faint through age,
And early mountest thy hatefull carriage.
But heldst thou in thine armes some Cephalus,
Then wouldst thou cry, stay night and runne not thus.
Doest punish me, because yeares make him waine?
I did not bid thee wed an aged swaine.
The Moone sleepes with Endymion euery day,
Thou art as faire as she, then kisse and play.
Ioue that thou shoulst not hast but waite his leasure,
Made two nights one to finish vp his pleasure.
I chid no more, she blusht and therefore heard me,
Yet lingered not the day, but morning scard me.

Christopher Marlowe

AMORES II, 4

I meane not to defend the scapes of any,
Or iustifie my vices being many.
For I confesse, if that might merite fauour,
Heere I display my lewd and loose behauiour.

I loathe, yet after that I loathe, I runne,
Oh how the burthen irkes, that we should shunne.
I cannot rule my selfe, but where loue please
Am driuen like a ship vpon rough seas.
No one face likes me best, all faces moue,
A hundred reasons make me euer loue.
If any eye me with a modest looke,
I burn, and by that blushfull glance am tooke.
And she thats coy I like for being no clowne,
Me thinkes she would be nimble when shees downe.
Though her sowre lookes a Sabines browe resemble,
I thinke sheele do, but deepely can dissemble.
If she be learn'd, then for her skill I craue her,
If not, because shees simple I would haue her.
Before Callimachus she preferres me farre,
Seeing she likes my bookes why should we iarre?
An other railes at me and that I write
Yet would I lie with her if that I might.
Trips she, it likes me well, plods she, what than?
Shee would be nimbler, lying with a man.
And when one sweetely sings, then straight I long
To quauer on her lips euen in her song.
Or if one touch the Lute with arte and cunning
Who would not loue those hands for their swift running?
And her I like that with a maiesty
Folds vp her armes and makes lowe curtesy.
To leaue my selfe, that am in loue with all,
Some one of these might make the chastest fall.
If she be tall, shees like an Amazon,
And therefore filles the bed she lies vpon.
If short, she lies the rounder: to say troth,
Both short and long please me, for I loue both.
I thinke what one vndeckt would be, being drest:
Is she attired, then shew her graces best.
A white wench thralles me, so doth golden yellowe
And nut-browne girles in doing haue no fellowe.
If her white necke be shadoed with blacke haire,
Why so was Ledas, yet was Leda faire.
Amber trest is she, then on the morne thinke I,
My loue alludes to euery history:
A yong wench pleaseth, and an old is good,
This for her lookes, that for her woman-hood.
Nay what is she that any Roman loues
But my ambitious ranging minde approues?

Christopher Marlowe

AMORES II, 10

Graecinus (well I wot) thou touldst me once,
I could not be in loue with two at once.
By thee deceiued, by thee surpriz'd am I,
For now I loue two women equally.
Both are well fauour'd, both rich in aray,
Which is the loue-liest it is hard to say.
This seemes the fairest, so doth that to me,
And this doth please me most, and so doth she.
Euen as a boate, tost by contrary winde,
So with this loue, and that, wauers my minde.
Venus, why doublest thou my endlesse smart?
Was not one wench enough to grieue my hart?
Why addst thou stars to heauen, leaues to greene woods,
And to the vast deepe sea fresh water flouds?
Yet this is better farre than lie alone,
Let such as be mine enemies haue none.
Yea let my foes sleepe in an empty bed,
And in the midst their bodies largely spread.
But may soft loue rowse vp my drowsie eyes,
And from my mistris bosome let me rise.
Let one wench cloy me with sweete loues delight
If one can doote, if not, two euery night.
Though I am slender, I haue store of pith
Nor want I strength but weight to presse her with.
Pleasure addes fuell to my lust-full fire,
I pay them home with that they most desire.
Oft haue I spent the night in wantonnesse,
And in the morning beene liuely nere the lesse.
Hee's happy who loues mutuall skirmish slayes,
And to the Gods for that death Ouid prayes.
Let souldiours chase their enemies amaine,
And with their bloud eternall honour gaine.
Let Marchants seeke wealth and with periured lips
Being wrackt carowse the sea tir'd by their ships.
But when I dye, would I might droupe with doing,
And in the midst thereof, set my soule going,
That at my funeralls some may weeping crye,
Euen as he led his life, so did he dye.

Christopher Marlowe

AMORES III, 1

An old wood, stands vncut of long yeares space,
Tis credible some godhead haunts the place.
In midst thereof a stone-pau'd sacred spring,
Where round about small birdes most sweetely sing.
Heere while I walke hid close in shadie groue,
To finde what worke my muse might moue, I stroue.
Elegia came with haires perfumed sweete,
And, I thinke, was longer of her feete.
A decent forme, thinne robe, a louers looke,
By her footes blemish greater grace she tooke.
Then with huge steps came violent Tragedie,
Sterne was her front, her cloake on ground did lie.
Her left hand held abroad a regal scepter,
The Lydian buskin in fit paces kept her.
And first she sayd: when will thy loue be spent?
O Poet carelesse of thy argument.
Wine-bibbing banquets tell thy naughtinesse,
Each crosse waies corner doth as much expresse.
Oft some points at the prophet passing by,
And this is he whom fierce loue burnes, they cry.
A laughing stocke thou art to all the citty,
While without shame thou singst thy lewdnesse ditty.
Tis time to moue graue things in lofty stile,
Long hast thou loytered; greater workes compile.
The subiect hides thy wit, mens acts resound,
This thou wilt say to be a worthy ground.
Thy muse hath played what may milde girles content,
And by those numbers is thy first youth spent.
Now giue the Roman Tragedie a name,
To fill my lawes thy wanton spirit frame.
This saied, she mou'd her buskins gaily varnisht,
And seauen times shooke her head with thicke locks garnisht.
The other smilde, (I wot) with wanton eyes,
Erre I? or mirtle in her right hand lies.
With lofty wordes stout Tragedie (she sayd)
Why treadst me downe? art thou aye grauely plaied?
Thou deignst vnequall lines should thee rehearse,
Thou fightst against me vsing mine owne verse.
Thy lofty stile with mine I not compare,
Small doores vnfitting for large houses are.
Light am I, and with me, my care, light loue,
Not stronger am I then the thing I moue.
Venus without me should be rusticall,

This goddesse company doth to me befall.
What gate thy stately words cannot vnlocke,
My flatt'ring speeches soone wide open knocke.
And I deserue more then thou canst in verity,
By suffring much not borne by thy seuerity.
By me Corinna learnes, cousening her guard,
To get the dore with little noise vnbard,
And slipt from bed cloth'd in a loose night-gowne,
To moue her feet vnheard in setting downe.
Ah howe oft on hard doores hung I engrau'd,
From no mans reading fearing to be sau'd.
But till the keeper went forth, I forget not,
The maide to hide me in her bosome let not.
What gift with me was on her birth day sent,
But cruelly by her was drown'd and rent.
First of thy minde the happy seedes I knewe,
Thou hast my gift, which she would from thee sue.
She left: I say'd, you both I must beseech,
To empty aire may go my fearefull speech.
With scepters and high buskins th'one would dresse me,
So through the world shold bright renown expresse me.
The other giues my loue a conquering name,
Come therefore, and to long verse shorter frame.
Graunt Tragedie thy Poet times least tittle,
Thy labour euer lasts, she askes but little.
She gaue me leaue, soft loues in time make hast,
Some greater worke will vrge me on at last.

Christopher Marlowe

Propertius

❲ The acknowledged master of Roman elegy is Sextus Propertius (born around 50 B.C. at Assisi, where inscriptions bearing his family name can be found in a crypt below street level; died 16 B.C. or later). This meter — a dactylic hexameter alternating with a dactylic pentameter *ad libitum* — was developed by the Romans to the point where they could almost claim it for their own, although it originated with the Greeks. Propertius' love for Cynthia formed the chief subject of his ninety-two elegies, together with etiological myths and Roman history. In his feverish, semi-neurotic self-absorption there is often a modern touch which Ezra Pound has re-created in his *Homage to Propertius*. His verse is less languid and more varied than that of Tibullus, but his Latin often curiously incoherent, indirect, and obscure. His moods range from hilarious elation to an unmanly self-pity. He is as frank as Catullus without the latter's tough realism and as sensuous as Ovid without Ovid's complacency. ❳

ELEGIES

I, 16

I, entrance door to Tarpeia's house, swung open, once,
On the occasion of triumphs. My decorum was well known.
Gilded chariots made me, of this address, famous. Tears
Of captives seeking mercy dampened my facade.
Now, injured by the nocturnal brawls of inebriates,
Pounded upon by unworthy hands, I am disconsolate often.
Never am I free from the suspended garlands of ill repute:
Torches lie always near me, saying to those not favored,
"Keep out!" There is nothing I can do to protect my owner
From these nights of infamy. A door of distinction, I
Have become the depositary of ribald verses.

Nor has she any vocation for respectability: lives, rather,
More shameless than a licentious age allows.
Add to this my graver concern — the long night watches
Of a lover pleading for admittance. He saddens me.
He gives my frame no rest; but addresses to me,
Everlastingly, this unchanging serenade:

"O door, more cruel than she whose door you are,
Why are you silent? Why are you closed to me now?
Why is it you never unbar yourself and admit me, her lover?
Never give her my secret messages — have you no feeling at all?
O when will this torture of waiting end?
Must I disgracefully sleep on a not warm doorstep?
Midnight, and the stars that grow fainter, and the air
Touched with Eous' frost — all pity me as I sit here.
You alone have no compassion on a man's suffering.
Alas! Only your silent hinges answer me.

"If my voice might carry, however faintly, through a chink:
And, reaching her ear, test its transforming power!
She may be more stubborn than flint or Sicilian rock;
She may be harder than iron or steel:
Yet she'll not have authority over her eyes —
Tears will come unwanted; and she will sigh.

"She lies now in the arms of another (what fortunate lover?)
While I talk to Zephyr of the late night hours.
You alone, door, are the prime cause of my dolor —
Never placated by the gifts I bring! Have I ever
Let my tongue run away with me, and insulted you
In the usual hoodlum terms of angry jest?
Why then provoke me to this noisy expostulation, and make me,
Anxiously, attend Venus all night in the street?

"Rather, I have often written poems for you, of a new
Kind. I have knelt and kissed your steps.
Before your pillars I have turned my head — how often! —
And left furtively, O faithless door, your rightful gifts."

This is his newfangled line. With addenda now current among
Excluded lovers. He outmatins the matutinal birds.

Thus have I achieved (what with the woman's vices and
Her lovers' constant scenes) a permanently bad reputation.

                                        Frances Fletcher

I, 21

You who flee to escape a bloody death like mine,
    Soldier, wounded among these hills of Etruria —
You who turn to the sound of my groaning your tearful eyes,
    I have stood next to you in the battle's fury.

Go, be safe, that your father and mother may cry with pleasure!
    Let not your tears tell my sister what I lament:
That I who escaped from the very midst of the swords of Caesar
    Could not avoid the hand of an unknown man!
And if any scattered bones shall ever be found in these
    Etrurian mountains, tell her that they are mine.

Asa M. Hughes

II, 5

Is it true, Cynthia, that throughout Rome you are notorious,
That your scandalous living is no secret thing?
Have I merited this culmination? You'll pay, deceiver:
I'll ride the wind elsewhere. From the crowd
Of women, many of them faithless, I'll light upon *one*
Who wants to be made famous by my song:
One who will not insult me by insensitive acts;
One who will have contempt for you — and you'll weep,
Alas! too late, my old love!
Now, while my anger is fresh, is the time to leave you;
Love will come again, believe me, once the pain is past.
The Carpathian waves, under the north wind, do not change so
    quickly;
Nor, when the south wind blows, does the black cloud swerve
So readily, as angry lovers are transformed by a word.

Get rid of this merciless yoke, Propertius, while you can.
You'll suffer, of course, but only the first night.
The evil of love, all of it, is little or
Nothing, once you have lived through it.
But, by imperial Juno's gentle laws, take care, Cynthia,
That you do not, through caprice, bring disaster upon yourself!
Not only does the bull charge his enemy with low-curved horns:
Even the sheep, when disturbed, strikes back at the offender.
I'm not going to tear the clothes from your perjured body;
Nor will my anger beat down your barred door:
Nor shall I, in a rage, pull out your braided hair;
Nor pommel you black-and-blue with my hard fists.

But I'll write — words you cannot, no,
Not in your lifetime, un-write:
    "Cynthia, compelling in beauty; Cynthia, frail in honesty."
Scorn as you will, Cynthia, the gossiping tongues,
This verse — believe me — will put the fear of God in you.

Frances Fletcher

II, 6

Corinthian Lais received no such crowds in her home —
Yet all Greece waited humbly for admission;
Menander's Thais, in whom Athenians delighted,
Had not so great a multitude around her;
Nor had Phryne — whom numerous lovers had made
So powerful, she could have rebuilt devastated Thebes.

Then, too, Cynthia, you lay claim to far too many
Relatives: those who have a perfect right to kiss you
Are never absent. I am jealous of the portraits, the
Names, of young men — not excepting the male child
In the cradle, who has not yet learned to talk.
Even your mother, if she kisses you many times, will arouse
My jealousy — and your sister; as also any other girl
Who stays with you all night. I'm jealous of
Everything: apprehensive (forgive me this apprehension) —
Suspecting, in my fear, the presence of a man
Beneath the woman's dress.

The fable is, such indiscretions as yours launched
A great war. In these beginnings you see the funeral pyre
Of Troy. The same mad course caused Centaurs
To smash embossed goblets; to fight the Lapiths.
Yet why should I look to Greece for illustrations?
You, Romulus, fed on the milk of a tough
She-wolf, generated this universal laxness: showed
How chaste Sabine women might be safely raped.
Love, because of you, now knows, in Rome,
No limit to its audacity. Admetus' wife was indeed
A fortunate being. So, too, was Penelope. And so
Is every woman, satisfied to love her husband's home!
What is the point of building temples of chastity for
The virgin, if the bride may do as she chooses?
The hand that first painted obscene pictures, and,
In moral homes, placed images of immorality —
That hand corrupted innocent young girls,
Forcing upon their attention a knowledge of its own
Lasciviousness. Let him groan in hell, who
By his insidious art, produced on earth dissensions
Inspired by his silently pictured delights!

Not with such representations did an earlier race
Relieve the monotony of its homes. No wall, then,

Showed painted scenes of illicit love.
Alas, cobwebs have veiled the altar — and rightly!
Weeds have grown over the abandoned gods.
What guards, therefore, shall I place over you? What
Sealed doors choose, over which no enemy may ever pass?
Protection, the closest, is powerless against
Insubservience. She is wholly protected, Cynthia,
Who will not stoop to sin. And yet no wife, nor mistress
Either, can ever take me from you.
For me you will always be mistress; and always wife.

Frances Fletcher

II, 8 *A* and *B*, 1–4

She is gone whom I loved so long, my girl that I loved so dear;
Stolen, my friend! and you can tell me not even to shed a tear?

No known hatred is bitter, compared with a lover's woe:
Slit my throat, and you'll find me a less implacable foe!

How can I bear to behold her in alien arms recline,
Now called *mine* no longer, who used to be known as mine?

"Everything goes in cycles"; — I know what you're thinking of —
"You conquer and then you are conquered: the spin of the wheel of
    love.

"Many a mighty leader, a puissant ruler, is dead:
"Thebes is a thing of the past, and the glory of Troy is fled . . ."

— Ah, but what presents I gave her, what poems I wrote her of old!
Yet never she said "I love you." She is iron: hard and cold . . .

And now I can see my madness, how deep my folly appears
To have borne such a house, such a woman, through all these reckless
    years . . .

John Angus Macnab

II, 9

What that man is, I often was: but in time, perhaps,
He, too, will be dismissed — and you'll love another even more.
For twenty years Penelope made it a point to live without
Lovers — a woman worthy, nevertheless, of attracting many
Suitors. By a pretence of devotion to Minerva's art —

By unravelling at night her day's weaving — she postponed
Marriage. Though she never hoped to see Ulysses
Again, she continued to wait for him — and grew old
Waiting. Briseis, too, embraced Achilles' corpse
And insanely battered her lovely face with her hands:
Only a captive of war, yet she wailed; and washed her lord's
Body free of blood. She placed it in tawny Simois'
Waters; then rubbed her hair with ashes. Small
As her hands were, they sustained the body's weight and,
After its burning, the mountainous ashes of great Achilles.
Neither Peleus nor your oceanborn mother, O Achilles!
Was with you then: nor Scyrian Deidamia,
Whom you left a widow. In those days Greece rejoiced in
Her faithful daughters. Even war had its virtue, its faith.

But you, Cynthia, found it impossible to go a single night
Without love — to stay alone for even one day, sinner!
Not only that: you two had great fun drinking; and
For all I know, spoke contemptuously of me. This
Man, too, is favored, though once before he left you
Flat. May the gods give you great pleasure
In your affair with the creature!
Is this my return for all the prayers I made, in your
Behalf, when the waters of Styx had virtually closed
Over your head — and we, your friends, stood weeping
At your bedside? My God, Cynthia, false sweetheart,
Where was *he* then? What did you mean to *him?*

What if I were a soldier, detained in faroff
India; or my ship at sea? I should like to know
What you would do then. But you lie and deceive
So naturally: this one art
Woman has never failed to master. The Syrtes
Do not change so quickly under a transient gale, nor leaves
So soon flutter in the winter winds,
As a pledge is forgotten by a woman in anger —
Whether the cause is serious, or slight to triviality.

If, however, this is the way you want it, very well:
Produce, Amores, yet sharper arrows, I pray:
Hit the mark, all of you, and relieve me of this life!
My death will be your greatest honor yet, Cynthia!
The stars; the early morning frost; the door
Opened secretly to admit me in my distraction — all
Support this truth: Nothing in existence has been, ever,

More desirable to me than you;
Nor in the future will be — though you continue obdurate.
I'll take no mistress into my bed. I'll remain
Celibate, since you refuse to have me. But oh!
If I have lived reverent of the gods, may that friend
Of yours turn to stone in the very act of love!
The Theban commanders, with their mother interceding, fell dead
After fighting no more bitterly for a throne
Than I will fight: nor shrink from death, even though
My mistress stands between us — if by fighting thus
I may kill my rival dead.

Frances Fletcher

II, 11

Let others write about you, or leave you all unknown,
Or praise you, if they want their seeds in barren desert sown!

Believe me, all your talents, that dark and final day
Upon one coffin Death shall pile, and cart them all away;

And passing by your graveside, the traveller's lip shall curl,
And none shall say of you: "That dust was once a gifted girl."

John Angus Macnab

II, 15

Happiness, happiness! blessed night! and bless you,
    Bed, changed to heaven by my happiness!
What happy talk we had, the lamp beside us!
    And what a happy struggle in the dark!
For now she wrestled with me, baring her bosom,
    And now she closed her shift to make a truce.
My eyes were heavy with sleep: she kissed them open
    And whispered, "Lazy sluggard, lying still!"
How often our arms slipped into new embraces!
    How long my kisses lay upon your lips!
Venus is spoilt by serving her in darkness;
    Surely you know, sight is the path of love.
They say that Paris sighed for naked Helen
    Once when he saw her leave her husband's room.
Endymion naked captured chaste Diana
    And held the goddess naked in his arms.
Now if you cling to clothes and sleep in nightgowns,
    Clothes will be torn, and you will feel my blows.

And if my righteous rage carries me further
　　You will have bruises to take home with you.
And drooping breasts must not prevent your pastime —
　　You have no secret child — you need not care.
While fate allows us, feast our eyes in passion.
　　The coming night is long and has no dawn.
Oh, that a chain would bind us, still embracing
　　Thus, irresolubly for evermore!
Why, take example from the quiet turtles,
　　The doves, who make a perfect married pair!
Folly to seek an end for this mad passion,
　　A real love can never reach an end.
Sooner shall earth deceive the waiting farmer
　　With changeling crops, the sun drive pitch-black **steeds,**
The rivers mount again towards their sources,
　　And fishes pant in the dry ocean-bed —
Sooner than I could change my burning passion
　　From her. I serve her now in life and death.
But if she grants me other nights, and others,
　　One year is lengthened to a happy life.
If she gives many, I become immortal!
　　In one such night, anyone is divine.
If all men sought to spend such quiet lifetimes
　　Or sleep a peaceful slumber, full of wine,
No cruel weapons would there be, nor warships,
　　Nor would the sea of Actium toss our bones,
Nor would our city, ground by her own triumphs,
　　Be tired of loosening her hair to mourn.
Posterity can praise this life with justice:
　　Our winecups are not blasphemous or cruel.
Only beware; leave not the feast in daylight!
　　If you gave all your kisses, they'd be few.
And as the petals leave a withered garland
　　To float in the abandoned mixing-bowls,
So now, for all our hopes, perhaps tomorrow
　　Will end our little life and our long dreams.

Gilbert Highet

II, 28 *A* and *B*

Jupiter, have compassion, finally, on that sick girl, my sweetheart;
The death of one so beautiful will be your crime.
We are in a season when the torrid air blazes;
When earth, in the first dry dog-days, seethes.
Yet the heat is not so much to be blamed, or heaven's crime,
As her own so frequent neglect of the gods' sanctity.

This fault destroys, has destroyed before, irresponsible girls.
Their vows, whatsoever, are eroded by wind and wave.
Was Venus pained that you should be mentioned in the same breath
  with her?
The goddess is jealous of any competitor in charm.
Or was Pelasgian Juno's temple beneath your notice?
Dared you deny Pallas has wonderful eyes?
You pretty women never spare your criticism:
Your injurious tongue, Cynthia, and your beauty, brought you to this
  estate.
But to you, living agitated through a cycle of
Much danger, a more soothing hour has come at last.

Io, transformed in appearance, passed her youthful years in mooing;
Now she, who as a cow drank Nilus' water, is a goddess.
Ino also, in early womanhood, was a wanderer on earth:
Now the sailor, when in trouble, prays to her as Leucothea,
Andromeda was to have been given to sea-monsters;
This same woman became Perseus' renowned wife.
Callisto wandered, a bear, through the Arcadian plains:
She now directs nocturnal sails by her star's light.

Suppose it *is* your destiny to go prematurely to rest:
That destiny may yet be favorable to you.
You'll tell Semele what a perilous thing is beauty;
And the woman, experienced herself in evil, will believe.
Not one of all the Maeonian heroines will contest
Your right to precedence in the place of honor.
In illness, then, try to reconcile yourself to fate:
God may change his mind — the day of rigor, its course.
Even Juno the consort will learn to tolerate you:
Even Juno is saddened when a young woman dies.

The rhombus sound, a whirl-and-boom beneath the magic song,
Now ceases. The fire has gone out; the laurel is dust.
The moon, unwilling, comes down less often from heaven;
And the bird of darkness utters its sinister warning.
One fatal boat, blue as midnight, will bear our two loves,
As one, on the voyage to deeplying rivers.
Yet have pity on two, not one, I pray!
I shall live if she lives. If she dies, I die also.
If you hear me, Jove, and save her, I promise to write
(My sacred art is pledge): "By Jove's power was my mistress saved."
Herself, she will perform the rites, then sit at your feet;
And, sitting there, will tell the long story of her perils.

                                                Frances Fletcher

II, 28 C

May your wellknown mercy, Persephone, remain steadfast:
And may you, O consort of Persephone, choose not to be too harsh.
So many thousands of beautiful women among the dead!
If it is possible, let one lovely creature stay here on earth.
You already have Iope; you have Tyro, of dazzling fairness;
Europa you have also, and the quite disreputable Pasiphae:
You have all the beauties who came, long ago, out of Troy,
Lost kingdom of Phoebus and ancient Priam — and out of Achaea,
   too:
And every Roman girl as lovely as these has died:
The devouring funeral fire possesses them all.

No one has beauty, or prosperity, forever:
Death attends each of us in the end.
Now that you are released, O my love-light, from a great danger,
Deliver to Diana the proper gifts of song and incantation;
Keep the watches, also, of that goddess once a heifer —
Ten votive night-watches pay her, because I ask it.

Frances Fletcher

II, 32

Who sees you, sins. Who has not seen you, therefore,
Will not desire you. Guilt, in this instance, is of the eyes.
For why, Cynthia, go in search of ambiguous oracles at
Praeneste (if, as you say, you do): or on excursions
To the walls of Tusculum? Why drive your chariot
To Herculean Tibur? Or so often to Lanuvium, along
The Appian Way?

I wish, Cynthia, you'd take your outings at home,
Whenever you're free. But people see you, a celebrant, in
Torchlight processions to the grove; see you carrying
Your torch for the goddess Trivia. They say I ought not
To have faith in you. Pompey's Portico, in fact, with its shady
Pillars, its dignity of cloth-of-gold hangings — this
Has grown too tame. So has the avenue where plane trees,
Thickly planted, rise in well spaced rows.
You are likewise bored with waters that fall from
Recumbent Maro, ripple lightly through the circular fountain —
Until all at once the Triton swallows the water.
You are too ingenuous. Your conduct suggests
Intrigue. You're running, mad woman, not from the city,

But from *my* sight! It's no use. With these foolish devices
You can't pull the wool over my eyes. Inept, you lay snares
For me who am erudite in that field.

For myself it matters less. For you, however, so complete
A rejection of your good name will have exactly the result,
Poor Cynthia, it should have. Only lately a rumor about you
Offended my ears. It was no good rumor: and
It ran the city end-to-end. After all, though, Propertius,
You should not believe all the gossip you hear?
Scandal is a penance beauty never escapes.

At all events, Cynthia, your reputation is not that of one
Who kills with poison. You, Phoebus, will testify
Her hands are clean on that score! Suppose you *have*
Passed a long lascivious night now and then: these small
Sins of the flesh disturb me not at all.
Tyndaris, in love with an alien, changed her country:
Yet, brought home alive, she remained unpunished.
Venus herself, they say, succumbed to Mars' sexual charms — yet
Her credit in heaven was still beyond reproach.
Mount Ida, it's true, holds that a goddess loved an anonymous
Shepherd and slept with him among the sheep — still,
A whole group of Hamadryads looked on, along with
Old Silenus himself, parent of the nymphs in question:
While you, Naiad, of the party also, gathered apples in
Ida's shadow; apples that fell into your uplifted hands.

In the light of this list of moral offenders, who now
Asks: "Why has she so much money? Who gave it to her? Why
Did he give it?" You are far too blessed, in this age, Rome,
If one woman goes against your conventions!
And Lesbia, before Cynthia, did exactly the same things — without
Retribution. Surely Lesbia's successor must be less censurable?
If anyone looks now for ancient Tatian virtues, and Sabine
Morality — well, he's a very recent arrival in our city.
You will more easily succeed in making dry land from
Ocean, and in gathering stars with your mortal hands,
Than in making our women follow the narrow path. This kind
Of restraint was in style when Saturn reigned. But in the
Era when earth was flooded by Deucalion's waters,
And since those old Deucalonic times, who — please tell me —
Has ever been able to enjoy a woman by himself?
The wife of the potentate Minos, they say, was once charmed
And seduced by a bull; and Danae, for all

She was shut in by metallic walls, and was chaste
In the bargain, could not deny great Jove.

And so, if you've definitely taken these Greek and Latin
Women for your models — go right ahead. Don't mind,
Ever, what *I* think!

Frances Fletcher

III, 1

Shades of Callimachus, and holy rites of Philetas,
Suffer me, I pray, to enter your grove.
I am the first, priestlike, to appear from a clear spring,
Uniting with Greek music the mysteries of Italy.
In what grotto, say, did you perfect your cadences?
Which foot marked the downbeat? What inspiriting water did you
    drink?
Oblivion to the poet who keeps Phoebus forever at war!
May my verse proceed neatly, thanks to a ready pumice:
By such writing fame raises me higher; and the Muse
Born of me goes triumphant with flower-wreathed horses.
In the chariot little loves ride with me;
And writers tag along at my wheels.
Why, with lax reins, compete with me?
No broad highway leads to the Muses.
Many there are, Rome, to enhance your annals
And, in song, fix Bactra as the limits of empire:
But, along a virgin path, I have brought
The pages of this work from the Sisters' hill,
To give you something to read in peacetime.
Award your poet, O Pegasid Muses, soft garlands;
No hard crown will become me.
But what the envious mob has deprived me of, living,
Fame shall repay, when I am dead, with interest two-fold:
For time, after one's death, magnifies all things.
The burial rites ended, a name has greater resonance.

For who would know about towers destroyed by a wooden horse,
Or rivers matching their strength with the Haemonian hero;
Or about Simois of Ida; or Jove's offspring, Scamander;
Or Hector making wheels thrice bloody, on the plain?
As for Deiphobus and Helenus, Polydamas and Paris,
That martial nonentity, their own homes would scarcely know them.

Men would have little to say of you, Ilion, and you,
Troy, twice captured by the Oetaean godhead.

And even Homer, narrator of your fate, has seen himself,
Generation after generation, increasingly exalted.
I, too, shall be praised by later Romans;
I foresee such a day, after my death.
My tombstone shall not call forth contempt!
Lycia's god has made certain of this; he knows my consecration.

Frances Fletcher

III, 2

Let us return, meantime, to the round of song;
And may my mistress, responsive, rejoice in the wellknown sound.
They say that Orpheus, with his Thracian lyre,
Tamed beasts, and brought wild rivers to a standstill;
Impelled to Thebes (they say) by music's art,
The rocks of Cithaeron sprang, of themselves, into a wall-shape.
And even Galatea, at savage Aetna's base, O Polyphemus!
Turned toward your singing voice her sea-dripping horses.
With Bacchus and Apollo for my sponsors, what wonder
A swarm of girls hangs on my words?
True, my house lacks the support of Taenarian columns;
It has no ivory room with gilded beams;
My orchards do not equal Phaeacia's growth;
Nor does the Marcian spring moisten my dedicated caves.

Yet, for companions, I have Muses. Readers prize my songs;
And Calliope is never bored with my music.
Lucky the girl my book has made known!
So many monuments of your beauty shall my songs stand.
For not the extravagant Pyramids trained toward the stars
Nor that copy of heaven, Jove's house in Elis,
Nor the magnificence of Mausolus's tomb
Can escape death's fixed extremity.
Either fire or rain robs them of their graces;
Or the years' stabs beat them at last, ponderous ruins,
To earth.

But I have sought a name, a genius, not perishable
In time. Deathless this ornament, this genius.

Frances Fletcher

III, 17

Now, O Bacchus, I turn humbly to your shrine:
Give me, father, peace of mind and fair sailing.

Yours is the power to control Venus when she rages;
Your wine is suffering's medicine.
Lovers are bound by you; and by you unbound:
O Bacchus, cleanse my spirit of this vice!
Ariadne, borne to the skies by your lynxes,
Surely witnesses, among the stars, your own love-knowledge.
This plague which lives, and has long lived, a flame
In all my bones, death, or your wine, alone can heal.

A night of soberness torments lovers at loose ends:
Now hope, now fear, plays at will upon their minds.
But if, O Bacchus, you will apply your gifts to
My fevered brain, and bring sleep to my body,
I will plant on my hills, in orderly rows, your vines;
And myself stand guard, lest wild creatures molest them.
If only I may fill my vats with purple must,
And my feet be grape-dyed in the winepress,
Your hornèd person will, henceforth, be enough to live for.
I shall appear before the world as your poet, O Bacchus!

I will tell how Semele, shaken by Aetna's violence, gave you birth;
Of Lycurgus maddened, and to no purpose, by the new vine;
And Maenads, three bands of them, gladdened by Pentheus' death.
I'll sing of curved dolphins, otherwise Tyrrhenian sailors,
Leaping from the vine-hung ship into deep waters;
And of sweetsmelling rivers, in Dia,
Whence Naxians drink your wine.
I shall present you, O Bacchus, with luxuriant ivy
Clustering around your white neck;
Your hair bound by the headdress of Lydia;
The fragrance of olive at your throat; and wearing
A long robe that strikes against your bare feet.
Dircean Thebes will beat the light timbrel;
Pans, goat-footed, will play on the pipe;
And Cybele, great goddess of the tower-crown,
Will bring to Idaean revels the clash of her raucous cymbals.
And from the bowl at the temple entrance, the wine,
Dipped up with utensil of gold, will flow
In celebration of your sacred rites, O Bacchus.

These things I will recite, not in modest speech,
But in the thunderous style of Pindar.
Only free me from this bondage to arrogance;
And let my despair be lost in sleep.

Frances Fletcher

III, 21

I am compelled to make the long trip to classic Athens,
In the hope travel will free me of this love-poison.
Seeing her constantly increases my morbid desire for the girl:
Love itself best supplies love's nourishment.
Everything I could try, to dispel this evil, I have
Tried. God himself shuts off my escape.
Yet she receives me only now and then; or will not see me at all:
And if she comes to me, she sleeps on the edge of the bed fully dressed.
There will be a cure, however. With a change of scene, love
Will be as far from my thoughts as Cynthia from my sight.

Get the ship launched, comrades! Draw lots
To see which two will sit at the oars, and when.
Hoist the auspicious sails to the mast-tip;
The breeze at the moment is a sailor's breeze.
O towers of Rome, farewell! Goodbye, my friends!
And, Cynthia, whatever you have been to me, adieu!

Now sails will carry me, inexpert guest of the Adriatic, away.
Now, with prayer, I must appear before the ocean-voiced gods.
The Ionian crossed, my boat will rest its tired sails
In Lechaeum of the placid waters:
After which, until the end, I must scurry hither and thither,
In the stretch where Isthmos obstructs the two seas.
The litoral, the harbor of Piraeus, will welcome me:
I shall ascend the long road of Theseus.
In Athens I shall start that work of the mind's cleansing —
Either in Plato's Academy; or in your gardens, O wise Epicurus!
Or I shall study the art of language, Demosthenes' power;
And search out the saltiness of your books, Menander.

I am certain to have a long feast of art works —
What precise hands have fashioned in ivory; or, better, in bronze.
The passing years, and the great expanse of seascape,
Will mitigate the hurt I bear within me silently.
If I die, it will be as a victim of fate, not scandalous love:
And the day of my death will be an honest day.

Frances Fletcher

III, 24

This faith in your beauty, woman, is false;
You have long been too arrogant because *my* eyes approved.

It was my love, Cynthia, adorned you thus:
Does it mortify you to owe distinction to my poems?
That love might believe you to be what you were not, I
Often praised your indeterminate person for various qualities —
Comparing your skin to the blush-pink of Eous, whereas
Its achieved freshness had nothing in common with the dawn-star.

And my father's friends could not divest me of this infatuation;
Nor with a whole ocean could any Thessalian midwife have cleansed
    me;
Now shipwrecked in Aegean waters — and not coerced
By either iron or fire — I have made this candid admission:
I was kidnapped and made to simmer in Venus's savage cauldron;
I was bound tight, hands behind my back.
But look! my victory-wreathed ships have touched port;
The Syrtes weathered, I have dropped anchor.

Though exhausted by agitation and tumult, I can think clearly at last;
My wounds have mended in a healthy body.
INTEGRITY, if there is such a deity, I present myself at your altar!
For whatever vows I made to Jove fell on deaf ears.

Frances Fletcher

III, 25

At the banquet tables of our social gatherings, I was ridiculed;
Anyone at all could find in me a subject for eloquence.
For five years I managed to serve you faithfully:
Now bite your fingernails and regret, often, my lost fidelity.
I am not moved by tears — by that art I was taken;
When you weep, Cynthia, it is habitually from stratagem.
Deserting you, I shall myself weep; but a sense of injury overcomes
    grief:
You do not permit me to wear my yoke becomingly.

O house of tears, lamenting still my resolution;
O door, provocative of my anger, yet still intact from violence: farewell!
And may the burden of old age, with its undiscernible years, oppress
    you;
May disfiguring lines overtake your beauty;
May you pull out, by the root, your white hair!
Reproached by your mirror for telltale wrinkles;
Excluded from choice circles; enduring the contempt of arrogance:
An old hag at last, may you suffer for your acts!

With these so gloomy prospects my poem endows you:
Learn to dread the full import of your beauty!

Frances Fletcher

IV, 1

PROPERTIUS:

All that you see here, stranger, where great Rome now stands,
Was once, before Phrygian Aeneas came, native hill and turf.
Where now rises the Palatine, sacred to Phoebus Mariner,
Evander's cows, refugees, sank down to rest. Where now,
For gods of clay, these gilded temples have been built,
A rough and artless shelter, formerly, was no shame.
Jupiter, Tarpeian father, thundered from the naked cliff;
Our oxen drank from Tiber, then a foreign stream.
Where Remus' shrine has been enhanced with steps, there stood,
Once, a single hearth: illustrious kingdom of the two brothers.
The Curia, now the lofty seat of a togaed senate,
Held fathers wearing skins tied with the rustic cord.
The trumpet called our early Quirites to assembly —
A hundred citizens, in a meadow, often made a senate.
No sinuous awnings hung in the concave theater;
Scenting the stage with saffron was not the custom.
No one looked abroad for his gods: the crowd, in suspense,
Felt awe and reverence during native rites.
For Pales' annual celebration, they made a hay bonfire: these
Rites, now revived, need a mutilated horse for sacrifice.

Vesta, poor, was pleased with garlanded asses;
Lean oxen brought in the mean images. Bleeding swine
Made the ritual of a simple Compitalia; the shepherd,
To music of the pipe, made, acceptably, ovine offerings.
Dressed in skins, plowmen struck women with rude thongs —
And today Fabius Lupercus, licentious, mimics old rites.
Nor did the rough soldier glitter in heavy arms: bare
Of defense, he fought with a flame-hardened stake.
Lycmon, in wolf-skin helmet, erected the first general's tent;
And Tatius had his headquarters among the sheep.
From this background came the brave Tities, Ramnes; Luceres
Of Solonium. From it Romulus drove in triumph his four white
Horses. Bovillae, then, was scarcely a suburb of Rome;
Gabii, a ghost town today, had a substantial population.
And Alba, born of the white sow's omen, stood supreme:
Fidenae was a long journey distant. A far cry, except in
Name, is today's Roman from his ancestors! Who
Could imagine him descended from the she-wolf's nursling?

You did well, Troy, to remove your exiled Penates here.
Ah, under what an augury did the Dardanian ship sail!
Already those Penates pledged the future: nowise injured,
When the wooden horse's belly opened up, discharging Greeks;
When Anchises clung to his son's neck, and flames,
Reverent, abstained from scorching the hero's shoulders.

There followed the brave Decii, and Brutus' consulship;
Venus herself, mother of Aeneas, carried Caesar's arms —
The victorious arms, in very truth, of a resurgent Troy,
A happy earth, O Julius, initiated your gods!
The shaking Sibyl's cauldron had forecast
Lands to be sanctified by Remus of the Aventine; and
Prophecies of the Pergamean seeress, made known, late,
To ancient Priam, had authentically announced: "Turn
The horse around, Greeks! You win in vain! Ilium
Lives. Jupiter will give arms to its ashes."
O Martian wolf, best of nurses to our state,
See what walls grew from your nourishing milk! Those walls,
I shall, given power, construct in reverent song — though
How limited the range of my voice!
Yet, however small the stream flowing from its confined
Source, it will flow in the service of my country.
For Ennius, poetry's shaggy crown: but bestow on me,
Bacchus, leaves from your ivy. So
May Umbria burst with pride of me and my books — Umbria,
Birthplace of the Roman Callimachus!
Whoever, from the valley, observes the heights above,
Let him esteem those walls as he esteems my genius.

Be kind, Rome — the work has its source in you.
Give me, citizens, bright omens. And, on my right,
At the beginning, let there be a bird singing.
I'll tell of rites and days; of early Roman place-names:
And to win *this* race my horse will have to sweat!

HOROS:

Whither so fast, Propertius, and off your track, into grand
Themes? Those threads are not spun from a ready distaff.
Apollo doesn't approve. Such poetry will hurt you.
Your lyre was not built for the music you demand of it.

I'll give you facts, on the most factual basis — or I'm a seer
Inept at twirling the zodiac on its bronze globe.
Babylonian Orops, offshoot of Archytas, begot me, Horos.

Conon is the remote ancestor of my house. No sign
Of racial degeneracy appears in me (the gods uphold me here!) —
And my books contain nothing, if not what you can believe in.
Constellations of the ecliptic, crossed and recrossed, now
Make the gods a source of profit. For gold, one understudies
Jupiter. Over every head now shine Jove's happy stars! And
The greedy orb of Mars; the portentous clusters of Saturn!
Everyone knows the menace of Pisces; of the furious Lion;
Of Capricorn wellwashed in Hesperian waters. Advantaged thus,
I may say: "Troy, thou shalt fall. Rome, thou shalt rise!"
And I may chant the long death-sleep of land and sea.

I said (did I not?) when Arria escorted her twin sons,
        (She gave arms to her sons, against God's will)
They would not be able to bring their spears home again?
And what happened? Why, two graves prove I was right.
For Lupercus, in the act of protecting his wounded horse's
Face, did not alas! protect himself when the horse fell.
As for Gallus, preoccupied, in camp, with standards in his keeping,
He fell before the bloodstained beak of his eagle.
Two youths foredoomed. Two dead sons of an avaricious mother!
True, too true — would it were otherwise! — that prediction of mine.

Also, when Lucina was in labor with Cinara, and
Her womb was slow in delivering its weight, I said:
"Make some vow to Juno that always goes over big."
Lucina had her child. My books got the credit! The sandstrewn
Cave of Libyan Jupiter does not explain things like this.
Nor does the entrail-filament speak for gods committed to it;
Nor the priest, who studies the crow's wings in flight;
Nor the underworld shade rising from magic waters. The course
To be watched is the heavenly one! The right path
Is by way of the stars! Truth comes from the five zones.
Now Calchas is a horrible example. Lacking astrology's
Wisdom, he freed ships adhering to the good rocks of Aulis.
He stained iron with the sacrifice of Agamemnon's
Daughter; and Atrides departed with bloodred sails. Nor
Did the Danaans return! Defeated Troy, suppress
Your grief! Behold again the Euboean inlets!
Nauplius put forth avenging fire under cover of night;
And Greece, weighted with spoils, swam to her death.
So you will, Ajax, conqueror, rape and abduct Cassandra
As she clings to the goddess's statue, and whom Minerva forbids
You to touch?

So much for history. Now I'll read your own horoscope.
Prepare yourself for bad news:
You come from ancient Umbria and an honorable family?
Am I right? I touch the general region of your birth?
Where misty Mevania gives off vapor in a hollow plain
And Umber Lake is warm in summer meadows, and
A wall rises at the summit of steep Asisium? (That wall,
Thanks to your genius, is not without fame.)

You gathered your father's bones, at an age you shouldn't
Have had to gather them; then came down in the world a few
Notches. Your entire property, cultivated, and where many young
Bullocks grazed, the regrettable surveying rod confiscated.
The gold locket was removed from your innocent throat. The
Toga of freedom was donned before your mother's gods. And soon
Apollo dictated to you a few scraps of his song. He forbade you
To thunder out oratory in exaggerated forensic style.
Compose elegy — a vicarious work. That's your real field!
So the world and his brother may write as you do! Keep on
With your campaign of the arms and the Venus — you'll be
A useful and hospitable target for Venus' little boys.
For whatever victories you have won by your work,
One woman snatches the prizes. It will, in fact,
Be useless to shake the embedded barb
From your chin — it will only grab you by the snout.
You'll see both day and night with her eyes; you'll shed
No tear but by her command. Useless
Your thousand watches. Useless to keep her locked up:
Through a chink in the door she'll arrange an assignation.

Now, whether your boat tussles with a storm in midsea;
Whether you go, a stranger, unarmed among the fortified;
Or whether a temblor makes a yawning fissure in earth: live,
At all times, in fear of the sinister-backed, eight-footed
                    CRAB!
                                        Frances Fletcher

IV, 2

Learn, you who wonder at my many forms,
The origin and ancestry of Vertumnus, deity.
Tuscan I am — from Tuscans sprung. I have no regrets
For leaving, in the midst of war, hearths of the
Volsinii. This my crowded city delights me. My pleasure
Is not an ivory temple: enough to be able to see the Roman

Forum. There, Tiber used to flow. They say the sound of
Oars, striking against water, could be regularly heard:
But, when Tiber ceded this field to his wards, the Romans,
They named me Vertum-amnis, River's Turning.

Or, again, you may think you see Vertumnus' form
In the turning year's first fruits, my offering.
For me the first clusters of purple grapes ripen;
For me the ear of corn swells with its milky content.
Here you see sweet cherries, reddening; here, the plums
Of autumn. And, on a summer day, berries.
The gardener, when he has bred apples from
A pear tree, makes votive offerings of the fruit.

You slander me, rumor, liar! I have myself to quote
As authority. Believe a god turned autobiographer:
My nature is adaptable to all forms.
Turn me into any shape you wish, I shall belong there.
Dress me in Coan silk, I'll be a very woman. If I appear
Wearing a toga, who will deny I'm a man?
Give me a sickle, and a fillet of twisted hay strands,
You'll swear it was my hands mowed the field.
Once, too, I was a soldier. I recall I distinguished myself.
Given a basket to carry, I shall turn harvester.
I'm sober at litigation proceedings: yet, crowned with
Roses of the reveller, I'll hear you cry "Crazy drunk!"
Put a turban on my head, I'll be Iacchus to a T: and,
If you will lend me a lyre, I'll become Apollo.
I hunt when supplied with nets; but, carrying a
Fowler's rod, I am the expert bird hunter's deity.
Vertumnus also shows as a charioteer: as the equestrian
Acrobat, moreover, in his graceful leaps from horse
To horse. Properly equipped, I'll take toll of the fishes:
And, in a loose robe, go the way of a street peddler.
In the guise of a shepherd, I can stoop on my crook;
Or traipse through summer dust carrying baskets of
Roses. Surely I need not mention (source of my greatest
Fame) garden produce, always at home in my hands?
The deep green squash; the pregnant gourd; the cabbage
Tied with filament of rushes: these make my reputation!
No flower blooms in the meadows that, fittingly,
Does not make my crown; does not droop upon my forehead.

From my actions (because, though one, I changed into each
And every shape) came my name in Latin, now my own

Tongue. You, Rome, have paid homage to my native race:
One of your thoroughfares is now the Tuscan street —
Commemorating military aid brought, long ago, by
Lycomedians, with the consequent defeat of Sabine Tatius.
I was present then: saw the weakening line, the castoff
Arms; the enemy running in disgraceful flight.
I ask only, Jupiter, that you keep the togaed
Throng of Romans passing back and forth, forever, before
My feet. Six lines remain: I'll not detain you, in haste
To answer your bail. This chalk marks the course's end. —
Once I was a maple bole, hacked out speedily by a
Sickle. I was an indigent god, in this my city,
Before Numa's time. And oh! Mamurius, creator of myself
In bronze — may Oscan earth lie gently on those artist
Hands: theirs the power that cast me infinitely varied, as
I am! The work is one; universal its honor.

Frances Fletcher

IV, 3

Arethusa sends this message to her husband Lycotas:
If one so often absent can yet be her husband.
If you find some portion blotted and irrecoverable —
Know it is because my tears have left blurred traces.
Should any letter waver in its track, perplexing you,
That will indicate my right hand's vanishing courage.

Bactra, in the East, has seen you repeatedly. So, too,
Has the Seric army with its heavy cavalry; and the ice-
Bound Getae; Britannia with its painted cars; India,
Of a different oriental color: all have now seen you.
Was this the meaning of my marriage? These the nights
Promised by old wives' tales when, virgin, I yielded to
Your assault? My marriage torch, burning darkly as I
Was led away, got its smoky flame from a smouldering
Funeral pyre. I was sprinkled with Stygian water. The fillet
Sat crooked on my head. Hymen was absent from my wedding.

My votive offerings (useless, alas!) hang on all the gates.
This cloak I'm weaving for you in camp — it is the fourth.
The harshest sentence upon him who first made a stockade
From an innocent tree; and built wailing tubas of bone!
More worthy he than Ocnus to twist the rope, sitting
Sideways at his work — and eternally feed your hunger, mule!

Tell me, does the leather cuirass chafe your arms?
The heavy spear leave callouses on your delicate hands?
Better these injuries than toothmarks on your throat,
Imprinted by some girl. Truly, then, I should sorrow.
The report is, your face looks haggard: I hope this
Means you miss me, and yearn to see me. Meanwhile,
Long winter evenings introduce the bitter nights.
I kiss, then, whatever arms of yours lie about: later,
Become restless, when coverings tumble on the bed and
Birds do not soon enough announce daybreak. I have, on
Winter evenings, my war work — spinning; and Tyrian wool,
Crimson-dyed, cut to the sword's length. I learn
In what direction Araxes, to be conquered, flows;
How many miles the Parthian horse travels without water:
And I study painted worlds on maps, in an effort to know
How the wise God disposes of his universe: what land
Lies sluggish under cold; what ones are torrid with heat;
What wind might favor boats on the way home to Italy.

One sister helps me with my affairs. And the pallid nurse
Insists, though not sincerely, it is the winter season
Causes your delay. O happy Hippolyte! Shieldless, she bore
Arms; wore on her soft hair the warrior's helmet — how brave!
I wish our Roman camps admitted women. A hindrance, I'd be
Your regiment's faithful hindrance. Scythian mountains (when
The Father congeals water into ice, more bitter
Than ordinary cold) would not deter me.

All love is great. Greatest, a wife's love for her husband.
That fire, to keep it living, Venus herself activates.
Why should the Tyrian seashell's purple glow, now, on my
Person? The aqueous crystal adorn my hands? All things lack
Sight; lack hearing. On the rare Kalends, one slave girl
Opens the shrine of the Lares, though not invariably.
My whining puppy Krauge is a pleasure — she, alone,
Is accredited to some small part of your bed. I cover with
Flowers the tutelary gods; decorate the compita with sacred
Vines. The crackling Sabine herb keeps the home fires
Burning. And if the little owl hoots from a nearby tree,
Or the stingy lamp has to be touched up with wine, that
Means a young lamb, next day, will be sacrificed;
And aproned priests work hard for better times.

Don't, please, think life's only glory lies in
Scaling Bactra's walls; in the loot of fine linen from some

Perfumed commander's body — when weights from the sling
Fall about you; and the trick-turned cavalry makes the bow sing.
Yet (once the Parthians are defeated, and a headless spear —
Distinguished service emblem — follows your triumphant horse)
Remember to keep faith with me.
On that condition alone I could wish for your return.
When you do come, I shall carry votive arms
To the Capene Gate. And my inscription will read:

FROM A GRATEFUL WIFE FOR HER HUSBAND'S SAFE RETURN

Frances Fletcher

IV, 4

Tarpeia's grove; Tarpeia's traitor-tomb; capture of
Ancient Jupiter's temple: of these I sing.
A life-giving pool lay hidden in an ivy-hung cove;
Native waters sounded in antiphonal response to woods
(Domicile, thick-shaded, of Silvanus): and here the soft
Shepherd's pipe led sheep, from outer heat, to drink.
This spring Tatius surrounded with a wall of maple
Stakes; fortified his camp with an encircling rampart.
Rome, then, what was it? When the trumpeter of the Cures,
With slow notes, shook Jove's regional sacred rocks?
Where laws, now, are promulgated for subject lands,
Sabine soldiers stood in the Roman Forum. Rome's walls
Were her hills. Where the Curia, now, stands
Enclosed, the warhorse drank from the famous spring.

From this source Tarpeia drew water for the goddess. And
The urn, made of clay, was heavy on her head.
Could one death, O Vesta, be enough for that bad girl
Willing to be a traitor to your altar's fire?
She saw Tatius exercising on the dusty field; saw
The confused radiance of embellishing armor and yellow
Plumes. Fascinated with the king's beauty, with his royal
Panache, she let fall the urn she carried.

Often, from this time on, she read omens in the omenless
Moon — pretended to need lustral water for her hair:
Often made gifts of argent lilies to persuasive nymphs —
As protection, against Romulus' spear, for her Tatius:
When she climbed the Capitol, alive with early fires,
It was always with arms scratched by brambles. And,
Sitting idly on the Tarpeian summit, she pitied herself,

Her lovesickness. (But Jove, her neighbor, was to have
No pity).

"O campfires and quarters of Tatius' guard,
O Sabine armor so attractive to my view,
If only I might sit, a captive, before your gods!
Captive, then I might look upon my Tatius! O
Hills of Rome, O Rome built on its hills, and
Vesta, whom my fault will shame — farewell! That horse,
That very horse whose mane Tatius himself smooths
Over his right shoulder — that horse will take me, in love,
To the camp! What wonder Scylla brutally cut her father's
Life-charm, a lock of hair — and saw her femininity
Transformed into wild dogs?
What wonder Ariadne betrayed the horned Minotaur,
Her half-brother, when, by a gathered thread, Theseus passed
Through the labyrinth? And myself. A paragon of infamy
For Italian girls! I, a traitor, yet ministrant to
Vestal fires! Forgive me — anyone who wonders why Pallas' flame
Has been allowed to die. I have wept, bitterly, at the altar.

"Tomorrow, rumor says, the entire city celebrates.
Come, Tatius, by way of the dewsoaked, brush-covered
Ridge. A slippery path, treacherous all the way. Its surface
Is deceptive, with unsuspected pools everywhere.
If only I knew the secrets of the Muse of Magic! Then
I might have passed on to you, my love, those charms!
For the embroidered toga of royalty suits you — not him,
Who, unhonored by a mother, was suckled by a she-wolf.
If, a stranger, a queen, I seem a menace in your native hall —
Yet, Tatius, my dowry (Rome herself, no trifling matter)
Goes with me. But if you won't be king, avenge the Sabine
Women — rape *me*, if only by the law of fair exchange! I
Can arrange an armistice between the engaged troops.
Dressed in a bride's cloak, I can, if you wish, be emissary
For peace. Hymen, your measures! Trumpeter, be quiet!
Marry me, Tatius, and (be certain) your war will end.

"Already the trumpet, closing the fourth watch, foretells
Dawn. The stars sink into the Ocean.
I'll try to sleep. I shall hope to dream of you.
O let me have you, a happy vision, before my eyes!"

She spoke. And relaxed into a disturbed sleep: unaware
Of new furies lying down beside her. For Vesta,

Holy guardian of Ilium's embers, fed
Her conscience; built a plethora of fires in her bones.

She sprang up — rushed off, like an Amazon on the banks
Of Thermodon the swift: her robe torn, her breast
Bare. It was the city's feast day (the Fathers called it
Parilia) — anniversary of the building of Rome's walls;
Yearly revel of convivial shepherds; carnival in the city;
A day when old pagan dishes are cooked with ceremony;
A day when, over scattered heaps of burning hay,
An inebriate mob shakes its unclean feet.
For Romulus decreed the sentry should be off-duty;
The trumpet silent; camp activities adjourned.

This, Tarpeia thought, was her hour. She met the enemy.
She made the contract, herself an integral part thereof.
The hill, quite difficult, was unwatched by reason
Of the feast. All happened quickly. Tatius silenced, with
His sword, the barking dogs. Everything, then, was silent.
Jove alone had not, in his own interests, gone off duty.

Tarpeia had betrayed the gate and, with it, the helpless
Country. Now she, herself, asked: "On what day
Shall we be married?" An enemy, Tatius yet abhorred
Treason. He said: "Marry me now. Mount
My royal couch!" Thus. And ordered her crushed
By his comrades' shields.
This dowry, virgin, you won by your service.

The hill is named, then, for Tarpeia, the leader.
O Vestal watcher, an unjust fate gave you this prize!

Frances Fletcher

IV, 5

May earth, O Acanthis, procuress, cover your grave with
Your namesake thorns; and your writhing shade know the drunkard's
Thirst. In the dust may your spirit rest uneasy; and Cerberus,
Avenger, terrify your ghost with his hungry howling!

Ingenious enough to soften Hippolytus, recusant of love;
The worst possible augury for concord between man and
Woman — she would compel Penelope to neglect news
Of her husband; and take into her bed lascivious Antinous.
If that woman wished, the magnet would not attract iron;

And a bird would be a vixen to its own young.
If she brought herbs from erring Vestals' graves, to the ditch
Of magic, indissoluble solids would dissolve in running water.
Bold to impose laws upon the enchanted moon, and to go
Incognita at night in a wolf's shape (that she might cunningly
Cause blindness in too-observant husbands) she tore out,
With her nails, the inoffensive eyes of crows.
She interviewed owls as to ways of extracting my lifeblood;
Gathered, for my harm, the mare's charm. A good talker,
She made her points: just as, flattering, she could, by
Experience in guilt, inflame to passion the roadside rocks.

"If the gold coast of the Dorozantes appeals to you,
And the shell proud beneath Tyrian waters:
If you want Eurypylan stuffs from Coan Minerva, or
Souvenir-antiques from cloth-of-gold couches:
Or any articles palm-bearing Thebes sends to market;
Along with gay pottery baked on Parthian hearths:
Perjure yourself for these things. Dump the gods in the trash.
Tell lies and conquer. Respectability never pays — to hell
With it! Pretend you've a protector: it enhances your value. Take
Advantage. Love, suspended for a night, is the more
Importunate! His anger, if he pulls your hair too hard, is useful:
You can force him to buy peace; to pay handsomely.
Then, having promised yourself to him, pretend the ensuing
Days are Isis' days — dedicated to celibacy. Have Iole remind you,
Openly, of the April Veneralia and giftgiving. Have Amycle
Keep telling you your birthday falls on the Ides of May.
He sits, an impatient lover, before you. But you, at ease
In a comfortable chair, are casually writing. If he's worried,
You've got him hooked!

"Always have fresh toothmarks on your neck. He'll think
Some rival gave them to you. Yet never go in for
Dramatic backbiting as Medea did: she had the nerve
To do the wooing — and paid for her boldness. Imitate
Thais, rather: expensive Thais, of Menander's world. In New
Comedy, Thais, a prostitute, fleeces the astute Scythians.
Adapt yourself to the man's manners. If he hits off a ditty,
Join in. Accompany his voice with your wine-thick voice.
See that your doorman checks on gift bearers. Let him who comes
Emptyhanded dream innocently on, supported by
The barred door. And don't look down on a soldier not made
For love! Nor on a sailor if he comes bringing gold. Nor those
Who, the bill of sale around their barbarian necks,

Were once marked with chalk, and vaulted in the Forum.
Whatever the hand bearing it, have a care for the gold.

"Listen to poetry, and what does it get you? Words, words.
If a man brings you verse, but never a Coan silk dress,
Pay no attention to the music of his artless lyre.
While the blood is in springtime — while time is unaged by
Wrinkles — live and profit. Tomorrow may steal the bloom!
Milesian roses in fragrant Paestum, roses meant to survive,
I have seen parched by the unseasonable scirocco."

Acanthis thus corrupted my mistress's mind: and
Through my drawn skin you could have counted my bones.
But O Venus Regina, receive now my gratitude — receive
A ringdove, its throat slit before your altar!
I saw her coughing more and more hoarsely: I saw
Bloodstained spittle seep through her hollow teeth;
I saw her evil soul expire upon mats inherited from beggars:
The tumbledown shed quaking with cold; the fire inert.
Her "funeral pomp" comprised stolen bands for her thin hair;
A soiled white mildewed bonnet: and that dog, long
Too vigilant on behalf of me and my anxiety (on nights when
I had to remove, with furtive fingers, the door's bars).

May the bawd's tombstone be an old broken-necked bottle:
Bring your strength, O fig tree, to weigh upon her grave!
All lovers, whoever you are, pelt this grave with stones —
    And, with the stones, mix maledictions.

Frances Fletcher

IV, 6

The priest performs rites: let there be silence during the rites.
Let the heifer be struck and fall before my altar.
Now may a Roman wreath and Philetan clusters hang side
By side; and the urn give up its Cyrenean waters.
Give me the fragrance of costos, the tribute of sweet incense;
Have the fillet of wool wound three times around the altar!
Sprinkle my head with pure water. And, on new shrines, let
The ivory flute pour forth its song from Phrygian
Jars. Opportunists, walk behind at a distance! Scatter your poisons
In another air. The new road is strewn with sacred laurel.
We shall restore, O Muse, the temple of Palatine Apollo:
An enterprise, Calliope, exalted enough for your
Patronage. These songs are made for Caesar. You, Jupiter,
I pray, attend while Caesar is celebrated!

A wide water, Actium's memorial of Caesar's war fleet,
Recedes toward the Athamanan shores of Phoebus' port —
Where a bay shuts out the murmur of Ionia's sea —
And, in response to sailors' prayers, forms a ready harbor.
Here the leaders of the world met. Their fleets, equally great,
Stood unequally favored by the omens. One,
Unworthily commanded by a woman, was fated for
Destruction at the hands of the Trojan Quirinus, great Caesar.

Under full sail the Augustan flagship advanced. Its
Protector was Jove. Its standard had been taught victory
For Rome. Nereus manoeuvred the ships into twin crescents;
Gaudy waters quivered under the sheen of arms.
One fleet, mobile, contended with a strong south wind:
And Phoebus, forsaking Delos (once floating, now fixed by him)
Came and stood over Augustus' stern. A strange fire shone:
Flashed three times in oblique manifestation.

Phoebus was not wearing his hair loose on his shoulders.
He came without his tortoise-shell lyre's unmartial music.
His aspect was such as when he gazed on Agamemnon, and
Decimated the Doric camps: or as when
He destroyed the Python, resting in its coils —
Serpent-terror of goddesses too timid to combat it.
He spoke. "O native of Alba Longa, world redeemer,
Augustus, known as greater than your Trojan forbears —
Win now at sea! Already the land is yours. My bow militates
In your favor. All the arrows in my quiver are yours.
Relieve the homeland's fear. Confident, with you for
Protector, the public has pinned its hope to your prow.
Unless you win, Romulus will have been wrong in his augury
For Rome: he will have misinterpreted the Palatine birds.
See, the enemy approaches too close — disgrace to Latins,
You being only *princeps,* any sea should suffer *royal* sails!

"Fear not, if the other fleet moves with a hundred winged
Oars to each ship. It labors in a stormy element.
No matter how many prows bear Centaurian rock throwers,
You'll find the shops hollow; their terrors, painted imitations.
It's the cause that makes or breaks a soldier's courage:
The cause unjust, troops lay down their arms. This
Is zero hour. Engage your fleet. I, who fix the hour,
Shall lead the Julian curved-beak prow with my laurelbearing
Hand." He spoke. And shot his quiverful into the enemy.
The next attack was Caesar's. And — for Phoebus kept his word —
Rome won. The woman paid.

Broken scepters floated in Ionian waters.
But Father Caesar, from his Idalian comet, said:
"I am a god. Victory proves you of our blood."
Then followed Triton with his trumpet-blast. All the ocean
Goddesses, around freedom's standards, clapped applause.
In shameful flight, *she* (at the mercy of her ship) sought
Nile. Her one triumph — death, by her own appointment!
The gods knew best! What kind of triumph would one woman
Have made: led through streets Jugurtha traversed before her?

And Phoebus acquired a shrine in Actium. His every arrow,
Aimed to hit, had accounted for ten ships.

And that is enough of war. Apollo, victor, now wants
The cithara. He would exchange arms for a music
Restful to the ear. So, let whiterobed guests come into
The grove. Place wreaths of roses about my neck. Let
Falernian wines flow freely. Drench
My hair with saffron of Cilicia. And, O Muse, inspire
Your imbibing poets! (You, Bacchus, are ever a stimulus
To Apollo whom you love).

One will tell of conquered Sygambri, in their marshes;
Another, of Ethiopian Meroe, and sunless kingdoms —
Not forgetting the late Parthian treaty, defeat's confession:
"Let him return Remus' standards. Soon he'll give his own.
Or, should Augustus spare something of the East from conquest,
Let him reserve this trophy for his sons.
Rejoice, Crassus, if, in black sands, you can rejoice:
By way of the Euphrates one can now reach your grave."

And so, with libation bowl, and song, night will pass:
Until daylight tosses its beams into my wine glass.

Frances Fletcher

IV, 7

The shades are real. Death is not the end. The
Ghastly wraith struggles free; escapes the grave.
Cynthia came to me, in a vision, and leaned over my bed:
Cynthia, lately buried near the humming highway's edge.
After love's death and burial, I slept by fits and starts —
But found my couch a lamentably frigid kingdom.

She had, with the hair that went with her to the pyre,
The same, the very same eyes. Part of her dress was

Burned. Fire had gnawed the beryl ring she always wore; and
Lethe's water had frayed the clear line of her lips.
Her slender hands, as she extended them, rattled: yet
Her presence, her voice, remained unchanged. She spoke:
"Perfidious lover (yet better than any woman dares hope for)
       Can sleep so soon possess you?
Already the memory of secret love in close-guarded Subura,
And my window worn with night's devices, has left you?
How often, from that window, I lowered the rope, in your cause:
And, descending in hand-over-hand motion, reached your arms!
We often celebrated Venus in the by-ways; and, breast
To breast, made our cloaks her thoroughfare. O silent
Pledge, whose falsely spoken words the south winds
       Were to sweep clean away!
No one called 'Cynthia!' as my eyes closed in death — though,
By your calling, I should have had one day's grace.
Nor did any mourner, on my account, rattle the split reed;
       Nor ease my head resting on a broken tile.
And further: Did anyone see you bowed in grief, at my grave,
       Or your black tunic glisten with tears?
If it was inconvenient to go beyond the gates, at least
You might have ordered my bier to proceed more slowly.
Why, ingrate, did you not yourself petition the winds
For my pyre? Make sweet my flames with nard? What sad
Omission, not to have showered me (the cost so little!)
With hyacinths; and broken a wine jar over my ashes!

"Let Lygdamus burn. Let the iron plates be red hot.
I knew his guilt, when I drank the death-filled wine!
Let clever Nomas hide, as she may, her secret poisons:
The burning shard will prove her hands bloodstained.

"One whose lowlived nights made her, lately, a public spectacle,
Now sweeps the ground with the golden cyclas of your giving.
And for the slave, naïvely garrulous, who spoke of my beauty,
She overweights wicked baskets of wool for spinning.
Because Petale took wreaths of flowers to my grave,
She now has her ankles bound to inhuman wooden blocks:
And Lalage hangs suspended by her twisted hair —
       Because she dared to invoke my name.

"That woman melted down (and you allowed it!) the gold
Of my image, to enrich herself by my burning. I'll not
Reproach you, Propertius, though you deserve it:
       In your books my reign was long.

I swear, by the fates' irreversible song,
I loved you faithfully. By this pledge, may Cerberus
Soften his voice for me! If I lie, let a serpent
      Hiss in my grave. Let him sleep in my bones.

"For my seat is not allotted along the infamous stream
Where a multitude of oarsmen row in divergent waters.
One group bears dishonored Clytaemestra. Another, Cretan
Pasiphae, fabricator of the false cow's image.
And look! another group sails by, in a wreathed and
Bean-shaped boat. Here the aura of the blessed sweetens
Elysian roses. Here sound Cybele's huge circular brasses;
And turbaned choruses strike strings with Lydian plectra.
      Here virtue has musical numbers.

"Andromeda and Hypermestre, those famous women of feeling,
Guiltless wives both, narrate their stories. The one,
In dismay, tells of arms made livid by her mother's chains:
      Of hands not meriting clammy rocks.
And Hypermestre tells how it happened she had not heart
To commit the outrageous crime her sisters dared. Thus,
      By tears in death, we heal life's love-anguish.

"I pass over the many injustices of your perfidy.
But if by chance you have some feeling for me still —
If Chloris' love philtre consumes you not wholly,
      Then do these things for me:

"Keep my nurse Parthenie, in her tremulous years, from
Want. She could have mulcted you — but did not.
And Latris, my delight, whose name means only 'slave' —
Don't let Latris hold the mirror for another mistress!
And all the verses, Propertius, you wrote for me:
      Burn them, please. Take me as your theme no longer.

"And prune the ivy on my tomb. Its aggressive clusters,
With their twisted tendrils, constrict my soft bones.
Where fruitful Anio spreads among greenbranched fields,
Write, on my column, as a tribute (brief: so one may read
In quick passage from the city) this verse:

    HERE, IN TIBURIAN EARTH, LIES GOLDEN CYNTHIA:
    HER FAME, ANIO, CAME TO REST ON YOUR BANKS.

"Nor think lightly of shades passing through blessed gates.
If, virtuous, they appear to you in sleep, know them real.

We wander by night. Night frees all the shadowy prisoners.
Even Cerberus, his bar withdrawn, roams where he will.
With daylight we return (so law requires) to stagnant Lethe.
We are transported. The mariner tallies his load.

"Though others possess you now, you will, soon, be mine
Alone. You will come where I am: our two shades commingled:
      Each permeating each."

Her charges ended. The gently bitter discourse ceased.
     And Cynthia's shade withdrew from me.

                   Frances Fletcher

IV, 8

Listen to what startled the neighbors, one night
On the aqueous Esquiline; sent them scampering through
The New Fields: and echoed, a scandal, in an obscure inn —
Without my assistance; but with damage to my reputation.

Lanuvium has long been the shrine of an ancient dragon —
    A few moments only, reader: this is rare!
An occult air-current catapults you down to the cave:
Along the drafty path the dragon's tribute must go.
    (And beware, virgin, of a path like this!)
The serpent emits, on the yearly occasions of his demand for
Food offerings, a loud hissing sound from earth's depths:
And girls dedicated to this rite are frightened to death.
They must confide a hand to the reptilian maw: and,
If the girl is virgin, the serpent snatches the offering.
The baskets of food she carries shudder from the impact.
Those proved by the dragon virgin, return to their parents:
And the farmers cry: "It will be a fertile year!"

To Lanuvium my Cynthia had been borne by cropped ponies —
    Juno, her excuse; Venus, her reason.
And, Way of Appia, I call you to witness Cynthia's triumphal
Progress, as she recklessly drove your rocky length!
Seated, she leaned over the pole; shook the reins where
The road was roughest. It was worth paying to see!
The silk-upholstered vehicle, owned by a smooth-shaven
Playboy, I'll let pass. So, too, dogs necklaced with Molossan
Collars. He'll end as they all do — eating, for pay, a
Gladiator's unholy food — once his so mortifying beard
    Takes toll of those satin cheeks.

Because Cynthia had so often deceived me with other
Lovers, I decided to switch, myself, both camp and cot.
A certain Phyllis lives near the Aventine Diana:
Sober, she's not much. Drinking, she does very well.
Another girl, Teia, from near the Capitolium, is normally
Modest. But one man won't satisfy her, drunk. Bent
On a night's diversion, I got in touch with them:
Fully prepared for a new intrigue; a new phase of Venus.

One couch, for the three of us, was hidden in foliage.
Was I on it, you inquire? Yes, between the two girls.
Lygdamus poured. The summer service was of glass. The
Scent of Greece was in the Methymnan wine. Yours, Nile,
Was the tibia! Yours, Byblis, the dancer to castanets!
Roses, of natural elegance, the essence, stood ready for
Throwing. Magnus himself, the dwarf, went into his routine:
Waved his ugly hands to the music's rhythm.

Yet, though the lamps were full, the flame flickered.
The table (another bad omen!) fell down and lay flat.
Also, each time I threw the dice (I wanted the auspicious
Venus numbers) the damned low-ciphered dogs leapt at me!
The two girls sang to a deaf man; bared their breasts
To a blind man. Ah me, I was off by myself to Lanuvium!

Suddenly hinges creaked slightly on the front door;
A sound was heard remotely at the entrance. And Cynthia
Threw back the folding doors. Her hair was a mess:
       She was in a rage but looked beautiful.
From limp fingers my goblet fell to the floor. I knew
My lips, not too controlled after wine, turned grey.
Lightning was in Cynthia's eyes — and, as a woman can,
She stormed. Rome captured could be no better drama!

She went full force at Phyllis' face with her nails.
Terrified Teia cried "Water! Water!" to put out the fire.
The pyrotechnics aroused the sleeping Quirites: and
The whole street reverberated crazily in the night.
Their hair rumpled by Cynthia's yanking, their tunics torn,
The girls ran for the first inn on a dark street.
Rejoicing in her spoils, Cynthia soon returned, a victor.

And proceeded to slap my face savagely. To place her mark
On my neck. To bite my flesh till it bled, especially in
The region near my eyes. (They deserved it.) At length

Her arms grew tired of pommeling me. Lygdamus, in hiding
On the left side of my bed, was made to come forth.
Put on the carpet, he cried out to my genius for help.
Lygdamus, I could do nothing! We were both captives.
A suppliant, I edged forward with the proper gestures,
And lay prostrate. Cynthia's feet scorned me. She spoke.

"If you want me to forgive you, then learn
The future terms of our contract.
You are not to walk, all spruced up, in Pompey's Portico;
Nor visit the Forum sanded for obscene combats;
Nor crane your neck and stare
At the women's section high in the theater.
You are not to hang around uncurtained litters.

"But Lygdamus is the chief cause of this quarrel — have
Him sold. Let him wear double chains on his feet."

She stated the law. I said, "I will obey." Proud
Of her achieved dominion, Cynthia laughed: then
Fumigated every spot the two strange girls had touched;
Cleansed the threshold with pure water;
Ordered my clothes changed again;
Touched my head three times with flame of sulphur.
I responded to treatment. The couch was made up fresh.
    And to sign our armistice required the whole bed.

Frances Fletcher

IV, 9

And in that faroff age when Amphitryoniades
Drove his cattle from your stables, O Erythea,
He came to the untamed uplands, the Palatine, thronged
With herds. Exhausted himself, he found a place for
His cows where Velabrum lay under shallow water.
Mariners sailed their boats through the city.

Cacus, keeper of the herd, was dishonest. He betrayed
Hospitality's god. With him the cattle were not safe.
A native, this Cacus, besides being a thief, had three
Faces, three voices. He had a tricky hideout in a cave.
To cover the tracks of theft, he dragged the cows backwards,
By their tails, to the cavern. But the god knew.
For the herd's lowing disclosed the thief's whereabouts.
In his anger the god broke down Cacus' door.

Struck three times by the club from Mount Maenalus,
Cacus lay on the ground. And Hercules said:
"Get along, bossies!
Get along, Herculean cows, last labor of our club.
O cows I have twice sought and twice found! Get along,
Bossies, and dedicate the Bovarian Fields with long mooing.
Rome's famous Forum Bovarium will rise from your pasture."
He spoke. And moved his dry tongue in his dry mouth.
But fruitful earth yielded no water anywhere.

Shortly, from within the green enclosure of a sacred grove,
He heard the laughter of cloistered women.
Here the Bona Dea had her close and fountains. And no man
Might look upon her rites without punishment.
Deep red wreaths covered the sacred entrance;
The ancient building, with its aromatic fire, was in decay.
Above the sanctuary hung leaves of the bright ornamental
Poplar. And birds sang within the rich foliage.

Here, at the entrance, the god fell on his face.
Dust was caked on his beard. Quite ungodlike he pleaded.
"O you who amuse yourselves in the sacred wood,
Give sanctuary, I pray. I have no strength left.
I have searched for water — I hear the sound of water —
Enough to fill one of my cupped hands is all I ask!

"You have heard of him who, but now, supported on his back
The heavens? I am he. Earth, grateful, calls me Alcides.
Who has not heard of the deeds of Hercules' club?
Of blows that never went wild against their wild prey?
And how for one man the Stygian darkness became light?
Though it were the rites of unmerciful Juno you celebrate,
That beldame herself would not deny me her springs.
But if, by chance, my face with its lion-mane beard,
And my hair burned by the Libyan sun, dismay any of you —
Then know I have, as well, done service in a Sidonian
Robe, a woman's robe; worked daily at the distaff, with
A band supporting my soft, though hairy, breasts; and,
For all my strength of arm, passed well enough for a woman."

Alcides spoke thus. But the fostering mother said
(She wore on her hair the priestess's red fillet):
"Be careful where you look, stranger. Leave this precinct.
Do as I say — move on. Betake yourself from this shrine.
It is forbidden to men. An inexorable law punishes violation.

A special altar, sacred to this house, guards the law.
Tiresias once looked on Pallas — saw her beauty plainly
As she bathed: she had laid aside her Gorgon-headed shield.
May the gods give you other springs — this water flows
From secret channels. It flows for women only."

Thus the austere priestess.
The god pressed with his shoulders against opaque pillars:
The gate could not support his raging thirst.
When he had assuaged his thirst by consuming a river, and
His lips were scarcely dry from drinking, he vowed:
"This corner of the world receives me and my fate.
This destined earth lies open to me, nearly revived.
O shrine (he said) made great by these hands! O
Ara Maxima, dedicated hereby to ranging herds! This
Altar shall never admit the worship of a woman:
And the thirst of Hercules shall be forever avenged."

His hands had purified earth. Hence the Sabines of Cures
Named him Sancus, the Purifier.
Hail, Sancus, to whom harsh Juno once more is kind!

O Sancus be with me and inhabit my book.

Frances Fletcher

IV, 10

Jupiter Feretrius? His origin? I'll make a start: write
Of three types of arms placed on his shrine by three leaders.
It's a steep road I'm ascending. The glory of it strengthens me.
Distinction never crowns a too facile work.

You, Romulus, were the first to lay down a prize before him,
When you returned, loaded with victory and spoils, from war.
It was when you conquered Acron of Caenina, as he advanced
Toward the gates; pinned him with a lance to his fallen horse.
This same Herculean Acron of Caenina, commanding the tower,
Was a terror, Rome, once. He threatened your destruction.
He dared to hope for spoils taken from Romulus' body:
Instead, gave up his own arms, his blood on them not yet dry.
Romulus saw him, before the hollow towers, leveling javelins;
And he took this measured oath before attacking:
"Acron will be your sacrifice today, Jupiter!"
True to his word, Romulus took the spoil to Jove's altar.

Father of Rome and its virtues, he was used to winning.
Born to a simple hearth, he withstood the rigors of camp;
He was as good a rider as plowman; and his wolf-skin helmet
Had a wolf's tail for ornament.
His buckler did not glitter with bronze-and-gold overlay;
And slain oxen furnished leather for his tough belts.

Not yet was there rumor of war beyond Tiber. The most distant
Conquests were Nomentum and captured Cora's sparse acres.
Yet, when it was a great achievement to defeat the Veians,
Cossus pursued them and cut down Tolumnius.
Ancient Veii, O pity! You were a kingdom then:
A king's gold throne stood in your Forum.
Now the rough shepherd's pipe sounds within your walls;
And, where your bones lie, they reap the corn.
Supported by his city, the commander held consultation.
While, with its bronze horn, the ram smashed at the wall,
Its penthouse concealed troops ready for action. And Cossus
Said: "It's better soldiership to fight on a plain."
Nor was there delay. Each side took its place in the field.
The gods fought with Latium's army. And Tolumnius' severed head
Spattered with blood Rome's horses.
Claudius Marcellus bent the attacking army from the Rhine:
He carried off the Belgian shield of the great leader,
Virdomarus. The latter claimed Rhine himself as ancestor:
Mobile, he could drive the chariot and hurl javelins, at once.
But as, barbarian in Gallic trews, he cast before the enemy,
A hooked torque split open his throat, then fell to the ground.

Three kinds of booty, then, are preserved in the temple. And
Jupiter Feretrius may mean the Slayer — as when a commander,
Under definite auspices, strikes down the enemy commander.
Or he may be the Carrier: as when arms are carried off, spoils
Of victory, on the victor's shoulders.

And this is the origin of JUPITER FERETRIUS.

Frances Fletcher

IV, 11

Cease, Paullus, to oppress my tomb with tears;
The black gate swings open for no prayers.
Once the dead have passed, subjects, into hell,
There is no escape. Entreaty softens not hard rock.
The dark hall's god may hear you pleading: but your tears

Will be drunk by deaf encompassing shores.
Olympian gods respond to vows — but once the infernal
Porter has received his fee, a ghastly gate shuts tight.
So the trumpet's dirge proclaimed, when death's torch
Was placed beneath my pyre, and flame ate my body.

Marriage with Paullus; ancestral triumphs; several
Children, pledges of my fame — how did these help me?
The Fates were not thereby kinder to Cornelia: a weight
Five fingers could gather up — that I am at present.
O nights known to the damned! And you, shallow, scarcely-
Moving waters; and little pools I touch with every step —
Know I came, unripe for death, yet with no poison in me!
May our father, Dis, impose light sentence on my shade.

Or, if some Aeacus sits as judge, and the urn near him,
Let him give verdict when my name is drawn: with Minos,
And Rhadamanthus as assessors; the Eumenides, austere,
Grouped near Minos' seat: and the court silent.
May you, Sisyphus, rest from stone-rolling. Let Ixion's
Revolutions cease to sound; the deceptive Tantalean waters
Contract; and cunning Cerberus pounce on no shades today —
Let his chain hang loose on its silent bar.
I shall plead my own defense. (If I perjure myself,
May the Danaids' tragic urn be the weight I have to bear!)

If even ancestral monuments entitled one to a birth of
Distinction, then African kingdoms prove my descent
From Numantian forbears. The many Libones, of my mother's line,
Are not less famous. My house has a dual claim to greatness.
Quite early I put aside my childhood dress; went out to
The wedding torches; wore a new fillet to bind my six curls:
I married you, Paullus. And left you alas! so soon.
The tombstone describes me as a woman but once married.
I appeal to those ancestors whom you, Rome, revere;
Beneath whose inscriptions you, Africa, lie injured.
And I call upon Perseus — inspired to action by descent from
Achilles, and from Hercules, who pulled down your mansions,
Avernus! You will testify no censor's law had to be modified
For me. No hearth blushed for shame of mine.

Cornelia brought no disgrace to so many standards:
She lived the cynosure of her family's dignity. My life
Was of one piece, without flaws of indiscretion. Between
Two torches — marriage and death — I lived in virtue.

Natural heredity dictated my laws — nor could fear
Of any judge make your conduct better.
Whatever harsh sentence the voting-urn may yield, no
Woman, sitting beside me, will lose in stature. Not you, O
Claudia, who towed Cybele's hesitant image to the shore —
Claudia, rare servitor of the tower-crowned goddess!
Nor you, Aemilia, whose white robe made vestiges of ashes
Burst into sheer flame, when Vesta removed her sacred fire.

Nor, Scribonia, gentle mother, did I ever give you offense.
Save for an early death, in what could you wish me changed?
A mother's tears honor me. The city's mourning, likewise.
My shade also finds support in Caesar's expressed sorrow:
Caesar fervently declares that, in me, his daughter had
A worthy sister. We have seen a god shed tears.

I wore the maternal stola of honor, once I had borne
Three children. Death took me from a fertile home.
Lepidus, Paullus — even now you bring me comfort.
It was your arms supported me at the last.
Twice I saw my brother shine in the curule chair:
In the very hour he became consul, Cornelia died. And O,
My daughter, born to mirror your father's high virtue,
Emulate me, and marry once, no more! Perpetuate, all
Of you, the family name. Charon's boat finds me a ready
Passenger — if many descendants give luster to my name.
To live, though a shade in hell, a legend of virtue
Among men: that is a woman's greatest triumph.

And to you, Paullus, I commend our children:
For them, my very ashes exhale solicitude. You,
The father, must wear a mother's mantle; on your
Shoulders falls the protection of them all.
If they grieve, embrace them for yourself and me.
But if you must grieve, conceal grief from them —
No tears, when they come near! Smile, or at least pretend!
The nights will be enough for remembering me: in sleep,
You will think you see me.
When you speak secret words to this my apparition,
Make each word distinct — as if I were to answer.
Yet, if another bed should stand facing the door, and
A stepmother, not quite at ease, reign there: then,
Children, accept your father's wife graciously.
Your good manners will win her friendship.
Be careful not to overpraise me, your mother. She might

Readily take offense, were her predecessor compared with her
Too freely. But if your parent continues happy in my memory:
If he still shows affection for my ashes: then watch,
Watch tenderly, for his first conscious signs of age.
Do what you can for him in his wifeless state.

May the years taken from me be added to your lives:
Thus you will bring comfort to Paullus in his old age.
This is as it should be — I never wore mourning for any child
Of mine. They were all present at my funeral.

My defense rests. Rise, O witnesses who mourn for me,
While earth gives its verdict on my life's conduct.
Heaven opens its gates to virtue. If I am judged worthy,
Let my spirit dwell aloft with the shades of my ancestors.

            Frances Fletcher

Tibullus

⟦ Albius Tibullus, of Gabii (c. 55–19 B.C.), is second only to Propertius in Roman elegy. He too was in love, first with Delia, then with
Nemesis, and turned his hypochondriac frustrations into poetry. He
wrote only twenty-five elegies in four books; the fourth contains
eleven poems partly by Sulpicia, the best known Roman poetess, and
partly by Tibullus or some other sympathetic friend of the lady (see
page 234). His themes are his love-affairs, both with women and
with a *puer delicatus* named Marathus, admiration for his friend
Marcus Valerius Messalla Corvinus (68 B.C.–A.D. 8), the quiet pleasures of old-fashioned country life, and for one elegy some events of
recent Roman history and the stories they recalled to Tibullus. "No
poet is more Italian," says Duff of Tibullus. There is a tender tranquillity in much of his poetry which contrasts strangely with the
violence of his romantic despair. Walter Pater appreciated this softer
mood in these elegies and described it beautifully in the first pages
of *Marius the Epicurean*. Hubert Creekmore's translation of the
complete poems of Tibullus should be exceedingly welcome for the
skill with which he has grasped in simple English the inner feelings
of the poet. ⟧

ELEGIES

I, 1

Hoards let others heap of tawny gold
And grip, of good ploughed land, their greedy acres,
Whom steady watch for near marauders scares
And war's dour pulsing drum repels from sleep!
My humble lot grant me a humdrum life
And grant my hearth a steady-shining fire!
For me, may I be happy to live on a little
And not for ever be pledged to the long march
But avoid the dogday heats in a tree's shadow
Upon a bank with water running by;
Nor feel it shame to handle the hoe sometimes
Myself, nor to jab at the slow ox with a goad;
Nor a great hardship to lift a lamb or a kid
Left by its dam, and myself carry it homeward.
Let myself, at the due time, graft the young vines

Like a true hodge, and deftly dig in the fruit trees;
So let Hope not cheat me, but always give me corn
Heaped high, and must foamy in a full vat.

For I pray, at least: wherever the garlands are hung,
By the lonely stump in the field, or the crossways stone;
And a due share of my fruit that each year ripens
Is always set aside for the god of the farms.
Blonde Ceres, do you, too, take from my hands a spiky
Wreath, to be hung up by your temple doors;
And let ruddy Priapus be put as a guard in the fruit trees
To scare away the birds with his nasty hook!
Ye, too, of a rich soil once, now of a poor,
The guardians, receive your gifts, my Lares!
Once a slain heifer was pledge for unnumbered cattle;
Now a poor lamb is hostage for my narrow fields.
A lamb shall fall, the country loons around
Shall cry, "Hail, harvests, Lares, and good wine!"
But ye, ye thievish wolves, my scanty flocks,
I pray, respect (great herds give proper prey!)
Here for my herdsman I make the year's lustration,
Appease with sprinkled milk the holy Bounds!
Be with me, Gods! Nor, from a humble board
And clean earth platters, scorn these, my gifts!
(Earthen at first the earliest farmers made
Their dishes, shaping them from easy clay.)

It's not as if I asked for my fathers' portion
That high-heaped harvests brought them long ago!
A small field's yield is enough; it's enough to lie
On my own divan, to stretch on the usual bed.
How I delight, as I lie, in the wind's rage
And at having my dear one safe in my gentle arms;
Or when Auster lets out of the bag his icy torrents
To sleep secure to the tune of the falling rain!
This lot be mine; his, rightly, wealth, who can
Bear the sea's fury and the dreary rains!
Oh, let what gold and what emerald there is go perish
Rather than one girl weep for my going away!
It suits you, Messalla, to battle on sea and on land
So that your gates may be showy with enemy trophies;
A trophy myself, I am bound in the chains of a beauty —
I sit like a doorman in front of her obstinate doors!
Praise isn't *my* passion. Delia, only with you
Let me stay, may the world call me weakling and slack.

And on you let me look, my last hour striking,
And clasp you, dying, with a failing hand.
You will weep for me then
(On my bed that will have to be burned),
You will give me kisses mixed with your sad tears.
You will weep; your bosom is not encased in iron
Nor within your tender heart does one find flint.
And from my burying, no brave boy at all
Nor pure young girl shall tearless go away.
Yet, Delia, spare — oh, fear to vex my spirit —
Your soft young cheeks then and your loose, wild hair.

Meanwhile, the Fates permit it, join we loves!
Too soon comes Death, his head all cowled in dark:
Too soon slack Age, when it will not be decent
To love, or speak soft things with greying hairs!
Now, now, pursue light love, while it's still no shame
To break down doors, and hearty brawls delight us!
In love, I'm both captain and private: trumpets and flags,
Away, bear your gashes to greedier men,
And your gains, too! I, safe on my garnered heap,
Your wealth despise, as I despise your hunger.

G. S. Fraser

I, 3, 1–10; 83–94

You will sail the dancing Aegean, Messalla, without me:
Oh, were I but remembered by you and my band!
I lie sick in Phaeacia, strange faces about me;
Only hold back, dark Death, hold back thy hungry hand.
Hold back, I pray, black Death! No mother mine is here
To clasp my charred bones to her sobbing breast,
No sister to shed warm a ritual tear,
Sweeten my ashes with Assyrian scent,
Shake her locks loose, and mourn before my monument.
No Delia — . She, they say, would never rest
But by some magic held me safe at home
Till she'd consulted every god in Rome . . . .
Now you, be chaste, be true. Never out of sight,
Let your good mother guard you day and night,
Tell you old tales and, setting down the light,
Draw the thin fibres from the distaff's crop,
While near, too long to heavy tasks applied,
The young maid's hands and eyelids slowly drop.
Then let me come, unlooked-for, unespied.

Let me seem sent from heaven to your side.
A sudden cry, no questions, no alarms,
But choked in your long tresses, as you are,
Run, Delia, barefoot, run into my arms,
For this I pray. Be this that purest star,
Radiant above the flush of crimson wings,
That to our loves a new Aurora brings.

George Santayana

I, 5

How well I'd bear the break, my anger spoke it:
Nothing more distant than defiance now!
Now, with a quick and clever boy to whip me,
I'm whirling like a top across the flags!

Brand my wild heart, and hurt it, that hereafter
It love not bragging: tame my bristling words!
And yet be kind. How once we put together
Our heads, made furtive plots, were fond, recall!
Think, when you lay cast down by wretched sickness,
Who was it sprinkled cleansing sulphur round,
And who invoked, lest mournful dreams beset you,
Quiet sleep, thrice scattering the sacred meal?
Cowled, in loose tunic, through the small hours' silence,
Who at the crossroads made the ninefold vow?
This payment mine, another has the profit,
Lucky, who draws the interest on my prayers!
I feigned, poor frantic man (the gods unfriendly!)
I should be happy then, if you were safe.

"Life on the land! Let Delia watch my harvests,
While on the hot, hard floor they thresh the corn,
Or watch the clusters in the full vat heaping
When rapid feet tread out the shiny must;
And learn to count my flocks; and, as a loving
Mistress, to dandle talkative small slaves;
Learn to give grapes as offering for vintage,
Spiked ears in pledge for corn, brimmed bowls for flocks.
She'll manage every man and every matter
And leave no task for me in all my house.
Messalla visits us . . . the sweetest apples
Delia will pluck him from the choicest trees:
Such a great man, she'll be an anxious hostess,
Prepare and serve his meals, a waiting maid!"

Such were my dreams that now the crosswinds carry
To scatter in Armenia's scented vales!

Often with drink I seek to rout these sorrows,
But sorrow turns wine itself to tears,
Often with girls; but on joy's very margin
Love, that recalls my love, abandons me.
The one who leaves me then will talk of witchcraft,
And say — oh, shame! — you know unholy charms!
And yet it is not words that could bewitch me,
But looks, soft arms, and girlish golden hair:
Such to Haemonian Peleus once was Thetis,
The sea-blue Nereid on her bridled fish!
These charms could charm me!
                 Some rich lover wants you,
And his accomplice is some crafty bawd!
May blood defile her food, her mouth be bloody
As it gluts brewage mingled with much gall!
May ghosts around her ply, their fate lamenting,
Yes, and the ghoul-bird skirl upon her roof!
Let her pluck grass from graveyards, dogged by hunger,
Seek pickings from the morsels left by wolves,
Howl through the streets with nothing round her middle,
Run at the crossways from wild yelping dogs!
So be it! A god confirms. Powers guard lovers.
Venus, renounced for no just cause, will rage.
So, Delia, leave this witch's griping lessons
In time, in time . . .
                 In love must riches win?
For your poor man is your most trusty servant,
Your poor man soonest cleaves to your soft side,
Your poor man, in the crush, a sturdy comrade,
Pushes your hips and somehow makes a way,
Your poor man will draw off your muddy leggings
And loose the coverings from your snowy feet.

(I sing in vain! Fine words will not win open
That door, who knocks must have a plenteous hand!)

You, who carry the day, of my fate be wary!
Light Luck turns lightly on her turning wheel.
Not in vain now one waits at the threshold,
Patient, and looks about him, and withdraws,
And seems to pass the house, but soon returning
Will hawk himself at Delia's very doors!

Sly Love has a dodge afoot. Be gay, I beg you,
While you can: your sloop still bobs in a clear sea!

G. S. Fraser

I, 9

If you had already resolved to blight my joyless love,
Why did you swear by the gods your faithfulness,
yet break it behind my back?
O pitiful prey, though perjury hide a while,
In time Vengeance will creep upon you with silent tread.
But spare him, gods above!
It's only fair that beauty may sin, just once, against your will
and go unpunished.

Pursuit of wealth!
For this, a peasant yokes to a handy plow his oxen
and sticks to hard work in the fields.
In hope of wealth, across wind-governed seas,
Pitching vessels steer a course by the fixed stars.
By money my boy has been captured.
O gods, turn all his profits to ashes and streams of water!
Soon he'll pay in full for my hurts:
Dirty labor will sap his beauty, the wind turn shaggy his curls,
The sun will blister his face, shrivel his hair,
Long marches will cripple his delicate feet.

So often I warned him: "Don't smirch your beauty with gold:
It frequently lends disguise to swarms of evils.
If anyone, enslaved to wealth, breaks faith with love,
Venus will use him fiercely, without mercy.
Bring fire to burn my head, instead of his,
And pierce my breast with a sword and cut my back with plaited
scourges.
But nurse no hope, my boy, to hide your plots for sinning:
The god who lets no guilt remain concealed knows all.
That same god lines up bottles before the mum accomplice
To make him babble a full confession in his cups,
And bids the sleep-sealed voice break forth unwillingly
To tell the deeds it would like to keep dark."

All this I used to say.
Now I'm ashamed I sobbed my words
and flung myself at your boyish feet.
Each time you swore you'd never sell your constancy
For any sum of minted gold or pearls,

Though Campania's fields be given as payment
Or Falernum's vineyards where the overseer is Bacchus.
                         With such words
You could have stripped me of belief that stars shine in the sky
                         and lightning spurts a dazzling streak.
And oh you'd even weep:
But blind to deceit, credulous, I'd wipe your streaming cheeks.

What wouldn't I do — if you weren't in love!
                         And with a girl!
I pray she'll take you as a model and turn fickle.
How often, so none should know of your courtship,
I've gone with you as lanternboy in far-spent night,
                         or when you had lost all hope,
Contrived for her to come and wait hidden behind the bolted door.
Then was I lost, wretched me, stupidly sure I was loved:
I might have been more cautious about your snares.
With reason stunned, I even wrote poems to praise you:
                         now I'm ashamed of myself and the Muses.
May Vulcan burn those songs with savage flames
                         and rivers dissolve them in currents of water.
Go, get away from me, boy,
You whose concern is selling beauty
                         and coming home with a handful of fat pickings.

As for you, old man who dare corrupt my boy with presents,
May your wife with endless intrigues flout you,
                         and go scot-free,
And after she's drained her lechers with secret bawdry,
Stretch fagged out beside you with sheets tucked between.
May stains of outsiders be always on your bed,
Your house be always open, free and easy, to rakes.
And none can claim that your lustful sister
Outguzzles her in goblets of wine or wilts more virile mates.
She, they say, keeps up her orgies
Till Lucifer's chariot wheels call forth the dawn.
No one could squander the nighttime better than she
Or better arrange well-varied positions for performance.
But your wife also thoroughly knows her stuff; yet you —
                         utter dunce —
Never see her limbs wriggling with tricks untried on you.
You don't imagine she's dressing her coiffure,
Combing her hair with a fine-toothed comb, for you?
You think such beauty as yours would move her to band her arms with
    gold

l parade the streets decked out in Tyrian frills?
· wants to appear lovely, yeah, but not to you —
ı∪ a youth for whom she'd damn your fortune and family too.
                    And she wouldn't do so from vice:
This elegant girl recoils from filthy, gouty limbs
                    and an old man's hugging.

And yet
          my boy has done it with him.
I do believe he could even roll and rut with a savage beast.
Did you dare sell others the fondling I should have,
                              crazy child,
Give others the kisses that were mine?
Well, you'll weep when another lad holds me captive
And proudly wields the scepter in your old domain.
I'll enjoy your punishment,
And to deserving Venus I'll raise a golden palm-wreath
                              with my story on it:

THIS, O GODDESS, TIBULLUS, SET FREE FROM DECEITFUL LOVE,
DEDICATES TO THEE, AND PRAYS YOU BE DISPOSED TO GRATITUDE.

                              Hubert Creekmore

I, 10

What man first forged the terrifying blade?
O he was steel, to steal away our breath.
Then murders spawned on earth, and wars were made,
and sudden shortcuts blazed the way to death.

Perhaps I blame him wrongly. We have turned
to evil use the sword-edge meant for beasts.
That is gold's curse. No battle-rages burned
when beechwood-cups were all that graced our feasts.
No forts or moats were found when in the shade
the shepherd drowsed among his varied flock.
Then I'd have never known a world dismayed
or felt my wild heart dread the trumpet-shock.

But now I'm dragged to war. Perchance some man
now shakes the spear-point destined for my side.
Rescue me, gods of home. A child, I ran
about your feet, and knew your love with pride.
I do not blush. From some old block you're hacked,
yet, Lares, my forefathers found you good.

Faith went more deep when all fine vestments lacked
and narrow shrines revealed a god of wood.
A grape-bunch made that god's affection wake,
a spiky wreath earned blessings for the home.
The favored man then brought a holy cake,
his little daughter brought the honeycomb.

My gods, beat off the shafts, preserve me sound.
Then to your shrine a hog I'll bid them bear;
and, purely clad, I'll come, my basket bound
with myrtle like the myrtle round my hair.
You'll love me. Let another bravely bleed
and, pleasing Mars, lay waste the battle-line.
While I am drinking, he'll recount each deed
and on the table draw the camps in wine.

Why do we call dark Death with crazy woe?
Crouching, she's coming at a gliding pace.
No cornlands, no pruned vineyards, lie below,
but hell's mad dog, the boatman's ugly face.
There, by the dusky pools, wan crowds are found
with broken holes for eyes and blackened hair.

I praise the man who draws his children round,
and, aging in his cottage, laughs at care.
He guides the sheep, his son the lambs, by day.
His wife prepares the water for his bath.
So let me live, till all my world grows grey
and back I'm wandering down memory's path.

Meanwhile let Peace command our daily tasks.
Peace taught the oxen yoked to plough the field.
Peace trimmed the vines and stored the juice in casks
that sons might drink of wine their fathers sealed.
In Peace the hoe and ploughshare gleam again;
rust gnaws in darkness through the blades of strife;
back from the grove the farmer drives his wain,
half-drunk, beside his children and his wife.
The shield and stake befit the cruel hand,
and gentle Venus flees their touch, distressed.
Come, gracious Peace, with cornsheaves walk the land
And pour us plenty from your shining breast.

Jack Lindsay

II, 1

Hush, all. Our crops, our lands we purify
the way our fathers chose in days gone by.
Come, Bacchus, grapes in bunches on each horn.
Come, Ceres, wreathing round your brow with corn.

The day is holy. Rest, earth. Rest, O plough.
The share's hung up. Now let all labouring cease.
Unstrap the yoke, and at the manger now
let oxen gay with garlands munch in peace.
These hours in happy worship must be spent,
so let no spinner touch the spinning-gear;
and if last night you were incontinent
and fell to Venus, keep away from here.

These powers ask pureness. Clean, your hands, and mine,
to draw the water. Clean, the clothes we wear.
The holy lamb now nears the gleaming shrine,
the files in white with olive in their hair.
We cleanse the farms. We cleanse the farmers too.
Gods of our fathers, drive all ill away.
Preserve our crops from drought and blighting dew,
our slowfoot lambs from pouncing wolves, we pray.

Then the sleek farmer, heaping lumps of wood,
will dream his teeming meadows in the flame,
while the farm's children (pledge the stock is good)
make huts of branches as a festal game.
The liver-markings show my prayers win.
Propitious gods have granted me the sign.
Bring smoked Falernian from the cobwebbed bin.
Undo the Chian jar and pour the wine.
Pour out the day with wine. It's holiday.
Be drunk and shameless, happy as you sprawl.
But don't neglect with every drink to say:
Good luck, Messalla. Say it, one and all.

The country and the country's gods I praise;
for they refined man's acorn-appetite
and bade him take the slabs of wood and raise
a leafy shelter for the rainy night.
They tamed the bulls, and for the waggon made
the curving wheel. Then savage times were past.
Fruits warmed the air and through the garden-shade

the irrigating waters flowed at last.
Gold grapes were pulped to juice by trampling feet
and sober water mixed with wines that cheer.
The fields bore corn, and through the glow of heat
earth's shock of yellow hair was shorn each year.

Across the meadow gads the bee of spring,
anxious to glut with sweetness every cell.
Then first the rustic, tired with furrowing,
struck up a tune to match the season's spell;
and on his oatpipe, full of food, he tried
to hymn the gods that he had made of wood.
It was a rustic, Bacchus, who first dyed
his body red, and danced the best he could.
To ease his hardship offerings were designed.
His special he-goat memorably bled.
And out of flowers the rustic lad first twined
A garland destined for the Lar's old head.

The country feeds the sheep whose glistening wool
Will give a deal of trouble to the girls.
Spin on, you wenches, spin and card and pull.
Your backs are stiff, but still the spindle whirls.
And women weaving in Minerva's toil
Sing as the clay-weights swing in clattering looms.
Desire was first engendered of the soil
Mid cattle and the mares' unsated wombs.
There first he bent his inexperienced bow,
Yet now he never misses once his mark.
These are not beasts he's shooting to lay low,
But girls and lads of courage, in the dark.

O chant the adored god. Call on him aloud
To bless your flock, but whisper your own claim;
Or shout them both. So merry are the crowd,
The Phrygian pipes, that none will hear your name.
O play and laugh. Now night has yoked her teams,
The bawdy stars are dancing in her wake.
Behind them darkens Sleep, and duskier Dreams
Waver and vanish in the stir they make.

Jack Lindsay

II, 4

I see enslavement to a mistress closing on me:
Goodbye now, former freedom of my fathers!

My fate is bondage — dismal, too.

> I'm kept in chains,

And Cupid never loosens the fetters on this woeful victim,
And whether I'm to blame or not, he burns me.

> Help! I'm burning up!

Cruel girl, take his torch away.

If I could just not feel such anguish,
How much I'd rather be a stone on frosty peaks,
Or a crag exposed to violent winds,

> pounded by shipwrecking waves of abysmal seas!

Now day is bitter and shades of night more bitter still,

> for every moment brims with tearful gall.

No use my elegies, nor Apollo, father of song:
Her cupped hand reaches always to solicit cash.

Leave me, Muses, if you can't help a lover.
I give you worship not so I may write an epic,

> or picture the path of the Sun

And how the Moon when her orbit is run,

> with horses turned, drives back.

Through poems I seek a ready sweet access to my mistress.
Go from me, Muses, if poems have no such power.

And yet I must get my hands on some gifts,

> by crime, by murder,

Lest I lie in tears before a locked-up house —
Or must steal the hallowed emblems from holy temples.
But first of all I must profane Venus:
She provokes the crime by giving me a greedy mistress;
Then let her suffer my sacrilegious hands.
A plague on anyone who mines green emeralds

> and dyes white fleece with Tyrian purple.

They breed up spurs to greed in girls,

> as gowns of Cos do too,
> and lustrous pearls from sun-red seas.

All these corrupt them; for these, the door endures a key
And a dog begins to guard the threshold.
But bring a wad of money and chaperones are won,
Locks don't hold and even the dog is silent.
What prize some god, in giving beauty to a greedy girl,
Bestowed upon a bundle of wickedness!
Because of this sobs and bickerings bellow.
In short, this shows why Cupid now wanders about,

> ill spoken of.

But you who slam the door on lovers outbidden by cash —
May blasts and blazes snatch the profits you cherish.
Still worse, may young men watch the fire with glee,
And not one move a hand to pour water on the flames.
And when death pounces on you, be there not a soul
To mourn or offer tributes at your gloomy funeral.
But she who was kind, who was not greedy,
though she live a hundred years,

Shall have friends to weep at the burning pyre.
And some old man, in homage to his love of long ago,
Will place a wreath on her seemly tomb each year
And, as he leaves, will murmur:
"Sleep well, sleep in peace;

And earth lie gently on your bones now free from care."

There's truth in what I urge, but how can truth help me?
I must pursue my darling according to her terms.
In fact, if she tells me to sell my ancestral home —
Well go, household gods, at auction and public sale!
Whatever philtres Circe and Medea listed,
whatever herbs in magic Thessaly grow,

Along with hippomanes that drips from loins of mares in heat
when Venus piques wild herds to rut —

All these my Nemesis may brew with countless other simples,
And if she'll turn on me a gentle smile,
I'll drink them all.

Hubert Creekmore

II, 6

Macer has joined the army, and what's to become of peaceable Cupid?
Can't he go along, like a man pack weapons on his back?
Though far campaigns take the soldier over land or shifting seas,
Can't Cupid march beside him with a spear?
Boy-god, I beg you, brand this rebel who quits your bower.
Still better, call the deserter back to your ranks.
However, if you spare soldiers,
here's one who'll be a soldier too,

Even the kind that fetches his water sloshing in his helmet.
I'm off to enlist, so goodbye Venus, goodbye girls!
The army's for me, I love the bugle calls!

I talk big, yes, but after I've bragged my biggest bombast,
A bolted door shakes out all the spunk from my spruced-up words.
I swore I'd never go near that door again —
swore up and down —

But my feet go right back by themselves.
If possible, heartless Cupid,
I wish I could see your arrows broken, your torch put out!
You torture my wretched heart, make me call dread curses upon myself,
                              and utter blasphemies insanely.
Long since, I'd have ended all in death,
But credulous Hope warmed me to life by saying tomorrow will be
    better.

Hope! She sustains the farmer,
Invests in the plowed furrows the seeds
The field will return at high interest.
She tries catching birds in snares, and fish on rods
                    after the bait has disguised the slender hook.
She comforts even the slave with fetters welded fast
                    on shanks that clank with iron,
For still he sings at his work.
Hope promises me a yielding Nemesis, but I'm refused.
Ah stubborn girl, don't thwart this goddess!

Be kind, I beg by the bones of your sister too early dead,
So the child sleep sweetly under soft-lying earth.
I hold her sacred, and I'll bring gifts to her sepulchre,
                    and wreaths all dripping with my tears.
I'll rush to her tomb and crouch there suppliant
                    and moan my fate with her mute ashes.
She won't allow her protégé to weep for you forever.
As if in her own words, I protest your backwardness,
Lest the neglected spirit send you nightmares,
And in your sleep your lamented sister loom beside the bed,
Looking as she did when, after falling headlong from the high window,
She went, blood-covered, to the rivers deep in Hades.

But I must hush, or I'll revive my girl's keen grief:
I'm not worth making her weep a single time.
It isn't right for her to spoil her speaking eyes with tears.

That bawd!   She's ruining us both!
                              My girl is good in herself.
That procuress, Phryne, is killing poor me,
      sneaking in and out with love-notes hidden in her breast.
Too many times, though I can recognize the sweet voice
                    through the hostile door,
The hag tells me she's not at home.
And when the night's been promised me, she brings a message —

My girl is sickly, it seems, or scared of some threat.
And I die from anguish, my desperate brain
Envisions someone clasping my darling close
                 and every position he holds her in.
Then I curse you, she-pimp, curse you!
If any tiniest part of my prayers affects the gods,
              you'll live with trouble to spare.

                               Hubert Creekmore

Domitius Marsus

◖ This somewhat shadowy contemporary of Tibullus is known only for this epigram on the deaths of Vergil and Tibullus and for a poem against the poetaster Bavius. He is mentioned by Martial as among the epigrammatists and by Suetonius, who says he agreed with Horace that Orbilius, Horace's teacher, was fond of flogging. Lord Byron, in his *Hours of Idleness,* has also translated the epigram:

> He who sublime in epic numbers roll'd,
>   And he who struck the softer lyre of love,
> By Death's unequal hand alike controll'd,
>   Fit comrades in Elysian regions move!

It is perhaps unnecessary to point out that Mr. Creekmore's version is the more accurate of the two. ◗

ON THE DEATH OF TIBULLUS

You, too, Tibullus, has unscrupulous Death sent
    Toward Elysium's fields, as Vergil's youthful partner,
And none remain lamenting love in gentle elegies,
    None singing splendid wars in heroic meter.

Hubert Creekmore

Sulpicia and Tibullus

❴ Hubert Creekmore's prefatory note to his privately printed translation of Sulpicia's poems (*No Harm to Lovers,* Blue Ridge Mountain Press, Parsippany, New Jersey, 1950) describes her and her work as follows: "Also present in Messalla's household was Sulpicia, the daughter of Servius Sulpicius and, most likely, Messalla's sister Valeria. Servius is thought to have been dead at this time, so that Messalla had become Sulpicia's guardian. The girl was of an ancient, aristocratic family, was said to have been beautiful, and was certainly adept at keeping pace with the intellectual, rather unconventional company about her. Though it may seem natural, from her association with so many poets, that she should begin to write poetry, it is strange that only six brief and very personal poems have come down to us — all concerned with the difficulties of her love for the young man Cerinthus — and that she never, so far as we know, wrote any more poetry. Except for a few fragments by other ladies, these six poems make up the extant body of classical Latin poetry by women."
❴ The exact contribution of Tibullus (see above, page 218) to the elegies of the fourth book, where Sulpicia's poems appear, is still obscure. It may even have been another person who wrote the poems which encourage her in her distress. Mr. Creekmore and I incline to the belief that it was Tibullus himself, her confidant and the intimate friend of Messalla. Mr. Creekmore has re-arranged the poems in a more reasonable order on the basis of the logic of their emotions (to risk a paradox) than that of the Latin texts. ❵

TIBULLUS IV, 2

The Matronalia, March 1

For you Sulpicia is decked, mighty Mars, on your festal day.
Come down from heaven and see for yourself, if you're wise.
Venus will forgive you. But, you lout, be careful not
to let your armor crash shamefully while you marvel.
　　When prickly Love would sting the gods,
　　he lights twin torches from her eyes.
Whatever she does, wherever she sets a footstep,
invisible Grace trails to see that all is correct.
If she shakes out her hair, then touseled hair is proper;
if she binds it up, she is worshipped for brushed braids.

Fevers, if she choose to walk in a Tyrian mantle —
fevers, if in a mist of snowy clothes she comes.
On eternal Olympus, fertile Vertumnus, like her,
has a thousand costumes and wears them all with style.

She alone of maidens merits soft Tyrian wool
    double-dyed in precious juices;
should have what the rich Arab farmer of fragrant soil
    reaps from his musky fields,
and all the pearls the swarthy Indian gathers from
    the crimson shores by waters of dawn.

Sing, Pierides, of her on this holiday Kalends;
Phoebus, sing, strutting your tortoise-fashioned lyre.
This observance is hers for many years over and over.
    No girl is more worthy of your band.

SULPICIA IV, 8

To Cerinthus

My hateful birthday is coming, and dismally I must spend it
    in the disgusting country, without Cerinthus.
What's more delightful than town? Are farmhouse or frigid stream
    in Arretium's fields environs fit for a girl?
(Messalla, you're too solicitous of me; relax:
    excursions, uncle, sometimes aren't exactly convenient.
You may drag me off, but here I leave my heart and soul,
    though you deny me them for my disposal.)

SULPICIA IV, 9

Later, to Cerinthus

That gloomy trip is lifted off your sweetheart's mind:
    did you know? Now she may have her birthday in Rome.
So let's all celebrate this day: it comes, a chance,
    (perhaps a bit surprising now) for you.

TIBULLUS IV, 6

Intercession, on Sulpicia's birthday, to her Guardian Spirit

Accept the holy mounds of incense, Juno of her birth,
from the tender hands of this accomplished girl.

To you she dedicates today — most joyously attired
to stand, a cynosure, before your altar.
She claims, O goddess, that you occasion this adornment,
but secretly she'd also like to please a certain someone.

So Heavenly One, be kind. Let no one sunder these lovers,
but link her with the youth in mutual fetters.
You would do well to join them so: for him no girl
more worthy to serve his love, for her no man.
Let prying chaperons not catch their love encounters;
let Love provide them with a thousand ways of bafflement.
Nod consent, and come in your light-filled purple robes:
three offerings, holy goddess, were made you of wine and cake.

The zealous mother orders her daughter's plea: but she,
undaunted, prays otherwise within her silent heart.
    She burns as the quick flames burn on the altar,
nor, though it were granted, would she wish to be cured.

Indulge them, Juno, so that in the coming year, their love,
now long enduring, may through their prayers remain the same.

Sulpicia IV, 11

To Cerinthus

Have you no tender thoughts, Cerinthus, for your sweetheart
    now when fever shivers my feeble body?
Ah, I'd never want to conquer bleak disease
    unless I believed that you desired it too.
What good for me to triumph over illness, if you
    can suffer, with indifferent heart, my torments?

Tibullus IV, 4

Plea and counsel

Come exorcise the illness of this lovely girl,
come down here, Phoebus, sporting uncropped hair.
    Believe me, and hurry; you'll never regret
applying to her beauty the medicine of your hands.
See that no blight invade her feeble limbs,
no morbid color blotch her pallid flesh.

Let rapid rivers discharge in the sea
  that sickness and corruption we dread.
Come, holy one, and bring whatever simples
or incantations relieve the ailing body.
Don't plague the boy who, fearing his girl's death,
    pledges countless vows to save her.
He prays, yes; but then, because she languishes,
he hurls rough words against the eternal gods.

Cast out your fear, Cerinthus; God does no harm to lovers.
Just love her always, and your girl is safe.
No need to weep; tears will be more in keeping
when she starts to doubt you. Now she's all your own;
no one but you fulfills her guileless thoughts
though a credulous group in vain awaits her glance.

Phoebus, give them your favor. You'll garner lofty praise
    for restoring two lives by saving one.
Then famous, you'll rejoice when the grateful pair
eagerly vie to pay their debt to your holy altar.
And the righteous host of gods will call you fortunate
    and covet, each for himself, your arts.

SULPICIA IV, 12

To Cerinthus

May I be, dear love, no more a caution so glowing
    as I feel I was a few days ago,
if I, in all my youth, have done a foolish thing
    for which I might confess to more repentance
than departing from you, left alone last night,
    because I yearned to cover my burning love.

TIBULLUS IV, 5

He speaks for the girl, on Cerinthus' birthday

This day, Cerinthus, which gave you to the earth for me,
to me shall ever be sacred and festival.
From birth you enthrall all maids in novel bonds,
the Fates proclaimed, and over them hold proud dominion.
Foremost I burn for you, yet joy in burning,

Cerinthus, if equal flame, sprung from mine,
leaps in you. Through your Patron Spirit, your eyes
and sweetest stolen ardors, I pray your love match mine.

Kind Spirit, please — here's incense — grant my prayer:
that when he thinks of me, he flush with thrilling warmth.
But should he now be sighing for some other,
O holy one, forsake the faithless altar of his hearth.

And Venus, be not unjust: make both of us your slaves
in equal bondage, or strike my chains away.
But rather let us each contain the other
with a mighty chain that no hereafter can dissolve.

His longings mirror mine, though hid within
for shame to speak his prayer-words out.
Yet, Spirit of His Birth, a god, you know all minds,
so promise. What matter if he plead aloud or mute?

SULPICIA IV, 10

To Cerinthus

I thank you indeed that, sure of me, you assume such license
lest, a dolt, I tumble suddenly into sin.
Pursuit of a toga, a strumpet packing her basket of wool,
may please you more than Sulpicia, daughter of Servius:
but some are troubled about us, in much concern lest I
should yield my place to some couch of vulgar love.

TIBULLUS IV, 3

Cerinthus forgiven; once more
Tibullus speaks for the girl

Spare my sweetheart, whether in grass-sweet meadow,
boar, or thickets of darkling mountains;
don't whet your cruel tusks defensively.
Let Love — his guardian, please — keep him safe for me.
For still the Delian Lady lures with love of hunting.
If only the forests would shrivel! the race of hounds expire!
What mania — what reason? — hurting those tender hands
to lock a cordon round the dense slopes —

or delight to probe the coverts of savage game
    and scratch white shins on bramble-thorns?

Yet, if I may range with you, Cerinthus,
I myself will pack the intricate nets across the scarps,
    will trail the spoor of darting deer,
unleash the iron collar of the leaping hound.
Then I'd like the woods, my darling, if in
the very snares, with love you pierced me as your quarry.
The boar before the trap will leave unhurt
to keep from breaking our rapture of vehement love.

But now, without me let there be no love. By Diana's canon,
innocent boy, touch the nets with innocent hands.
May any slithering female who decoys my love
chance among raging beasts and be slit to ribbons.

So yield your zeal for hunting to your elders
and run straight back into my encompassing heart.

SULPICIA IV, 7

To Cerinthus

At last comes such a love that gossip that I conceal it
    would be more shame than to some friend reveal it.
The Cytherean, persuaded by my poetry's charms,
    has brought him here and placed him in my arms:
Venus kept her promise. Let those chatter of
    my joy who never found their own in love.
I'd wish, in trusting words to letters, never to need
    them sealed so none before my love might read;
I'm glad of my guilt; and loathe, for Rumor, to arrange
    my air. Let's tell that it happened — a fair exchange.

TIBULLUS II, 2

He need speak no longer in behalf of Sulpicia and Cerinthus
(but if he did speak of them, this is what he said)

EPILOGUE AS EPITHALAMIUM

Let's speak of good omens only: The Spirit of Birth draws near
    The altar: all men or women here, be silent.

Let fire consume the holy incense, burn the perfume
   The languid Arab sends from his opulent country.
Let the Genius, whose sacred hair our graceful garlands
   Must adorn, approach and see his oblations.
Pure spikenard must trickle down his brow; with holy
   Cakes he must be stuffed, with neat wine sotted:
So may he then bestow, Cornutus, what you ask.
   Now quickly — why do you balk? He grants it — ask him!
I guess you'll wish your wife's love always loyal: by now
   The gods, I fancy, know your prayer by heart.
You'd never choose instead the world-wide spreading fields
   Which sturdy farmers plough with mighty oxen,
Nor all the pearls that generate for favored India
   Where the tides of the Eastern Sea run red.
Your wish comes true: look — on murmuring wings Love flies
   To you, brings golden cords about your marriage,
Bonds that ever will endure, though sluggish age
   Spread wrinkles on your cheeks or gray your heads.
Let it thus befall, Birth-Spirit, bring them children,
   And new broods bouncing around ancestral feet.

                             Hubert Creekmore

Sulpicia ll

⟮ The second Roman poetess of this name is assigned either to the first or to the fourth century A.D. Her satire refers to the age of Domitian (A.D. 81–96), a gloomy tyrant who struck terror into the hearts of writers and thinkers in his time. ⟯

THE SATIRE, 20–34

Look back. Two powers have raised Rome's lofty head:
Valor in war, Wisdom in peace, were these.
But valor, trained at home, soon crossed the seas;
Sicily fell; down Carthage towers were hurled;
The other empires crashed. Rome ruled the world.

Then, as a victor in the Stadium,
Alone, undaunted, feels his flesh succumb —
So Rome, when back she stood to face her pains,
Now faltered, bridling peace with lengthy reins.

She re-created Grecian law and thought
At home. The empire which her arms had bought,
She swayed with foresight and redeeming grace;
And thus, and only thus, she kept her place.
Else vainly would the Father's voice have spoken:
"I give her empire that will last unbroken."

Jack Lindsay

Carmina Epigraphica

(Epitaphs from the *Anthologia Latina*)

❡ The Latin Anthology from which these poems are taken is a collection of 1,858 complete pieces and fragments from epigraphic sources exclusively, in various meters, saturnians, senarii, hexameters, and elegiacs. Most of them are printed in the great *Corpus Inscriptionum Latinarum;* very few can be dated accurately, but they range from the third century B.C. to the second century A.D. They are written by humble people for their dead and are inscribed upon tombstones; some were composed for the bereaved by more professional writers, although few of the authors are known. There is a simple pathos in many of them all the more touching for their lack of careful polish. They represent a large body of poetry which reflects the education and tastes of the average Romans; they show a higher taste and sense of propriety than most modern funereal verse and should be more carefully studied than they have been. So far as I know, none have been translated by anyone except Mr. Lucas. ❡

1

Short is my say, O stranger. Stay and read.
Not fair this tomb, but fair was she it holds.
By her name her parents called her Claudia.
Her wedded lord she loved with all her heart.
She bore two sons, and one of them she left
On earth, the other in the earth she laid.
Her speech was pleasing and her bearing gracious.
She kept house: span her wool. I have said. Farewell.

(Rome, 2d cent. B.C.)

2

Here lies a scoffer, who had a good life and made a good end.

3

AN OLD GENTLEMAN OF SEVENTY-SEVEN

Happy on earth he was — the happiest
That ever lived — good, simple, truly blest.

He never grieved, his heart was always high,
He never cried for death as old men cry,
He was afraid of death and thought he'd never die.

(Ostia, 3d cent. B.C.)

4

A MATRON

Earth, lightly lie upon my *middle* age.

5

The rich man builds a house, but the wise a tomb.
For that is but our lodging; this our home.
There for a while we sojourn; here abide.

6

Mourn not my loss; tears change not destiny.
Thus is man's life; as from the lemon-tree
The ripe fruit falls or green is gathered.

(Aix in Provence: 2d cent. A.D.)

7

I was not, I was; I am not, I would not be.

8

I have escaped, O lingering age, your shame.

9

Women and wine and baths bring life's decline.
Yet what *is* life but women, baths, and wine?

(Rome)

10

Now only what I ate and drank is mine.

11

I bid my heirs pour wine even on my dust; let my soul's butterfly be drunken in her flight, my bones be so thickly overgrown with grass and flower, that whoso reads this stone which bears my name, may say: "Whatever the devouring flame has spared, whatever turns to ashes when the body burns, here slumbers well."

(Near Cordoba, Spain: in prose)

12

Lovely as is the rose to men, when first it flowers in spring,
So to their eyes that saw me, I too was a lovely thing.

(Age of Augustus: Via Aurelia)

13

Grieve not, mamma, it was to be.

14

AGATHE, AGED FIVE

All my life I played, and all were fond of me,
   For, know, I had a boy's look, not a girl's —
Only my parents knew their Agathe —
   Close-cut before, behind streamed my red curls.
O feasters all, drink to my name tonight
And say "Upon her may the earth be light!"

(Rome)

F. L. Lucas

Persius

《 Aulus Persius Flaccus (A.D. 34–62) was a modest, retiring, studious young man probably reared by maiden aunts. He died at 28 after composing six brief satires, a total of 650 lines, and a short choliambic poem. They are full of especially abrupt transitions, digressions, curious indirection, and almost private reference; they require close study. Their subjects include the decline of Roman literary taste, prayer, moral lassitude and dangerous desires, political unfitness (Alcibiades may equal Nero in the fourth satire), the Stoic paradox that all men except the true Stoic are slaves, and the spending of one's money for the right things. Persius more than any other Roman writer resembles those poets of our time who have been accused of talking to themselves; he is well worth overhearing. 》

CHOLIAMBS

I've wet no lip in the Nag's spring
And dreamed no dream, that I can bring
To mind, on doublehead Parnassus
To issue forth in this degree,
A poet suddenly.

Wan Pirene and Helicon's girls
I leave to those whose marble curls
The obsequious ivy wreath caresses.
Half Philistine, to the bards' devotions
I bring my own notions.

Who crammed the parrot's human screech
And taught magpies the trial of speech?
Doctor of arts, sponsor of wit,
The belly will contrive pursuit
Of tongues that should be mute.

But if another prospect shines
Of slippery coin to pay their lines,
Our poetess-magpies and poet-
Ravens you'd think were chanting themes
In Pegasean streams.

Robert A. Brooks

SATIRE I

Alas, man's care, and O the vacuity
In things! "Who'll read that?" Asking me? Why, no one.
"No one?" We two aside, being nobody.
"A wretched shame." Why? that Polydamas
And the Trojan Dames should favor Labeo,
Not me? Nonsense.
            Whatever muddy Rome
Makes light of, still don't engage yourself to go
Chastening the lying tongue that marks its scale,
Nor search outside yourself. For who in Rome
Is not — if I might — but should speak, having viewed   10
The grey years come on us, our living stale,
Whatever we changed toys for, and pursued,
Learned as uncles — then will you give me leave?
No? What to do? but bray; my guts are rude.

We write shut up like sages, verse or prose,
Some spacious thing, to exercise the soul
And stretch the lungs. Now for the public pose;
Coiffure, clean toga with the birthday stone
(Sardonychal splendor): up to the speaker's station:
Recite: the throat is syrupy: the eyes   20
Languish duly, hinting at copulation.
Then see, in no strict mode or quiet tone,
Our high patricians palpitate, as song
Enters their loins trilling, to scrape the bone.
(Old pimp, collecting scraps for others' ears,
Till, stripped, you beg them to be left alone.)

"Why learn, unless the germinal, the wild fig-tree
Once inborn, splits the heart's case to appear?"
Look at your pallor and old age. Lord, must it be
Nothing at all for you to know, unless   30
Another comes to know your knowingness?

"But think of fame: to draw the indication
Of tongues and fingers pointing, to provide
Legions of schoolboys with their recitation,
Is it all nothing?"
            Discovered, dining well
And well drunk, the sons of Romulus. They seek
What tales celestial poesy has to tell.
Enter one appareled in a violet cape,

Droning some mouldy morsel through his nose;
All Phyllises, Hypsipyles, the bards'   40
Drippings he redistills, and shuffles woes
Over his lisping palate.
                    Our heroes cheer.
The poet's dust receives the accolade;
The headstone presses lighter on his bones.
The banqueters applaud; now from the shade,
Now from the mound and beatific ash
Let violets spring. "Mocking," you say, "denotes
A loftiness in the nose. Will any man deny
Wanting the people's well-deserved votes,
His words entrusted to archival store,   50
Encedared poems which fear no second use
As haddock-wrappings or excelsior?"

Opponent, O whoever you may be
I've made to contradict, by no means, when
I write, if something turns out decently,
Do I fear praise; my bowels are not of bone.
But the end and term of right I will refuse
To be your "excellent" and "nicely done."
Shake out this "nicely"; what do you find
That's not inside? Look, Attius' Iliad   60
Blind drunk on hellebore, see, elegy
Dictated belching by some Aenead,
And at the bottom, all that's written from
The citron couches of celebrity.
You serve hot tripe, donate an ancient coat
To your gooseflesh retainer, and "Honesty,
Please, honesty" you ask; "say what you think
Of me." How can he? Let me speak his piece.
You and your poetic trifles, baldhead,
Carrying that paunch in front, a yard of grease —   70
O Janus, whom no stork's bill nips behind,
Nor fingers flapping like pale donkeys' ears,
Nor tongues as long as thirsty hounds unwind —
But you, patrician blood, whom god ordains
To live with blind backsides, must turn around
To find what mockery the rear sustains.

What's the general word? "What but our song
At last flows in soft lines, joined smooth enough
To slip the searching nail? He sights along
His verse as one might snap the ruddled line   80

One-eyed. Whether the given theme's decay
Of morals, railing on vice, or feasts of kings,
His Muse gives greatness to her protégé."
See now, we teachers have them introduce
Great souls of sentiment, when all their art
Has been Greek miniatures, not workmanlike
Enough to describe trees in a grove, impart
Fat countrysides, hearths, marketbaskets, pigs,
Straw smoking at the feasts —
                      yet here's the birth
Of heroes; Remus, and Cincinnatus came   90
Shining his plow-teeth in the furrowed earth.
Fumbling, his wife dresses the magistrate;
Oxen are audience; the lictor bears
The plowshare home again. "O wondrous poet!
But is there anyone still left who cares
For varicose Accius, mouthing in his beard,
Pacuvius and his warty heroine,
'Her woesome heart bolstered on bitter grief'?"
Seeing blind fathers pour this discipline
Upon their boys, then do you ask whence came   100
That goulash style upon the lips of all,
That viciousness wherein our shaven sprouts
Caper for pleasure in the lecture-halls?

Not yet ashamed? A grey head comes to grief,
And still you can't defend him, without the itch
To hear applause. Call Pedius a thief;
What's his reply? He balances the writ
In shaved antitheses, displays the scale
Of learned tropes, is praised: "Done beautifully."
Beautiful? Ah, Romulus, you twitch your tail.   110
Shall I wag too? And when the shipwrecked beggar
Sings his ballade, shall I produce a tip?
Singing too, when from your shoulder hangs
Yourself, painted astride the broken ship?
Truth that's not sweated up at night he'll plead
Who'll weigh me with the burden of his need.

"But grace and craftsmanship have settled in
Our raw verses. Look at our sentence-ends:
'Berecyntian Attis,' and this: 'The dolphin
Who clave the azure Nereus,' so again: 120
'We have taken a rib from the long Apennines.'
'Arms and the man . . . ?' All foam and corky growth,

Dead branches on a great tree, bark-swollen lines."
What then for reading soft and dissolutely?
"They filled with Bacchanal crescendoes the wild horn,
The Bassarid ready to carry away the torn
Proud steer-head, Maenad leopard-mount with ivy rein
Evoe redoubled cries, while echo turns refrain."
Would this happen, with one paternal trace
Of testicles among us? This eunuch stuff   130
Swells with the earliest spittle to the lips;
Maenad and Attis, floating on the scum,
Hammer no desks, and gnaw no fingertips.

"What need is there to rasp the tender ear
With biting truth? Beware lest great thresholds
Grow chill toward you; from noble noses hear
The watchdog snarl." Naturally, from now
All's bright to my eyes. I'll not hesitate.
Hurray for everyone, splendid for all,
You're wonderful — do you approve the estimate?   140
"No nuisances permitted here" you say;
Paint up two snakes; "A holy place, boys, go
Outside to urinate." I'm on my way.
Lucilius slashed this town, and well you know
Still, Lupus, Mucius, what broke his wisdom tooth.
Sly Horace, while his friend laughs, pricks each pose
In turn, and plays around the unlocked heart,
Dangling the people on one upturned nose.
May I not let it out? Not secretly?
Not whispered in a ditch? Nowhere? Yet here's   150
My book to spade it in. O I have seen,
And I have seen — *they all have asses' ears.*
This secret joke, this nothing, makes me glad;
I won't barter it for any Iliad.

Scorched by Cratinus' breath, when you grow pale
With Eupolis' anger, with Aristophanes,
Listen for notes refined from a higher scale.
Whose ear is purged so, may I satisfy,
Not one transported with cheap levity
On seeing Greek shoes, who manages to cry   160
"Blind" in the blind man's face, whose vanity
Enfolds himself, the smasher of short measure,
Puffed with provincial honors, in Arretium;
Nor yet the astute one, who mocks for pleasure
All numbers, cones, the philosophic sum

Traced in the sand; uproariously he's cheered
If some whore of early evening plucks the beard
Out of the preacher's face.
                    To these I'd show
Play programs before lunch, then Callirhoe.

                                        Robert A. Brooks

SATIRE III

I. DIALOGUE

"Still at it? Morning stares between the shutters,
Swelling the thin cracks with light. While you snore
The froth out of that heady Falernian,
Five shadows circle on the creviced floor.
Is this your life, scholar? Some hours now
'The Dogstar's crazy sun' has baked the harvest —
'Lo, rests the herd beneath the spreading bough'."
A friend speaks.
                    "What's that? What? Come here, quick,
Here, where's that boy?" pumps up the crystal bile;
"My head!" bleats like the Arcadian pastureland.   10
Forthwith the book, the parchment, hued and slick,
The jointed reed, the sheets run to his hand.
And then we agonize: the ink's too thick, and clots;
More water; but that pales the sepia;
The reed must drip a double tale of blots.

"Poor fool, and every day more destitute,
Have we come so far? Now why not bawl for mush
Like a king's son, or a pigeon's, and dispute,
With such tantrum talents, your nurse's lullaby?"
"With this pen can I work?"
                                "Who takes that alibi,   20
That byway twittering? The game's on you.
When your wits drain, you are despised. Flaws speak;
Fresh-made jars, rung bitterly, renew
That malice in their answer. Your quality
Is clay still, soft and spongy. Run now, now;
Be fashioned on the wheel's infinity.

Your father left a decent crop, a farm,
The heirlooms unattached; is it enough
To keep the cult utensils safe from harm?

Or would you split your lungs more properly   30
Because you burgeon on the Tuscan stem,
Parade before the censor? O thousandth sprout! O panoply!
Medals for the mob. Beneath them, on the hide
Is where I know you; shamelessly enough,
Like Natta's, your wardrobe of virtue's come untied.
But Natta, comatose in sin — fat grows to stuff
The nerve's perception — innocent of shame,
Conceives no loss, and lies so deep-
Drowned, his breath will not boil up again
To our sea-surface. No, that comes too cheap.   40

Great father of the gods, may our tyrants' rage,
When lust, venom's color, dreadfully propels
Ability, incur no other punishment:
Let them perceive the Good, and, looking, rot
At her farewell. Did that brassy choir lament
Louder inside the Bull of Sicily,
Or the sword, hung between the gilded beams
And purpled throats below, distil more agony
Than 'Going, I am going headlong' spoken low
And inward, paling the heart alone, for cause   50
The woman in his bed can never know?

I was childish too; I remember the old trick
Of blearing my eyes with oil, if I was sick
Of spouting words for Cato's benefit —
'Advice on Suicide' — and getting praised
For such by Teacher, who was a nit-wit,
While Father summoned company and sat
And sweated joy to hear.
                              My prayers would call
Then, reasonably enough, for infinite riches
Rolled on the bones, asked auguries of crapping out   60
With snake-eyes, excellence in penny-pitches,
And skill at whipping tops, to beat them all.

But you've learned more; for habit's sagging line
Was straightened in that classroom, where the scrawl
Of trousered Medes is Wisdom's countersign,
The Painted Porch. The tonsured scholar's night,
Metaphysic vigil on beans and barley stew,
Was yours as well; the Samian's parable, Y
Displaying its two forks, revealed to you
The stony climb which rises to the Right.   70

Still at it, slack and sprung. Your snoring head
Rocks, and unravels both its cheeks widespread
To belch out yesterday. Have you a sight,
A bow at stretch? Or do you wander after crows,
Clod-marksman, flinging shards of broken clay,
And never see the path your foot follows,
Making your life extempore, from Time's decay?"

II. DIATRIBE

You'll see them cry for hellebore in vain
When dropsy swells the skin; turn, meet the plague
Before it seizes you, and so retain   80
The mountainous fees you'd promise Craterus.
Learn, fools, and understand the world's design,
What it is we are, what life is made for us,
What order, where and why the supple swerve
Around the mark, what means for wealth, and ends,
Those uses harshly minted in the coin,
What beneficence you owe to nearest friends
And nation, what person have you in God's plan?
Where is your province in the state of man?

Learn, don't envy him, whose earthen vials   90
Rot in his well-stocked warehouse, service-fees
From fat Italian farmers, pepper-piles
And ham-memorials of Marsian clients,
Or undecanted wealth of anchovies.

Here someone smelling like a goat (his class,
Centurions) will say, "My head's enough for me.
I don't take after your Arcesilas
And wretched Solons, crooked heads and looks
Stuck to the ground, gnawing their secrecies,
Mumbled or raving mute, whose mouths grow hooks   100
To hang word-balances, who ponder dreams
Of ancient invalids: 'In all creation
Nothing of nothing born, nothing to nothing
Can be resolved.' Is this your dissipation?
Should a man forsake his dinner, in this cause?"
At this the people laugh, the brawny youth
Twitches its nose with duplicate guffaws.

"O doctor, look me over, there's a wheeze
And a bad taste in my mouth. I think I've got

A palpitation too . . . Look at it, please." 110
Rest is prescribed, but when three nights have seen
The blood run quiet, he begs a flask of wine
(A moderate thirst, the blandest Sorrentine)
And goes out to the baths. "Well, friend, you're pale."
"It's nothing." "Something, nothing, take care of it.
Your skin's like mud, and bloated . . ." "You look worse.
If you're to be my keeper, you can quit
Right now. I buried him some while ago.
How come you're left?" "Go ahead, I'm through."
Blown with his feast, a whited paunch, with slow 120
Miasmas oozing sulphurously from
His guts, he bathes.
 A shudder secretly
Slips in among the cups and shakes them, hot
Out of his hands. Teeth rattle nakedly,
The morsels fall anointed from his lips.
Hence horns and tapers, and our dear defunct,
Laid high at last and restful on his pall,
Mud-smeared with perfumes, stretches toward the door
Stiff heels. A Roman from today, his slave
Caps head with freedom, hoists him to the grave. 130
"Fool, take my temperature, and feel my heart;
No fever there. Feel hands and feet; no chill."
Envisage cash, then, or the tenderest
Smile from the pretty girl next door, and will
Your heart dance soberly? Serve food congealed,
Tough beans, or flour culled from the vulgar mill;
Then try your taste. The tongue secretes
An ulcerous spot, putrescent and refined,
Nobly allergic to plebeian beets.

You tremble, when fear's frost has shivered down 140
The gooseflesh on your limbs. When fires are lit
Then your blood bubbles, your eyes are sparks of rage.
You say and do such things as would befit
A madman: mad Orestes will swear to that.

 Robert A. Brooks

SATIRE VI

Has winter brought you to the Sabine fire,
Bassus, and brought to life your somber chords,
A manly music moving on the lyre?
Craftsman of the Roman lute, of ancient words,

Still young in moving laughter, you will come
Tuning to old age with an honest thumb.

The Riviera warms my solstice days;
My own sea lies in winter quarters, trenched,
Under the mountain wall, with a thousand bays.
"The gulf of Luna, Romans, mark it well";   10
So Ennius' heart spoke, once he'd popped his ear
Awake from being Homer, Quintus again
After that Pythagorean bird.
                              And here
I'm careless of the mob, and all the menace
Of the sickly southern wind for man and beast,
Careless too if my neighbor's corner field
Is fatter than my own. Let them be increased,
Even the baser born. I will not shrink
To hooped senility or dine without sauce
Or peer at some stale vintage-mark across   20
My nose, to damn the wine before I drink.
Someone will disagree. Now, horoscope,
Bring forth the twins: one star and opposite mien.
Birthdays alone, one hires a salad bowl
And dressing, to anoint the naked bean.
The other chap, munching through his broad estate,
Approves himself sound-toothed and large of soul.
I shall use and use, though not with elegant airs
Enough to serve *filet de sole bonne femme*
For all my freedmen, or know the sex of fieldfares   30
By their savor. This is the Right, when life is clear
Up to the harvest and your granary.
Grind out and harrow: another crop is in the ear.

But conscience speaks: a reeling hull is struck
Upon the Bruttian rocks; your wretched friend
Has laid up all his treasure and his luck
Dumbfounded in the deep Ionian sea.
He is flung upon the shore, and with him blown
The great gods of the quarterdeck; the gulls
Come down to roost along the timbered bone.   40
Break up the living turf in acrefuls;
Enlarge his barrenness, lest he wander green
And ghostly painted in a shipwreck scene.

But your heir will rise in wrath, to slash
His outlay for the funeral feast. You've clipped

His patrimony; now he'll yield your ash
Unscented to the urn, oblivious
If all the perfumes fade, if the cassia spoils
In sinful union with polluted oils.
"Will you get off scot-free, diminishing   50
The sum of my estate? Bestius can wring
The Greek philosophers: 'And so it goes.
Once our country wit, untainted with the seas,
Has come to market with pepper and mangoes
Our mowers spoil their porridges with grease.'
Fear this beyond the shade."

                  Now you, whoever
My heir may chance to be, come down
A little further from the mob. Dear fellow,
Hadn't you heard? Caesar has sent the crown
Of victory abroad, for his majestic   60
Carnage among the tribesmen. Now is the time
To sweep dead ashes from your altars; now
Comes on the whole triumphal pantomime
(Staged by our loving Empress): trophies on
The temple doors, the battle-dress of kings,
Barbaric furs, war-chariots, the monstrous Rhine.
To the gods and Caesar, therefore, for all such things
Magnificently achieved, I offer a hundred
Bouts of gladiators. Who has the face
To tell me no? The worse for you. Come, oil   70
And ravioli free, for all the populace;
Do you forbid it? Speak up, loud and clear.
"Oh no," you say; "the farm is worn bone-bare."

So. My paternal aunts may all be dead,
No cousins, not once or twice removed, childless
My mother's sister, no survivors bred
From grandma's line; I still can go
Up to Bovillae, on the Beggar's Row,
There to appoint — Manius my legatee.
A clod? A child of earth? Inquire of me   80
My ancestor four generations back,
But give me a little time, I'll find his name.
His father then? And his? At last we come
To a son of earth, and Manius, of the same
Accredited lineage, stands forth my great-
Great-great-great uncle.

                How is your claim
Nearer than his? Are you the runner, to tear

The torch from my hand, before the course is done?
I am your Mercury, I come to you here
A god, as he is painted. Will you decline?   90
Will you be happy with remainders? "Something
Is short from the sum." The shortage is for me.
Your count is whole, whatever it may be.
Never ask what happened to the pile
That Tadius once left me; don't moralize:
"Lay up your capital. Assume your style
Of life from dividends. Leave the rest to me."
The rest?
Now oil, now salad oil luxuriously
Imbrue upon my cabbages. Shall I   100
Cook up hog-jowls to celebrate my day,
With nettles, smoke, and dirt for seasoning,
So that your grandson, bloated on paté,
Once his fastidious gland starts hiccuping,
May discharge in a patrician womb? Shall I
Shrink to a spider's thread and let him feast
Till his belly shakes, to counterfeit a priest?

*   *   *

[Sell your soul for profit, trade cunningly,
Shake out the pockets of the teeming world,
Yield to no other in chicanery,   110
Prod fat barbarians on the auction block,
Double your goods. "I've done it. Three, fourfold,
Ten return into my pouch. Set me a bound."
Chrysippus, it's the answer to your mound.]

Robert A. Brooks

Lucan

❨ Marcus Annaeus Lucanus, born A.D. 39 at Cordoba, Spain, and forced by Nero to commit suicide in A.D. 65, wrote much, but all we have is the historical epic on the civil war between Caesar and Pompey. It is a triumph of poetical rhetoric, full of gory fighting, Stoic heroism, tragic conversations, gloomy apostrophes, and character sketches of famous contemporaries. Perhaps the quietest scene is the return of Marcia to her first husband, the Stoic Cato. Lucan's learning and his weakness for declamation hamper his poetry; but poetry it nevertheless is in a special way. His book conjures up most vividly the bloody atmosphere and tension of a conflict immensely decisive for later history and does this as no prose account could. ❩

THE CIVIL WAR II, 326–391

THE STOIC'S WEDDING

Meanwhile, as chilly night gave way to dawn,
A knocking sounded: leaving her husband's tomb,
There entered Marcia, filled with pious grief.
A nobler husband took her maidenhood,
Then, when the rich reward of marriage grew
To a third child, another home received her
To fill it too with offspring, a fertile mother
Linking the houses. Now her husband's ashes
Laid in the urn, she came in pitiful stress,
Tearing dishevelled locks, beating her bosom
With blow on blow, defiled by funeral ash —
For thus she would please Cato. She addressed him:
"While strong and fertile blood was in me, Cato,
I did your bidding, gave two husbands children.
My womb is tired now: let me return to you
And let no other husband take me. Grant
Again our early union; let my tomb
Bear the vain title *Marcia, wife of Cato*.
Let future ages know whether I left you
As a gift or as a castaway from marriage.
You will not share prosperity and peace
With me; I come to share your cares and labors.

257

So let me follow your camp. Must I be left
Further than Pompey's wife from the civil war?"
Her pleading moved her husband's heart. The crisis,
The fates crying "To arms!" were strange for marriage;
Yet simple union and a sober wedlock,
With gods alone to witness, pleased their thought.
No crowned threshold and hanging garlands of joy,
No gay white ribbon linking door and posts,
No torch-procession, couch with ivory dais,
No coverlet of gold embroidery,
No towering marriage-crown, no solemn entrance
Of the bride, stepping across the threshold lightly;
No saffron veil shielding her downcast face —
A flimsy garment for her modesty —
No jewelled belt girding her flowing garments,
Necklace, or scarf resting light on her shoulders
And flying freely from her slender arms.
She kept the state of grief: she gave her husband
Only the embrace a mother gives her sons.
Her simple robe was veiled with funeral weeds.
There was no marriage-jesting, and the husband
Did not submit to the gay old Sabine songs.
No kin, no family faces smiled on them;
They wed in silence, with one witness — Brutus.
And Cato neither freed his solemn face
Of shaggy hair, nor would admit a smile —
When he first saw the fatal weapons raised,
He suffered his unshorn grey locks to hang
Over his brow, and his beard mourned on his cheeks;
For he alone, free of ambition and hate,
Wept for the human race — nor did he now
Resume his nuptial rights: even a just love
His strength refused. Such was the rule of Cato,
Such his unyielding will — to keep sure limits,
To follow nature, spend his life for his country,
To live not for himself but for the world.
To conquer hunger was a feast; a palace
For him was a plain roof; a precious garment
For him was the rough-haired toga of the Roman
In time of peace; the only use of love
Was offspring: he begot and loved for Rome.
Justice and rigid honor — these he worshipped,
And virtue serving the world. No act of Cato
Was touched by pleasure and the greedy self.

Gilbert Highet

Petronius

(Gaius Petronius, Arbiter Elegantiarum, who was forced by Nero to kill himself, is best described by a kindred spirit, Tacitus, in the *Annals,* 16.17–19 (A.D. 66), as a polished, sardonic *bon vivant* with amazing courage and wit. He is best known, of course, for his satirical novel about the Roman underworld, the *Satyricon.* His poems, some of them contained in this novel, are, however, among his most characteristic writings. They are both passionate and mocking, realistic and sensitive. The influence of Epicurus and Lucretius is heavy in the scepticism of Petronius; but the worldly philosopher could also become a frank, unrestrained lover, caught in the trap of his emotions. There is no single book on Petronius; E. T. Sage's edition of the *Satyricon* is useful for some remarks.)

I

O restless, caressing eyes,
You say a certain special thing.
Pleasure and light love sit there,
And sensuousness sits between.

II

With your beautiful hair and seemly
Years and candid face, sweetly,
As I lay still, you gave me
Caressing kisses. If now I never
May see you waking, I hope sleep
Holds my eyes bound shut forever.

III

That night will long delight us, Nealce,
That first cuddled you upon my breast,
The bed, and the image above it,
And the secret tongue with which you gave
Yourself, so softly, into my power.
For these, we can let age gain on us,
And enjoy the years which a little while
Will erase. It is fitting so

To prolong our love as we grow old,
And let what happened so suddenly,
Never suddenly stop.

IV

Waking, my eyes, and in the night
My soul, seek you. Overcome
By my body, in my lonely bed,
I see you beside me, lying,
In the lying visions of sleep.
You would conquer sleep
If you really came to me.

V

Good God, what a night that was,
The bed was so soft, and how we clung,
Burning together, lying this way and that,
Our uncontrollable passions
Flowing through our mouths.
If I could only die that way,
I'd say goodbye to the business of living.

VI

Fornication is a filthy business,
The briefest form of lechery,
And the most boring, once you're satisfied.
So let's not rush blindly upon it,
Like cows in rut.
That's the way passion wilts
And the fire goes out.
But so, and so, feasting without end,
Lie together kissing each other.
It's a lazy shameless thing,
Delights, has delighted, always will delight,
And never ends, but constantly begins again.

VII

Why do you frown on me, you puritans,
And condemn the honesty of my latest poems?
Be thankful for fine writing
That makes you laugh instead of weep.
What people do, an honest tongue can talk about.

Do you know anybody who doesn't enjoy
Feasting and venery?
Who forbad my member to grow hot in a warm bed?
Father Epicurus himself commanded us
To become really sophisticated in this art.
Further, he said this was the life of the gods.

VIII

I had just gone to bed
And begun to enjoy the first
Stillness of the night,
And sleep was slowly
Overcoming my eyes,
When savage Love
Jerked me up by the hair,
And threw me about,
And commanded me to stay up all night.
He said, "You are my slave,
The lover of a thousand girls.
Have you become so tough that you can lie here,
All alone and lonely?"
I jumped up barefoot and half dressed,
And ran off in all directions,
And got nowhere by any of them.
First I ran, and then I lingered,
And at last I was ashamed
To be wandering in the empty streets.
The voices of men,
The roar of traffic,
The songs of the birds,
Even the barking of dogs,
Everything was still.
And me alone,
Afraid of my bed and sleep,
Ruled by a mighty lust.

Kenneth Rexroth

IX

Outward looks are not enough,
Beauty is no common stuff —
Of merriment it is compact,
Playful grace in every act,
Witty laughter, laughing wit:

These are things that go with it,
These surpass the simple graces
In beautiful and silly faces.
Art is for beauty; and I say:
Take the lovely fool away! —
If she strips from foot to head
And doesn't ask me into bed.

X

So, contrary to Nature's normal ways,
The raven lays her eggs in autumn days,
The she-bear shapes her cubs with her own tongue.
Without coition fish bring forth their young.
The tortoise, sacred to Apollo, knows
How to hatch eggs by breathing through the nose.
No fornication has produced the bee
Whose cells now hum with busy soldiery.
No single law in Nature fixed we see;
She loves to work in vast variety.

XI

You send me apples hot with gold, Martia.
You send me fruit of the shaggy chestnut too.
Thank you for your apples, Sweetface, thank you for your nuts,
But what I want is you.
Come, gild your gifts; come with unripe apples —
You have only to breathe on them and watch the honey-gloss fall.
But if you say you can't come, at least send kisses on the apples,
And hungrily I'll eat them all.

XII

In the soldier's helmet doves
Have made a nest — see
How Venus loves Mars.

XIII

This is nobleness, this is the one claim
To honor, this it is:
That a man's hands
Have shown no fear.

Jack Lindsay

SATYRICON 126, 18

Can it indeed be, Jove, you have grown old?
Now if ever were the moment to put on
Brute forehead and the bull's horns, or unfold
The outrageous beauty of a busking swan.

This is the only Danaë. Desire
To touch her body where she lies — and all
That once was god, involved in such a fire,
Must change to fame and as a gold rain fall.

John Peale Bishop

Martial

([Marcus Valerius Martialis (born in Bilbilis, Spain, c. 40, died there
A.D. 104) is the most prolific and entertaining of the Latin epigrammatists. He began as a writer of greeting-card sentiments and developed into a sparkling, keenly perceptive satirist. His 1,561 poems in
several meters including the elegiac (used by other poets for love and
more serious themes) hold up to scorn and ridicule a Roman galaxy
of fakes, sycophants, snobs, misers, confidence men, spongers, and
many other ridiculous characters whose names are usually given.
Mingled with these epigrams, each with its witty sting at the end in
the ordinary manner of the epigram, are a few poems in straight-face
addressed to ordinary simple people or on the pleasures of a quiet life
outside noisy Rome. Other poems are distinguished largely for their
peculiarly Roman obscenity. Martial, who is rarely bitter and almost
always amusing, is one of the most satisfying of Roman poets. His
work is a mine of information on Roman daily life.])

EPIGRAMS

I, 16

Some of these poems are good, some are medium, many are poor stuff;
    Avitus, read and believe: no book is made otherwise.

Robert R. Schnorr

I, 30

Once a surgeon, Dr. Baker
Then became an undertaker,
Not so much his trade reversing
Since for him it's just re-hearsing.

T. W. M.

I, 38

Mine was the book, Fidentine, till you ravished it for your recital.
    You've been making it yours: take it, recital and all.

Robert R. Schnorr

I, 75

He who prefers to grant only half of the total which Linus
    Tries to borrow from him, only prefers to lose half.

Robert R. Schnorr

I, 98

    Gouty-footed Colonel J.
        Counsel's services enlists;
    When the moment comes to pay
        Gout has doubled up his fists.

T. W. M.

I, 109

Issa's more full of sport and wanton play
    Than that pet sparrow by Catullus sung;
Issa's more pure and cleanly in her way
    Than kisses from the amorous turtle's tongue.
Issa more winsome is than any girl
    That ever yet entranced a lover's sight;
Issa's more precious than the Indian pearl,
    Issa's my Publius' favorite and delight.
Her plaintive voice falls sad as one that weeps;
    Her master's cares and woes alike she shares;
Softly reclined upon his neck she sleeps,
    And scarce to sigh or draw her breath she dares.
Her, lest the day of fate should nothing leave,
    In pictured form my Publius has portrayed
Where you so lifelike Issa might perceive,
    That not herself a better likeness made,
Issa together with her portrait lay,
    Both real or both depicted you would say.

W. F. Gosling

II, 5

    Believe me, sir, I'd like to spend whole days,
    Yes, and whole evenings in your company,
    But the two miles between your house and mine
    Are four miles when I go there and come back.
    You're seldom home, and when you are deny it,
    Engrossed with business or with yourself.

Now, I don't mind the two mile trip to see you;
What I do mind is going four to not to.

J. V. Cunningham

II, 59

Look round: you see a little supper room;
But from my window, lo! great Caesar's tomb!
And the great dead themselves, with jovial breath
Bid you be merry and remember death.

Robert Louis Stevenson

II, 68

That I now call you by your name
Who used to call you sir and master,
You needn't think it impudence.
I bought myself with all I had.
He ought to sir a sir and master
Who's not himself, and wants to have
Whatever sirs and masters want.
Who can get by without a slave
Can get by, too, without a master.

J. V. Cunningham

II, 88

Though you never recite, you would like to pass for a poet.
Pass for whatever you like; never, though, — never! — recite.

Robert R. Schnorr

III, 9

That fellow Singer, it is said,
Against me wrote a song.
But when a man is never read
To say he writes is wrong.

T. W. M.

IV, 32

The bee in amber hides, yet gleams unspoiled
As if its native nectar held it frozen.
It won due honor for the days it toiled:
This seems the death it would itself have chosen.

Geoffrey Johnson

IV, 41

Upon the platform Croker
    All muffled up appears,
But how we'd like that choker
    To muffle up our ears!

T. W. M.

IV, 69

You serve the best wine always, my dear sir,
And yet they say your wines are not so good.
They say you are four times a widower.
They say . . . A drink? I don't believe I would.

J. V. Cunningham

V, 9

I wasn't well, and at my call
    The doctor came to sound me;
And after him five score in all
    Of students crowded round me.

Five score of ice-cold hands they laid
    On heart and lungs and liver:
I had no fever yesterday,
    But now I'm all a-shiver.

G. I. C.

V, 34

Mother and sire, to you do I commend
Tiny Erotion, who must now descend,
A child, among the shadows, and appear
Before hell's bandog and hell's gondolier.
Of six hoar winters she had felt the cold,
But lacked six days of being six years old.
Now she must come, all playful, to that place
Where the great ancients sit with reverend face;
Now lisping, as she used, of whence she came,
Perchance she names and stumbles at my name.
O'er these so fragile bones let there be laid
A plaything for a turf; and for that maid
That ran so lightly footed in her mirth
Upon thy breast — lie lightly, mother earth!

Robert Louis Stevenson

V, 56

Lupus, you question carefully
The teacher who will oversee
The schooling of your son; I say,
From orators keep him away.
Don't let the boy just loaf about;
If he writes verses, kick him out.
But if he wants to learn a trade
By which a lot of coin is made,
Then let him learn to play a tune
On flute or saxophone, and croon.
Yet if he proves too dull by far
To strum a lucrative guitar,
You'll have to make the boy, I fear,
An architect or auctioneer.

L. R. Lind

V, 76

By daily sipping poison Mithridates used to think
In time he'd make himself immune from any deadly drink.
And you take like precautions, too, if that's your daily dinner:
At least you'll never die of hunger, miserable Cinna.

T. W. M.

VI, 19

It's not a case of poisoned cup,
    Assault, or slitting throats;
I've had to have my neighbor up
    For stealing my three goats.

You dwell on Punic faith and fury,
    Pontic wars and Cannaes,
But this they're asking on the jury,
    "Prove he stole the nannies."

And now with gestures various
    You've told in ringing notes
Of Sulla, Mucius, Marius,
    Please mention my three goats.

T. W. M.

VI, 57

On your bald, dirty head you wear,
  Phoebus, a lot of grease paint hair;
You need no razor for your knob:
  A sponge would do a better job.

L. R. Lind

VI, 65

"An epic epigram," I heard you say.
Others have written them, and so I may.
"But this one is too long." Others are too.
You want them short? I'll write two lines for you:
  As for long epigrams let us agree
  They may be skipped by you, written by me.

J. V. Cunningham

VII, 16

Thus, Prince, of all my goods bereft,
  With not a farthing in my coffers,
One course alone to me is left,
  To sell your presents. Any offers?

T. W. M.

VII, 83

When Handiman shaves Herr von Wolf
  So heavy is the going
That when at last he towels his chin
  Another beard is growing.

T. W. M.

VII, 86

Once I used to be called to join your parties,
At a time when you hardly knew me, Sextus:
What is wrong now, what's happened lately, tell me,
After so many years of trusted friendship,
That your messenger's passed your best friend's threshold?
But I know what the cause is: Never have I
Sent you platters of hammered Spanish silver,
Nor light togas or cloaks to wear upon them . . .

Why, you're trading instead of giving dinners,
Feeding presents instead of friends, dear Sextus!
But I know that you'll say, "My slave has blundered."

Robert R. Schnorr

VIII, 9

Seventy-five percent of his debt did the wine-bleared Hylas
   Offer to pay you back; half-blind, he still offers half.
Do snap it up, I advise, for there is a time-limit on it:
   Once he has lost all his sight, everything will be lost.

Robert R. Schnorr

VIII, 10

"Of late our friend has bought a purple-dyed toga,
   A very good one; still, it was a great bargain . . . "
"So well bought, eh?" — "Indeed; our friend just won't pay, sir."

Robert R. Schnorr

VIII, 16

You, Casey, long a baker,
   Now pleading at the Bar,
You ask big fees, and spend them,
   You owe too much by far.
You're still the baker, Casey,
   The one we used to know,
You make a good turnover,
   And still you knead the dough.

T. W. M.

VIII, 29

Epigrams should, I suppose, please their readers by saying it briefly:
   Why — though your lines are concise — why do they fill a whole
     book?

Robert R. Schnorr

VIII, 69

You, Vacerra, admire the ancients only,
And you praise only buried poets, don't you?
You will pardon me: that much, dear Vacerra,
I would not pay to give you satisfaction.

Robert R. Schnorr

VIII, 76

"Tell me honestly, Marcus, tell me, please do:
How d'you like it? I'd love to know, my Marcus . . . "
You keep asking me, when you read your poetry,
Or whenever you plead your clients' causes —
Asking, Gallicus, praying, praying, asking . . .
Well — it seems I just can't refuse to answer.
Listen then; here's the truth and nothing but it:
You would probably not be fond of MY truth.

Robert R. Schnorr

IX, 10

So you would like to become Mrs. Prisca? — Well, I understand that.
Priscus won't like the idea . . . which I can understand too.

Robert R. Schnorr

IX, 59

Mr. Flint goes up the West,
Walks for miles without a rest,
Where the gilded city squanders
All her money, there he wanders . . .
Views the tables in the shops,
Makes the men unwrap the tops,
Sees on high carved ivory legs,
Has them taken off the pegs.
Several times he measures well
A sofa made of tortoise-shell;
"No," he sighs to those in charge,
"My cedar table's just too large."
The bronzes, too, with knowing grin
He sniffs, to test their origin.
Statues then attract the fellow,
Carps at works by Donatello.
Then decries a crystal vase,
Shows a speck of glass that mars:
Picks a set of porcelain,
Sighs, and says, "I'll call again."
Feels an ancient piece of plate,
Tries a cup to test its weight,
Goblets, too, perhaps made grand
Once by Benvenuto's hand.
Emeralds that the craftsman mounts

On gold engraved he duly counts,
Every jewel large and clear
That tinkles from the snow-white ear.
On every jeweler's tray he fixes,
Hunts for perfect sardonyxes.
In the bidding then he cries
For jaspers of unusual size.
    And now when sinks the sun,
All wearied out, his shopping done,
Himself he takes it, in the end,
— Two penny mugs they would not send!

                        T. W. M.

X, 23

Now Antoninus, in a smiling age,
Counts of his life the fifteenth finished stage.
The rounded days and the safe years he sees,
Nor fears death's water mounting round his knees.
To him remembering not one day is sad,
Not one but that its memory makes him glad.
So good men lengthen life; and to recall
The past is to have twice enjoyed it all.

               Robert Louis Stevenson

X, 43

Smith's seventh wife has joined the batch
That's buried on his cabbage patch.
From what he's planted on that field
He must have had a famous yield.

                        T. W. M.

X, 47

To bring yourself to be happy
Acquire the following blessings:
A nice inherited income,
A kindly farm with a kitchen,
No business worries or lawsuits,
Good health, a gentleman's muscles,
A wise simplicity, friendships,
A plain but generous table,
Your evenings sober but jolly,
Your bed amusing but modest,

And nights that pass in a moment;
To be yourself without envy,
To fear not death, nor to wish it.

Gilbert Highet

XI, 18

You've bestowed a suburban farm on me, Sir.
Yet I've more of a farm right in my window.
Dare you call this a farm? I like your humor.
Look: this rue is the only grove it yields me;
One shrill grasshopper's wing would give it shadow;
One little ant can in just one day devour it,
And a rose's corolla overtops it.
You won't find any taller trees than spikenard,
Or maybe even some green pepper in it.
Why, my cucumber has to grow straight upward,
Since my farm, I'm afraid, can't house an earthworm.
Though perhaps it may feed one caterpillar,
For a gnat it would be a starving diet
(I might try to employ a mole to plow it).
Not a mushroom can seed, no fig will smile there,
And the violets must keep closed their blossoms.
A mouse makes raids, like the famous Calydonian
Boar, on my farmland's border, scares the farmer.
Also, all of my crop might by one swallow
Be swept off to its nest with little effort,
For not half a Priapus can be placed there,
Though he leave both his scythe and scepter elsewhere . . .
Still, there's hope that my crops may net a spoonful,
Plus a nutshell with wine of my own vintage.

After all, your mistake consisted only
In one letter: when you said FARM, I should have
Humbly asked for the bill of FARE . . .

Yours truly,

Robert R. Schnorr

XI, 42

Dull are the topics you want me to treat in my epigrams, Mister;
Livelier verses you want . . . Whose is the fault, Sir, I ask —
Do you expect me to bring Hyblean and Hymettos honey,
When you feed Attic bees nothing but Corsican thyme?

Robert R. Schnorr

XI, 67

Nothing you give while alive; but you promise a legacy, Maro.
Maro — if you are no Moron, you know what I wish.

Robert. R. Schnorr

XII, 47

Generous and jealous, soft and hard of heart —
I cannot live with you, nor live apart!

Richard A. Bell

Juvenal

❴ Decimus Iunius Iuvenalis (c. A.D. 60–131) was born at Aquinum, the birthplace of St. Thomas Aquinas, suffered exile and poverty, and wrote sixteen satires which are among the most powerful examples of this Roman genre we have. Gilbert Highet, in a brilliant book, *Juvenal the Satirist,* describes his subjects: "Of the sixteen poems, twelve deal with the maladjustments of contemporary society, considered from different points of view: the relation of husbands and wives, of friends true and false, of parents and children, of civilians and soldiers, and so on. Two (4 and 15) treat recent historical events. The other two, 10 and 13, are on moral topics: crime and punishment, and the true aim of human life."

❴ Juvenal's style is conditioned by his anger and despair at the world's inequities; it is distinguished by a remarkable talent for penetrating epigrams and memorable phrases. Although some of the targets of his indignation now seem trivial to us, all are attacked in a white heat of fury that still stirs the most complacent reader. Injustice, cruelty, vice, poverty, and humiliation are among his themes; no one except Swift and Voltaire has made such enduring literature out of his hatred for such evils. There is no good readable verse translation in modern English of all the *Satires*. Perhaps the most famous, by way of Dryden and Samuel Johnson, are the Third, on the ills of city life; the Sixth, on marriage and women; the Eighth, on the vanity of family position and snobbery; and the Tenth, on the goals and wishes of human life. ❵

SATIRE I

On Poets Who Recite in Public —
and Other Sinners

Must I be always merely a listener? Never reply
Though bored so often by the "Theseid" of Codrus the hoarse?
Shall this man, unpunished, spout long-robed comedies at me,
And that man elegies? Huge "Telephus" wear out the day
Or "Orestes," written all over a big book's margin,
And then on the back, and not yet finished at that?
No man knows his own house as well as I know
"The grove of Mars" and "the cave of Vulcan," nearby
"The cliffs of Aeolus"; how the winds fare, what shades

Aeacus tortures, whence somebody carries the gold   10
Of "the stolen Fleeceling," how big the spears that were tossed
By the Centaur Monychus: Fronto's plane trees and halls
Cry out, their marble and columns shattered with all
The noise that the endless, unwearied reciters have made.

You'll get the same stuff from the greatest and smallest of poets.

And *I* once pulled back my hand from the ruler, and *I*
Once gave schoolboy advice to Sulla: go home and sleep
Like an untroubled private citizen! — Mercy is foolish,
When you run into so many bards all around you, to spare
The paper that's sure to be wasted.
                       I'll tell you why,   20
If you have the time and the patience, I've decided to run
The same course that Lucilius ran, in the satire-race.
When soft eunuchs marry, when Mevia sticks a wild boar
And holds a man's hunting spear close to her naked breast,
When a man who used to cut hair in my barber shop
When I was a boy now rivals the richest alone,
When the scum of the Nile, when a slave like Crispinus, who comes
From Canopus, can hitch a Tyrian cloak from his shoulder
And wave the gold "summer-ring" on his sweating finger,
Unable to bear the weight of a heavier gem: 30
It's hard *not* to write satire. For who is so patient
With big-town injustice, so tough, as to control himself
When along comes Matho the lawyer in a shiny new car
Full of himself, and after him comes the stool-pigeon
Who turned in his prominent friend, who's eager to tear
What's left of the high-born already gnawed to the bone,
The man Massa fears, whom Carus feels out with a bribe,
To whom Thymele was sent by a scared Latinus?
When men who earn legacies by night-work push you back,
Men raised to heaven by the best way of all to succeed —   40
The lust of a rich old woman? Each lover will share:
Proculeius one-twelfth of her money, but Gillo eleven-
Twelfths of the loot, to the measure each worked on the job.
Let each take the wages of blood, and so let him turn
Pale like a man whose bare heel treads on a snake,
Or an orator ready to speak at the altar in Lyons.

Why should I tell how my heart burns dry in its rage
When I see the people shoved back by the mob that surrounds
A man who has cheated, debauched his ward, or another

Condemned by a judge that was bought, who loses his name   50
But keeps all the cash? The exile Marius drinks
Deep in the afternoon and enjoys the gods' anger,
While you, poor Province, can win your law suit and still groan.
    Shouldn't I think these scandles worth Horace's lamp?
Why shouldn't I rave at them? Should I tell a tale
Of Hercules, Diomedes, the labyrinth's roar,
How Icarus fell in the sea while his father flew off,
When a scoundrel will take from a man in love with his wife
The money she cannot receive as a legal heir,
Well trained to stare at the ceiling or snore in his cups,   60
His sniffing nose still awake? When a man who has run
Through a family fortune at race tracks yet thinks it is right
To expect the command of a cohort? Although he is broke
And out of his class, he whirls down the Flaminian Way
Headlong in his racer, like Automedon, while he holds
The reins and shows off for his mistress dressed in a man's coat.
    Wouldn't you like to fill up a big note-book with facts
As you stand at the cross-roads, where borne on the necks of six men
You see a forger pass by, sticking out here and there
From a carrying-chair, the curtains drawn back, while he lolls   70
Like a lounging Maecenas, who turned himself elegant, rich,
By means of a tiny will and a moistened seal?
    There passes a powerful matron who mixes a drink
When her husband is thirsty (it's made of toad's blood and wine!);
More bold than Lucusta, the poisoner, she teaches her more
Naïve neighbors to carry their husbands out, blackened and dead,
In funeral processions where people will gossip and stare.
If you want to be something you have to dare deeds that are fit
For Gyara, the small prison-island, at least for a jail.
Uprightness is praised, and it freezes. Men owe to their crimes   80
Their gardens, commands, fine tables, their silver ware,
With its goblets where goats stand out in heavy relief.
What seducer of greedy daughters-in-law will allow
Anyone to sleep, what tarnished brides, what adulterous
Teen-ager? If nature won't let me, my rage makes me write
Such verse as I can, or the kind Cluvienus can write.
    From the time when the clouds drew the water up to the sky,
And Deucalion sailed up a mountain to question his fate,
When the stones grew, warm and soft, into human beings,
And Pyrrha revealed naked girls to the men of the earth,   90
Whatever men do, their prayers, fear, anger, or pleasure,
Their joys and their discourse, I've put them all into my book.
And when could you find more vices abounding? When

Did the gullet of greed open wider? When did the dice
Draw more to the tables? They don't bring their wallets along,
They bring a whole safety deposit box: you will see
The battles they wage while their treasurers back them up.
Isn't it clearly insane to throw away thousands
And not give as much as a shirt to a shivering slave?
Which of our grandfathers built himself so many homes   100
In the country, or ate by himself a seven-course dinner?
Just look at the measly handout they put on the porch
For a bunch of reliefers, poor devils, to fight over now.
The boss looks you over, afraid that you're claiming a share
As a stand-in for somebody else, with that somebody's name:
When he knows you, you get it. He tells his assistant to call
The aristocrats too, since they beat at the door with the rest.
"Give some to the Judge, give some to the Justice of Peace!"
"But I was here first," says a freedman once born just a slave.
"Why should I worry or fail to defend my place?   110
Although I was born near Euphrates (a fact I deny,
In spite of the pierced ears that give me away), I'm the owner
Of five shops that bring me in forty thousand apiece.
What good is high birth if Corvinus the noble tends sheep
Down at Laurentum while I have more money than any
Two millionaires? So let the high-hats await
Their turn. My money talks louder than honors." Let each
Of those prominent men give way to a slave whose feet
Were whitened with chalk only yesterday when he came here.
The holiest god of them all is the power of Wealth,   120
Even if, fatal Money, as yet you don't live in a shrine
Of your own: we have built no altars to Cash in Hand
As we worship Peace, Virtue, Faith, Victory, and
At the temple of Concord, where storks make a noise at the door.
    But when the big men add up at the end of the year
The money raked in from their handouts, how much will they have?
What can we reliefers expect for our share? We shall need
To pay for our coats and shoes, our bread and our heat.
The litters come crowding, for fifty cents each; here's a man
Whose sickly or pregnant wife follows him; here is another   130
Who's clever at tricks: he points to a closed, empty chair
And says, "My Galla's in there; give my share, and be quick!"
— "Galla, stick out your head." — "Don't bother her, she is asleep."

    The day is marked off in a beautiful sequence of chores:
First handout, then forum, then law courts, then statues, where some
Egyptian named Arabach dares to set up one of his;

You can answer the calls of nature beside it, you know.
The weary old paupers go home from the doors of the rich;
They're hopeless, although their hope of a dinner goes last.
They have to buy cabbage, poor devils, and fuel for a fire.   140
Meanwhile, their king will be hogging down all of the best
That the sea and the forest produce, while he lies on a couch
All alone. For at one of their beautiful tables, immense
And antique, they can eat up a fortune in food by themselves.
Soon there won't be reliefers. But who can stand riches so mean?
How huge is a gullet which swallows whole pigs by itself,
A beast that was born to be shared? You'll pay for it yet,
Old man, when bulging with peacock still raw in your guts,
You take off your clothes and go bathing: swift death and no will!
What a story, what fun, for the tables where others will dine   150
When your body's brought forth to be cheered by your angry friends!
    Posterity cannot add to these customs of ours;
Our descendants will do the same things and want the same things.
Vice stands at her peak: use your sails, and spread all the canvas!
Here probably you may say: "Where's the man for the task?
Where's the freedom of style that once matched such a burning of
        soul?"
— "Whose name do I dare not speak? What difference if now
Mucius pardons my words or not? Write up Tigellinus,
And you'll be burnt like a torch where the victims stand
Clutching their throats for the smoke as they roast to death.   160
Your carcass will make a broad groove in the midst of the sand.
    Shall a man who has poisoned three uncles ride by and look down
At me in his pride as the cushions swing back and forth?"
— "You're right. When you meet you had better just button your lip.
You'll be charged with informing if you merely say, 'There's the man.'
You can safely describe how Turnus battled Aeneas;
And no one is shocked when he hears how Hercules died,
Or how he chased Hylas so long, the boy with the jug.
But whenever Lucilius takes up the sword of his satire
And rages about, then his hearer, whose heart is stone-cold   170
With its crimes, will flush and grow sweaty with conscience of sin.
Hence come anger, tears. Think over these things before you
Hear bugles sound; when once your helmet is on,
It's too late to pull out of battle." Then I'll try to find
What I can get by with in writing of those who are dead
Along the main highways from Rome, to the south and the north.

                                                    L. R. Lind

SATIRE III

LIFE AT ROME

Although I am sorely vexed by an old friend's leaving the city,
Nevertheless I praise him because at populous Cumae
He intends to live and to give one citizen to the Sibyl.
It is the gateway to Baiae and a pleasant shore of delightful
Retirement. And I prefer even Prochyta to the Subura.
For what have we seen so wretched, so deserted, we would not think it
Worse to dread conflagrations and the constant falling of buildings
And all the thousand perils of the scarcely civilized city —
To say not a word of the poets reciting their verses in August?
But while in a single wagon his household is being loaded,   10
He has stopped at the ancient arches and the dripping gate of Capena;
Here where Numa went out to meet by night his mistress,
The grove of the sacred fount and the shrines are rented to Jews —
For every tree is commanded to pay its share to the people,
And the wood has become a beggar, with the Muses driven out from it.
We go down to the vale of Egeria and the imitation grottoes.
How much more present would be the deity of the water
If grass enclosed its wavelets with verdant borders,
And marbles did not violate the native pumice-stone!
Here, then, Umbricius spoke: "Since," he said, "there is in the City   20
No place for honest crafts, no just reward for my labors,
My means are less today than they were the day before,
And tomorrow will wear away still more from my little stock,
I purpose to go where Daedalus put off his wearied wings,
While still I'm newly gray, while my age is fresh and sturdy,
While Lachesis has something to spin, and my own feet carry me,
Without the need of a staff to support my aged hand,
Let me leave my native land, let Artorius and Catulus stay,
And those who turn black into white, and those who find it easy
To contract for a building, rivers, ports, a sewer to be dried,   30
Or for a corpse to be carried to burn on the funeral pyre,
And to offer themselves for sale as if they were put at auction.
At one time these blowers of horns and constant arena-attendants,
These bawlers, were known through the towns; now they set forth
     public shows,
And when the thumbs of the mob are turned down, they will kill
     anyone,
Just as the crowd may desire: done with shows, they contract for
     privies.
And why should they not do all things? Since they are such as
     Fortune

Raises from humble and low condition to heights of affluence,
Whenever she has a mind to show she knows how to play jokes.
What can I do at Rome? I am not a good hand at lying;   40
If a book is bad, I can't praise it, nor ask for it everywhere:
I don't know the motions of stars; and I will not and cannot promise
The death of a father; and never have I looked at the entrails of frogs.
Let others take to a wife the notes that her lover sends her,
And know what his message is; nobody shall be a thief
By my aid: and for these reasons, a companion to no one at all,
Like the maimed and useless corpse of a paralyzed hand, I go.
For who is sought after now, unless he's a confidant
And one whose eager mind boils over with hidden secrets?
No obligation he has, he thinks, and will give you nothing,   50
Who has made you the sharer with him of only an honest secret.
Dear will he be to Verres, who can, whenever he wishes,
Accuse Verres himself. Don't set so much value upon all
The sand of the dark Tagus river and the gold it rolls into the sea
That you should lie sleepless of nights and take bribes that should be
       rejected,
And, sorrowful, always be feared by your friend of the highest rank.
That people which is most dear to our men of wealth at present
And which most especially I flee, I'll hasten now to confess;
Nor shall I be hindered by shame. I cannot bear, O Romans,
A city of Greeks: though what portion comes from the dregs of
       Achaea?
Long ago the Syrian Orontes flowed into the Tiber river
And brought its tongue and its customs and its crooked harps with its
       pipers,
And its native timbrels as well, and its girls at the Circus bidden
To prostitute themselves. Go there, you whom a barbarian
Harlot with painted head-dress can charm. Our rustic compatriot
Wears now, O Romans, a robe worn by parasites at a dinner,
And on his perfumed neck hangs the prize of victory.
This man from lofty Sicyon, that man from Amydon migrated,
Another from Andros or Samos, from Tralles or Alabanda,
Has sought the Esquilian Mount or the hill named after its willows;   70
The intimates of great houses and the lords who will soon be our
       masters.
Quick wit and shameless boldness and readiness of speech
And loquacity more torrential than Isaeus' flow: what do you think
He is? And he's brought with him whatever fellow you please:
Grammarian, rhetorician, geometrician, painter,
Anointer, augur, tight-rope walker, physician, wizard:
All things he knows; a hungry Greekling will climb into heaven
Should you command it. In short, no Moor he was or Sarmatian

Or Thracian, who put on wings, but one born in the midst of Athens.
Shall I not flee from the purple garments of such as these,   80
Shall he sign his name before me, or lie at table above me,
Who was brought to Rome by that wind which carries us plums and
    figs?
Is it of no importance that my childhood breathed the air
Of the Aventine and was nourished by the Sabine olive?
What! because a nation most skilled in flattery praises
The speech of an unlearned friend or the face of one deformed
And declares the weakling's long neck equal to Hercules' shoulders,
Holding Antaeus aloft from earth, admires a squeaking
Voice which is worse than the squawk of a hen pecked by a rooster!
We also may praise such things, but only these people find credence.
Does the comedian play better the dramatic part of Thais,   91
Or a wife, or uncloaked Doris? A very woman he seems,
Complete in all her parts, including those from the waist downward.
Yet they won't ever applaud one of their own Greek actors:
The nation itself's a comedian. Do you laugh? With uproarious
    laughter
He's shaken. He weeps if he sees his friend in tears — not that he
    grieves.
If in winter you ask for a little fire, he puts on a great-coat;
If you chance to say you are warm, your Greek will burst into a sweat.
We are not, then, equals; he's better who, both night and day, can
Put on another man's face. Why, he is prepared to throw kisses,   100
To praise if his friend has belched well or if he has made water nicely,
If his drinking cup makes a gurgle when the friend has turned it
    mouth downward.
Moreover, there's nothing that's sacred or safe from their ravaging
    lust:
Not the lady of the house, nor the daughter, before this a virgin, or
    even
The still beardless bridegroom, or else the son, who was hitherto
    chaste.
And if there aren't any of these, he'll ravage his friend's aged grand-
    mother.
All the family secrets they'll know, and thus they are more to be
    feared.
And since I have mentioned the Greeks, why, go to the schools and
    learn
Of a crime of more villainous nature. It was Egnatius, a Stoic, who
    murdered
Bareas; an informer his friend, an old man his pupil — a man   110
Nourished on that same shore where Pegasus dropped one of his
    feathers.

There's no room for a Roman here, where some Protogenes rules,
Or Diphilos, or Erimanthos, who by the vice of his nation
Never will share a friend, but he must own his alone.
For when in his friend's facile ear he has dropped a bit of the poison
Natural to him and his country, I am removed from his threshold,
My days of long service forgotten — never of smaller account
Is the loss of a client. Moreover, what is the reward of his duty
(Not to flatter myself), or the merit of a poor man here if he troubles
As a client to rush about in the midst of the night when the Praetor
Hustles the lictor along toward the homes of those childless old
     women,   121
Albina and Modia, so that his colleague shan't greet them before him?
Here the son of a free-born man gives the wall to a rich man's slave,
And the latter donates a sum as large as a tribune's salary
To great Calvina or Catiena, that again and again he may tremble
Over her body; but you, when the face of a well-dressed harlot
Attracts you, must hesitate to hand her down from her litter.
Produce a witness at Rome as just as the goddess of Ida;
Let Numa himself step forth, or he who saved frightened Minerva
From the burning shrine: at once they'd question his income; his
     morals   130
Would be their last inquiry: the first — how many slaves has he?
How many his acres of land? How many and how fine his dishes?
As much as the money he holds in his chest do they value his word.
Though you swear by the gods Samothracian and as well by our
     native altars,
A poor man is thought to despise their thunders and heaven itself,
Though the very gods forgive him. Why? Because this same poor
     fellow
Gives matter and cause for jests to all, if his cloak is dirty
And torn, or his toga soiled, and one of his sandals is gaping
With the leather broken, or if in the tear that he has stitched
Not one patch only displays the coarse and lately-sewn thread!   140
Poverty has nothing harsher to bear in itself, than that
It makes men ridiculous. The usher says, 'Let him go, if he has
A sense of shame, and get off a gentleman's seat, he whose fortune
Does not satisfy the law, and allow to sit there in the Circus
The sons of pimps instead, born in some brothel or other.
Here let the son of some spruce public crier applaud among
The cultured scions of gladiators, the children of fencing masters':
For thus it pleased stupid Otho, who made this distinction between us.
What son-in-law is accepted here if his fortune is less
And his money-bags unequal to the girl's? What poor man is made
     heir?   150
When does he sit in council with Aediles? The penniless Romans

Should long ago in a body have departed for other lands.
They do not rise with ease whose family's narrow resources
Hinder their talents; at Rome the attempt to advance is made harder.
A wretched lodging costs much, and so does the feeding of servants,
And a simple little dinner means an enormous expense.
We are ashamed to eat from earthen vessels, though you would
Feel it to be no disgrace if suddenly you were taken
To the country of the Marsians and to a Sabine table,
Content there with a Venetian cape of coarse blue wool.   160
There is a great part of Italy, if we will admit the truth,
Where no one dresses in togas except a dead man, and even
The majesty of festal days is cherished, if ever,
In a theater grown over with grass, and the well-known farce returns
To the stage, while the cleft cut in the actor's pale mask frightens
The country child who sits in his mother's lap. There appearance
Is equal, and you will see alike the senate and people.
The costume of glorious honor, white tunics, alone are sufficient
For the great Aediles. But here our fine dress costs more than our
     means;
Here something more than enough is sometimes stolen from some one.
Here we all live in ambitious poverty. Why do I linger?   171
At Rome everything has its price. What will you give that sometimes
You may speak to Cossius or gaze on Veiento, while he, still closing
His mouth, remains in silence. One of them is shaving his beard,
The other is dedicating the locks of his boy-favorite.
The house is full of cakes — that you must buy if you want them.
Keep that ferment for yourself; every client must offer tribute
And by our tips increase the hoard of a sleek, well-fed slave.
Who at cold Praeneste has feared that his house would tumble,
Or at Volsinium placed among its tree-grown hills,   180
Or at rustic Gabii or on steep Tibur's summit?
We inhabit a city supported by slender props
Throughout its greater part; janitors shore up falling places
And, when he has covered up the gap of some long-aged crack,
He tells us to sleep securely, while the house is beginning to totter.
I must live in a place where there are no conflagrations,
No scares by night; already Ucalegon begs for water,
Already he's moving his wretched sticks; your third floor smokes
     already,
And you know nothing of it. For if the alarm's on the ground floor,
The garret will burn, where only the roof protects from the rain,   190
Burning the last man in it, under the nests of the soft doves.
All Codrus had was a bed, shorter than Procula, the dwarf;
Six little pitchers were all the ornament of his cupboard,
And a small jug beneath them, a statue of reclining Chiron

Under the marble slab of his shelf, and an old chest containing
His Greek books; barbarous mice kept gnawing those marvellous
    poems.
Codrus had nothing, in short: who will deny it? And yet
The poor man lost all that nothing, and this is the crown of his sorrow,
That when he is naked and begging for scraps, nobody will feed him,
No one will take him in or give him a roof for shelter.   200
Should the great house of Asturicus fall, the matrons go towelled,
The nobles go into mourning, the Praetor postpones all his cases.
Then we lament the city's misfortunes, *then* we hate fire.
While it is still ablaze, someone runs to give him marbles,
To contribute to his expenses. One brings white, naked statues,
Another some famous work of Euphranor or of Polyclitus,
Another brings the antique adornments of Asian gods.
One will give books and cases, and Minerva's statue, to place
Amongst them; another, a peck of silver: so Persicus lays up
Better and more possessions, most splendid of destitute humans,   210
And is now with justice suspected of having fired his own home.
If you could be dragged from the Circus, an excellent house at Sora,
At Fabrateria or Frusino can be hired for the same sum a year
For which you rent only shadows to dwell in now at Rome.
There you will have a small garden, and a shallow well that needs
No rope to draw up water, which with easy draft is poured
Over your tender plants. Live there, loving your mattock,
Manning a well-kept garden from which you might give a feast
To a hundred Pythagoreans. It is something, wherever you wander,
To become the lord of one lizard. Many a sick man at Rome   220
Dies for the lack of sleep (but bad food brought on his illness,
Lying on his fevered stomach), for what hired flat allows rest?
Only the rich sleep well in the City. This is the cause
Of disease — the passing of wagons in the narrow curve of the streets,
And the noise of the standing teams, snatch away sleep from Drusus,
As they would from a beast of the sea. If duty calls, the rich man
Is carried over our faces in a fine Liburnian litter,
While the crowd gives way before him, and on the way he reads,
Or writes, or sleeps, perhaps, for a litter with windows closed
Easily brings on slumber. He will get there before me;   230
As I hurry, the crowd in front obstructs me, the people who follow
Push at my back in their crowding; one strikes with his elbow, another
With a litter-pole; a third bangs my head with a beam,
A fourth with a keg. My legs are thick with mud; the next minute
I am trodden on by a huge foot, and the nail of a soldier's
Boot sticks into my toe. Do you see how much smoke arises
Where the hand-out basket draws crowds? A hundred guests, and
    each of them

Is followed by his own kitchen and cook; Corbulo scarcely could bear
So many heavy vessels, so many things placed on his head
As one small miserable slave carries with neck held rigid,   240
Fanning the flames with his running and keeping the food in his pots
    hot.
Now the patched tunics are torn; now a long pine-tree is shaking
In a wagon that keeps on coming: another carries in it a fir-tree.
They nod up above us and threaten the crowd; but if an axle
Of a cart carrying stones has broken and poured its mass over the
    people,
What is there left of their bodies? Who finds their limbs and their
    bones?
The whole of a common man's body perishes, just like his soul.
Meanwhile his family, unknowing, wash their dishes and blow up their
    fire,
Grate with the bath-oil scrapers, collect their towels and oil-flasks.
The boys rush about with their tasks, but *he* sits now by Styx-
    river   250
And, newcomer as he is, dreads Charon; the poor man cannot hope
For the boat on that muddy torrent, since he doesn't have even a
    penny
To bring out of his mouth for the fare. Consider now some other
And different dangers of night: how high are the towering roof-tops
From which a potsherd may strike your head, when cracked and
    broken vessels
Are thrown from the windows, how heavily they can mark
And injure the very pavement! You can be regarded as foolish,
And improvident of sudden fate, if you go out to your dinner
Without having made your will: as many deaths await you at night
As there are open windows to watch you as you pass by.   260
Therefore you should desire, and should carry a pitiful prayer
Along with you, that they be content to empty their slop-pails.
A drunken and quarrelsome man, who has not yet knocked over a
    victim,
Suffers like some Achilles mourning all night for Patroclus.
He lies on his face; and then turns over again on his back.
Only fighting will make some men sleep; but though he is old in his
    evil,
And heated with wine, such a man shuns another whom a scarlet
    cloak
And a long troop of attendants warns that he should be avoided,
And a great number of lights and torches set in a bronze socket.
I, who am used to have only the moon above as my escort,   270
Or the brief light of a candle whose wick I trim and take care of,
Will be scorned by such men; learn now the start of a quarrel —

If that can be called a quarrel where you strike and I only am beaten.
He faces you, roars to you, 'Stop!' There's no choice but to obey,
For what can you do when a madman attacks you, and he is the
    stronger?
'Where do you come from?' he bawls: 'With whose cheap wine and
    beans are you bloated?
'What cobbler ate a sliced leek and a piece of boiled sheepshead with
    you?
'What, won't you answer? Speak up, or else I'll kick you on your
    shins.
'Tell me, where do you live? In what synagogue shall I seek you?'
Whether you try to speak, or whether you shrink back in silence,   280
The result is always the same; they strike you in either case:
And then these furious men have you served with a summons to court.
This is a poor man's freedom; when beaten, he may implore,
And bruised with fists, may entreat that he be allowed to go home
With a few teeth left in his mouth. Nor is this the worst you may fear,
For you will be robbed by a burglar, when all the houses are shut
And every fastened padlock of the chained shop is quiet.
Sometimes the sudden cut-throat does his work with a sword;
Whenever the Pontine Marshes and the Gallinarian forest
Are made safe by an armed guard, then the highwaymen all rush here
As if to a game-preserve. In what furnace, on what anvil   291
Are not heavy chains manufactured? So much iron is used for fetters,
You may fear a dearth of ploughshares, a famine of hoes and spades.
Happy our fathers of old, happy the by-gone ages
Which once, under kings and tribunes, saw Rome content with one
    prison.
To these I have given I could add other and more potent reasons;
But my team is calling, the sun's going down, and my time's come for
    leaving.
My muleteer long ago gave a hint by shaking his whip,
So goodbye, and don't forget me; and whenever Rome shall restore
    you
Hurrying for refreshment to your beloved Aquinum,   300
Tear me also away from Cumae to your Helvine Ceres and Diana.
I also, a listener to your satires (if it won't shame them)
Shall come all booted and spurred into your chilly fields."

                        Miriam Allen deFord

SATIRE VI, 474–493

But you should know what Everywoman does
At home all day. Suppose her husband turns

His back to her in bed. God help the housemaid!
The lady's maids are stripped, the coachman's thrashed
For being late (punished because another
Slept), rods are broken, bleeding backs are scourged
And lashed: some women keep a private flogger.
She scourges while her face is made up, talks
To her friends, examines a gold-braided frock
And thrashes, till the thrasher tires, and she
Screams "Go now!" and the inquisition's over.
She rules her home more savagely than a tyrant.
Has she an assignation, wants to look
More beautiful than usual, quick, he's waiting
Under the trees, or in Queen Isis' brothel —
Poor Psecas combs the mistress's hair, her own
Tattered, with naked shoulders and bare breasts.
"This curl's too high!" At once the oxhide thong
Lashes the wretch: her crime was a coiffure.

Gilbert Highet

SATIRE X

THE VANITY OF HUMAN WISHES

In all the lands there are, from Cadiz to
The Ganges and the dawn, few men can tell
True good from bad, its opposite, and dispel
Their cloud of error. What do we fear with reason,
Or what desire? Which plans do we take up
So well conceived we do not change our minds,
Repenting our attempt and its success?
The easy gods have ruined whole families,
Granting their very wish. In peace and war
We ask for what will harm us. The torrent flow   10
Of eloquence has brought death to its owner.
And he has perished who trusted muscle-strength.
But more are choked by too much heaped-up coin,
By fortunes that surpass what fathers leave
As much as British whales surpass the dolphin.
So, in his dreadful days, Nero gave orders
To close Longinus' and too-rich Seneca's gardens
And ring the Lateran palace with a cohort.
A soldier seldom comes into a garret!
Although you carry in the night away   20
Those few plain silver dishes, you will fear

Some sword or club, the shaking of a reed's
Tall shadow in the moonlight. An empty-handed
Traveler will sing before a thief.
The first of prayers, well known in all the temples,
Is "Give me wealth, and may it grow, and may
My money-box be largest in the town."
But no one drinks his poison out of clay
Cups; you'll be afraid when someone offers
You jewelled goblets or when Setine wine   30
Winks at the brim in a bowl of solid gold.
Now will you praise the wise men, one of whom
Laughed when the other set foot outside his door,
While the latter wept? It's easy enough to sneer
And snicker: the wonder is where he found enough
Tears for those eyes. Democritus shook his sides
With constant laughter, although in those cities
There were no robes with purple stripes or borders,
No fasces, no sedan chairs, no tribunal.
What if he had seen the praetor riding by   40
Aloft in his tall car amid the dust
The circus raised, in Jove's own tunic, wearing
A Tyrian gown and carrying a crown
So large no neck could bear the weight of it?
A sweating public slave holds up the crown
Above the praetor's head and, that he may
Not grow conceited, rides at the great man's side.
Add now that bird upon his ivory scepter,
The blowing horns on this side and on that,
The clients in long line, the white-clad Romans   50
Beside his bridle (his free-lunch-money stuck
Deep in each purse has made them all his friends.)
The wise man found good cause for laughter in
Each man he met; his wisdom shows the world
The greatest men, who set the great examples,
Can rise in stupid towns, in Meat Head Land.
He laughed at the cares and pleasures of the mob,
And sometimes at their tears, while for himself
He ordered grim-faced Fortune go hang and stuck
His obscene middle-finger out at her.   60
So what we pray for, and properly wax the knees
Of the gods' statues as we pray, is fruitless
And dangerous. Their envied power hurls men
Headfirst, their long and noble list of honors
Swallows them up. Their statues all come down,
Pulled by a rope. An ax chops up the wheels

They rode on, even the legs of the poor horses
That drew their chariot. Now the fires crack,
Now, bellows-blown, the furnace flames, and great
Sejanus' head, the people's favorite, melts   70
Down its bronze. That face, of all the world
Once second in command, is turned to pitchers,
To dishpans, skillets, and to chamber-pots.
Put up the laurel at your doorway, lead
A huge chalked bull up to the Capitol!
Sejanus by a hook is dragged along
For all to see; the people cheer: "What lips,
What face he had! — I never liked the man,
Believe me. — What was the charge against him? Who
Squealed on him? What evidence, what witness? —   80
None: just a big, long, wordy letter came
From Capri. — Fine! I'll ask you nothing more."
    But what does the mob of Remus say? It follows
Fortune as ever and hates the men condemned.
The same crowd, if the Etruscan goddess Nortia
Had favored Etruscan Sejanus, if in his safe
Old age the Emperor had been murdered, would
In that same hour have called Sejanus August.
Now when nobody buys the votes we sell,
Cares flow away; the folk who once conferred   90
A general's rank, the fasces, legions, all,
Now holds off, anxious only for two things:
Bread and the circus games.
                                            "I hear that many
Will die. — You're right: inside a great big furnace. —
My friend Bruttidius seemed a little pale
When last I saw him by Mars' altar. I'm
Afraid that conquered Ajax will take vengeance
Upon him for a poor defense. — Let's run
Headlong and while he lies upon the bank
Let's trample on the enemy of Caesar.   100
— But let our slaves look on so none of them
Will rat on us and drag his trembling master,
A noose around his neck, into the court."
These were the words at that time on Sejanus,
These secret murmurs of the crowd. Would you
Like to be greeted as Sejanus, have
The wealth he had? To give, as he did, chairs
Of office, high commands, and be considered
The guardian of an Emperor who sits
On that thin ledge in Capri with his flock   110

Of fortune-tellers? Certainly you'd like
To have your body-guard, your noble knights,
Your private barracks; and why should you not?
Still those who have no wish to kill would like
The power to kill. But what extreme good fortune
Is worth it if your happiness is matched
By equal measure of unhappiness?
Do you prefer to wear the bordered gown
Of this man dragged to death, or to be safe
As plain commissioner of weights and measures   120
At Gabii or Fidenae, smashing up
The vessels of short weight like any poor
Town aedile in deserted Ulubrae?
You will admit Sejanus did not know
What he should wish for: when he craved too much
Honor and too much wealth, he was preparing
The stories of a mighty tower from which
His fall would be the greater and the crash
Of headlong ruin immense. What was it then
That threw down Crassus, Pompey, and the man   130
Who led the conquered Romans under his whip?
Why, highest power sought by every means,
Devout prayers heard by hostile deities!
Few kings descend to Ceres' son-in-law
Without a wound or slaughter, and few tyrants
Die a dry death.
              Whoever worships Wisdom
And brings his penny on her holiday
(A frugal gift to pay a frugal mistress),
Accompanied by a house-slave with his satchel
Begins to hope for eloquence and fame   140
Such as Demosthenes and Cicero had.
Yet eloquence brought death to each great speaker;
The boundless flowing fountain of his genius
Gave each to ruin. Cicero's genius cut
His head and hands off. Petty lawyers never
Poured out their life's blood on the speaker's stand.
"O Rome born blessed while I was your consul!"
He might have scorned the swords of Antony
If he had always spoken in this style.
Rather write poems that make their readers laugh   150
Than you, unwound the second on the roll,
Divine *Philippic* of conspicuous fame.
It was a dreadful death that swept him off
Whom Athens marvelled at as he stormed along,

Handling the reins in a crowded theater,
Born to unkindly gods and evil star,
Whose father, blear-eyed from the soot and glow
Of red-hot metal, sent from coal and tongs,
Where Vulcan beat out swords upon his anvil,
To study public speaking in a school.   160
    The spoils of war nailed to the trophy-stumps,
Breast-plates, cheek-straps that hang from a broken helmet,
A yoke with its pole cut off, the figure-head
Of a captured warship, and a prisoner shown
With hang-dog look high on a triumphal arch:
These are considered greater-than-human goods.
For these each Roman, Greek, barbarian
General longs, for these he risks and labors.
So much the greater thirst for fame than virtue!
For who would throw his arms around sheer Virtue   170
Shorn of rewards?
                    Yet often the vain glory
Of a few men has overwhelmed a country,
Their lust for praise and for a title, clinging
Upon the stones that guard their ashes, stones
Which evil strength of barren fig tree rends,
Since even sepulchers are doomed.
                    Weigh up
Hannibal in the scales; how many pounds
In that supreme commander? This is he
Whom Africa could not hold, a Moorish land
Beaten by Ocean, east to the luke-warm Nile,   180
South to the Ethiopians, and to other
Elephants. He conquers Spain, he leaps
Over the Pyrenees. His way is barred
By nature, Alps, and snow: he cracks the cliffs
And splits the mountain side with vinegar.
Now he holds Italy, he presses further still.
"Nothing is done," he says, "until my army
Breaks down the gates of Rome, and I shall place
My flag in mid-Subura." What a sight,
What picture worth the painting, to see the one-   190
Eyed leader riding on his elephant!
How did he finish? O glory, he was beaten
And fled break-neck to exile. There he sits
A mighty, marvellous suppliant of King Prusias,
Waiting until that tyrant chooses to wake.
No swords, no stones, no spears will kill that man
Who turned the whole world topsy-turvy once;

His little poison-ring shall yet avenge
The field of Cannae, so much Roman blood.
Forward, you madman, race across the Alps,   200
To please small school boys and become — a speech!
     One world is not enough for Alexander;
Forlorn he fidgets in the earth's short limits
As if caged up at Seriphos or Gyara.
Still, when he enters Babylon, that town
Walled in by bricks, he will be satisfied
With a sarcophagus. Lone death declares
How much a man's poor body's worth. The tale
Of history says that ships once sailed through Athos
(What things the lying Greeks will dare to tell!);   210
How solid sea gave surface to chariot wheels
And laid a pavement for those very ships;
How the steep rivers faded and the brooks
Were drunk dry while the Persian gulped his breakfast —
And all those songs drench-winged Sostratus sings.
But how did Xerxes come back from Salamis,
He who whipped the winds that never suffered
Such punishment in Aeolus's cavern,
He who tied Neptune up with chains and fetters,
And thought it merciful not to brand him too: 220
Which of the gods would wish to serve this master?
But how did he return? In just one ship,
Ploughing through bloody water dense with corpses!
All that he won for wishing so much glory.
     "Give me long life, Jove, give me many years!"
This only, this, though sick or well, you pray for.
Yet how continuous and how long old age,
How full of ills! Deformed and ugly face
Unlike its former self, a wrinkled hide
Instead of skin, the hanging cheeks, the grooves   230
Like those an old baboon carves on her jowls
Deep in the shaded jungle of Africa.
Young men differ in so many ways:
This one is handsomer than another; he
Still better than a third, while one man's stronger —
Old men have one appearance only: voices
That tremble like their legs, their heads are bald,
Their noses drip like a baby's; they must chew
Their bread with toothless gums: and so revolting
They are to wife and children and themselves   240
That even fortune-hunters pass them by.
Their torpid taste finds no more joy in wine

Or food; love fades into a long oblivion,
And if they try, their little tool lies still
And helpless even though they work all night.
Can grey hairs hope for anything from passion?
Should not desire be suspect with reason,
Attempting Venus when it's impotent?
Now see how one more sense is lost. What joy
Can old men take in song, however great   250
The singer, even the harper Seleucus?
What pleasure to shine with those who wear bright robes?
What difference does it make where he may sit
In the vast theater when he scarcely hears
The blare of horns and trumpets blown all together?
The slave who names his caller or tells the hour
Will have to shout to make an old man hear.
     Further than this, the little blood that flows
Through his cold body warms with fever only.
Diseases, forming ranks, leap all around him: 260
(If you should ask their names, I'd be prepared
More easily to tell you Oppia's lovers,
How many patients Doc Themson killed one autumn,
How many partners Basil cheated, how
Many the wards that guardian Hirrus ruined,
How many men tall Maura squeezes dry
In one day, or how many of his pupils
Hamillus has corrupted; I could much sooner
Tell you how many country homes the man
Who shaved my heavy beard when I was young,   270
Making his razor rasp, possesses now.)
That man suffers in his shoulder; this
In loins, that in his hips; here is another
Has lost both eyes and envies the one-eyed man.
This man's pallid lips accept their food
From someone's fingers. That other man whose mouth
Used to gape wide whenever he saw his dinner
Now opens his beak like any little swallow.
Whose hungry mother flies up with loaded bill.
But worse than any loss of limb is loss   280
Of memory, which cannot name his slaves,
Cannot recognize the friendly face
With whom he dined the night before, nor those
Children whom he created and brought up.
For with a savage testament he cuts
Off all his heirs, and wills his total wealth
To Phiale — so powerful the breath

Of that girl's tempting mouth: she carried on
For many years in a dark cell under an arch.
    And though the senses of his mind are strong,   290
Yet he must bury sons, must sadly view
The pyre of his beloved wife and brothers,
The urns that hold his sisters' ashes. These
Are penalties the long lived pay, to see
Calamity renewed within their homes;
In lamentation and perpetual grief,
In mourning garments always to grow old.
The king of Pylos (if you can believe
Great Homer) lived almost as long as crows,
Happy no doubt because he put off death   300
So many generations that he counted
His years by hundreds, and so many times
Drank up the new-made wine in every season.
    Yet wait a bit, I beg; see how he wails
Against the laws of fate, his too-long thread
Of life when he sees brave Antilochus'
Beard burning in the flames, and asks each friend
Around him why he's lived so long, what sin
Was his that made him worth so long a life.
Peleus too, when he mourned for lost Achilles,   310
Spoke thus; Laertes, when he mourned Odysseus.
Had Priam died while Troy was still unscathed,
With Hector and his brothers bearing the pall
While Trojan daughters wept, when first Cassandra
Began the wail, and Polyxena tore her veil,
If he had died more early and before
Paris began to build bold ships — what good
Did his long day bring him? He saw all things
In ruin, and Asia fallen in flames and steel.
He laid aside his crown and took up arms,   320
That tremulous soldier, and he died in front
Of great Jove's altar like an aged ox
Who thrusts a thin and wretched neck toward his
Master's knife, now done with the thankless plough.
Priam died at least a man's death; yet
His wife lived on to bark like a savage dog.
    I hasten to our Romans; I'll pass by
The king of Pontus, and Croesus, whom the voice
Of just and eloquent Solon ordered: "Look
To the last lap of all in your long life!"   330
Long life it was that brought to Marius
Exile and prison and Minturnan swamps

And made him beg his bread in conquered Carthage.
What citizen could nature have brought forth
In all the earth more blessed, what could Rome
Create, if crowded by long lines of captives,
By all the pomp of war, he had breathed his last
Just when he stepped from his German chariot?
Provident Campania gave fevers
He might have wished, to Pompey; but the prayers   340
Of many cities won: his luck, and Rome's,
Preserved him to be beaten and lose his head.
Lentulus never suffered this; Cethegus
Escaped this fate and died unmutilated,
And Catiline's entire corpse lay scratchless.
An anxious mother begs in a little voice
Good looks for her boys, and in a louder voice
Begs beauty for her girls as she goes by
The shrine of Venus, dwelling on details.
"Why shouldn't I?" she asks. "Latona took   350
Pride in Diana's beauty." But Lucretia
Forbids us to desire a face like hers.
Verginia, dead, would gladly take the hump
Rutila wears and give her loveliness
In fair exchange. A handsome son will make
His parents walk in fear and misery:
Good looks and chastity are seldom joined.
Although his home possesses a tradition
Of strict behavior like the ancient Sabines,
And kindly Nature with her lavish hand   360
Gives him chaste character, a cheek that blooms
With modest blood (what better could she give,
More careful and more powerful than any
Guard, to any youth?) he will not be
Allowed to grow to manhood. Spendthrift, pervert,
Vice will dare to tempt his very parents.
You can depend on money! No ugly boy
Was ever castrated by a cruel tyrant
In his high castle; Nero never raped
A bow-legged youth, or scrofulous, or one   370
Who had a hump upon his back or belly.

    Go now, rejoice in your son's youthful beauty,
Whom greater perils await. He will become
Public in his adultery and fear
His punishment from angry husbands, fall
At last like Mars, no luckier, into a net.
And now and then a husband will exact

More penalty than the law allows: he'll slay him,
Cut him to pieces with a whip, or stuff him
With mullets — common fate of gigolos.
Your Endymion will become some matron's
Lover. Soon, when Servilia pays him money,
He'll be *her* lover, just to take her jewels.
For what can any woman in love deny
Her lover, whether she's Oppia or Catulla?
Her passion is a woman's greatest weakness.
"But how does beauty harm the chaste?" What profit
Was chastity to Hippolytus, resolution
To Bellerophon? As though she were despised,
Phaedra grew angry when she was rejected
No less than Stheneboea; both of them
Stirred up their wrath. A woman is most savage
When to her hatred shame gives stimulus.
Choose the advice you think that we should give
To him whom Caesar's wife intends to wed.
Best and most handsome of a noble house,
That wretched youth is dragged to death by means
Of Messalina's very eyes. She sits
Draped in a flame-red bridal veil; the bed
Of matrimony stands in her open garden;
A dowry of one million sesterces
She brings, in ancient manner; witnesses
And fortune-tellers too are at her side.
You thought all this was secret, known to few?
She will not marry except by proper law.
Tell me what you've decided: if you say "No!"
You'll die before the lighting of the lamps.
If you complete the marriage you'll be given
A small delay until the whole affair,
Now known to town and people, reaches the ear
Of Caesar: he will be the last to know
The scandal in his house. But meanwhile you
Obey the order if you wish to live
A few days longer. In the better way,
Or easiest, you'll have to stick your neck,
So white and pretty, out for the hangman's sword.
    Then shall men pray for nothing? If you ask
Advice from me, you'll leave it to the gods
To give what's good for us and what is useful
To the Roman state: in place of what is pleasant
They'll give what fits us best.
                    Man is more dear

380

390

400

410

420

To them than to himself. We are led on
By impulse of soul and by our blind desire
To ask for wives and children: but the gods
Know of what sort our wives and sons will be.
Yet, so that there may be something you can pray for,
As you devote the entrails and prophetic
Sausages made from white pigs on the altar,
Why, pray for a sound mind in a healthy body!
Ask for a brave heart not afraid of death   430
That will not place long life among the gifts
Of nature, that can bear whatever troubles,
That knows no anger, wishes nothing, thinks
The works and woe of Hercules are better
Than love and banquets and the downy cushions
Of Sardanapalus. I'm pointing out
The things that you can give yourself: the path
To peaceful life, the only one, leads on
Through virtue. Fortune, you would have no power.
If men had wisdom; it is we who make   440
A goddess of you and place you in the skies.

L. R. Lind

Seneca

❰ Lucius Annaeus Seneca, son of the rhetorician of the same name and uncle of Lucan, was born at Cordoba, Spain, in 4 B.C. and took his own life at Nero's orders in A.D. 65, accused no doubt falsely of complicity in Piso's plot against Nero's life. He was Nero's tutor for seven years and an imperial administrator; the first five years of Nero's reign were a period of good rule largely because of Seneca's official activity and influence upon the emperor.

❰ Seneca was a philosopher who wrote much on ethics and natural science from the Stoic point of view. He also wrote nine tragedies on epic subjects, chiefly made up of rhetorical speeches and lyric choruses which greatly impressed the Elizabethan dramatists and inspired them to imitation. He seems to have been somewhat neurotic; his psychological state is revealed in his plays as well as in his philosophic writings. The intense passion and morbid violence of the plays are extraordinary; they were probably not meant to be acted but to be read. The chorus-sapphics could not have been sung in the Greek manner. The Elizabethan translators, so highly praised by T. S. Eliot in a famous essay, are still the only ones who have brought any measure of spirit and literary quality as English verse into their translations. ❱

THYESTES 344–357, 391–403

Wealth can never produce a king,
Robes of purple will not avail,
Nor broad brows of a kingly cast,
Nor great gates with a gleam of gold;
Nothing dug from a western mine,
Nothing dredged from the yellow flood
Tagus holds in its lucent bed,
Nor whatever from harvest fields
Boiling Libya threshes out.
King is he who has lost all fear,
All ill thoughts of an angry heart;
Whom no lawless ambition moves
Nor that ever fickle applause
Of massed men with their headlong haste.
He who stands upon solid ground

299

Sees within his own soul all things,
Meets his fate with a cheerful mind
Nor complains when it's time to die . . .
Let him have power's proud hall who will
Fly so high on a slippery peak;
Let sweet peace be enough for me:
Let my life in the silence flow
Quite unheeded by fellowmen.
So when all of my days have passed
Undisturbed by the world's loud noise,
Let me die as a plain old man.
Death comes hard for the man who lives
Known too well to his fellowmen,
Still unknown to himself in death.

Asa M. Hughes

THYESTES 391–403

Climb at Court for me that will
Tottering favor's pinnacle;
All I seek is to lie still.
Settled in some secret nest
In calm leisure let me rest,
And far off the public stage
Pass away my silent age.
Thus when without noise, unknown,
I have lived out all my span,
I shall die, without a groan,
An old honest country man.
Who exposed to other's eyes,
Into his own heart ne'er pries,
Death to him's a strange surprise.

Andrew Marvell

HERCULES FURENS

Chorus

Let th' ayre complayne, and eke the parent great
Of haughty Sky, and fertile land throughout,
And wandring wave of ever moving freat.
And thou before them all, which lands about
And trayn of Sea thy beames abroade dost throe

With glittring face, and mak'st the night to flee,
O fervent Titan: bothe thy settinges loe
And rysing, hath Alcides seene wyth thee:
And knowne lykewise hee hath thy howsen twayne.
From so great ills release yee nowe hys brest,
O Gods release: to better turne agayne
His ryghter mynde, and thou O tamer best
O sleep of toyles, the quietnesse of mynde,
Of all the lyfe of man the better parte,
O of thy mother Astrey wynged kynde,
Of hard and pyning death that brother arte,
With truth mingling the false, of after state
The sure, but eke the worste foreteller yet:
O Father of all thynges of Lyfe the gate,
Of lyght the rest, of nyght and fellowe fyt,
That com'st to Kyng, and servaunt equally,
And gently cherysshest who weary bee,
All mankynde loe that dreadfull is to dye,
Thou doost constrayne long death to learne by thee.
Keepe him fast bounde wyth heavy sleepe opprest,
Let slomber deepe his Limmes untamed bynde,
Nor soner leave his unright raginge breaste
Then former mynd his course agayne may fynd.
Loe layd on ground with full fierce hart yet still
His cruel sleepes he turnes: and not yet is
The plague subdude of so great raging yll
And on great club the weary head of his
He wont to laye, doth seeke the staffe to fynde
With empty handes his armes out casting yet
With moving vayne: nor yet all rage of minde
He hath layd downe, but as with Sowthwind greate
The wave once vext yet after kepeth still
His raging long, and though the wind now bee
Asswaged swelles, shake of theis madde and yll
Tossinges of mynde, returne let piety,
And vertue to the man, els let be so
His mynde with moving mad toste every waye:
Let errour blynd, where it begun hath, go,
For naught els now but only madnes maye
Thee gyltles make: in next estate it standes
To hurtles handes thy mischiefe not to know.
Now stroken let with Hercules his handes
Thy bosome sounde: thyne armes the worlde allow
Were wonte to beare, let grevous strypes now smyte
With conquering hande, and lowde complayning cryes,

Let th' ayre now heare, let of darke pole and nighte
The Queene them hear, and who ful fyercely lyes
That beares his neckes in mighty chaynes fast bounde,
Low lurking Cerberus in deepest cave.
Let Chaos all with clamour sad resound,
And of broad sea wide open wasting wave.
And th' ayre that felt thy weapons beter yet, but felt them though.
The breastes with so great yls as these beset,
With litle stroake they must not beaten bee.
Let kingdomes three sound with one playnt and crye,
And thou neckes honour and defence to see,
His arrowe strong longe hanged up on hye,
And quivers light the cruell stripes now smyte
On his fierce backe his shouldars strong and stout
Let oken club now strike, and poast of might
With knots ful hard his breaste load all aboute.
Let even his weapons so great woes complayne
Not you pore babes mates of your fathers praise,
With cruell wound revenging kinges agayne:
Not you your lims in Argos barriars playes,
Are taught to turne with weapons strong to smite
And strong of hand yet even now daring loe
The weapons of the Scithian quiver light
With stedy hand to paise set out from bow.
And stags to perce that save them selves by flight
And backes not yet ful maend of cruel beast.
To Stigian havens goe ye of shade and night
Goe hurtles soules, whom mischiefe hath opprest
Even in fyrst porch of lyfe but lately had,
And fathers fury goe unhappy kind
O litle children, by the way ful sad
    Of journey knowen.
    Goe see the angry kynges.

Thomas Newton

MEDEA

Chorus

What sharpe assaultes of cruell Cupids flame
Wyth gyddie heade thus tosseth to and froe
This bedlem Wyght, and divelysh despret dame
What roving rage her pricks to worke this woe?
Rough rancours vile congeales her frosen face,

Her hawty breast bumbasted is wyth pryde,
Shee shakes her heade, shee stalkes wyth stately pace.
Shee threates our king more than doth her betyde.
Who would her deeme to bee a banisht wyght,
Whose skarlet Cheekes doe glowe with rosy red?
In faynting Face, with pale and wanny whyght
The sanguyne hewe exyled thence is fled.
Her chaunging lookes no colour longe can holde,
Her shifting feete still travasse to and froe.
Even as the fearce and ravening Tyger olde
That doth unware his sucking whelpes forgoe,
Doth rampe, and rage, most eger ferce and wood,
Among the shrubs and bushess that doe growe
On Ganges stronde that golden sanded flood,
Whose silver streame through India doth flowe.
Even so Medea sometime wantes her wits
To rule the rage of her unbrydeled ire,
Nowe Venus Sonne, wyth busie froward fits,
Nowe Wrath, and Love enkyndle both the fire.
What shall shee doe? when will this heynous wyght
With forwarde foote bee packing hence away
From Greece? to ease our Realme of terrour quight,
And prynces twayne whom she so sore doth fray:
Nowe Phoebus lodge thy Charyot in the West,
Let neyther Raynes, nor Brydle stay thy Race,
Let groveling light with Dulceat nyght opprest
In cloking Cloudes wrapt up his muffled Face,
Let Hesperus the loadesman of the nyght,
In Western floode drench deepe the day so bryght.

John Studley

Statius

❨ With Publius Papinius Statius (born in A.D. 40 or 45 at Naples, died there in 96), the decline of Roman poetry under the influence of declamatory rhetoric and learned imitation begins to become pronounced. He wrote *Silvae,* thirty-two pleasant poems in five books on many topics often autobiographical, the *Thebais,* an epic on the Oedipus cycle pervaded by his love for Vergil, and an *Achilleid,* which he left unfinished. The dreamy languor and graceful ease of his Neapolitan surroundings make many of his shorter poems most charming reading. The most famous poem of the *Silvae* (meaning "woods," or material to be worked up into polished form) is his invocation of Sleep, here superbly translated by J. V. Cunningham. ❩

SILVAE V, 4

What was my crime, youthful most gentle god,
What folly was it that I alone should lack,
Sweet Sleep, thy gifts? All herds, birds, beasts are still,
The curved mountains seem wearily asleep,
Streams rage with muted noise, the sea-wave falls,
And the still-nodding deep rests on the shore.
Seven times now returning Phoebe sees
My sick eyes stare, and so the morning star
And evening, so Tithonia glides by
My tears, sprinkling sad dew from her cool whip.
How, then, may I endure? Not though were mine
The thousand eyes wherewith good Argus kept
But shifting watch, nor all his flesh awake.
But now, alas! If this long night some lover
In his girl's arms should willingly repel thee,
Thence come, sweet Sleep! Nor with all thy power
Pour through my eyes — so may they ask, the many,
More happy —; touch me with thy wand's last tip,
Enough, or lightly pass with hovering step.

J. V. Cunningham

Hadrian

(The emperor Hadrian (A.D. 76–138, reigned 117–138) was a patron of the arts and of philosophy and, like many patrons, a minor artist himself. The poem to his soul is the single bit of his verse which has survived.)

TO HIS SOUL

Little soul, like a cloud, like a feather,
My body's small guest and companion,
Where now do you rest, in what places —
Stripped naked, and rigid, and pallid,
Do you play as before, little jester?

Elinor Wylie

Aulus Gellius

⟦ Aulus Gellius (c. A.D. 123–c. 165, birthplace unknown) is famous for his encyclopedia of miscellaneous information, the *Attic Nights*. He was a member of cultured circles at Rome and Athens and a student of philosophy. The poem translated here is a rare event in the pages of his encyclopedia (19.11); it was written not by Gellius but by "a not uncultured young man" of his acquaintance who paraphrases an epigram of Plato on Agathon. Sir Stephen Gaselee, the translator of this poem, has traced the influence and the imitations of this idea in world literature: "The Soul in the Kiss," *The Criterion*, II (1924), 349 ff., the magazine edited by T. S. Eliot. ⟧

ATTIC NIGHTS 19.11

THE SOUL IN THE KISS

My lips apart
The lip I sip
And fragrant breath
Of my sweet-heart,
Till nigh to death
My poor soul leaps
From inmost deeps
And tries to force
A way across

And if a minute's more delay
Should make us in our kissing stay,
The poor thing would be all away,
And I — a dead man I should be;
For then my darling I should fill,
So living still
Though not in me.

Stephen Gaselee

Sulpicius Lupercus Servasius, Jr.

《[Nothing is known of this writer except that he lived in the fourth century A.D. and was probably not from Africa. **]》**

Rivers level granite mountains,
Rains wash the figures from the sundial,
The plowshare wears thin in the furrow;
And on the fingers of the mighty,
The gold of authority is bright
With the glitter of attrition.

Kenneth Rexroth

The Vigil of Venus

❨ The *Pervigilium Veneris*, a charming poem in honor of the Spring festival of Venus, is of unknown authorship, written perhaps in the reign of Hadrian or of Antoninus Pius, A.D. 117–161, or in the fourth century. E. K. Rand and others have argued for the earlier date; but there seems equally good evidence for the later one. The poem is easily the most remarkable of all manifestations of the new romantic spirit in Medieval Latin from which grew the secular Latin and vernacular lyric of later times. Its sensuous, passionate quality has caused it to be associated for centuries with Catullus and even printed with his poems; the last example of such an edition is Mackail's, 1912. The rhythm or verse-form was used in widely separated periods of Latin literature by the playwrights Plautus and Terence, by the soldiers at Caesar's triumphs in a kind of folk-song (compare the poem preserved by Flavius Vopiscus, translated by Edgar Allan Poe, page 323, and dating from a much later age), by St. Augustine in a hymn, and by early Irish hymn writers. ❩

I

Tomorrow let loveless, let lover tomorrow make love:
O spring, singing spring, spring of the world renew!
In spring lovers consent and the birds marry
When the grove receives in her hair the nuptial dew.

Tomorrow may loveless, may lover tomorrow make love.

II (III)

Tomorrow's the day when the prime Zeus made love:
Out of lightning foam shot deep in the heaving sea
(Witnessed by green crowds of finny horses)
Dione rising and falling, he made to be!

Tomorrow may loveless, may lover tomorrow make love.

III (II)

Tomorrow the Joiner of love in the gracious shade
Twines her green huts with boughs of myrtle claws,
Tomorrow leads her gangs to the singing woods:
Tomorrow Dione, on high, lays down the laws.

Tomorrow may loveless, may lover tomorrow make love.

308

IV

She shines the tarnished year with glowing buds
That, wakening, head up to the western wind
In eager clusters. Goddess! You deign to scatter
Lucent night-drip of dew; for you are kind.

Tomorrow may loveless, may lover tomorrow make love.

V

The heavy teardrops stretch, ready to fall,
Then falls each glistening bead to the earth beneath:
The moisture that the serene stars sent down
Loosens the virgin bud from the sliding sheath.

Tomorrow may loveless, may lover tomorrow make love.

VI

Look, the high crimsons have revealed their shame.
The burning rose turns in her secret bed,
The goddess has bidden the girdle to loose its folds
That the rose at dawn may give her maidenhead.

Tomorrow may loveless, may lover tomorrow make love.

VII

The blood of Venus enters her blood, Love's kiss
Has made the drowsy virgin modestly bold;
Tomorrow the bride is not ashamed to take
The burning taper from its hidden fold.

Tomorrow may loveless, may lover tomorrow make love.

VIII

The goddess herself has sent the nymphs to the woods,
The Boy with girls to the myrtles; perhaps you think
That Love's not truly tame if he shows his arrows?
Go, girls! Unarmed, Love beckons. You must not shrink.

Tomorrow may loveless, may lover tomorrow make love.

IX

Bidden unarmed to go and to go naked
Lest he destroy with bow, with dart, with brand —
Yet, girls, Cupid is pretty, and you must know
That love unarmed can pierce with naked hand!

Tomorrow may loveless, may lover tomorrow make love.

x (xiv)

Here will be girls of the farm and girls of the mountain
And girls who live by forest, or grove, or spring.
The mother of the Flying Boy has smiled
And said: Now, girls, beware his naked sting!

Tomorrow may loveless, may lover tomorrow make love.

xi

Gently she asks may she bend virginity?
Gently that you, a modest girl, may yield.
Now, should you come, for three nights you would see
Delirious bands in every grove and field.

Tomorrow may loveless, may lover tomorrow make love.

xii (x)

Venus herself has maidens as pure as you;
So, Delia, one thing only we ask: Go away!
That the wood shall not be bloody with slaughtered beasts
When Venus flicks the shadows with greening spray.

Tomorrow may loveless, may lover tomorrow make love.

xiii (xii)

Among the garlands, among the myrtle bowers
Ceres and Bacchus, and the god of verse, delay.
Nightlong the watch must be kept with votive cry —
Dione's queen of the woods: Diana, make way!

Tomorrow may loveless, may lover tomorrow make love.

xiv (xiii)

She places her court among the flowers of Hybla;
Presiding, she speaks her laws: the Graces are near.
Hybla, give all your blossoms, and bring, Hybla,
The brightest plain of Enna for the whole year.

Tomorrow may loveless, may lover tomorrow make love.

xv

With spring the father-sky remakes the world:
The male shower has flowed into the bride,
Earth's body; then shifted through sky and sea and land
To touch the quickening child in her deep side.

Tomorrow may loveless, may lover tomorrow make love.

XVI (XVII)

Over sky and land and down under the sea
On the path of the seed the goddess brought to earth
And dropped into our veins created fire,
That men might know the mysteries of birth.

Tomorrow may loveless, may lover tomorrow make love.

XVII (XVI)

Body and mind the inventive Creatress fills
With spirit blowing its invariable power:
The Sabine girls she gave to the sons of Rome
And sowed the seed exiled from the Trojan tower.

Tomorrow may loveless, may lover tomorrow make love.

XVIII

Lavinia of Laurentum she chose to bed
Her son Aeneas, and for the black Mars won
The virgin Silvia, to found the Roman line:
Sire Romulus, and Caesar her grandson.

Tomorrow may loveless, may lover tomorrow make love.

XIX

Venus knows country matters: country knows Venus:
For Love, Dione's boy, was born on the farm.
From the rich furrow she snatched him to her breast,
With tender flowers taught him peculiar charm.

Tomorrow may loveless, may lover tomorrow make love.

XX

See how the bullocks rub their flanks with broom!
See the ram pursue through the shade the bleating ewe,
For lovers' union is Venus in kind pursuit;
And she tells the birds to forget their winter woe.

Tomorrow may loveless, may lover tomorrow make love.

XXI

Now the tall swans with hoarse cries thrash the lake:
The girl of Tereus pours from the poplar ring
Musical change — sad sister who bewails
Her act of darkness with the barbarous king!

Tomorrow may loveless, may lover tomorrow make love.

XXII

She sings, we are silent. When will my spring come?
Shall I find my voice when I shall be as the swallow?
Silence destroyed the Amyclaeans: they were dumb.
Silent, I lost the muse. Return, Apollo!

Tomorrow let loveless, let lover tomorrow make love.

Allen Tate

Ausonius

❪ Decimus Magnus Ausonius (born at Bordeaux, c. A.D. 310, died there in 394) is the best Latin poet of the fourth century, one of several poets who enriched Gallic culture in that age. His poems contain a great deal of biographical detail. He was a professor of rhetoric at the university of Bordeaux, happily married, and later a tutor to Gratian, who became emperor in 375. Ausonius reached the consulship in 379. He is the first secular Christian-Latin poet to compose literature, not propaganda or polemic, in Western Europe. His best poem is a long description of the Moselle river, *Mosella,* full of keen and delicate perception. The *cento,* or patchwork poem, on *Nuptials* is an incredibly ingenious and obscene re-arrangement of many lines from the poetry of Vergil. Ausonius is a cultivated dilettante who chose no great subjects for his verse but nevertheless a man of great charm, the last pagan Latin author (although he also gave lip-service to Christianity) to preserve the flavor of ancient Roman poetry. Classical Rome greets the Middle Ages in his person. ❫

TO HIS WIFE

Love, let us live as we have lived, nor lose
    The little names that were the first night's grace,
And never come the day that sees us old,
    I still your lad, and you my little lass.
Let me be older than old Nestor's years,
    And you the Sibyl, if we heed it not.
What should we know, we two, of ripe old age?
    We'll have its richness, and the years forgot.

Helen Waddell

ON NEWBLOWN ROSES

Spring, and the sharpness of the golden dawn.
Before the sun was up a cooler breeze
Had blown, in promise of a day of heat,
And I was walking in my formal garden,
To freshen me, before the day grew old.

I saw the hoar frost stiff on the bent grasses,
Sitting in fat globes on the cabbage leaves,

And all my Paestum roses laughing at me,
Dew-drenched, and in the East the morning star,
And here and there a dewdrop glistening white,
That soon must perish in the early sun.

Think you, did Dawn steal color from the roses,
Or was it new born day that stained the rose?
To each one dew, one crimson, and one morning,
To star and rose, their lady Venus one.
Mayhap one fragrance, but the sweet of Dawn
Drifts through the sky, and closer breathes the rose.
A moment dies: this bud that was new born
Has burgeoned even fold on even fold;
This still is green, with her close cap of leaves,
This shows a red stain on her tender sheath,
This the first crimson of the loosened bud;
And now she thinks to unwind her coverings,
And lo! the glory of the radiant chalice,
Scattering the close seeds of her golden heart.
One moment, all on fire and crimson glowing,
All pallid now and bare and desolate.
I marvelled at the flying rape of time;
But now a rose was born: that rose is old.
Even as I speak the crimson petals float
Down drifting, and the crimsoned earth is bright.

So many lovely things, so rare, so young,
A day begat them, and a day will end.
O Earth, to give a flower so brief a grace!
As long as a day is long, so long the life of a rose.
The golden sun at morning sees her born,
And late at eve returning finds her old.
Yet wise is she, that hath so soon to die,
And lives her life in some succeeding rose.
O maid, while youth is with the rose and thee,
Pluck thou the rose: life is as swift for thee.

Helen Waddell

THE SORT OF GIRL HE PREFERS

Here's the mistress that I choose.
Careless brawls she won't refuse,
And bawdy words she'll often use;
Lovely, lively, loose in act,

She'll smack and let herself be smacked,
And smacked will snuggle to a kiss.
But if she's not at all like this
And lives a chastely straightened life —
I tremble: she will be my wife.

Jack Lindsay

ON SCRIBE PERGAMUS,
A SLAVE WHO VAINLY FLED

Slow Pergamus, you always were a dunce;
And then you ran, but you were caught at once.
So now your lettered brow, beneath the brand,
Endures the task neglected by your hand.

Jack Lindsay

TO THE NYMPHS PURSUING HYLAS

Nymphs, wanton out your hour.
Your cruel love has no power.
This lad shall be a flower.

Jack Lindsay

THE OLD MAN NEAR VERONA
WHO NEVER LEFT HIS FARM

Happy is he that owns ancestral lands
Where all his days from youth to age are cast.
There, where the baby crept, the old man stands
And sees, beyond his farm, the years go past.

For no tumultuous miseries he craved;
No unknown waters slaked his wandering thirst;
The seas, for gain or pay, he never braved;
With raucous lawsuits he was never cursed.

His inexperience looks upon the stars
More freely, ignorant of the town nearby.
The changing crops are all his calendars;
Apples mean autumn, spring a blossoming sky.

The sun goes down and rises still from earth,
And toil is all the clock that makes his day.
He knew the acorn whence the oak had birth,
And groves are ageing with his locks of grey.

Somewhere in India is Verona mapped,
And Lake Benacus the Arabian Sea.
Yet still the greybeard finds his strength unsapped,
And grandsons watch him bustling sturdily.

Let others seek Iberia, thewed for strife.
They know more ways, he knows the way, of life.

Jack Lindsay

SINGING ON THE MOSELLE 163–168

A folk rejoicing in labor, husbandmen busy and nimble
Move and work on the heights and along the slopes of the valley,
Singing their country ditties. To some the traveler journeying
Under the bank responds; and some from his vessel the sailor
Mocks in answering song because they are late to the vineyards.
Echoes ring from the rocks and the shore and the trembling forests.

Howard Mumford Jones

EPIGRAMS

On the Sicilian strand a Hare well wrought
Before the hounds was by a Dog-fish caught;
Quoth she; all rape of Sea and Earth's on me,
Perhaps of Heav'n, if there a Dog-star be.

The Cyniks narrow houshold stuffe of Crutch,
A stool and dish, was lumber thought too much;
For whilst a Hind drinks out on's palms, o' th' strand
He flings his dish, cries, I've one in my hand.

A treasure found one entring at death's gate,
Triumphing, leaves that cord was meant his fate,
But he the gold missing which he did hide,
The Halter which he found, he knit, so dy'd.

Vain Painter, why dost strive my face to draw,
With busy hands a Goddesse eyes nere saw?

Daughter of Air and Wind; I do rejoyce
In empty shouts (without a mind) a Voice.
Within your ears shrill echo I rebound,
And if you'l paint me like, then paint a sound.

Her jealous Husband an Adultresse gave
Cold poysons, which to weak she thought for's grave.
A fatal dose of Quicksilver, then she
Mingles to hast his double destinie;

Now whilst within themselves they are at strife,
The deadly potion yields to that of Life,
And straight from th' hollow stomack both retreat,
To th' slipp'ry pipes known to digested meat.
Strange care o' th' Gods! the Murth'resse doth avail,
So when fates please ev'n double poysons heal.

Because with bought books, Sir, your Study's fraught
A learned Grammarian you would fain be thought,
Nay then buy Lutes and strings, so you may play
The Merchant now, the Fidler the next day.

Richard Lovelace

THE GRAVE OF HECTOR

This is the grave of Hector: Troy lies in this small room —
The men, and the topless towers, that perished in his doom.

Anonymous

Paulinus of Nola

❪ Pontius Meropius Anicius Paulinus, born at Bordeaux in A.D. 353, was a student of Ausonius; their correspondence is extant. He became a politician and administrator, married a wealthy woman, and lived with her on his estate in Spain. He later turned to Christianity at Nola, in Campania, Italy; in 409 he was made bishop of Nola and died in 431. ❫

TO AUSONIUS

I, through all chances that are given to mortals,
   And through all fates that be,
So long as this close prison shall contain me,
   Yea, though a world shall sunder me and thee,

Thee shall I hold, in every fibre woven,
   Not with dumb lips, nor with averted face
Shall I behold thee, in my mind embrace thee,
   Instant and present, thou, in every place.

Yea, when the prison of this flesh is broken,
   And from the earth I shall have gone my way,
Wheresoe'er in the wide universe I stay me,
   There shall I bear thee, as I do today.

Think not the end, that from my body frees me,
   Breaks and unshackles from my love to thee;
Triumphs the soul above its house in ruin,
   Deathless, begot of immortality.

Still must she keep her senses and affections,
   Hold them as dear as life itself to be.
Could she choose death, then might she choose forgetting:
   Living, remembering, to eternity.

Helen Waddell

FOR ST. FELIX' DAY

Spring wakens the birds' voices, but for me
My Saint's day is my spring, and in its light
For all his happy folk the winter flowers.
Keen frost without, midwinter, and the year
Rigid with cold and all the country white,
But gone the harder winter of the soul.

Even as the gentle swallow knows the days
That are his friends, the white bird with black wings,
And the kind turtle-doves, and no bird sings,
But silently slips through the ragged copses,
Till the day comes that the thorn trees are loud
With the greenfinches, then what shining wings
And what gay voices, so I know the day
Year after year that is St. Felix' Feast,
And know the springtime of my year is come,
And sing him a new song.

Helen Waddell

Avianus

❨ The Romans loved the terse wisdom, the embodiment of moral principles, in fables. Aesop the Greek in the sixth century B.C. was the first European fabulist, followed by Babrios in the second century A.D. Ennius, Lucilius, and Horace used them in their Latin satires; Phaedrus, a freedman of Augustus, published a collection of eighty-three. The Romans used fables in their elementary education. Avianus, whose dates are around 400 A.D., wrote forty-two fables whose style is heavily influenced by Vergil. His style is simpler than that of Phaedrus; his book was a favorite in Europe during the Middle Ages. Had he lived to complete it the late Prof. W. A. Oldfather's critical text of the fables of Avianus, based on the most complete manuscript evidence, would have been definitive; it is to be hoped that this edition will some day be published. ❩

THE WOMEN AND THE WOLF

A country-nurse once told her weeping boy
"A wolf will eat you if you cry again."
A credulous wolf, who overheard with joy,
Remained all night before the doors, in vain.
The weary child soon drifted into sleep;
With disappointed hope the listener burned —
Back to his forest-lair he had to creep;
His bitch perceived that fasting he'd returned.
"Where is the usual snack?" she asked. "And why
With wasted jaws come crawling in dismay?"
"Don't stare," he said. "I heard a wicked lie.
It's luck that, famished out, I got away.
What profit could I ever hope to gain
When hearkening to the prattle of a nurse?"
Thus often must a worried man complain,
Who, trusting woman, finds her art a curse.

Jack Lindsay

THE CRAB

A crab once tried to turn and bumped instead
On washing rocks his rugged carapace.

His mother, who desired to go ahead,
Admonished thus her son with moral face:
"Come, leave these crooked ways and mend your gait;
Don't dodge aside on any weak pretence:
With ready effort take the road that's straight;
And tread the unwinding path of innocence."
The son replied: "Then go in front of me
And show me what is right. I'll do it then."
A man, defaulting, is a fool if he
Accuses faults revealed by other men.

Jack Lindsay

Claudian

([Claudius Claudianus, an Eastern Greek born perhaps c. A.D. 370 in
Alexandria, Egypt, spent the years 395–404 in Italy, where he wrote
poems of flattery in Latin to those from whose favor he might profit.
He proved himself an able poet in the foreign tongue he had adopted,
writing political, mythological, and shorter pieces. His work is full of
rhetoric and exaggeration; his longer and more famous poems are *The
Rape of Proserpine* and a series of political panegyrics and epithalamia. Claudian is sometimes called the last pagan Latin poet; but he
was a Greek by birth and certainly no more entitled to this melancholy honor than was Ausonius.])

EPITAPH

Fate to beauty still must give
Shortened life and fugitive;
All that's noble, all that's fair
Suddenly to death repair.
Here a lovely woman lies,
Venus in her hair and eyes;
Since with these she must divide
Heaven's envy, here she died.

Howard Mumford Jones

Flavius Vopiscus

❮ This obscure man from Syracuse, Sicily, is better known as one of the six Scriptores Historiae Augustae of the fourth century A.D., who wrote thirty lives of the later emperors modelled on the biographies of Suetonius. His particular small collection of lives was completed before the death of Diocletian in 316. He is not the author of this soldier's song, which he records in his life of Aurelian, who built the great wall still to be seen around the city of Rome. The translation is the only one Poe seems to have made. ❯

AURELIAN 6

TRIUMPHAL SONG OF THE ROMAN ARMY

A thousand, a thousand, a thousand,
A thousand, a thousand, a thousand,
We, with one warrior, have slain!
A thousand, a thousand, a thousand, a thousand,
Sing a thousand, over again!
Soho! — let us sing
Long life to our king
Who knocked over a thousand so fine.
Soho! — let us roar,
He has given us more
Red gallons of gore
Than all Syria can furnish of wine!

Edgar Allan Poe

St. Ambrose

❨ St. Ambrose was born at Treves (c. A.D. 330/340; died 397), educated at Rome, and became bishop of Milan in 374 as well as a counsellor of the emperors Gratian, Valentinian II, and Theodosius. He drew upon Cicero's *De Officiis* (On Moral Duties) for his own influential work of almost the same name, *De Officiis Ministrorum* (c. 391), on Christian morality, borrowing by way of Cicero from Stoic ethics the distinction between reason and the passions, the idea of the sovereign good, the classification of virtues and duties, the values of conscience, etc. His hymns are well edited by A. S. Walpole, *Early Latin Hymns,* Cambridge, England, 1922. Four great hymns are attributed to Ambrose by St. Augustine: *Aeterne rerum conditor, Deus creator omnium, Iam surgit hora tertia,* and *Veni, redemptor gentium;* eight others are doubtful. ❩

AETERNE RERUM CONDITOR

Builder eternally of things,
Thou rulest over night and day,
Disposing time in separate times
That Thou mayst lessen weariness;

Now crows the herald of the day,
Watchful throughout the wasting dark,
To walkers in the night a clock
Marking the hours of dark and dawn.

The morning star arises now
To free the obscure firmament;
Now every gang and prowling doom
Forsakes the dark highways of harm.

The sailor now regathers strength,
The channels of the sea grow calm;
And now Peter, the living rock,
Washes his guilt in the last crow.

Then quickly let us rise and go;
The cock stirs up the sleepy-head,

And chides again the lie-a-bed;
The cock convicts them who deny.

And to cock-crow our hopes reply;
Thy grace refills our ailing hearts;
The sword of brigandage is hid;
And faith returns where faith had fled.

Jesu, look back on us who fall,
Straighten the conduct of our life;
If Thou lookst back, denials fail,
And guilt is melted in a tear.

Thou Light, illumine with Thy light
Our sleeping lethargy of soul;
Thy name the first our lips shall choose,
Discharging thus our vows to Thee.

J. V. Cunningham

Prudentius

❰ Aurelius Prudentius Clemens, the first great Christian Latin poet, was born in Spain in A.D. 348 and died in 405. He wrote didactic and lyric poetry. Among his more considerable works are the *Peristephanon, Psychomachia,* and *Hamartigenia.* The *Cathemerinon* is a collection of twelve hymns, the first six for appropriate hours in the Christian day. The *Hymn for Morning* is the second of these. A selection of the poems of Prudentius as well as of other Christian Latin poets is published by O. J. Kuhnmuench, *Early Christian Latin Poets from the Fourth to the Sixth Century,* Chicago, 1929. ❱

PER QUINQUENNIA IAM DECEM

My first half century was done
With long ago, the year that's just begun
The fifty-seventh I've enjoyed the rolling sun.

The end is near and near the day
The god long since assigned for my decay —
What useful thing have I contrived in so long stay!

My childhood was a tearful time
Under the smacking ferule; then the prime
Toga brought me to lies and vice and even crime!

Then wanton lust and wild excess
Befouled my youth — alas, I now confess
In sorrow and shame — with filth and mire of worthlessness!

Contention next gave instruments
To my vexed soul and often my intense
Evil desire to conquer bred harsh consequence.

Twice in administering the law
I held the reins over proud towns and saw
The good given their rights, the evil struck with awe.

My gracious Prince at length relieved
My army service and myself received
As his close helper: nearly regal rank achieved!

So life flew by; my hair, grown white
Unnoticed, flashed old age — for I had quite
Forgot under what consul I first saw the light.

The snow flakes on my head disclose
How often since the sun's brought round the snows,
How often to meadows freed from frost returned the rose.

Asa M. Hughes

HYMN FOR MORNING

　　Black clouds and mists and sullen night —
This world's confused and murky gloom —
Disperse — begone — the Dawn is come:
Christ enters: in the East is light . . .

　　So fades the darkness from our hearts:
Made bare the guilty fears that filled
Our breasts are presently dispelled,
Our God is King: the clouds depart . . .

　　Once with the Angel Jacob dared
By night to wrestle unafraid,
Nor from unequal combat stayed
Until the morning light appeared.

　　But when the gathering dawn was high,
Presumption fled, he knew his fault:
His sinew shrank and he was halt,
Lamed in the hollow of his thigh . . .

　　We by this parable are taught
That whoso clings to darkness close
And yields not unto God, shall lose
The rebel strength by which he fought.

　　More blest is he who, maimed from strife,
Each limb unruly cut away,
Wasted and lamed, when comes the day,
Is called to enter into Life . . .

Basil Blackett

FOR THE BURIAL OF THE DEAD

Now, Earth, to thy keeping we send him:
In thy fostering bosom we leave him.
He's a man: to thy care we commend him:
He is dead, he is noble; receive him.

In this body a soul had his dwelling,
By the breath of His Maker was fashioned:
In wisdom and knowledge excelling:
For the Christ and His Kingdom impassioned.

In thy mantle enfold him and shield him,
In trust: for His Author and Maker
Ever mindful shall bid thee to yield him
His own, of His image partaker.

When the day of the just comes in splendor,
When hope is fulfilled, from thy portal
Even such, as I give, thou shalt render
Him again, unto glory immortal.

What if time with his mouldering finger
His bones under ashes shall smother,
And of dust but a handful yet linger —
But a handful of ashes our brother —

What if flesh that to atoms is scattered,
And on wind blowing whither it knows not
Through the empty inane shall be scattered,
That a man be destroyed, God allows not . . .

For the faithful a highway is builded:
Unto Paradise bright it shall guide them:
And the keys unto men have been yielded
Of the garden the serpent denied them.

There, hallowed in house of His Father,
Whence outcast he wandered and weeping,
To Thy bosom, we pray Thee, Lord, gather
This soul, this Thy servant, here sleeping.

Heap violets, boughs blossom-laden,
Many leaves on his resting place strew:
Cold stone with his epitaph graven
With perfume and fragrance bedew.

Basil Blackett

Boethius

《 Anicius Manlius Severinus Boethius, born at Rome, A.D. 480, executed by Theodoric in 524, was an adviser to Theodoric, king of the Ostrogoths, and a philosopher whose famous work is the *Consolation of Philosophy*, one of the most influential books of the Middle Ages. It is written in the form of a Menippean satire, in prose mingled with thirty-nine poems. Boethius composed it in prison. He also produced commentaries on works of Aristotle and Cicero and theological tractates. Gibbon called him "the last of the Romans." His noble character shines throughout the pages of his masterpiece. 》

From the CONSOLATION OF PHILOSOPHY

OPENING POEM

Lo! I sing cheerily
   In my bright days,
But now all wearily
   Chaunt I my lays;
Sorrowing tearfully,
   Saddest of men,
Can I sing cheerfully,
   As I could then?

Many a verity
   In those glad times
Of my prosperity
   Taught I in rhymes;
Now from forgetfulness
   Wanders my tongue,
Wasting in fretfulness,
   Metres unsung.

Worldliness brought me here
   Foolishly blind,
Riches have wrought me here
   Sadness of mind;

329

When I rely on them,
   Lo! they depart —
Bitterly, fie on them!
   Rend they my heart.

Why did your songs to me,
   World-loving men,
Say joy belongs to me
   Ever as then?
Why did ye lyingly
   Think such a thing,
Seeing how flyingly
   Wealth may take wing?

Alfred the Great (attributed)

Venantius Fortunatus

¶ Venantius Honorius Clementianus Fortunatus was born near Treviso, Italy, c. 540, and died c. 603. Educated at Ravenna, he came to France by way of the cities of the Rhineland on pilgrimage to the shrine of St. Martin of Tours, writing poems of flattery to the bishops he visited along the way. This journey is recorded in the eleven books of his poems, collected at the wish of his friend Gregory, bishop of Tours. He became bishop of Poitiers, whither he had been drawn by his admiration for the saintly life of the former queen of Chlothar, Radegunde. Venantius is sometimes called the first of Medieval Latin poets. Iovinus, to whom he wrote a poem translated here, was governor of Provence. The *Vexilla Regis Prodeunt,* one of Venantius' great hymns, was written in honor of a fragment of the Holy Cross brought to Poitiers; the hymn became a Crusaders' marching song. ❱

VEXILLA REGIS PRODEUNT

The banners of the King go forth,
Glistens the Cross's mystery
That flesh's Builder in the flesh
Was on a gibbet hung.

His vitals were transfixed with nails,
He stretched out his hands and feet:
For grace of our redemption
This Host was sacrificed.

Upon the cross He hung, wounded
By the point of a dire lance.
That he might wash us of our sins
He dripped water and blood.

Fulfilled is all that David sang
In his prophetic song of Faith,
Declaring to the nations,
"God from wood has reigned."

The tree is fit and glorious,
Adorned with purple of the King,

331

Chosen by honorable gift
To touch such sacred limbs.

Blessed it is upon whose arms
Has hung the ransom of an age;
It has become the body's scales
And taken spoil of hell.

You pour a sweet smell from your bark,
You outdo nectar in your taste.
Fertile with a joyous fruit,
In noble triumph you praise.

Hail altar, hail the Victim
For glory of the passion
By which life has accomplished death
And through death life restored.

Albert Cook

TO THE NOBLE AND PATRICIAN IOVINUS, GOVERNOR OF PROVENCE

The fallen ages fly away, we are tricked by the fugitive hours . . .
So we too, unlike each other, all move to the same end,
    No one draws back his foot once it has touched the threshold . . .
What protection are weapons to men? Hector falls and avenging
        Achilles,
    Ajax, the Achaean wall with his shield, is dead . . .
Charming loveliness slips away, Astur the most handsome has fallen,
    Hippolytus huddles in death, and Adonis survives no more.
Where is song, I ask? Orpheus who entranced the world
    With his high notes lies dead, the voice of his lyre is silent.
What of poetry? Vergil, Ovid, Menander, Homer,
    Whose naked bones their sepulchers cover in dripping slime?
When the last day comes, their songs are no good to the Muses,
    There is no joy in drawing out their last lingering melody.
Thus, as the moments fall, the present flies,
    When the dice are snatched from our hands the gaming table is taken
        away . . .
There is nothing left when good men die but a blessed flower,
    The fragrance of those who were just rises sweet from their tomb.

L. R. Lind

Octavianus

❮ Octavianus is the editor of the *Anthologia Latina*, a collection of poets who flourished down to the end of the third century A.D. The Anthology was compiled around the year 532 at the request of a Vandal prince. Emil Baehrens discusses the meager history of the book in the preface to his edition of the *Poetae Latini Minores*. The following poem is attributed to Octavianus. ❯

PAINTED PASSION

Paint a whitelimbed girl for me
Such as love himself might fashion;
So that nothing hidden be,
Paint her with a lover's passion.
Through her silken garments show
All her body's rosy wonder —
Love will set your sense aglow,
Longing tear your heart asunder.
Call it, when your work you scan,
"portrait of a wretched man."

Howard Mumford Jones

St. Columban

❲ Columbanus (St. Columban), born in Leinster, Ireland, in 543, lived in Gaul around 590, and was a great teacher and an apostle to Burgundy, Switzerland, and Italy. He was a skilled versifier who wrote "the oldest surviving quantitative verses of Irish origin" (Raby). The ascription of the *Boating Song* to him is probable. Columbanus founded the monastery of Bobbio in the Apennines midway between Genoa and Piacenza, an important seat of learning and manuscript-copying during the Middle Ages. ❳

BOATING SONG

Heia, men, our shout goes out and echoes back, heia!
The placid face of the sea is dimpled smilingly.
The bed of ocean is smooth, the storms are put to flight,
And the restless weight of the waves has fallen out of sight.

Heia, men, our shout goes out and echoes back, heia!
As our oars together dip, a quiver seizes the ship.
The sea and the sky are beaming to befriend us in our need,
The wind will marry our sails and belly them out with speed.

Heia, men, our shout goes out and echoes back, heia!
Our prow is cleaving the foam like a dolphin racing for home.
The timbers shake and wheeze at each sinewy stroke we make,
And we leave behind in the trough a winding whitening wake.

Heia, men, our shout goes out and echoes back, heia!
The dolphins leap from the waves, but heia is what we call.
The tossed waves foam from our oars, but heia comes from us all.
Our songs ring back from the shores — *heia all, call heia!*

Jack Lindsay

Alcuin

⟨ Alcuin (c. 735–804) went from York Cathedral in England, where he had collected a fine library, to Aachen (or Aix-la-Chapelle) to become Charlemagne's Master of the Schools. He taught there ten years, then retired to Tours, where he died in the abbey of St. Martin. He wrote much on grammar and other subjects. ⟩

TO THE CUCKOO

Now from the topmost boughs resounds the song of the cuckoo,
And the parti-colored world brings to blossom the buds of the flowers;
Now the young vine puts forth from the shoot the wine-bearing jewels,
And now in the golden land the nightingale, never-tiring,
Pours its melody forth, uplifting our ears to its music.

Howard Mumford Jones

Paul the Deacon

⟨ A companion of Alcuin during the ninth century at Charlemagne's palace-school and a close friend of that monarch, Paulus Diaconus (Paul the Deacon) came from Lombardy; among his works is a History of the Lombards. After 774 he retired to Monte Cassino, a great center of learning. He wrote some Horatian odes and acquired a reputation for his knowledge of Greek. The poet here laments the death of Charlemagne's daughter. ⟩

ADELHEID

Within this sepulcher
A little girl lies buried;
She was called at baptism Adelheid.
Charles was her father, Charles the Mighty,
The bearer of two diadems.
Nearing the Rhone
She was snatched from the threshold of life.
Far distant
Her mother's heart was stricken with sorrow.
She died, never beholding
The triumph of her father,
And now in the kingdom of the blessed
The Infinite Father
Has her.

Howard Mumford Jones

St. Peter Damian

❪ Peter Damian or Damiani (1007–1072) was born at Ravenna, where he opened a school. He left teaching for the Church, became cardinal-bishop of Ostia, and grew famous for his preaching and practice of asceticism, which caused him to live in a world of strange fancies and terrors produced by his own imagination. ❫

THE GLORY OF PARADISE

For the springs of living waters pants my parchèd soul athirst:
Still my spirit, prisoned, exiled, longs its bars of flesh to burst,
Straining, yearning, pining, burning for the home it knew at first.

Here it moaneth and it groaneth, faint with sin, by care fordone;
In surrender sees the splendor of the glory that is gone:
Sting of present sorrow sharpens memory of bliss foreknown.

In that realm of perfect peace and joy and happiness untold
Pearly mansions gleam to heaven capped with domes of burnished
     gold,
And the dwellings of the saints are decked with riches manifold.

For the building of that city only precious stones are meet:
Polished gold, and clear as crystal, is the paving of the street.
There no filth, nor slime, nor mire can befoul the passer's feet.

Winter's ire, summer's fire, that fair city never knows:
In its gardens, sweet with balsam, spring eternal breathes and blows,
White with lily, bright with crocus, red with ever-blooming rose.

Green its fields and clean its pastures; flow with honey stream and rill:
Fragrant scents and luscious juices aromatic herbs distill:
Fruits that fall not bend the laden boughs of orchards flowering still.

Moon and sun and stars unsleeping keep their constant watch aright:
Christ, the Lamb, upon that city sheds His never-failing light:
Day perpetual reigneth alway: never intrudeth Time nor Night.

Lo! the visage of each saint there, as the Sun, in glory glows:
Victors, jubilant, triumphant, sharing heaven's sure repose,
They rehearse their well-fought battles and recount their conquered
    foes.

They are cleansed from taint of evil, lust of flesh and passion wild:
Member wars no more with member, mind and body reconciled:
They shall dwell in peace forever, holy spirits undefiled.

They have turned from all that changeth to the changeless source of
    all:
They behold the very beauty of the Godhead actual:
Sweet and living waters drink they from the fount perennial.

They have caught the rhythmic measure that is life's eternity,
Life from change and chance immune, abundant, active, joyous, free.
Age enfeebles not and sickness saps not their virility.

Therefore is their Being timeless: fleetingness is fled away:
Ardor, vigor, valor fill them: gone corruption and decay:
Immortality is master over death's dead mastery.

Knowing Him who knoweth all things, nought can be to them
    unknown:
Each his fellow's secrets sharing shares with all the rest his own:
In refusing and in choosing all their several wills are one.

Diverse gifts, unequal merits bring no inequality:
Thine is what thou lovest in others — this is heaven's charity:
Thus belongs what each possesses to their whole community.

Surely, wheresoever the body, must the eagles gather there:
One the Bread and One the Body which the saints and angels share:
Citizens of earth and heaven thus their unity declare.

Always filled yet always eager for that true and living Bread:
Pangs of hunger gnaw them never: never are they surfeited:
What they have they still desire: still they crave and still are fed.

Anthems new and hymns of glory tuneful voices ever sing:
Organ's music charms their ears with harmonies re-echoing:
Laud they Him who made them victors: praise they Him who is their
    King.

Happy souls, that stand in presence of the King of Heaven on high,
And behold beneath their feet this Earth and Sun and Moon and Sky
And the clusters of the Stars that whirl in space eternally.

Christ, who art the soldier's palm-wreath, bring me to Thy city blest:
Let me enter there, Thy veteran, and unarm at Thy behest,
To receive my portion there, and dwell with Thine elect at rest.

Grant me strength to battle on undaunted in this ceaseless war:
Grant me peace when I have fought my fight and earthly life is o'er:
Be my guerdon to possess Thee utterly for evermore.

Basil Blackett

Hildebert of Le Mans

《 Hildebert (born at Lavardin, France, 1056; died as archbishop of Tours, 1133) became leader of the cathedral school and archdeacon at Le Mans in 1091, bishop in 1096. His interests were both secular and ecclesiastical under the dukes of Normandy. His visit to Rome in 1100 inspired him to write a verse description of the pagan ruins he saw there. He wrote sermons, letters, saints' lives, a treatise on theology, and many poems, chiefly on religious subjects. His biography was written by A. Dieudonné, *Hildebert de Lavardin*, Paris, 1898. 》

ORATIO AD DOMINUM

I

Save me, Lord! thou King Eternal!
From those dark domains infernal,
Where is weeping, where is wailing;
Where all prayers are unavailing;
Where each soul doth self-inherit
Proof of its own damned demerit; —
Tortures reaping, ever crying,
From the worm that is undying;
Where no hope can come to sever
Life from death in hell for ever!

II

Me to Zion take in pity!
David's Zion, tranquil city.
Built by God, of light: its portal
Cross of Christ, the wood immortal:
Key that locks, the tongue of Peter;
Turned, the songs of gods not sweeter:
Walled, heaven-high, the scaleless story,
Guarded by the King of Glory!

III

In this city, light eternal
Reigns for ever — peace supernal;
Odors flow in such completeness,
Heaven is filled with songs of sweetness.

IV

There the soul knows no corruption,
Frailty none, nor interruption;
None too little, none dilated —
All in Christ are consummated.

V

Heavenly city! glorious city!
Built upon the rock of pity!
City, in whose gates are gathered
All I longed for, all I fathered!
Now I greet thee, thee I sigh for,
Whose possession I would die for!

VI

With what warm congratulations
Meet in thee the joyful nations!
How delighted stand they gazing
At the walls, with glory blazing —
Hyacinth and chalcedony —
Heaven's own wealth their patrimony!

VII

In this city's streets, for greeting,
Clouds of blessed souls are meeting —
Singing songs, such as the pious
Moses sang for rapt Elias!

Thomas Holley Chivers

SENECA'S EPITAPH

Toil, trouble, praise and blame through office won,
Go, and vex other lives, now mine is done.
God calls me from you; with the world's travail
Accomplished, earth that welcomes me I hail.
Take to your somber rocks my body too:
My soul I give to Heaven, my bones to you.

L. R. Lind

Abelard

([Peter Abelard (1079–1142) was a great medieval hymn writer as
well as a prominent university professor. He refuted the theories of
William of Champeaux, becoming a central and controversial figure at
Paris. The story of his famous love-affair with Heloise he told in his
History of Calamities; the tragic pair are buried in Père Lachaise
cemetery in Paris. Helen Waddell has written a charming novel
called *Peter Abelard* (London, 1933).])

RUMOR LETALIS

I am constantly wounded
By the deadly gossip that adds
Insult to injury, that
Punishes me mercilessly
With the news of your latest
Scandal in my ears. Wherever
I go the smirking fame of each
Fresh despicable infamy
Has run on ahead of me.
Can't you learn to be cautious
About your lecheries?
Hide your practices in darkness;
Keep away from raised eyebrows.
If you must murder love, do it
Covertly, with your candied
Prurience and murmured lewdness.

You were never the heroine
Of dirty stories in the days
When love bound us together.
Now those links are broken, desire
Is frozen, and you are free
To indulge every morbid lust,
And filthy jokes about your
Latest amour are the delight
Of every cocktail party.
Your boudoir is a brothel;
Your salon is a saloon;

Even your sensibilities
And your depraved innocence
Are only special premiums,
Rewards of a shameful commerce.

O the heart-breaking memory
Of days like flowers, and your
Eyes that shone like Venus the star
In our brief nights, and the soft bird
Flight of your love about me;
And now your eyes are as bitter
As a rattlesnake's dead eyes,
And your disdain as malignant.
Those who give off the smell of coin
You warm in bed; I who have
Love to bring am not even
Allowed to speak to you now.
You receive charlatans and fools;
I have only the swindling
Memory of poisoned honey.

Kenneth Rexroth

Bernard of Clairvaux

¶ Bernard of Clairvaux in France (1090–1153) was the most famous of Cistercian monks. He founded the abbey at Clairvaux in 1115. A great and simple mystic, his devotion expressed itself best in the verses in which he praised Jesus. ¶

IESU, DULCIS MEMORIA

Jesus to cast one thought upon
Makes gladness after He is gone;
But more than honey and honeycomb
Is to come near and take Him home.

Song never was so sweet in ear,
Word never was such news to hear,
Thought half so sweet there is not one
As Jesus God the Father's Son.

Jesu, their hope who go astray,
So kind to those who ask the way,
So good to those who look for Thee,
To those who find what must Thou be?

To speak of that no tongue will do
Nor letters suit to spell it true:
But they can guess who have tasted of
What Jesus is and what is love.

Jesu, a springing well Thou art,
Daylight to head and treat to heart,
And matched with Thee there's nothing glad
That can be wished or can be had.

Wish us good morning when we wake
And light us, Lord, with Thy daybreak.
Beat from our brains the thicky night
And fill the world up with delight.

344

Be our delight, O Jesu, now
As by and by our prize art Thou,
And grant our glorying may be
World without end in Thee.

Gerard Manley Hopkins

St. Thomas Aquinas

([St. Thomas (c. 1225–1274) was born at Aquino in Italy, where his father was a count. He was educated at Montecassino, studied at Naples, and joined the Dominican order. From 1245 to 1248 he studied at Paris, later at Cologne, under the famous scholar, Albertus Magnus. The Aristotelian studies of Thomas Aquinas, carried on in Latin translations, resulted in his monumental *Summa Theologica*, a synthesis of Aristotle in harmony with Christian doctrine. He composed beautiful church offices and sequences still included in the Roman Breviary and Missal. He is the patron saint of students, for whom he wrote a famous prayer.])

RHYTHMUS AD SS. SACRAMENTUM

Godhead here in hiding, whom I do adore
Masked by these bare shadows, shape and nothing more,
See, Lord, at thy service low lies here a heart
Lost, all lost in wonder at the God thou art.

Seeing, touching, tasting are in thee deceived;
How says trusty hearing? that shall be believed;
What God's Son has told me, take for truth I do;
Truth himself speaks truly or there's nothing true.

On the cross thy godhead made no sign to men;
Here thy very manhood steals from human ken:
Both are my confession, both are my belief,
And I pray the prayer of the dying thief.

I am not like Thomas, wounds I cannot see,
But can plainly call thee Lord and God as he:
This faith each day deeper be my holding of,
Daily make me harder hope and dearer love.

O thou our reminder of Christ crucified,
Living Bread the life of us for whom he died,
Lend this life to me then: feed and feast my mind,
There be thou the sweetness man was meant to find.

Bring the tender tale true of the Pelican;
Bathe me, Jesu Lord, in what thy bosom ran —
Blood that but one drop of has the world to win
All the world forgiveness of its world of sin.

Jesu whom I look at shrouded here below,
I beseech thee send me what I thirst for so,
Some day to gaze on thee face to face in light
And be blest forever with thy glory's sight.

Gerard Manley Hopkins

Thomas of Celano

❮ The medieval hymn, *Dies Irae*, is ascribed to Thomas of Celano, a Brother Minor and biographer of St. Francis; he lived in Germany from 1221 to 1223, but little else is known of his life. This hymn is the most magnificent expression of that apocalyptic vision of the last judgment which shadowed the lives of so many in the Middle Ages. For what we know of him, see A. G. F. Howell, *The Lives of St. Francis of Assisi by Brother Thomas of Celano*, London, 1908. ❯

DIES IRAE

DAY OF JUDGMENT

Day of sorrows, dreadful day,
When the world shall pass away,
So David and the Sibyl say.

Ah, what terrors shall appal;
Systems ruining shall fall,
When the Judge his roll doth call.

To that Tribune, strangely led,
Men shall gather, trumpeted
From the regions of the dead.

Life and Death shall there be dumb,
When, arising from the tomb,
To be judged the Nations come;

And His record, page on page,
He shall scan, and give each age
Sentence and a righteous wage.

When our Lord shall mount His throne,
Vengeance shall o'ertake its own
All that's hidden shall be known.

If the righteous then do quake,
What reply can sinners make,
What defences can they take?

Mighty and majestic Lord,
Savior of the Just, accord
Me the mercy of Thy word!

O remember then what sorrow,
Thou, my Christ, for me didst borrow:
Aid me on that dread tomorrow!

Tired with seeking after me,
Thou didst buy me on the Tree:
Shall Thy labors fruitless be?

Judge of righteous vengeance, then
On that day recall again,
Thou didst purchase Peace for men.

When I weep with culprit face,
Reddening for my guilty case,
Grant a suppliant, Lord, Thy grace!

Mercy was assured of Heaven,
And the thief by Thee was shriven —
Let their hope to me be given!

Thou art good, Thou will not spurn me;
Prayer unworthily shall earn me
Rest, ere fires eternal burn me.

From among the goats Thou'lt lead me;
At Thy right hand (Thou wilt heed me!)
Pastured with Thy sheep I'll feed me.

When the wicked to eternal
Death are plunged in fire infernal,
Take me to Thy bliss supernal!

Suppliant from the dust I send
My contrite heart on Thee to tend:
Care for me, Father, at my end!

Day of vengeance, mournful day,
When our dust to life shall sway,
And culprit men their judgment see —
Then, O my God, deliver me!

Howard Mumford Jones

Bernard of Morlas

❰ A monk of the abbey of Cluny, Bernard wrote around A.D. 1140 a satire three thousand lines long in a leonine rhyme called *trinini salientes* and dedicated to the abbot Peter of Cluny; the title of the poem is *On the Contempt of the World* and its introduction is influenced by Horace's *Art of Poetry*. It is full of a peculiarly medieval pessimism marked by a deep scorn for the fleeting life of this world and by gloomy warning against the sins of mankind. Bernard describes the golden age and then discusses women and love with revulsion. He condemns the sins of pride and avarice, atheism, magic, and sodomy. The corruption of the papacy and the imminent ruin of Rome are described in bitter tones. The material of the poem is drawn from the Bible and from the classical Latin authors, such as Juvenal. Unfortunately, the verse-form with its rather monotonous jingling rhymes is unsuited for a lengthy narrative. Hugo of Trimberg and Bernard of Clairvaux wrote poems on the same theme, inspired by Bernard of Morlas. ❱

DE CONTEMPTU MUNDI

O land without guilt, strong city, safe built in a marvellous place,
I cling to thee, ache for thee, sing to thee, wake for thee, watch for
    thy face:
Full of cursing and strife are the days of my life; with their sins they
    are fed,
Out of sin is the root, unto sin is the fruit, in their sins they are dead.
No deserving of mine can make answer to thine, neither I unto thee;
I a child of God's wrath, made subject to death, what good thing is
    in me?
Yet through faith I require thee, through hope I desire thee, in hope
    I hold fast,
Crying out day and night that my soul may have sight of thy joy at
    the last.
Me, even me hath the Father set free, and hath bidden come in:
In sin hath He found me, from sin hath unbound me, and purged me
    of sin.
In His strength am I glad, whom my weakness made sad; I that slept
    am awake;
With the eyes that wept, with the spirit that slept, I give thanks for
    His sake.

Things weak he makes sure, things unclean He makes pure, with his
 fresh watersprings;

Throughout all lands He goeth, for all things He floweth, and halloweth
 all things.

O home of salvation, a chosen nation, a royal race

Doth build and possess thee, increase thee and bless thee, engird and
 embrace;

Every heart boweth down to that grace which doth crown thee, O
 Sion, O peace!

Time is there none in thee, stars neither sun in thee rise not nor cease;

Of the saints art thou trod, and made glorious of God; thou art full
 of thy Lord;

And the sound of thee rings from the great ten strings of the deca-
 chord.

Thou hast lilies made sweet for their maiden feet who were clothed
 with lowliness;

And roses blood-red, as a saint's blood shed, in the beauty of holiness.

With His wings He shall cover thee, He that rules over thee even the
 Son,

The Mystic Lion, the Lamb out of Sion, the God which is One;

Purged of all revelling, clear of all travailing, pure of all strife,

Land of glad hours, made fair with new flowers, and sweet with new
 life.

Algernon Charles Swinburne

Carmina Burana

❲ First presented at Frankfurt in 1937, the brilliant musical settings of Carl Orff, the German composer, for twenty-four of the *Carmina Burana* have made these medieval songs much better known to the non-scholarly public than before. The text of the *Carmina Burana* (so named from the Benediktbeuern manuscript No. 4660 in the Staatsbibliothek at Munich which contains them) is a collection of about 250 Latin and German poems from the first half of the twelfth century. Other anthologies of a similar nature are the Cambridge Songs (ms. Gg. 5. 35, Cambridge University, 49 poems of the eleventh century), the love poems of Santa Maria de Ripoll (12th century, Barcelona), the Arundel poems (Brit. Mus. ms. 384), the Vatican ms. Lat. 4389, and the Basel ms. D iv. 4. Earlier collections of such poems were made (e.g., at St. Gall, in Switzerland, at Fulda, Bamberg, etc.) from the eighth century to the eleventh and have a common ancestor in the *Anthologia Latina*. The variety of themes in the *Carmina Burana* ranges from poems full of erotic passion and the love of nature to moral subjects which include satire against ecclesiastical abuses, the corruption of the world, and the unfeeling selfishness of patrons. Their carefree rhythms describe tavern life, love among the shepherds, the exaltation of fleshly pleasures, and the full rejection of asceticism and the narrow pedantry of the lesser schoolmen. The authors of these poems were the "clerici vagantes," wandering theology students of the "family of Golias." This tribal eponym is probably drawn from Latin *gula,* synonymous with gluttony, or from Goliath, the rebellious giant slain by David; both etymologies tend to merge. This group of poets, whose identifiable members are Hugo Primas of Orléans, the Archpoet of Cologne, Walter of Chatillon, Serlo of Wilton, Peter of Blois, and Philippe de Grève, are among the first critics of the Medieval Church and its hierarchy; their loose behavior was condemned by Church Councils as early as the thirteenth century. They are the spiritual companions of the troubadours and Minnesingers pointing the way toward the secular poetry of later Europe. ❳

Potatores exquisiti

Fellow topers fine and dandy,
Even if your thirst be scanty,
Pass the bottle quick — be handy —
Fill your mugs with ale, no shandy;

Toss your wine off: swill your brandy:
    Drink contagious:
And be sure the jests you bandy
    Are outrageous.

If you cannot carry liquor,
Out you go, sir! Slick, slick, slicker!
This is not the place to dicker:
Nothing spoils a party quicker
    Than temperance:
Proves a man without a flicker
    Of social sense.

Lurks there here some lout uncivil
Who with heady wine would cavil?
To the doorway show the devil:
Death would be a lesser evil:
We don't want to share our revel
    With a blister.
If he isn't drinking level,
    Let him fester.

Comes your turn to lead the table:
Drink ahead of all the rabble,
Till your legs begin to wobble,
And your speech is senseless babel.
There remains where all's unstable
    One salvation:
Drain the biggest bowls you're able
    In rotation.

Wine and water, keep your station!
God and Goddess, no flirtation!
Liber is his appellation:
Liberty is his vocation.
Water means annihilation
    Of vinous graces:
Wine sustains debilitation
    By her embraces.

Godhead well you may ascribe her:
With the name of Sea Queen bribe her:
Only some indecent giber
As Bacchus' consort would describe her.

He of water an imbiber
    Profanation:
Baptism for Father Liber
    Is damnation.

                    Basil Blackett

Flora, the Pictured Flower Who Is a Girl

Suscipe flos florem

Flora, take this flower; it means my love;
And by that flower I'm seized with too much love.
This flower, sweetest Flora, smells always sweet,
For like the dawn your beauty is complete.
Flora, see my flower and seeing smile.
Take it, Flora; your voice is a nightingale's.
Kiss the flower; it suits your ruby mouth.
The pictured flower is but an ornament;
Who paints a flower paints not the flower's scent.

                    L. R. Lind

Nobilis, precor

Gracious Lady, pity!
    Have pity on my pain!
The sword-thrust of your beauty
    Has pierced me: I am slain.
My being's inmost city
    Your love has captive taken.
        Aid! Oh aid!
    Graceless Love
    Rules all above.
        Aid! Oh aid!

Entangled are your tresses
    With the fibers of my heart:
Close the fire presses:
    Anguished is my smart.
My soul in deep distress is
    And all my powers depart.
        Aid! Oh aid!
    Graceless Love
    Rules all above.
        Aid! Oh aid!

Your lips with fragrance rarer
   Than roses scent the air:
You're lovelier and dearer
   Than all the girls there are:
Than lily you are fairer,
   Than honey sweeter far.
     Aid! Oh aid!
   Graceless Love
   Rules all above.
     Aid! Oh aid!

Your beauty mocks the splendor
   Of heaven's pavilion.
My humble suit I tender
   At Venus' judgment throne.
My life I must surrender
   Unless you help your own.
     Aid! Oh aid!
   Graceless Love
   Rules all above.
     Aid! Oh aid!

Basil Blackett

The noble wood displays

The noble wood displays
Green leaves and flower-sprays.
Where can my lover be?
Once he was kind to me.
He rode off under the bough.
Ah, who will love me now?
The wood is thick with flowers.

Jack Lindsay

Juliana

Juliana, one sweet spring,
Stood with her sister, marveling
To see the fruit-trees blossoming.

  Sweet love, sweet love!
To miss thee now would be a thing
  Past thinking of.

See how bloom bursts from the tree,
And how the birds chant amorously;
So maidens melt in some degree:
 Sweet love, sweet love!

See too the lilies, how they flower;
So maidens clustered in a bower
Sing the high god's resistless power:
 Sweet love, sweet love!

Could I but hold in close embrace
That girl in some leaf-shadowed place,
Joy! What joy to kiss her face!
 Sweet love, sweet love!

George F. Whicher

In taberna quando sumus

When we're at the tavern we,
Care not what this world may be,
But we set ourselves to dicing —
Sport of all sports most enticing.
Would you glance at our high jinks
Where one small coin pours out the drinks?
Would you have that scene unfurled?
Listen to me, I'll tell the world.

We play, we drink, it's thus, my friends,
We burn the candle at both ends.
Of those who most frequent the game
Some lose their shirts and mourn the same,
Some pile fresh garments on their backs,
Some hide their nakedness in sacks;
All thought of death each man postpones
When for the drinks we roll the bones.

First we throw a round to settle
Who shall pay, like men of mettle;
Next we drink to captives, then
Drink a third to living men;
Fourth, to Christians truly bred;
Fifth, to cheer the faithful dead;
Sixth, vain woman when she errs,
Seventh, Diana's foresters.

Eighth, to brothers born to roister;
Ninth, to monks that slip the cloister;
Tenth, to voyagers and sailors;
Eleventh, to discord-making railers;
Twelfth, to all who penance pay;
Thirteenth, to wanderers by the way;
And at the last to king and pope
We all inordinately tope.

Host and hostess, *he* drinks, *she* drinks,
Even the parson on a spree drinks,
The captain drinks, nor drinks alone,
The tapster drinks with greasy Joan.
They drink, they drink, a motley rout,
The stay-at-home, the gadabout,
The ignorant, the erudite,
The swift, the slow, the black, the white.

They drink, the poor man ill at ease,
The no-account gone overseas;
They drink, the boy, the reverend man,
Prelate and dean both clink the can.
They drink, the sister with the brother,
They drink, they drink, old maid and mother,
What hundreds, nay, what thousands think!
Drink, drink, drink, drink, drink, drink, drink.

To quench their thirst what would avail
A hundred mugs of penny-ale,
When all are drinking without measure
And all in drinking find their pleasure?
Whoever treats these thirsty folk
By morning will be stony broke.
They sponge on us? We treat? Not much!
Good fellows, listen! *This is Dutch.*

George F. Whicher

Amor habet superos

Love controls the gods above:
    Jove takes Juno's orders;
South winds pressing waves with love
    Rule in Neptune's borders;
Love alone is master of
    Hell's relentless warders.

For joy of love with love I dally;
I love a maiden virginally:
Sweet is bloom without fruition,
And bliss that leads to no contrition.

Love in yielding natures born
    Very lightly presses.
Those who hold his power in scorn
    Feel his sterner stresses;
Lo, he tames the unicorn
    Through a maid's caresses.

Bright my flame and kindled soon;
    Fair the maid, none fairer.
Joys that keep our hearts in tune
    Day by day grow rarer.
Fervid as the sun at noon
    Glows the love I bear her.

When I play with Cecily
    Prudent fears are needless:
Of her young transparency
    Never am I heedless.
Lilies guard her purity —
    I would keep them weedless.

Such a flower as she, 'twould ill
    Serve my turn to break it.
I can leave the grape until
    Ripeness overtake it.
Thirst for happier issues still —
    May I live to slake it.

Dalliance with the stronger sex
    Pleases girls completely.
Jealousies need not perplex
    Those that mingle sweetly,
Nor should any rancor vex
    Kisses given discreetly.

Simple girls I like whose lips
    Boast no false carnation.
Married women making slips
    Cause me no sensation;

I despise the kind that drips
   Cheap sophistication.

Never mind what others do,
   Girlie, since I say so,
Let me keep some awe of you,
   It is best to play so;
We are innocents, we two,
   And we mean to stay so.

All I want is that we should
   See each other's faces,
Speak, join hands, and when we would
   Lightly give embraces,
And be just as good as good
   When I take you places.

             George F. Whicher

Exiit diluculo

The farmer's daughter
  goes out at dawn
    with her flock,
      and wool to spin
       and a staff.

In her flock are
  a sheep,
    an ass's colt,
      a billy-goat,
       a nanny-goat,
         a bull-calf,
         and
           a heifer calf.

Hard she looks
  at the man of books
    seated alone
      in a grassy spot:

"What are you doing there,
  studious sir?
    come play with me —
      why not?"

             George F. Whicher

Tempus instat floridum

The time draws near for flowers to spring,
Birds appear and sing and sing,
Earth now comforts everything.
   Ah, my dear, well I see
Love has little joy for me.

Not to think of, not to tell —
For a while I hid my fear,
And I loved, I loved too well.
Now my fault must all be clear,
For I feel my body swell;
Childbed and its pangs are near.

For this my mother rates me,
For this my father hates me;
Both do their best to hurt me.
I sit at home outlawed,
I dare not stir abroad,
Nor anywhere divert me.

When in the street I venture out,
People stare that meet me
As if a monster walked about.
Each notes my shape, and judges;
One man another nudges;
And no one cares to greet me.

Nudging elbow so loose-jointed,
Finger always my way pointed,
Am I such a holy show?
Wagging head and curling lip,
Death's too good for me, *you* know,
Just because of one small slip.

Where shall I go, I alone,
I a byword now become
In the mouths of all and some?
What more can I know of grieving
Since my own true love is leaving
Till the storm be overblown?

From my father's countenance
He has fled to farthest France,

Leaving me alone to face
All the gibes, all the disgrace.
In despair I could die,
And I cry and cry and cry.

George F. Whicher

Ver redit optatum

Spring returns, the long awaited,
    Laugh, be glad:
Spring with blossoms decorated,
    Purple-clad.
Birds prolong their accords of song there
    How sweetly!
Trees renew their youth now,
Song brings joy in truth now,
    O completely.

While the youngsters welcome flowers
    New in bloom,
And refresh themselves with showers
    Of perfume,
Maidens meet them, in cadence greet them,
    So featly.
Through the fields they wander,
Flower-decked, growing fonder,
    Indiscreetly.

George F. Whicher

[FRAGMENTA BURANA (1901)]

O comes amoris, dolor

What grief keeps company with love!
The torments I am weary of —
    Is there no means of curing?
Small wonder that I dread love's fire;
She plays the mischief, she is dire
    Whom most I find alluring,
Whose matchless beauty might eclipse
The face that launched a thousand ships
    And send Lord Paris touring.

I'm hers alone, would she were mine!
She plays me like a fish on line,

No love to me returning.
Within a vale her dwelling lies,
To me it seems a paradise
   Fit for the Lord's sojourning:
He formed the radiant being there,
In spirit pure, in feature fair,
   For whom my heart is yearning.

This vale exceeds all vales beside,
A vaunted vale, the valley's pride,
   Where rose bloom veils each alley;
Available to birds, a vale
Where sun and moon themselves regale
   And longest love to dally;
The nightingales reveal thy worth,
Most valuable of vales on earth,
   O sweet and pleasant valley.

Yet why should I in grief demur
At being kept away from her
   Who scorns her faithful wooer?
Her very name, at last accounts,
I must not venture to pronounce
   Like one who really knew her;
It cost me her regard to try:
Such looks she gave me, as if I
   Were less than nothing to her!

               George F. Whicher

Vidi viridi Phyllida sub tilia

Under green
I have seen
A girl below a linden tree

Chicory
Tall as she
All along a summer lane

Color clear
Quick and pure
And a mediaeval strain.

               Rolfe Humphries

Obmittamus studia

Let's away with study,
  Folly's sweet.
Treasure all the pleasure
  Of our youth:
Time enough for age
  To think on Truth.
So short a day,
And life so quickly hasting
And in study wasting
  Youth that would be gay!

'Tis our spring that slipping,
  Winter draweth near,
Life itself we're losing,
  And this sorry cheer
Dries the blood and chills the heart,
  Shrivels all delight.
Age and all its crowd of ills
  Terrifies our sight.
So short a day,
And life so quickly hasting,
And in study wasting
  Youth that would be gay!

Let us as the gods do,
  'Tis the wiser part:
Leisure and love's pleasure
  Seek the young in heart
Follow the old fashion,
  Down into the street!
Down among the maidens,
  And the dancing feet!
So short a day,
And life so quickly hasting,
And in study wasting
  Youth that would be gay!

There for the seeing
  Is all loveliness,
White limbs moving
  Light in wantonness.
Gay go the dancers,
  I stand and see,

Gaze, till their glances
   Steal myself from me.
So short a day,
And life so quickly hasting,
And in study wasting
   Youth that would be gay!

Helen Waddell

Volo virum vivere viriliter

I would have a man live in manly fashion,
Yea, I shall love, but given an equal passion:
So to my mind should love be,
And no other,
And herein myself I see
A better man than Jupiter.
I know not how to pray
In the old vulgar way.
Would she have me love her?
Then shall she first love me.

Well do I know the pride of woman's spirit,
And with sardonic eyebrow I contemn it.
Shall I put the greater last?
Set the ox behind the plough?
This common guise
Of wretches I despise,
And rather choose myself to play
Than be the toy that's thrown away.

She who fain would please me, I shall please,
First shall she show her favour, for returning.
So shall we throw the main,
She shall not think me chaff,
Herself the grain.
I shall Love's servant be,
But with an equal yoke for her and me,
I'll have no woman laugh
At me flung prostrate by her coyness spurning.

Free am I, and I boast myself as free.
Hippolytus was chaste, I chaste as he.
Nor with sudden wooing
Shall she be my undoing.
Tender eyes and hands seducing,

Let her pleasure in me find,
Love me most sincerely
This forwardness towards me designed
Pleases in the female mind.

Alas, alas, what is it I have sung?
My song was all a lie, I am undone,
Lady, thy prisoner I!
Thy loveliness forgot,
Thy sweetness heeded not,
Worthy am I of all thy cruelty.
I do confess my guilt,
Then chide me as thou wilt,
But let thy chamber my tribunal be.

Helen Waddell

De ramis cadunt folia

Down from the branches fall the leaves,
A wanness comes on all the trees,
   The summer's done;
And into his last house in heaven
   Now goes the sun.

Sharp frost destroys the tender sprays,
Birds are a-cold in these short days.
   The nightingale
Is grieving that the fire of heaven
   Is now grown pale.

The swollen river rushes on
Past meadows whence the green has gone,
   The golden sun
Has fled our world. Snow falls by day,
   The nights are numb.

About me all the world is stark,
And I am burning; in my heart
   There is a fire,
A living flame in me, the maid
   Of my desire.

Her kisses, fuel of my fire,
Her tender touches, flaming higher,
   The light of light

Dwells in her eyes: divinity
    Is in her sight.

Greek fire can be extinguishèd
By bitter wine; my fire is fed
    On other meat.
Yea, even the bitterness of love
    Is bitter-sweet.

Helen Waddell

Gaudeamus igitur

Let us live, then, and be glad
    While young life's before us!
        After youthful pastime had,
        After old age hard and sad,
    Earth will slumber o'er us.

Where are they who in the world,
    Ere we kept, were keeping?
        Go ye to the gods above;
        Go to hell; inquire thereof:
    They are not; they're sleeping.

Brief is life, and brevity
    Briefly shall be ended:
        Death comes like a whirlwind strong,
        Bears us with his blast along;
    None shall be defended.

Live this university,
    Men that learning nourish;
        Live each member of the same,
        Long live all that bear its name;
    Let them ever flourish!

Live the commonwealth also,
    And the men that guide it!
        Live our town in strength and health,
        Founders, patrons, by whose wealth
    We are here provided!

Live all girls! A health to you,
    Melting maids and beauteous!

Live the wives and women too,
 Gentle, loving, tender, true,
Good, industrious, duteous!

Perish cares that pule and pine!
 Perish envious blamers!
  Die the Devil, thine and mine!
  Die the starch-necked Philistine!
 Scoffers and defamers!

John Addington Symonds

Hugo Primas of Orléans

❨ Hugo of Orléans in France (1093–c. 1160) is mentioned by several writers in the twelfth and thirteenth centuries but is best described by Richard of Poitiers in his *Chronicle* (A.D. 1142): "In these days there flourished at Paris a certain teacher named Hugo, called Primas by his associates, a man ugly in form and face. This man was devoted to worldly literature from his early youth and gained fame on account of his wit and knowledge. He stood out so among the professors of rhetoric in facility of verse-making and in eloquence that he is said to have made everyone laugh who listened to those verses which he composed in a declamatory style on a shabby cloak given him by a certain bishop." Primas was a nickname (such as "Archpoet") which played on the meanings for chief, chairman of a church council, and metropolitan of a diocese. Hugo wrote poems on Orpheus and Eurydice and on the return of Odysseus, but his short occasional poetry is the best known and loved for its satire and mocking wit. He was a predecessor of François Villon in his description of the hard life a poet could lead. He was skilled in classical allusion and parody, and versatile in handling leonine hexameters, rhymed elegiacs, sequences, and tirade-rhymes, using the latter to revenge himself on those who had rebuffed or slighted him. ❩

ON THE GIFT OF A CLOAK

PRIMAS

Scum of churchmen! clergy's dregs!
Pain in the neck, who gave me
An unlined cloak to save me
From winter's cold, i' fegs!

BYSTANDER

Who was it then presented
This — shall we say — integument?
It wasn't bought or rented?
It's yours?

PRIMAS

Yes, mine; I meant
Merely to say I mind it
That he who gave it tore away what lined it.

BYSTANDER

But who then was the donor?

PRIMAS

A certain prelate gave it me — the owner.

BYSTANDER

He gave this gift so proud!
He might as well have given you a shroud.
For service in all weathers
What good's a cloak with neither fur nor feathers?
You'll see, when snow is driving,
You'll catch your death of cold — there's no surviving.

PRIMAS

Poor mantle, what abuse could thin you?
No fur, no padding in you!
Think you, thus sadly aging,
To fend me from the blast, the storm's mad raging,
To shield me and protect me
So piercing cold will not affect me,
That in your keeping surely
I may withstand the wintry winds securely?

THE MANTLE *thus responded:*

No pelt, no fleece is left, my fur's absconded;
Worn smooth am I, and like a head bare
My texture's threadbare.
The biting north to chill you
Will drive his lances through me fit to kill you.
There's no escaping
The wind's assault while all these holes are gaping;
A thousand vents in each direction
Will strip you of protection.

PRIMAS

You think we're in for freezing?

THE MANTLE

I do, and you with cold are wheezing.
But till some fur is added,
It's little help you'll get from me, unpadded.
Know what, Primas? I together
With peltries could repel this pelting weather;
Buy furs, and thus augmented

I'll fight the storm and keep you well contented.
Your plight I pity truly,
And if I could, would help you duly,
But when it comes to hair my make-up
Is less like Esau than like Jacob.

George F. Whicher

The Archpoet of Cologne

《 The most famous of the Goliards and perhaps the greatest, the poet who bore this name was a Rhinelander born perhaps around 1130 of a knightly family; not long before 1161 he became a companion of Reinald of Dassel, who was archbishop of Cologne and Frederick Barbarossa's envoy to Italy. Witty and wild, the spirit of the Archpoet was tamed for a short period as a teacher of letter writing and as jester-extraordinary at Reinald's court. The last we hear of him is at Salerno, Italy, where he turns up ill and penniless. He wrote ten poems that can be certainly identified as his, all realistic and clearly autobiographical. There is nothing servile in them, although like Hugo of Orléans he practically begged his living. Their humor is headlong and irresistible. The last poem was written around 1165; the locale of the poems shifts from Germany to Italy and France. The *Confession of Bishop Golias* is his greatest poem, a synthesis of all the gay and blasphemous elements in Medieval Latin secular poetry. The Archpoet and Hugo Primas are pagan spirits whose poetry heralds the more earthly vernacular verse of the Renaissance. 》

OMNIA TEMPUS HABENT

All things have their time; as for me I crave but a moment,
Only the time to recite before you a handful of verses.
Here in your court, sacred prince, garments so slovenly make red
Cheeks full loath I can tell you with girlish blushes to mantle.
Hail to you, O Vastness, our realm's protection and fastness,
Whose views are long and well-planned, and enforced with a strong
    hand.
Rose of the Church, rosier priest never bore mitre and crosier,
Long live our Nestor, in the ship of state pulling the best oar.
Pious and just, question I have whether to make a suggestion,
Right sure 'twere treason to advise one so famed for his reason:
What would it make crumble if the great should cherish the humble?
Open to wretches your heart, since that is the way of the pure heart.
Let your hand save, or grant poverty's victims your favor;
You, a tramontane scion, are the help tramontaners rely on.
Small hope mine of living were it not for the chance of your giving.
Freezing and starvation have deprived me of all animation,
Winters with shivers fill me, till I know their bleakness will kill me.

Constantly I'm coughing, consumption is just in the offing;
Pulse-beats scarce existent are a warning that death is not distant.
Proof of my neediness is that my shoes are as poor as my dress is.
Hence as is most meet I importune you with words of entreaty:
Wearing such rags and tatters in your presence — believe me, it matters!
So may success greet you as in largess you're mindful of me too.

George F. Whicher

THE CONFESSION OF BISHOP GOLIAS

Inwardly fired with vehement wrath,
In bitterness I will speak my mind:
Made of material light as lath,
I am like a leaf tossed by the wind.

Though it were just for the wise and brave
To place their seat on the rock of will,
Fool, I am like the flowing wave
That under one sky is ever unstill.

I am borne on as a pilotless ship,
As a vagrant bird through the cloudy haze;
Ungoverned by reins, ungoverned by whip,
I gad with my kind, I follow their ways.

I walk the broad path in the fashion of youth,
Forgetful of virtue, entangled with sin;
Avid of pleasure more than of truth
I die in soul but take care of my skin.

Most worthy prelate, your pardon I pray,
I die a good death, swing on a sweet rope,
At sight of the ladies I still get gay;
Whom I cannot by touch, I sin with in hope.

Who placed on a pyre will not burn in the fire?
Or dallying at Pavia can keep himself chaste?
Where Venus goes hunting young men for hire,
Drooping her eyelids and fixing her face.

Hippolytus placed in Pavia today
Would not be Hippolytus "when the dawn came";
To the bedroom of Venus still runs the broad way,
Nor in all those towers is the tower of shame.

Again, I'm charged with playing strip poker:
When play casts me out in my naked skin,
Shivering, I sweat while my mind plays stoker,
And I write better verse than I did within.

The tavern, thirdly, I note in this summing
Up of the life I will ever have led
Till I hear the holy angels coming,
Singing rest eternal unto the dead.

For I propose in the tavern to die
That wine may be near when the throat grows hard,
And the chorus of angels may joyfully cry,
"O Lord, be kindly to this drunkard."

The lamp of the soul is lighted by wine,
Sotted with nectar it flies to the sky;
Wine of the tavern is far more divine
Than watery wine that the priest raises high.

They say a poet should flee public places
And choose his seat in a quiet retreat:
He sweats, presses on, stays awake, and erases,
Yet comes back with scarcely one clear conceit.

The chorus of poets should fast and abstain,
Avoid public quarrels and brawls with their neighbors:
That they may compose what will ever remain,
They die in a cell, overcome by their labors.

Nature to such gives a suitable crown:
I never could write on an empty purse;
Myself when fasting a boy could knock down;
Thirsting and hunger I hate like a hearse.

Never's the spirit of poetry given
Except when the belly is fat and sleek;
While Bacchus is lord of my cerebral heaven,
Apollo moves through me and marvels I speak.

Behold, of my vice I was that informer
By whom your henchmen indicted me;
No one of them is his own accuser,
Though he hopes to sport through eternity.

So I stand before the blessed prelate
Urging that precept of our Lord, wherein
He casts the first stone, nor spares the poet,
Whose heart is wholly devoid of sin.

I've charged myself with whatever I knew
And vomited up my long cherished dole;
The old life passes, gives way to the new;
Man notes appearance, Jove sees the soul.

Primate of Cologne, grant me your blessing,
Absolve the sinner who begs your grace;
Impose due penance on him confessing;
Whatever you bid I'll gladly embrace.

J. V. Cunningham

Walter of Chatillon

❡ Walter of Chatillon, in spite of the resemblance of some of his poems to those of the Goliards and the inclusion of a few of them in the *Carmina Burana,* was not a Goliard but a highly respectable churchman and politician. He was born at Lille, France, not later than 1135. By his friend John of Salisbury he was called Walterus de Insula but received the better-known name from his service as a teacher at Chatillon-sur-Marne. He studied at Paris, Bologna, and Reims, where he received a canonry. He became chancellor to Henry II of England but left after the murder of Thomas à Becket, whose death he deplored in a poem attacking Henry II. Archbishop William of Reims made Walter his secretary. His last canonry was at Amiens; the date of his death is unknown.

❡ In addition to a distinguished epic on Alexander the Great (*Alexandreis*) he wrote more than fifty short satirical, moral, religious, and erotic poems; some of the latter resemble the French pastourelle. He used accentual rhymed verse and may even have invented the vigorous, rolling Goliardic measure in trochaic septenarii, often with *auctoritas* (a line from a classical Latin poet quoted as the fourth line of a stanza); in any event, he founded an extensive school of poets who used chiefly the Goliardic measure. The *Apocalypse of Golias* is attributed to him in a Paris manuscript. His satirical poems condemn the corruption of the clergy and of secular princes. The Latin texts of his poems are scattered in several collections edited by Karl Strecker, Thomas Wright, F. A. G. Müldener, C. Blume and G. M. Dreves, Migne (*Patrologia Latina* 209), and Jacob Schmeller, the first editor of the *Carmina Burana.* ❣

LOVE'S TEMPERATURE

In the chill of Autumn
    When the lily dies,
While outwardly I shiver,
    Flames within me rise.
I, a fool by industry,
    The laws of logic break
Because two contrarieties
    I undertake.

Now the changing face of Jove
    Alters the face of things;

375

But no appearance changes now
    My soul's determinings.
The north wind forces into ice
    The breath of every man;
All, except my steadfast vow,
    Will change, and can.

On violets and cowslip flowers
    There lies no glassy dew;
They wither; all the lilies fade:
    I stand, and flower anew.
While Niobe's true to me,
    Niobe, whom I hold,
I shall remain the only man
    Unchilled beneath the cold.

While I gaze upon her eyes
    Like two stars above,
And on the flowers of her mouth
    Fit for gods to love,
I feel that I have won far more
    Than treasures of old kings,
While I clasp her, while our flesh
    Clings again, and clings.

To the well-deservèd yoke
    Of Love I bow my head.
There may be those who scoff at me,
    Who say my honor's dead.
But if the world will let me live
    And serve in love's own guise,
Though everyone will call me mad,
    I'll think I'm wise.

L. R. Lind

Quem pastores laudaverunt

(This anonymous carol of the fourteenth century is printed in the
Oxford Book of Carols, No. 79.)

Shepherds him with praise attended,
When at last their fear was ended
By the host of angels splendid.
   Born is now our glorious King.

Unto him came wise men, offering
Gold and incense, myrrh of suffering,
Fearless hearts with these things proffering
   To the glorious new-born King.

Christ, begotten of God the highest,
Who in Mary's arms now liest,
Unto thee, who all suppliest,
   Let eternal praises ring.

Barbara J. Hodge

Latin Poets of the Renaissance

❡ These were very numerous, and few of them attained real distinction. Their immensely prolific production was a striking indication of the extent to which Latin literature had captured the fancy and challenged the poetic talents of the scholars and public men of the Renaissance in Europe. Huge collections of their poetry were issued: the *Carmina Quinque Illustrium Poetarum Italorum* (1719), the *Delitiae Poetarum Italorum* published by Gruter in 1608, the anthologies of Toscanus and Gherus, the Florentine anthology in eleven volumes, and the numerous editions of the works of single neo-Latin poets not only in Italy but all over Europe testify to the fascination which Latin exercised upon these men. They flourished under patrons and in academies of learning, as at Naples in the sixteenth century. Their poems are often imitations of Catullus, Vergil, Horace, Ovid, and lesser Latin poets, but sometimes as in the works of Petrarch and Poliziano they transcend the bounds of imitation and can be regarded as valuable writings on their own merits. Of the few that can be represented in this book, we may conveniently group for discussion those given here in translations by Aldington.

❡ Antonio Beccadelli (1394–1471) was born at Palermo and hence is called "Panormita." He studied civil and canon law at Siena and Bologna, found patronage with the Visconti at Pavia, and joined Alfonso of Aragon at the court of Naples. His *Hermaphroditus* (1445) in two books is a collection of amorous and satirical epigrams modeled on Martial's poems; its subject-matter is the licentious student-life of Siena. His only other work is a series of anecdotes from the life of Alfonso.

❡ Giovanni Pontano (1442?–1503) studied at Perugia, sought his fortune also at the court of Alfonso and was aided in his career by Beccadelli. He was a diplomat. His writings include two books of elegies, *Parthenopei;* the *Lepidina,* which describes Neapolitan scenery and customs as well as the joys of conjugal love; and *Naenia, Lepores, Tumuli, Hendecasyllabi seu Baiarum,* and *Urania* (on astronomy).

❡ Andrea Navagero (1483–1529), known as "Naugerius," was a disciple of several learned men, including the philosopher Pomponazzi, and a friend of Aldus Manutius the elder. He edited classical texts and gave funeral orations in Latin for the republic of Venice. He became librarian to Cardinal Bessarion in 1516. He was an ambassador to Madrid, took part in the arrangements for freeing Francis I, who had been captured at the battle of Pavia, and became acquainted with the Spanish writer Boscán. His Latin poems, some of them included in the *Carmina Quinque* etc., Venice, 1548, are called *Lusus;* their inspiration is idyllic and elegiac. *Opera Omnia* were issued in a second edition at Venice, 1754.

❲ Marc-Antonio Flaminio (1498–1550) was the precocious protégé of Pope Leo X. On literary and diplomatic journies he visited widely in Italy. For fifteen years he was a secretary to Bishop Giberti at Verona and then to Cardinal Polo, who took him to the Council of Trent. A friend of the poetess Vittoria Colonna, he wrote eight books of pastoral poems, *Lusus Pastorales,* and some religious poetry, *De Rebus Divinis Carmina.*

❲ Girolamo Amaltheo (1507–1574) was a professor of medicine at Padua, a practicing physician at Ceneda, Serravalle, and Oderzo. He was a classicist of considerable ability and wrote elegant Latin epigrams. His brothers Giambattista and Cornelio were celebrated Latin poets of the sixteenth century.

❲ Of Francesco Franchini and Antonio Mario, almost nothing is known except their poems in the anthologies; even the great *Enciclopedia Italiana* and the very useful *Dizionario Letterario Bompiani* say nothing about them.

❲ Angelo Poliziano (1454–1494) will be discussed under his Latin name, Politian, below (page 386). ❳

Antonio Beccadelli

ELYSIA

Elysia, most beautiful of golden-tressed girls, what praise can ever define your excellent beauty and merit? For your lips outdo the rose, your eyes the heavenly stars, and your throat the snow: robed, you are Helen: naked, goddess Dian herself. When you speak, though you speak little and that but seldom, you alone seem worthy to speak and to speak often. How shall I make clear to others your able fingers, your duties and accomplishments? You avoid the thousand ways of idleness, and yet among your many labors you sing, O sweetest, and unknowingly steal away a score of hearts with your sweet voice. And though you are rightly the glory and ornament of the lyre and the dance, yet you are seldom at revels. When you do go, putting aside your duties for a little, then Love and the Graces go with you; wherever you pass there is a breathing of violets and roses; and if you pass at night then night becomes day. Whatever praise and beauty belong to the Gods and Goddesses are yours also. And this, too, is happiness, that you, a chaste and very lovely girl, are the pleasure of a chaste and beautiful husband. You are the glory of women and he of men.

May Heaven give you both many years, and may Venus, in spite of your shyness, often join you together.

Richard Aldington

Giovanni Pontano

FANNIA

Girl, more beautiful than a soft rose, which the spring winds bring forth and which the Mother of dark Memnon waters with dew in a garden, and which in the early morning decks the boughs, surrounded with wet shining leaves — when Phoebus and his horses have traversed the reddening sky, then the short glory of the flower dies and the tired petals droop; the blossom falls from the naked stem and its short honour perishes.

Thus beauty flowers in its first years. When unlovely age comes on, alas! the shining colour will fade from the golden face and wrinkles will mark it; the glitter of the hair will perish, the glory of the forehead and the white teeth; a narrow breast-fold will hide the unlovely bosom with its drooping breasts: they will shine no more with dawn-like jewels, no longer will a thin girdle enclose them. You will hear no prayers of a sad lover begging at your door; you will see no garlands hung on your door-posts, the gift of the excluded lover; but alone, sought of none, you will spend your nights lying in a cold bed.

Then let us enjoy the sweet and flowering spring of youth and its short-lived flower; after five lustres already age begins and, though hidden, creeps on. Then, O soft wind of my desires, let us live white days and spend unbroken nights, lit by Hesperus at dawn.

Richard Aldington

Andrea Navagero

TO DEMETER

Great Ceres, now that the seed is sown, we, the rustic band, dance in unskilled chorus in your honour. Grant that no soaking rain rot the seed, no heavy frost crumble the furrows. Let no sterile crop of useless oats arise, no weed that harms the fair harvest. May the gusts of Eurus not crush the thick standing corn to the earth; may no hail break it; may no greedy birds and beasts of the earth steal the grain.

May the fields return plentifully and with large increase the seeds we have trusted to the well-tilled soil.

So be it. And now we pour forth the narrow-waisted beakers of white milk, and of honey mingled with mellow wine. Let the sacrifice be led three times about the sown fields before the slain beast falls by the sacred altar. And now the rites are ended. After the reaping new honours shall be offered you, and sweet-smelling garlands shall bind your braided hair.

Richard Aldington

Marc-Antonio Flaminio

TO THE MUSE OF SIRMIO

Muse, you who cherish the comely white shore of Sirmio and teach the sacred grove of olives to murmur of beautiful Lesbia — we dedicate to you an altar of green turf and three bowls of honey and bubbling milk.

We call you with entreating voice, Goddess, to the poor but reverent offering, call you to celebrate Hyella on your sweet lyre. There has never lived, in any land, a more beautiful girl than she, nor will there ever be one more worthy of your song.

Then leave the green places and the waves of Benacus. For here the breath of light Favonius murmurs. The air is delighted with the music of birds. The meadows glimmer with flowers. The pure fountains cool the dryads of the woods with glass-clear waters. Thither return the chaste bands of Artemis when they weary of slaying the deer in the sharp burning sunlight.

Come then, O white maiden, and speak your songs to me, so that Hyella may be immortal even as your most lovely Lesbia.

Richard Aldington

Girolamo Amaltheo

OF THE DUST IN AN HOUR–GLASS

The dust in the hour-glass which returns again and again upon its narrow path of old was Alcippus. When he looked on Galla's eyes he was as fire; and suddenly from fire he became ashes.

O restless dust, from you unhappy lovers may know that for them there can be no rest.

Richard Aldington

Francesco Franchini

LUCIA

I am naked, and naked Lucia holds me in her arms, and, panting, gives me sweet kisses. I am overcome, looking upon her beauty and gracefulness, and it seems to me that I have Venus herself for mistress. Rightly exulting, I say to her: "Beautiful Adonis now yields to me; yield thou also, father of Aeneas!"

Richard Aldington

Angelo Poliziano

SIMONETTA

When la bella Simonetta was borne forth on her black bier, and loveliness still breathed from her dead face, the Love-God seized that hour, when no man dreaded him, to cast a thousand rays from her closed eyes.

He took captive a thousand souls with her form and exclaimed (exulting over Death): "She is still mine. She is still mine," said Love; "not yet, O Death, canst thou take her utterly. Even in death she is mine." And then Love moaned, for now he sees no more days of triumph, but of tears.

Richard Aldington

EPITAPH FOR GIOTTO, THE PAINTER

I am he through whom dead painting lived again. Swift as my hand was, it was subtle. Nature herself lacks what my art lacks; to none is it given to paint more or better.

Do you wonder at the bell-tower that rings with holy bronze? From my design it grew towards the stars. I am Giotto. Why should I count my works? My name can stand in place of long-drawn praise.

Richard Aldington

Antonio Mario

THYRSIS

Thyrsis. Nymphs, who dwell among the waters of the Rhine, Pan, gay keeper of flocks, twi-horned Satyrs, hear me! Grant that Phyllis may love me more than she loves Amyntas, or swiftly heal me with death.

Alcon. O father, O Faunus, often we sang your love; I hung a pine-wreath upon your horns, and when Lydia shall bind your brows with crimson garlands, let her not scorn me for ever.

Thyrsis. Hills, unshorn hills, soft meadows, Rhine flowing gently by, tell me, did Phyllis teach you to love her when she sang, or did she hurt you with her beauty?

Alcon. Pools, mossy pools, you touch her face and her white limbs; tell me, did Galatea burn you with the fire of love? Or did she sit upon the green bank, playing with the glass-blue ripples?

Thyrsis. Whiter than swans, softer than the vine, fairer than a garden with fountains, Iollas, my love, came to me. I sang my love with the slender pipe. He mingled kisses with my singing.

Alcon. Nobler than violets, gentler than summer air, kinder than the shadowing plane-tree, Lycoris tended flocks with me, wandered with me through the meads, closer embraced than vine and elm.

Thyrsis. The fields break in a wave of blossoms, the air sounds as with echoes from sea-shells; the woods are green, the olive-tree buds. This is the likeness of laughing Lycidas.

Alcon. The light rises from Olympus, coloured like a crocus; the ice gleams in the white frosts. The dew drips from a garden of crimson roses; this is the likeness of mournful Varus.

Thyrsis. Here are gentle winds, cone-bearing cypresses, and caves; here the little rills flow through the grasses. Here Lycidas wove baskets from rushes, and slew the frightened deer with his shafts.

Alcon. Now the cold pools and the pastures, Varus, delight me no more; the Gods here are of no account. Come here to me, and the cold pools and the pastures shall gladden me; nothing shall be dearer to me than these fields.

Thyrsis. Let Iollas bring back my gladness, let Phyllis no longer scorn my piping; then if Orithyia bear wreaths in her hands, O Faunus, I shall deck your horns with these gifts.

Alcon. If the milky rivers flow in these banks, if the genista is yellow with honey, if the fleece is purple with the juice of Tyre, Lydia, then you shall hear my song.

Richard Aldington

Janus Vitalis Panormitanus

《 His Italian name was Giano Vitale (or Giovanni Vitali) and he was called Panormitanus because he was born at Palermo. His life falls in the last half of the fifteenth century; he is known chiefly for his short poems, many dedicated to contemporary writers. 》

ROME

You that a stranger in mid-Rome seek Rome
And can find nothing in mid-Rome of Rome,
Behold this mass of walls, these abrupt rocks,
Where the vast theatre lies overwhelmed.
Here, here is Rome! Look how the very corpse
Of greatness still imperiously breathes threats!
The world she conquered, strove herself to conquer,
Conquered that nothing be unconquered by her.
Now conqueror Rome's interred in conquered Rome,
And the same Rome conquered and conqueror.
Still Tiber flows on swift waves to the sea.
Learn hence what Fortune can: the unmoved falls,
And the ever-moving will remain forever.

J. V. Cunningham

Jacopo Sannazaro

❲ Jacopo Sannazaro (1458–1530) was born at Naples and died there. He was a prominent member of the Academy founded by Pontano; the Latin name he bore among this group of literary men was Actius Sincerus; his home was a villa on the lovely hill of Posilipo, a gift from Duke Federico. He is known for his *Piscatory Eclogues*, admirably edited by Wilfred P. Mustard, 1914; they form part of the large literature of imitation in pastoral poetry in Europe which goes back to Vergil's own imitation of Theocritus, the Greek founder of the type. These poems are dialogues between fishermen and sea gods. His artificial epic, *De Partu Virginis*, cost him the labor of twenty years; in Italian his best known poem is the *Arcadia*, a landmark in the development of that kind of poetry which praises the delights of rural life and cherishes the beauty of nature among men who have turned away from the life of cities, courts, and worldly ambitions. In this poem he praised his lady friends, Carmosina Bonifacia and Cassandra Marchesa, and described the countryside around Naples. It may be set beside Boccaccio's *Filocopo* and Guarini's *Pastor Fido*, famous poems of the same genre. One of his most delightful Latin poems is an ode in honor of his Villa Mergellina, destroyed by foreign troops under the prince of Orange. ❳

TO PENTADIUS

It is not, y' are deceav'd, it is not blisse
What you conceave a happy living is;
To have your hands with Rubies bright to glow,
Then on your Tortoise-bed your body throw,
And sink yourself in Down, to drink in gold,
And have your looser self in purple roll'd;
With Royal fare to make the Tables groan,
Or else with what from Lybick fields is mown,
Nor in one vault hoard all your Magazine;
But at no Cowards fate t' have frighted bin,
Nor with the peoples breath to be swol'n great,
Nor at a drawn Stiletto basely sweat.
He that dares this, nothing to him's unfit,
But proud o' th' top of Fortunes wheel may sit.

Richard Lovelace

Politian

❨ Politian (1454–1494) was actually named Angiolo Ambrogini; I reprint here the description of him which I wrote as a footnote to the selections from his poems in my anthology, *Lyric Poetry of the Italian Renaissance* (Yale University Press, 1954), 234–235: "He called himself Poliziano from the name of his birthplace, Montepulciano. Tutor to the sons of Lorenzo de' Medici, he was a famous and precocious scholar who became professor of Greek and Latin literature at Florence in 1480. He was one of the greatest Humanists of his century, wrote the first masque, Orfeo; Stanze per la Giostra, a long, melodious, and colorful poem about the tournament in which Giuliano de' Medici won the prize on January 28, 1475; and many popular poems, including both ballate and rispetti. . . . There is in the poetry of Poliziano a lusty joy in earthly things and a love of nature combined with a sophisticated polish that reminds one of the later Renaissance. A charming New Yorker Profile by A. Moorehead (February 24, 1951) is devoted to Poliziano."

❨ J. A. Symonds admired his Latin poetry extravagantly. Politian wrote the *Sylvae,* four long hexameter poems entitled *Nutricia,* a history of classical poetry; *Rusticus,* an introduction to pastoral verse; *Manto,* a eulogy of Vergil; and *Ambra,* in praise of Homer. His shorter poems are not of great value, slight, delicate, and charming as they are. His Italian poetry represents his greater claim to fame. ❩

Ecce autem dulces labris pater ingerit uvas

Now Father Autumn heaps the vat
With burden of the vine,
And through the press sweet juices flow
Beneath the stamping heel.

A wanton brood of revellers
Crowd round and drink their lade,
Pressing their lips against the tank
To suck the musty streams.

With purple hand one crushes out
The heart blood of the grape;
Another wets the eager lips
Of comrade and of mate,

386

Staining his chin and panting chest
This rustic Bacchus reels
To stagger with uncertain feet
Along the drunken road.

D. C. Allen

Protinus extremo cum jam Boreas autumno

When Boreas at the autumn's end
Broods on the earth, the leaves descend,
After a first taste of the frost,
Like children from their mother's arms;
Then the felled trees unfearful lie
Sturdy and tough before decay;
And so the rustic meditates
His heart filled with the silent care
Begotten by the impending year.

From what trunk may he hew a cart
Servile to oxen, and what bough
Will make a yoke or curving plough?

Without delay old beeches high
Are top-shorn, and the great oaks fall,
Chaonian giants, then the elms
Are reft of branches. Laurels sing
Under the axe incessantly.
To these the warm smoke of his hearth will bring
New shape and use and altering.

D. C. Allen

Ruris opes saturi, gnavoque agitanda colono

Grant me for celebration on my pipe of seven reeds
The glut of rural riches and the labors without cease
Of the yeoman toiling endless and the honor holy, pure,
Of earth forever fruitful. Bless these reeds which yesterday
The happy Tityrus gave me on the Mantuan river's shore
And said, "O youth, beloved, recommence the Ascrean song."

O mighty Pan, be present underneath this arch of stone
And while the burning Phoebus tarries in the middle sky
Give me the breath of music when the mateless dove complains
And the throat-encircled woodbirds reiterate their cries.

Here the pine, dear to you, murmurs softly in the aimless air;
Here the cypress dark and conehung whistles mildly and the water,
Clear and bubbling, chased by boiling strength, is driven
Through the clamor and the clatter of a thousand colored stones.
And here your wanton Echo, lurking in the neighboring shade,
Is hard upon our traces, the huntress of our song.

D. C. Allen

Dulce mihi quondam studium fuit

Study was once my dearest joy, but jealous Poverty
Adorned in torn and greasy rags has surely frightened me;
And now that poets are a joke throughout all Italy,
I think that I shall take the hint and join the bourgeoisie.

D. C. Allen

Johannes Secundus

❮ Jan Everaerts, born at The Hague in 1511 as one of nineteen children, is better known in the history of Latin lyric poetry as Johannes Secundus, author of the *Basia*. He died before the age of twenty-five; but he was distinguished for high affairs in both church and state. After studying at Bourges he became secretary to the archbishop of Toledo and later to the bishop of Utrecht. He died at Tournai in 1536. The annotated edition of his works by Burmann-Boscha, 1821, runs to more than 600 pages. He describes in his poems his travels to Bourges and to Spain. Among his poems are *Silvae, Funera,* and the *Amores,* in elegiac verse. The first book, called *Julia Monobiblos* (in imitation of Propertius), describes his first love. The *Basia* are unabashedly sensuous poems addressed to a dark Spanish girl whom he called Neaera. Their pagan frankness is unusual even for the neo-Latin poetry of the Renaissance. His gaiety and wit look forward to the Cavalier poets of England; in fact, most of the Caroline and Restoration poets owe something to him and read him carefully. ❯

THE THIRD KISS

BUTTERFLY KISSES

When I asked you for a kiss
　　You said "Yes";
And I felt your lips on mine
　　Lightly press
For a moment: then, as tho'
You had touched a snake, they go.

Do you call that thing a kiss,
　　Or profess
That a moment's lingering makes
　　A caress?
Such a kiss can only fan
Desire in a hungry man.

F. A. Wright

389

THE THIRTEENTH KISS

LOVE, LIFE AND DEATH

Faint from our dear encounter, love, I lay
And panting let my languid fingers stray
Around your neck; my lips were parched and dry;
I scarce could breathe, and death seemed drawing nigh.
I saw the waves of Styx before me roll,
I saw old Charon waiting for his toll,
I saw and trembled; till your kisses fell
Wet on my mouth and brought me back from hell,
Bidding the ferryman to wait no more,
But sail without me to the further shore.

F. A. Wright

THE SEVENTEENTH KISS

NEAERA'S LIPS

As some red rosebud, in the darkness born,
Unfolds its dewy petals to the morn;
So do my lady's lips the day delight
Bedewed by me with kisses through the night.
And as a cherry-tree shows white and red
When summer comes before the spring has fled;
So do her cheeks as setting for them stand
Like snow-white violets in a virgin's hand.
O woe is me! Your kisses burn my heart.
Why must I leave you and perforce depart?
Ah, let those lips like roses still remain
When evening brings me to your bed again.
But if another lover should them seek,
May they outpale the pallor of my cheek.

F. A. Wright

ELEGY I, 5

GATHER YE ROSES

And shall one woman rule me all my years
And be the cause of all my smiles and tears?
Shall I be constant all this life of mine,
I who so soon must dwell with Proserpine?

Whether my mistress kind or cruel be,
It matters not: death waits in watch for me.
Come, join your lips to mine, as pigeons use;
Let neither tongue nor teeth their part refuse.
A hundred kisses: nay, a thousand even:
And then the final gift: I mount to heaven.
What profits it with frowns to mar your grace?
Too soon will wrinkles spread on that fair face.
Nay rather pluck the rose, while yet you may,
Ere life's bright spring by fate is swept away.
See, I am here: together let us tread
The flowery path before its blooms fall dead.

For whose delight do you those bright eyes guard
And those full breasts that bondage find so hard?
Those tapering fingers and those skilful feet,
Those lips perfumed with kisses honey-sweet?
For whom do you array those locks of gold?
Who shall your smiles and wanton jests behold?
Will you all these for crusty Charon save
Who sweeps in crazy barque the Stygian wave?
Nay, let the dead take pleasure where they can,
And for your lover choose a living man.
Come to me, sweetest; rest within my arm,
And let me lie upon your bosom warm,
To expire in kisses with delicious pain
And from your kisses win back life again,
My life or yours: but let it, sweet, be thine:
I draw your breath and you, dear love, draw mine.

F. A. Wright

OCCASIONAL POEMS

The Ladies of Bourges

The ladies of Bourges are a very poor crowd,
   And beauty is rare in this city:
There are just two or three of them — that is allowed —
   Who can fairly be reckoned as pretty,
And ten more of whom you can hardly complain;
The others are really portentously plain.

And yet the young sparks of the town are content,
   And do not find fault with their features,

Nor seem to regard it a hard punishment
  To spend a long night with such creatures.
For myself, I'd as soon to a tigress be led
For her partner, or take a she-wolf to my bed.

F. A. Wright

To a Lady Who Used Cosmetics

Seek not in borrowed hues your cheeks to dress,
Naked is Love, and loveth nakedness.

F. A. Wright

The Foolish Husband

Tom and Dick were in love with the fair Mrs. Brown,
So to get her old husband to roam about town
They gave him a suit of most superfine cut;
And he swallowed the bait, the ridiculous mutt.
In that suit every day he goes swelling around
From morning to night: he can always be found
In some market or bath place or gay house, and stops
For hours at a time in the arcades and shops.
They have nothing to fear: Tom and Dick can both come
At dawn or at mid-day; he's never at home.
And young Mrs. Brown's quite content, it appears,
With the service she gets from her two cavaliers.

F. A. Wright

George Herbert

¶ George Herbert (1593–1633), a saintly country parson in the village of Bemerton, Wiltshire, England, came of a rich and powerful family and had won distinction as Public Orator at Cambridge University. He is best known for his *The Temple*, called the most popular of Anglican poems. He was at various times in his career a soldier, statesman, philosopher, poet, and preacher. His prose work *A Priest to the Temple* describes the ideals of a parson's life. He was a fine musician, and his love for music is revealed in his melodious although somewhat difficult verse, expressed in vivid images and unusual combinations of rhyme and length of line. Herbert is one of the most important poets of the group known as Anglican Catholics, who began to flourish under Charles I and Archbishop Laud, when a return to asceticism as well as an emphasis on metaphysics characterized some of the best English poetry. ◗

Hoc, Genitrix, scriptum proles tibi sedula mittit

Mother, your faithful child writes to you;
Cease now your hymn of praise and pause to read
(To hear from theirs is music to the saints).
The cares that troubled you are still our own;
Alas, we weep and darken the clear days;
Our evening cheeks are like a double cloud.
Meanwhile the King prepares a mighty fleet
For some great exploit, but we only weep
And that for you is more important news.
They were to sail, but favoring winds held off;
Had they blamed rain, they might have blamed our tears.
Tilly presses the Danes; sea war the French;
And weeping us. Throughout the English Court
Weeping is now the password among men.
So Time moves slowly while the thousand wheels
Of the swift year are slowed by many tears.
I would have written more, but what to me
Are laurel wreaths or nectar fitly poured
When I no more may spend the day with you?
And while tears ask a share of all I write
True tears erase the shining tears of words.

D. C. Allen

Horti, deliciae Dominae, marcescite tandem

Gardens delightful to her, you must fade;
You have adorned her coffin; you cannot endure.
Your glory threatened by the frightening thorn
Recalls in vain your lady's careful hand.
The flowers smell of earth and funeral,
And root and roses where her body lies are dead.
The violets bow their dark heads to the ground
And gravely show her only dwelling now.
You are no gardens but a burial place
Since each bed keeps the absent mistress sure.
Die all of you! Nor ever afterward shall spring
A bud or flower to seek the lady lost!
Sink to your roots! Seek your ancestral tomb!
Lo, God has given you unpurchased graves.
Go die! Or at the best live little more
And evening's dew shall mark your death with tears.

D. C. Allen

Dum librata suis haeret radicibus ilex

While strengthened by its roots the oak
Stands firm against Volturnian stroke,
But let the cruel axe strike the tree
It wanders in vain liberty.
I am the oak, for once I grew
Stronger than cedars near to you;
Without you I am tempest lost,
Like the wide seascape I am tossed.
Mother, you were my anchoring stone;
With clutching shell to you alone,
A barnacle to rock I clung;
The sisters drear have not unstrung
Your fate from off the spindle but
In your death, too, my thread is cut.
Wandering, I am the Odyssey;
Your death, the Iliad to me.

D. C. Allen

In Natales et Pascha concurrentes

Cum tu, Christe, cadis, nascor; mentemque ligavit

You died and I was born, O Christ;
   One little hour tied

My soul to flesh and put you on the tree.
Born with unequal fates, O woe to me;
Why did you give me life that you denied?
    But I shall die with you;
Accept from me the life which you contemned
Or grant a life like yours to me anew.
Oh, if to me you give this sweet bequest,
    Born of your bitter throes,
  Then shall my life be double blessed
And sanctified the first day of my breath
As through each day the calm of Easter flows.

D. C. Allen

Richard Crashaw

❴ Richard Crashaw (1612–1649), a younger contemporary of Herbert, became a Catholic at thirty-three and died in Rome as secretary to a cardinal. In his poetry he combined the influences of Italians such as Marini with the passion of the Spanish mystics, exerted upon his own deep mystical tendencies and admirations for the saints, as for St. Teresa, to whom he wrote *The Flaming Heart, Upon the Book and Picture of the Seraphical Saint Teresa,* a fine hymn. His first book was called *Delights of the Muses;* in 1646 he published another collection of poems, *Steps to the Temple.* He is one of England's greatest devotional poets and a translator of some attainments, especially of Catullus. ❵

EPIGRAMMATA SACRA

Book I

ii

In asinum Christi vectorem

Matth. 21.7

The former one could chide his lord;
Of praise you have no single word.
That you are dumb more curious is
Than all the chattering of this.

ix

Æthiopus lotus

Act. 8

How clean this holy black comes from the pool!
Who washes Æthiopians is no fool;
A snow white soul glows in a pitch black skin,
Seeing this sable house, the Dove flew in.

396

xxxi

Vincula sponte decidunt

Act. 12

Hard jailor who chains Peter, you shall know
By iron to be softer. For your pains,
The links unbind themselves, the fetters flow;
Go, fool, and put a chain upon your chains!

xxxviii

Ad Judaeos mactatores Stephani

Act. 7.60

In vain they roll and scatter, the vagrant, straying stones.
Hurtless, it cannot hurt him, this storm of savage hail;
He does not feel its fury; he can its ill endure
The stone hearts in their bosoms will be his painful bale.

lxi

Christus Vitis ad Vinitorem Patrem

Joann. 15

Behold the purple tendrils of your vine
Creep on the ground; creep to the bitter loss
Of leaf and fruit. O great Vinitor, come
And lift me with a vine stake. What? The Cross!

lxxii

Si Filius Dei es, dejice te

Matth. 4.6

So you will not believe he is God's son
Unless he leaps to see his bidding done;
But you will know he is God's child when
He hurls you from the evil hearts of men.

lxxvi

Beati oculi qui vident

Luc. 10.23

When kindly Christ walked in our way
And gave to blind the light of day;
Happy were those with eyes; I find
Them just as happy who were blind.

lxxxiv

Piscatores vocat

Matth. 4.19

Fishes, secure within the ocean, play!
For we are fish, too, in another way.
Not to be taken is your wished-for fate,
But we are safe when we have seized the bait.

xcvi

Aquae in Vinum versae

Joann. 2

Whence came this purple color not its own?
Such rosiness to water is unknown.
Discern, O guests, the present Deity;
The modest nymph has blushed her Lord to see.

Book II

(From Bodl.MS.Tanner 465)

xi

In Beatae Virginis verecundiam

The Virgin is not humble, but her son,
On whom she looks as in her lap he lies,
For he is God and he has made it so
That she sees Heaven when she lowers her eyes.

xxix

Pisces multiplicati

Marc. 8

Within your silent words what nets pass secretly
With which not fish you take but all the fecund sea.

D. C. Allen

O Deus, ego amo te

⟨ This anonymous sonnet, whose history is outlined in the note at the end of this anthology, dates from 1676; two great religious poets have had some connection with it: St. Teresa, to whom the Spanish version has been attributed, and Gerard Manley Hopkins, who translated the Latin text into English. ⟩⟩

O God, I love thee, I love thee —
Not out of hope of heaven for me
Nor fearing not to love and be
   In the everlasting burning.
Thou, thou, my Jesus, after me
   Didst reach thine arms out dying,
For my sake sufferedst nails and lance,
Mocked and marred countenance,
   Sorrows passing number,
   Sweat and care and cumber,
Yea and death, and this for me,
   And thou couldst see me sinning:
Then I, why should I not love thee,
Jesu, so much in love with me?
Not for heaven's sake; not to be
Out of hell by loving thee;
Not for any gains I see;
But just the way that thou didst me
I do love and I will love thee:
What must I love thee, Lord, for then?
For being my king and God. Amen.

Gerard Manley Hopkins

Notes

THE EARLY ROMAN WRITERS. *Pages 1–6.*

ENNIUS: Latin text in E. H. Warmington, *Remains of Old Latin,* I, Loeb Classical Library, 1935, p. 154. Bergk assigns the fragment to Book 16 of the *Annales.*

NAEVIUS: A fragment from a play possibly called the "Girl from Tarentum." It is in trochaic meter; text in Warmington, II, 1936, p. 98.

The fragments of Lucilius together with Pacuvius are found in Warmington's volumes.

PLAUTUS. *Pages 7–16.*

F. A. Wright, *Three Roman Poets,* London, G. Routledge and Sons Ltd., 1938, pp. 27–87, prints these translations:

Mostellaria 84–117. Philolaches' half-drunken observations on mankind.

Curculio 95–110. An apostrophe to wine by Leaena, an old woman who has just smelled the libation to Venus poured by Phaedromus.

Casina 217–227. Lysidamus, the old man who is his son's rival for the favors of the girl from Casinum, sings this song when the bailiff Olympio wins the lot-casting which brings her, by a pseudo-marriage, within the power of Lysidamus.

Curculio 147–149. A canticum, or solo, in cretic meter with rhyme, sung by Phaedromus.

Truculentus 565–575. Cyamus' lament for the fate of his young master, who is in the clutches of the courtesan Phronesium.

Asinaria 215–226. Cleareta, the madam, describes her profession to the young man Argyrippus.

Amphitryo 218–247. Sosia, the servant of Amphitryo, describes the campaign from which he and his master have just returned.

The translations by Gilbert Highet are from his *Roman Drama in Translation: Illustrative Material for Comparative Literature 252,* mimeographed, Columbia University:

Miles Gloriosus (The Braggart Soldier). The boastful captain, Pyrgopolinices ("much-conquering tower"), is flattered by the parasite, Artotrogus ("bread-eater"). **brush plaster:** reed-thatched roof. **To keep my teeth from teething:** Artotrogus flatters in order that the captain may feed him and thus prevent his teeth from growing through disuse. When Pleusicles, the young Athenian, wishes to rescue his beloved courtesan Philocomasium from the braggart captain who has carried her off to Ephesus, Periplecomenus, a friend of Pleusicles' father, strikes an exaggerated attitude of lofty planning which burlesques a military staff-meeting; Palaestrio, the faithful servant of Pleusicles, eggs on Periplecomenus with fitting admiration. **foreign poet:** perhaps Naevius, the Roman poet, who had been jailed for lampooning the Metelli and who was supposed to support his chin with his hand while thinking. In the next scene Sceledrus, the captain's servant, through a skylight discovers Philocomasium in the arms of Pleusicles next door. Later, Palaestrio persuades the captain that the wife of his neighbor Periplecomenus is in love with him. To receive the courtesan Acroteleutium, whom Palaestrio has induced to play the role of the neighbor's wife, Pyrgopolinices sends Philocomasium away in charge of Pleusicles, her lover in disguise; Palaestrio goes along with Philocomasium at her request. Then Milphidippa, Acroteleutium's maid, invites the soldier next door to visit her mistress. There he is discovered by Periplecomenus, who with her servants beats and strips the braggart; they let him go on promise of proper behavior thereafter.

Mercator 40–84. Charinus, son of Demipho and in love with Pasicompsa, speaks in the prologue.

On Plautus, see G. E. Duckworth, *The Nature of Roman Comedy,* 1952.

CATULLUS. *Pages 27–52.*

10. This translation is an interesting imitation of the Phalaecean, or hendecasyllabic, meter which Catullus uses so often. No imitation in English can avoid much dependence upon stress-accent; but I feel that the original Latin verse in all meters had more stress when read aloud than most scholars will allow. This meter most frequently opens with a trochaic foot and in English imitation usually continues rather uniformly in the same meter.

11. Printed in *The Partisan Reader,* 1946. This version is revised from the earlier one in Fitzgerald's *A Wreath for the Sea,* New Directions, 1943. A skillful imitation of the lesser Sapphic meter, which Catullus uses only here and in poem 51. It is an answer to Lesbia's offer of reconciliation as well as to an offer of foreign service from Furius and Aurelius. With the last lines compare Tasso, *Orlando Furioso* 18.1060: "come purpureo fior languendo muore/che'l vomere al passar tagliato lassa"; and Robert Burns' extended use of the same image in "To a Mountain Daisy."

14. Catullus writes to Calvus, who has played a practical joke on his friend by sending him a book of third-rate poems by some contemporary poets. Vatinius was a politician attacked by Calvus and, on another occasion, defended by Cicero; see Catullus 53 and Cicero, *In Vatinium.*

17. The delightful poem to Colonia, a suburb of Verona. It is in Priapean meter. **Salisubsilian:** Catullus' joke-word for the Salic jumping priests who performed for Mars in March.

31. Sirmio, the home of Catullus, was on the shore of the Lago di Garda, a peninsula jutting northward into the lake. The so-called grotto of Catullus at the tip of the peninsula is a Roman villa of the early Empire. Note the echoes from this poem in Tennyson's "Frater Ave atque Vale."

51. Catullus' imitation of Sappho's second ode. He changes much and substitutes an entire stanza for Sappho's fourth stanza.

63. "The most famous of his poems," says Robinson Ellis in his commentary; certainly it is one of his most fascinating. The sixteen-syllable galliambic meter is to be read with the jangle of a tambourine in mind (or ear); in its rapid and feverish movement it fits the strange theme: the self-castration of Attis, a devotee of Cybele, the great earth-mother goddess of Asia. The subtle shift from masculine to feminine adjectives immediately after Attis performs his ritual mutilation cannot be reproduced in English. Theodore Martin, *The Poems of Catullus,* mentions English imitations of the meter in Tennyson's "Boadicea" and George Meredith's "Phaethon." Although it is apparently iambic-anapaestic it sounds much like the trochaic septenarii of the *Pervigilium Veneris.* Anaclasis, or substitution of double trochees for the ionics which are supposed by an older theory to form the basic foot in this meter, makes trochaic reading easy. For a good study, see J. P. Elder, "Catullus' Attis," *American Journal of Philology* 68 (1947), 394–403; also E. T. Merrill's text, Ginn and Co., 1893, pp. xlviii–xlix.

84. The famous poem on the Roman cockney who pronounced "commoda" as "chommoda" and "insidias" as "hinsidias." Compare L. R. Palmer, *The Latin Language,* London, 1954, p. 230: "The aspirate was lost in certain country dialects (e.g., *arena, edus, ircus, olus,* etc.). Ignorant reaction against this mark of *rusticitas* produced hyperurbanisms which prompted Catullus' mockery of Arrius' *hinsidias;* cf. the comment of Nigidius (Aulus Gellius 13.6.3), 'rusticus fit sermo si aspires perperam.'"

DECIMUS LABERIUS. *Pages 54–55.*

Latin text in O. Ribbeck, *Scaenicae Romanorum Poesis Fragmenta,* II, 3d ed., 1897, p. 339.

PUBLILIUS SYRUS. *Pages 56–57.*

Text in J. W. and A. M. Duff, *Minor Latin Poets,* Loeb Classical Library, 1934. Only a brief selection is given here.

VERGIL. *Pages 58–96.*

Text in Loeb Classical Library Vergil.

Copa: the Barmaid. The arbor-god (stanza 6) is Priapus, who with his prodigious phallus served as an ancient scarecrow.

Eclogue II. An unusual rendering, quite faithful to the text and the more remarkable because of the stanzaic form with closing alexandrine. The original is in dactylic hexameters. In this Eclogue Vergil imitates Idyll XI of Theocritus, where the Cyclops Polyphemus laments his failure to win the love of the sea-nymph Galatea.

Eclogue III. An incomplete translation, beginning with line 60 and ending with 107; this portion includes only the singing-match. **Bavius, Maevius:** traditionally bad poets.

Eclogue IV. Translation privately printed by New Directions, 1939. This is the so-called Messianic Eclogue; see the discussion as to the child who is to be born in H. J. Rose, *A Handbook of Latin Literature,* 2d ed., 1950, and notes by T. E. Page, text-edition, 1907.

Eclogue V. A friendly contest between two shepherds; one tells of the death of Daphnis, the other of his deification.

Georgic I. This translation includes the following lines only: 124–146, 178–186, 160–168, 204–222, 231–251, 259–266, 272–275, 291–296, 301–311, 316–350, 355–382, 387–389, 393–416, 424–435, 438–514. Some passages are translated out of their order in the Latin text. This Georgic treats the growing of crops and is mingled with much weather-lore. It closes with a lament on the troubled times, 37–30 B.C.

For an excellent complete translation of the four Georgics, see that by C. Day Lewis, Oxford University Press, 1947. A new translation is the one by Smith Palmer Bovie, University of Chicago Press, 1956.

HORACE. *Pages 97–142.*

Ode I, 1. An imitation of the Lesser Asclepiad meter.

Ode I, 2. An imitation of the Sapphic strophe, in which Horace wrote 25 of his 104 odes. **Father:** Jupiter. **Pyrrha:** the Greek Eve. **Proteus:** The keeper of Neptune's sea-calves, he drove them into the mountains during the great flood of Greek legend. **Maia's son:** Mercury.

Ode I, 3. The First Asclepiad strophe, in which Horace wrote twelve odes, is imitated here. Lines 14–18, 27–36, are omitted. **Cyprian foam:** Venus (Aphrodite) was born of the sea-foam. **Aquilo:** the North Wind.

Ode I, 4. The woodland god is Faunus.

Ode I, 5. Gilbert Highet's translation is a clever imitation of the Third Asclepiad strophe, in which Horace wrote seven poems.

Ode I, 11. Chaldaean figures refer to astrology.

Ode I, 13. Translation from George F. Whicher, *On the Tibur Road,* Princeton University Press, 1911.

Ode I, 18. An unusually clever imitation of the Greater Asclepiad strophe in which Horace wrote only three poems.

Ode I, 25. Three versions, each by an excellent living poet, are printed for their instructive differences in approach and handling.

Ode I, 27. Horace stills a drunken brawl by extracting from a young guest the name of his current sweetheart, a mercenary courtesan.

Ode I, 33. An imitation of the Second Asclepiad strophe.

Ode I, 38. Imitates the Sapphic strophe.

Ode II, 1. **Metellus' year:** 60 B.C.; Pollio is writing a history of the Civil War, which actually began in 49 B.C. when Caesar crossed the Rubicon. **tragic Muse:** Pollio was celebrated for his tragedies. He was also a well-known lawyer. **Cato:** He killed himself at Utica after Caesar won in Africa. **Juno:** patron goddess of Carthage. **Jugurtha:** against whom the Romans fought long and hard in Africa (111–105 B.C.). **Hesperia:** Italy, at civil war. **Daunian:** Apulian, in the sense of Italian. **Cean:** referring to Simonides of Ceos, who wrote sad patriotic poetry; an adjective suggesting pathos. **Dionean:** Dione was the mother of Venus.

Ode II, 7. **Venus-throw:** the highest throw of the dice, when the faces turned up were all different; this throw decided who was to be the master of ceremonies at the banquet.

Ode II, 8. A brilliant modernization like Nims' version of I, 25.

Ode II, 14. This version is briefly analyzed by L. P. Wilkinson, *Horace and His Lyric Poetry*, 1946, pp. 154–155.

Ode III, 1. Translation reprinted by permission of the V. Rev. M. C. D'Arcy, S.J., of London. Readers familiar with Hopkins' original poetry will recognize his translations as characteristic in their curious choice of words, the wrenching effect of their word-order, and the startling images. This is a masterly translation, truly Horatian in economy and compactness. It is unfortunately not complete, lacking lines 45–46. **Sinner who saw the blade that hung:** the tyrant Damocles of Sicily.

Ode III, 2. An imitation of the Alcaic meter, but with a movement rather slower than that of the Latin because of the crowded lines.

Ode III, 13. A fine imitation of the Third Asclepiad strophe; a famous ode.

Ode III, 23. Imitation of the Alcaic. Lines 6–8 are omitted and a few others much condensed.

Ode IV, 7. Perhaps the most famous of modern translations of Horace. Of this poem in the Latin, Housman once said, "That I regard as the most beautiful poem in ancient literature." Compare Ode I, 4, for the sentiment. W. H. Alexander has a good explanation of line 13 in *University of California Publications in Classical Philology* 13 (1947), 231–232. He paraphrases thus: "the moon too, like everything else in nature, suffers obvious losses, but the swift passage of time makes these good right before our eyes in the heavens, just as time also in its flight makes good the losses that the weathers (i.e., the seasons) suffer. But as for us, there is no possibility of renewal." *caelum* in the sense of "weather" lies behind *caelestis* here in the Latin text.

Epode XV. An imitation of the Third Archilochian strophe. The lack of synchronism between the English verse and prose stress is greater than that in the original, but the number of syllables is the same.

Satire I, 5. Horace describes a journey to Brundisium, either in 40 or 37 B.C.   **Line 28, legates on a great affair:** This refers either to the treaty of peace made between Octavian and Antony in 40 B.C. or to the agreement in 37 B.C., when Antony agreed to assist Octavian against Sextus Pompey.   **37, Mamurran town:** Formiae, the modern Formia.   **46, legal pillage:** Officers traveling on public business often stopped at inns reserved for them.   **51, Tell, Muse, I pray:** In mock-epic style Horace describes a slapstick vaudeville skit put on for the entertainment of the travelers at the villa of Cocceius by two rustics, Sarmentus, a small slave, and Cicirrus, a huge ugly fellow who has had a wen recently removed from his forehead. The tone of the skit is that of Fielding, *Tom Jones,* IV, viii, "A Battle Sung by the Muse in Homerican Style, and Which None But the Classical Reader Can Taste."   **78, Atabulus:** a local name for the scirocco, a hot wind.   **87, a little town with name too queer:** Porphyrio, a commentator on Horace, calls it Equos Tuticus, which cannot be got easily into a hexameter.   **101, I've learnt that gods:** Epicurean doctrine.   **104, Brundisium:** Horace had traveled 340 miles in from 12 to 15 days from Rome.

Satire I, 8. A bawdy joke played by the scarecrow garden god Priapus on two witches who are collecting the vile materials for their magic in a real estate addition recently made from a slave-burial ground. The point of the joke lies in the fact that olive wood, of which the statue of Priapus was made, splits easily.

Epistles II, 3. The Art of Poetry is one of Classical Antiquity's most famous and important documents in literary criticsm. Its sources are found among the Hellenistic critics, especially Neoptolemus of Parium (third century B.C.). The three parts of the poem deal with poetry (1–41), the poem (42–294), and the poet (295–476); in this translation, 1–45, 46–358, 359–606. The first part discusses content, invention and use of poetic themes; content must be simple and unified. The second part includes the problem of form (*ars*) and is much more extensive since form was highly significant in classical literary theory: the various types of poetry, especially tragedy and satyric drama, are then described. The third part passes from *ars* to *artifex* in discussing theories concerning the poet himself and criticizes Roman poets for neglecting form and relying too much on *ingenium,* individual talent. The last section analyzes the nature and ends of poetry. The entire treatise follows the plan of works on prose rhetoric such as Cicero's *Orator.* The main outlines of *The Art of Poetry* can be checked with Neoptolemus' essay on poetry preserved in Philodemus, *On Poems,* edited by C. Jensen, 1923.

The emphasis throughout *The Art of Poetry* is on propriety, the effective tone and appropriate meters for each literary type, the value of slow composition and laborious correction, moderation in diction and rhetorical figures. The purpose of poetry is to instruct and to please at the same time; judicious eclecticism is the rule of Horace as he discusses the works of famous poets and sums up his literary principles. The poem has been much imitated, followed, and translated by later classical-minded poets and critics, by Boileau, Philip Sidney, Dryden, Pope, and Croce. Standards of taste are established in it which have exerted great influence. In its form *The Art of Poetry* is a letter addressed to the Pisos, a father (consul in 23 B.C.) and his two sons. It combines advice to authors with a mature, conservative attitude toward life; it is witty, satirical, even to some extent a tract for the times. While Horace concentrates on poetry, he considers its inter-relations with the other arts — painting, music, the dance, sculpture, and handcrafts — in terms of their common principles. John Hawthorne, the translator, sums up excellently the ideas raised by *The Art of Poetry* as "the proper subject-matter of poetry, its source, the relation between literature and life; the relation between art and nature, the purpose and value of art, the end of poetry; tradition and originality, training and natural talent, lifelike representation and imagination; style (arrangement and consistency); verse-forms and their appropriateness; character-drawing; language (archaism, modernity, invention); audience-reaction; faultiness and excellence in art; the nature of criticism; the essentials of good writing; and the pitfalls of the rich, untutored, would-be genius."

Line 38, Aemilius' school: of gladiators.   65, Caecilius: (c. 219–166 B.C.), a writer of comedy.   66, Varius: friend of Horace, author of a tragedy, *Thyestes*.   68, Cato: (234–149 B.C.), the Censor, who wrote on agriculture.   95, Archilochus: a Greek lyric poet and satirist of the seventh century B.C.   96, Iambic: the meter used for lampoons, short poems which ridiculed people.   108–150, Thyestes . . . Orestes: All these are characters in Greek drama and mythology. See Gayley's *Classic Myths* and Robert Graves' *The Greek Myths*.   267, Satyrs: followers of Dionysus described as monsters half-man, half-goat; a satyr-play for comic relief ended a Greek dramatic trilogy.   286–288, Davus, Pythias, Snub-nose (Simo): characters in Roman comedy.   299, knights: of the Roman equestrian (capitalist) class.   305, trimeter: a line of six iambic feet varying with spondees.   341, Old Comedy: Greek comedy of the fifth century B.C., chiefly that of Aristophanes.   355, Pompilius: Numa Pompilius, second king of Rome, founder of the Roman religion, according to Livy.   359, Democritus: Greek philosopher, c. 460 B.C., who developed the atomic theory.   361, Helicon: a mountain in Boeotia sacred to the Muses.   401, as: originally a pound of bronze (12 ounces) used as currency.   419, Lamia: queen of Libya, whose children were killed by Hera; she became a monster who ate children.   442, Choerilus: a second-rate epic poet who described the career of Alexander the Great.   460, Messalla: Messalla Corvinus, patron of Tibullus.   461, Aulus: Aulus Cascellius, a prominent lawyer in Cicero's day.   482, Maecius: Maecius Tarpa, censor of plays for Pompey's theater, built in 55 B.C., and president of the guild of poets at Rome.   488, Orpheus: the famous musician of Greek mythology; his wife Eurydice returned to Hades when he turned round to look at her as he was bringing her home.   491, Amphion: mythological lyre-player.   502, Tyrtaeus: Spartan poet of the seventh

century B.C. who wrote martial poetry.   **551, fox's face:** the fox who
flattered the crow in Aesop's fable.   **568, Aristarchus:** chief librarian at
Alexandria, Egypt, 180–145 B.C., the editor of Homer; he is called by
J. E. Sandys "the founder of scientific scholarship".   **588, Empedocles:**
a Greek philosopher of the fifth century B.C., a pre-Socratic.

OVID. *Pages 143–176.*

The latest complete version of the *Metamorphoses* is Rolfe Humphries'
blank-verse translation, Indiana University Press, 1955.

The *Tristia* are poems written at Tomi (modern Constantsa, Rumania,
on the Black Sea) where Ovid, after one of ancient Rome's great unsolved
scandals, was exiled by Augustus Caesar and where he died, still begging his
friends for release from his lonely captivity.

The *Amores* in Christopher Marlowe's magnificent English are among
the few great classics of translation from Latin poetry. Rolfe Humphries
has also translated all of Ovid's love poems: Indiana University Press,
1957.

PROPERTIUS. *Pages 177–217.*

Propertius is one of the most modern in feeling and tone of all the Latin
poets, but he did not find a translator who could reproduce his peculiar
ironic, half-tearful, half-mocking quality until Frances Fletcher undertook
a complete translation in free verse. He writes the elegiac distich, a dactylic
hexameter varying with a dactylic pentameter, the meter used by Catullus,
Tibullus, and Ovid as well. The numbering of the elegies follows the text
by Butler and Barber, Oxford University Press, 1933. Two new texts have
recently appeared, one by E. A. Barber, Oxford Classical Texts, 1953, more
dependable than the one by M. Schuster, Teubner, Leipzig, 1954; the latter,
however, contains a full bibliography and useful indexes. The bibliography
has been used in a handy exegetical or explanatory apparatus.

I, 21. The translator adds the note: "Irregular 5's and 6's with rhyme,
near-rhyme, and assonance."   **I who escaped:** Gallus, someone known to
Propertius, who died in the Perusine War, 41 B.C., fighting on Antony's
side against Octavian. The appeal is addressed to a fellow-soldier near
Perugia. Butler and Barber in their note (pp. 186–187) reject the *ne* in
line 6 and read *haec* with Beroaldus: the meaning thus becomes, more
appropriately as they think, "Save yourself, and by your tears let your sister
know that I am dead, and whatever bones she may find on the Etruscan hills,
let her know that *these* (here where I lie) are mine." But it may be that it
is the humiliating nature of his death (*acta:* possibly at the hands of

bandits since he expressly states that he escaped from the swords of Caesar) that Gallus wishes to conceal from his sister; there is no need to assume, as Butler and Barber do, that she is the fellow-soldier's sister and the betrothed of Gallus.

II, 5. **Juno:** Propertius implores Cynthia in the name of Juno, the goddess of marriage, as though Cynthia were his wife. Line 25–26 have been omitted but can be translated as follows: "Let some rustic seek such a quarrel as this,/ Around whose head the ivy has not twined"; insert just before "But I'll write. . . ."

II, 9. **Deidamia:** daughter of Lycomedes, king of Scyros, with whom Achilles fell in love and by whom he had a son, Neoptolemos, while living in Scyros disguised as a woman to avoid being drafted for the Trojan war. **Theban commanders:** Polynices and Eteocles, sons of Oedipus, in the story of the Seven against Thebes; see the play by Aeschylus. Compare Butler-Barber, pp. 207–208, for comment on the clash of these concluding lines with the rest of the elegy.

II, 28 A and B. Propertius begins to address Cynthia at "Was Venus pained. . . ." **Juno's temple:** Butler and Barber say *templa* "is impossible in this context"; but it is quite in harmony with "her own so frequent neglect of the gods' sanctity."

II, 28 C. **that goddess once a heifer:** Isis. Butler and Barber make out a good case for the following translation: "Pay your vows to Isis [ten nights of worship without sexual intercourse] and then pay me ten nights of your embraces." They add, somewhat unnecessarily, "His ten nights are to balance the ten nights of abstinence."

II, 32. **Maro:** a statue used as a fountain at Rome. **Triton:** the sea-god. **Tyndaris:** Helen of Troy, daughter of Tyndareus. **wife of Minos:** Pasiphae; the bull was sent by Neptune to Minos for sacrifice. Pasiphae fell in love with it and gave birth to the Minotaur, half-brother to Ariadne (see Elegy IV, 4).

III, 1. **Callimachus, Philetas:** Alexandrian Greek poets in whose steps Propertius declares he is following in his elegies. **triumphant:** three metaphors are used: a triumph, a chariot, a race. **bactra:** Balkh, capital of Bactria in Parthia. **Sisters:** the Muses. **Simois, Scamander:** rivers at Troy. **Hector . . . Paris:** Trojan heroes in Homer's *Iliad*. **Oetaean godhead:** Hercules. **Lycia's god:** Apollo, patron of poets.

III, 2. **music's art:** Amphion's lyre-playing. **Galatea and Polyphemus:** The Cyclops vainly wooed the sea-nymph Galatea; see Theocritus, *Idyll* VI. **Taenarian columns:** black marble from Taenarus in Sparta. **Phaeacia:** the orchard of Alcinous in Homer, *Odyssey* VII, 112. **Mar-

cian: the Marcian aqueduct at Rome.   **Calliope:** the muse of epic poetry.
Mausolus's tomb: the Mausoleum of Halicarnassus, tomb of the king of
Caria, which has given its name to all similar structures.

III, 17. An elegy in honor of Bacchus and thus filled with his legends.
Ariadne: Bacchus, god of wine and revels, found her abandoned by Theseus
in the island of Naxos; he placed her in the sky where her golden crown
formed a constellation of nine stars.   **lovers at loose ends:** excellent for
vacuos . . . amantes.   **Semele:** Beloved by Zeus at Thebes, she gave birth
to Bacchus.   **Aetna's violence:** The volcano Aetna in Sicily is used to
describe the thunder and lightning with which Zeus destroyed Semele.
Lycurgus, Pentheus: kings who opposed Bacchus and were killed by his
followers, the Maenads.   **Tyrrhenian sailors:** changed into dolphins
because they tried to kidnap Bacchus.   **Dia:** identified with the island of
Naxos.   **Pindar:** the greatest of the Greek lyric poets in fifth century B.C.
Athens. His home was Thebes.

III, 21. **Lechaeum:** the port of Corinth on the Corinthian Gulf.
long road of Theseus: the long walls of Attica from the Piraeus to Athens.

III, 24. **Eous:** the morning star.   **Thessalian midwife:** Thessaly was
famed for magic and for witches; compare Apuleius, *The Golden Ass.*
Syrtes: dangerous sandy shoals with shifting currents off the coast of Tunis
and Tripoli in Africa.

IV, 1. In this curious elegy Propertius essays to write on the grand theme
of Roman history but is brought back to his proper subject — love — by the
astrologer Horus, who reads his horoscope for him.   **Conon:** a famous
Alexandrian mathematician and astronomer.

IV, 2. An explanation of the origin of the Roman god Vertumnus, what
is known as an etiological myth, a favorite subject with Propertius.
Voltunna, the Etruscan original of Vertumnus, abandoned Etruscan
Volsinii during its war with Rome, 264 B.C.   **Iacchus:** Bacchus, god
of wine.   **To answer your bail:** Compare Horace, *Satires* I, 9, 36–37,
where the bore Horace has met must also answer his bail and thus releases
Horace.   **chalk:** marking the end of the race course.   **Mamurius:** a
famous artist in the time of Numa, one of the seven kings of Rome; hence
legendary.

IV, 3. A charming elegy in which a Roman soldier's wife writes him a
letter, complete with an account of her war-work, her map-study of his
campaigns in various theaters of war, chiefly the Orient, and the inevitable
expression of her fear that he may be unfaithful to her.   **Seric:** from
Seres, the Chinese, but used vaguely and in general of far-off, exotic peoples.
Ocnus: a hard worker who, for his failure to control his wife's extravagance,
did penance in Hades by twisting ropes of straw which were eaten up by a

donkey as fast as they were made. Ocnus sat sideways at his work and never saw the donkey as he ate the straw-ropes.   **Hippolyte:** the Amazon queen whom Theseus carried off.   **Kalends:** Arethusa's interest in the family festival for the Lares has dwindled because of her desolation.   **compita:** shrines of the Lares set up at the cross-roads. An annual festival, the Compitalia, was celebrated for them.   **trick-turned:** The Parthians had a nasty habit in war of running away at breakneck speed, then suddenly reining up their horses and turning to shoot arrows at their pursuers.

IV, 4. The story of the traitress Tarpeia; she fell in love with the Sabine commander who was attacking the Capitol and received the reward of her treachery by being crushed to death by Sabine shields.   **Cures:** the Sabines, from the name of their chief town. This elegy illustrates one of Propertius' favorite themes: love, etiological myth, and Roman history.

IV, 5. A curse upon the dead procuress who has turned Cynthia away from Propertius. This poem is another demonstration of the poet's peculiar gift for the macabre; see also IV, 7: there is something closely akin to the morbid vividness of certain poems of Baudelaire in this aspect of the elegies. **Hippolytus:** son of Theseus, whom Phaedra, wife of Theseus, destroyed by arousing her husband's jealousy.   **Dorozantes:** a fanciful distant people who probably never existed except in the imagination of Propertius. The word does not appear in Harper's Latin Dictionary.   **Eurypylan:** from Eurypylus, king of Cos, according to legend.   **Isis' days:** Compare Elegy II, 28 *C* and Butler-Barber, p. 254.   **Iole, Amycle:** Cynthia's servants.

IV, 6. A poem in praise of Augustus and his naval victory at Actium, off the west coast of Greece, in 31 B.C. Cleopatra, who fought with Antony in this battle against Octavian (later Augustus), is commonly represented by the Latin poets as an evil siren (see Horace, *Odes* I, 37, and elsewhere); she was actually a very resourceful and able leader who succeeded in escaping safely from the battle with a fleet of sixty ships.   **Roman wreath:** clusters of ivy-berries, sacred to Bacchus, symbolic here of victory and its celebration. **Philetan clusters:** the laudatory elegiacs of Propertius, called Philetan from Philetus (more correctly, Philitas) of Cos, ranked by Quintilian as second only to Callimachus among Greek elegiac poets; see Butler-Barber, introduction, xlvi.   **Cyrenean:** refers to Callimachus of Cyrene.   **Phrygian:** Flutes were usually of Phrygian make; they are mentioned here with jars from which wine was poured in the sacrifices celebrating military triumphs. **Calliope:** the muse of epic poetry, appropriately mentioned in a poem of praise for national triumph, although the departmentalization of the Muses as presiding over special forms of art and literature is not yet an accepted convention in the Augustan period.   **Quirinus:** a name given to Romulus after his death and now used of Augustus as the second founder of Rome. **Nereus:** a god of the sea.   *princeps:* a modest title in comparison with *rex,* king, a term which aroused hate and fear in the Romans with its implications of absolute power during the Republic.   **Centaurian:** This

refers to the Centaurs, creatures half-man, half-horse.   **Triton:** a sea-god.
Jugurtha: the Numidian chief led in triumph at Rome by Marius after his
capture in 106 B.C.   **Sygambri:** a German tribe on the right bank of
the lower Rhine.   **Meroe:** a reference to the story of Andromeda,
daughter of Cepheus, king of Ethiopia. The Ethiopians were beaten by the
Romans in 22 B.C.   **Parthian treaty:** by which the Roman ("Remus")
standards captured from Crassus in his defeat in 53 B.C. at Carrhae were
returned: a diplomatic victory for Augustus; see his will, the *Monumentum
Ancyranum,* paragraph 29.

IV, 7. Propertius dreams of Cynthia, dead. The poem has been translated also by Robert Lowell in *Lord Weary's Castle,* 1947, although incom-
pletely; he keeps what is essential, however: the reproaches of Cynthia's
ghost, her accusation of poisoning, and her pleading for her slaves. F. L.
Lucas also has a version in imitation of the elegiac distich in *The London
Mercury* 24 (1931), 392–394; it omits the mythological decoration of
lines 55–70.   **broken tile:** may have been used to prop her head on the
bier or might have fallen on her head: Butler-Barber, p. 361.   **Notus:**
the south wind.   **Chloris:** the girl who has replaced Cynthia in the
affections of Propertius and who is accused of poisoning Cynthia with the
help of Nomas, the slave of Propertius.   **Petale, Lalage, Parthenie,
Latris:** Cynthia's maids.

IV, 8. Propertius' best attempt at humor: the story of his ill-fated effort
to seek comfort for Cynthia's unfaithfulness in the arms of *two* other girls.
aqueous: because it was well supplied with water by at least three aque-
ducts.   **Juno, her excuse:** Cynthia has driven to Lanuvium, southeast of
Rome, under the pretext of worshipping Juno at the famous shrine there;
she has actually gone to keep an appointment with one of Propertius' rivals,
a man destined (so Propertius thinks and hopes) to end as a gladiator,
lowest of the low, in an occupation sought only by those in extreme straits.
Byblis: This is Palmer's emendation for *Phyllis* (mss.), which Butler-
Barber consider inappropriate because she is supposed to be a guest. But
what would be more natural for Phyllis, a frequenter of cabarets and probably an entertainer in them, than to snatch a castanet and go into her favorite routine between courses?   **Venus-numbers:** four dice were used by
the Romans, marked on four sides only: I, III, IV, VI (the highest, or
Venus-throw); the lowest was I, I, I, I ("snake-eyes" for the modern crap-
shooter).

IV, 9. An etiological myth about the foundation of the Ara Maxima by
Hercules.   **Amphitryoniades:** Hercules, as the son of Alcmene, wife of
Amphitryon, by Jupiter; see Plautus, *Amphitryo,* and its thirty-eight imitations down to the one by Jean Giraudoux.   **Erythea:** a legendary island
in the West, from which Hercules drove off the cattle of Geryon.   **Cacus:**
Hercules' host; he lived on the Aventine hill at Rome; also a primitive fire-
god with three heads. Compare the description of the fight between Her-

cules and Cacus in Vergil, *Aeneid* VIII, 185–279.   **Bona Dea:** the Good
Goddess, of the women only.   **Alcides:** a patronymic; Hercules was the
grandson of Alceus.   **Sidonian robe:** Hercules, dressed as a woman,
served Omphale, queen of Lydia, in her household in expiation of the
murder of his friend Iphitus; the queen, meanwhile, wore the lion-skin of
Hercules.

IV, 10. Another etiological myth. Propertius gives the etymology of
Feretrius as from *fero,* bear, or from *ferio,* strike.   **Romulus:** descendant
of Aeneas, first of the seven kings of Rome.   **Acron:** Sabine king of
Caenina, near Rome; he attacked Rome because of the Roman rape of the
Sabine women.   **M. Claudius Marcellus:** He defeated the Insubres, a
tribe of Cis-Alpine Gauls, at Clastidium in 222 B.C.

IV, 11. This noble elegy, the greatest work of Propertius, was written in
16 B.C. and is a funeral oration spoken by Cornelia, the dead lady herself.
She was descended on her father's side from Scipio Africanus, the younger,
who conquered Carthage, and on her mother's side from the Libones, a clan
of Roman aristocrats. She addresses first the judges of the dead and then her
family. Her husband was Lucius Aemilius Paullus Lepidus, whose sons had
his last two names.   **Charon:** the ferry-boatman of the river Styx.
Sisyphus, Ixion, Tantalus: famous rebels against the gods, who are punished in Hades.   **Danaids:** For killing their husbands on the wedding
night the daughters of Danaus, with one exception, were compelled to pour
water into a broken vase (not a sieve; this, like the lantern of Diogenes, is
merely a vulgar error).   **Cybele:** the great mother of the gods worshipped
in Asia. See Catullus 63.   **Claudia:** Claudia Quinta, after praying, pulled
the ship bearing the image of Cybele off the shallows when it ran aground
in the Tiber river in 205 B.C. as it was being transported to Rome. Claudia's
own statue was later placed in the temple of the goddess.   **You, whose
linen raiment:** Aemilia, a Vestal virgin of thirty years' service, rekindled
Vesta's fire by placing her robe in the ashes, also after making a prayer. She
and Claudia are outstanding examples of Roman chastity.   **Lepidus,
Paullus:** the sons of Cornelia.   **censorship:** Her daughter's virtue was
worthy of a censor's daughter.

It may be useful to discuss here the *Homage to Propertius,* by Ezra Pound,
a series of poems which has brought Propertius to the attention of many
readers who do not know him in Latin and has done more than any other
single work to rescue Propertius from undeserved neglect. The controversy
over the *Homage* has reached formidable proportions: a short bibliography
includes the various printings in *Quia Pauper Amavi* (1919, *Personae*
(1926) and its re-issues in 1934 and 1947 by Faber and Faber and New
Directions; articles or studies by W. G. Hale, in *Poetry: a Magazine of
Verse* 14 (1919), 52–55; T. S. Eliot, *Selected Poems of Ezra Pound*
(1933), xxiii, and in *Poetry* 68 (1946), 328, 335, 337; R. P. Blackmur,

The Double Agent (1935), 37–44, and in *Poetry* 68 (1946), 340–341;
James Laughlin, "Ezra Pound's Propertius," *Sewanee Review* 46 (1938),
480–491; and Lawrence Richardson, "Ezra Pound's Homage to Propertius,"
Yale Poetry Review (1947) No. 6, pp. 21–29.

The controversy is neatly summed up by T. S. Eliot in a much-needed
remark about Pound's erudition: "Pound's 'erudition' has been both exaggerated and irrelevantly underestimated: for it has been judged chiefly by
scholars who did not understand poetry, and by poets who have had little
scholarship." (*Poetry* 68, 337). Speaking of the *Homage* itself he says
(p. 335): "I am aware of the censure of those who have treated it as a
translation; and if it is treated as a translation, they are of course right."
Further, (introduction to *Selected Poems of Ezra Pound,* xxiii): "If the
uninstructed reader is not a classical scholar, he will make nothing of it; if
he be a classical scholar, he will wonder why this does not conform to his
notions of what a translation should be. It is not a translation, it is a paraphrase, or still more truly (for the instructed) a *persona.* It is also a criticism of Propertius, a criticism which in a most interesting way insists upon
an element of humor, of irony and mockery, in Propertius, which Mackail
and other interpreters have missed." ... "the poem ... would give difficulty
to many readers: because it is not enough a 'translation,' and because it is,
on the other hand, too much a 'translation' to be intelligible to any but the
accomplished student of Pound's poetry."

Blackmur's analysis of the *Homage* (*Poetry* 68, 341) throws some light
on Pound's method of writing poetry "suggested" by Propertius: "Pound
used what he could catch of the mood in Propertius' mind — not the mode
of his language — and responded to it with what he could make out of the
best current mood and mode of his own time; that is why his versions of
Propertius are called an Homage, and that is why they seem written in a
mode of language (the prose tradition combined with composition in the
musical phrase) which is an addition to the language itself."

Laughlin's detailed study points out the shortcomings of the *Homage* as
translation in the conventional sense, emphasizes the special technique
Pound uses, and defines the exact method employed as follows: "Pound
uses Propertius' ideas as a springboard for his own. He uses the Latin
language as a catalyst for his own. There are spots where he seems only to
have glanced at the texture of a word, ignoring its dictionary meaning, to
form his version. It has occurred to me that 'Variations on themes of
Propertius' would be a more accurate title than 'Homage to Propertius'"
(p. 483). He too says: "Pound's 'Propertius' ... cannot be called a translation. He would not call it that himself." Finally, Laughlin makes clear
that the *persona* Eliot mentions here is quite the reverse of all of Pound's
other *personae,* Provençal or Chinese; Propertius speaks through the mask
of Pound himself.

Richardson, a Latinist himself, further explains the problem by a close
comparison with the Latin text: "Often Pound has omitted any hint of the
ordinary translation and substituted into his text the garbled collage of sense

possible if one takes only a few words and fits them on to what has gone before. It is this that has misled readers into thinking that Pound did not grasp the matter of Propertius; they have rigid ideas of translation and are ready to understand a variety of possibilities in the recasting of Latin thought into English verse, but they do not understand the value of possibilities that appear in the Latin itself as it strikes the eye, imagination, and wit. These reactions are the very stuff with which Pound works to transmit the flavor and intricacy of Propertius."

Of the 92 elegies Pound has used only 14, sometimes mingling parts of different elegies in the same selection. The list follows: III, 1 (and 2), 3, 16, 6, II, 10 (to line 20, followed by II, 1, to line 50), I, 13 *A* (conflated with III, 5, line 16, and 4, lines 1–6), II, 15, 28 (done as two, with division at *Deficiunt*), 29 (and 29 *A*), 30 (the opening imitates I, 15, and the end II, 24), 34. Meyerstein in his translation refers to Yeats' "A Thought from Propertius" (i. e., II, 2, 7–10) in *The Wild Swans at Coole* (1919).

TIBULLUS. *Pages 218–232.*

The text of his poems by Kirby Flower Smith, American Book Co., 1913, contains also the works of Sulpicia attributed to Tibullus and the works of Sulpicia herself, with very full notes and an introduction which includes a study of the Latin elegy and a page of excellent criticism on Propertius (p. 67). Smith's erudition in classical Latin elegy was made richer by his interest in Renaissance Latin pastoral, of which his colleague, W. P. Mustard, was a master.

I, 1. In the concluding lines Tibullus turns to Messalla and Delia, his sweetheart. **Ceres:** goddess of the harvest. **Priapus:** the grotesque garden-god. **Lares:** the household gods of whom Tibullus is so fond and to whose worship he lends a haunting beauty; see Pater's meditative first pages of *Marius the Epicurean.* **Pales:** an old pastoral divinity who was worshipped with libations of milk. Her birthday, April 21, was regarded as the birthday of Rome and celebrated as a festival. She is not mentioned by the translator, but the lustration of the land made in connection with her worship is maintained in the word "Bounds."

I, 9. The last poem of a group whose central figure is the boy Marathus, with whom Tibullus, in his curious bisexual manner, is in love. Marathus has begun an affair with a repulsive old man, for gain, and Tibullus scolds him. The irony of the situation lies in the fact that Marathus himself is in love with a girl, thus providing Tibullus with a second rival.

I, 10. Lines 53–64 are omitted. This is perhaps the best-known of all ancient protests against war, although Tibullus, of course, is afraid only for his own skin.

II, 1. This elegy celebrates a country festival of purification, either the Ambarvalia in May or the Feriae Sementivae in January. **Messalla:** Marcus Valerius Messalla Corvinus (64 B.C.–A.D. 8), Tibullus' lifelong friend and patron and leader of a literary circle. Lines 32–36 are omitted. For lines 47–48, *rura ferunt . . . ,* here translated "The fields bore corn . . . ," compare E. A. Robinson's sonnet, "The Sheaves": "As if a thousand girls with golden hair/ Might rise from where they slept and go away." **Desire:** Cupid. Lines 72–82 are omitted except for "in the dark" (*tenebris,* 76).

II, 4. In K. F. Smith's words, "Tibullus describes and deplores his misery as a lover of Nemesis." She is the second of his female loves. **sun-red seas:** actually the Red Sea is meant.

II, 6. Macer is probably the poet Aemilius Macer of Verona, a friend of Tibullus. He died in Asia in 16 B.C., perhaps at the end of this very campaign. Hope vs. Nemesis was a favorite literary conflict. **That bawd:** the go-between or *lena,* against whom Tibullus turns his anger as the supposed cause of the rift with Nemesis.

DOMITIUS MARSUS. *Page 233.*

Text in K. F. Smith, *The Elegies of Albius Tibullus* (1913), p. 173.

SULPICIA AND TIBULLUS. *Pages 234–240.*

Sulpicia is one of two Roman poetesses of the same name whose works have survived. The elegies of Tibullus are collected in two books; the third and fourth books, so divided by fifteenth-century Italian scholars, consist of poems attributed to him or written by Sulpicia; see Smith's introduction, pp. 77–87, and his notes (pp. 487–516) on Sulpicia. The twelve poems translated here by Hubert Creekmore tell the love-story of Sulpicia, a ward of Messalla and probably his niece, and Cerinthus, a rather tongue-tied youth whom she seems to have rushed off his feet.

The Matronalia. This was the women's counterpart of the Saturnalia, celebrated on the first of March in holiday dress and with the giving of gifts. **Vertumnus:** As divinity of gardens and shifting seasons he could assume bewitching forms at will. He was the husband of Pomona, who presided over fruit trees. **Pierides:** the Muses.

The arrangement of these poems is discussed in Smith, pp. 81–82. In the order followed by Jack Lindsay in his translation (*I Am a Roman,* pp.

150–151) these brief poems tell a vivid story as follows: 1) Sulpicia glories in having at last won Cerinthus to her. 2) She pouts because Messalla, ignorant of her wish to see Cerinthus on her birthday, has arranged a day in the country for her. 3) The country visit, to her great relief, is called off. 4) She writes in fury to inform Cerinthus that gossip about his unfaithfulness has reached her; the poem is full of bitter feminine irony. 5) Ill, she writes an appealing note to Cerinthus. 6) A brief apology for her abrupt departure the evening before. Elsewhere in Latin poetry only Catullus and Propertius give us this sort of immediate, surface, personal passion in their poetry.

SULPICIA II. *Page 241*

Only lines 20–34 of the satire are translated here. The poem was first printed in an edition of Ausonius by Ugoletus in 1496, and appears in the Loeb Ausonius, translated by H. G. Evelyn-White, who calls it a school exercise of the fourth century A.D. (Vol. I, p. 271). R. Peiper also prints it in his edition of Ausonius, and Buecheler in his edition of Juvenal, 4th ed., 1910. Besides this satire, Sulpicia left a brief and very candid fragment of verse addressed to her husband Calenus (W. Baehrens, *Fragmenta Poetarum Romanorum*, p. 370). She is mentioned by Martial in X, 35, 38. The references to Calenus in both of her poems, the satire and the fragment, as well as those by Martial, clearly identify Sulpicia with these writings. As we know from Tacitus, the age of Domitian was well worthy of satire. **Father's voice:** Jupiter. The last line in the satire is from Vergil, *Aeneid* I, 279.

CARMINA EPIGRAPHICA. *Pages 242–244.*

Latin text in *Anthologia Latina,* II, 1, Carmina Latina Epigraphica, edited by Franz Buecheler (Leipzig, 1921); II, 2 (Leipzig, 1897).

PERSIUS. *Pages 245–256*

Choliambs. The poem hangs on a number of disparaging references to symbols of poetic inspiration. The "Nag's spring" is the spring Hippocrene on Mt. Helicon, reputed to have been struck from the rock by the foot of Pegasus ("Pegasean streams") and claimed by many poets as the source of their art. Mt. Parnassus (line 3) was used in a similar way by the Roman poet Ennius, among others, who located his dream-vision of Homer on this mountain. Pirene was another spring, on the acropolis of Corinth, also connected with Pegasus and sacred to the Muses ("Helicon's girls").

Satire I. **Line 1:** The line is quoted from the first book of Lucilius, the originator of Roman satire, who lived in the second century B.C.   **4–5:** Persius satirizes the captious nobility of Rome as Trojans, since they liked to trace their lineage back to Aeneas and his company (cf. line 62). Polydamas is mentioned in the *Iliad* as a carping critic. Attius Labeo, mentioned also at line 60, was a contemporary poet who catered to noble tastes by making a literal translation of the *Iliad* into Latin.   **40, Phyllises, Hypsipyles:** subjects of romantic tragedy and love-elegy; types of pathos. **60, 62:** See lines 4–5 and note.   **71, Janus:** the god of gateways, represented with two faces.   **78–81:** The first metaphor is from cabinet-work, where a join in the wood was tested by running the thumbnail across it. The second is from carpentry, where a chalked string was stretched and snapped against a board to mark a straight line.   **90–94:** This is the legend of "Cincinnatus at the plow." In the fifth century B.C., according to the story, T. Quinctius Cincinnatus was summoned from retirement on his farm to become military dictator at a time of crisis and defeat.   **96–98, Accius, Pacuvius:** Roman writers of tragedy in the second century B.C.; they were considered old-fashioned and out of date, like the legend of Cincinnatus, by the literati of Persius' time. Line 98 is quoted from the *Antiope,* a tragedy of Pacuvius.   **113–114:** Compare Satire VI, line 43 and note. **122, Arms and the man . . . ?** Persius' interlocutor quotes the beginning of Vergil's *Aeneid,* in order to dismiss it as antique and overblown.   **145, Lupus, Mucius:** contemporaries of Lucilius and butts of his satire. **150–152:** Persius refers to one of the fables about Midas. He grew asses' ears, but managed to conceal them from everyone except, naturally, his barber. The barber found that keeping the secret on pain of death eventually became oppressive, so dug a ditch, whispered it in, and filled up the hole. But reeds grew on the spot, and sang the story whenever the wind moved over them.   **155–156, Cratinus, Eupolis, Aristophanes:** the three principal writers of the Old Comedy at Athens (fifth century B.C.), a style marked by complete freedom of speech and strong personal attacks. **160, Greek shoes:** as a distinctive part of the national dress, would be marked with scorn by parochial Romans.   **162:** Persius refers to a petty provincial magistrate, one of whose jobs would be the inspection of weights and measures. Compare Juvenal, p. 291, lines 120–122.   **169, Callirhoe:** probably the title of a popular contemporary play.

Satire III. **Line 1:** The scene is a student's rooms after a night of heavy drinking. Persius, in the character of a fellow-student paying an unwelcome early visit, speaks first.   **26, wheel:** the potter's wheel, on which clay takes form.   **31, the Tuscan stem:** Tracing ancestry to the Etruscans was fashionable among the Roman nobility.   **32, Parade before the censor:** One of the ceremonies of the census was a parade by the equestrian class, or knights, of Rome before the censor. This class included most of the wealthier Romans.   **45–46:** Persius refers to Phalaris, tyrant of Agrigentum in Sicily during the sixth century B.C., who roasted his victims alive inside a brazen bull.   **47, the sword:** of Damocles.   **54–55:** This was a typical exercise in rhetoric assigned to schoolboys. They were required to provide an exhortation to some historical figure (in this case the younger Cato) at a critical moment in his career. **66, Painted Porch:** the symbol and home of the Stoic school of philosophy. The Porch, or Stoa, was in Athens, and was decorated with pictures of the Athenian victory over the Persians (Medes) at Marathon. **68, the Samian's parable, Y:** Pythagoras of Samos used the parable of the letter Y to indicate the choice of the good and evil ways of life. **81, Craterus:** a famous physician. **97–98:** The ignorant centurion picks two well-known names of philosophers, Arcesilas (third century B.C.) and Solon (sixth century B.C.), whose actual doctrines and lives are completely irrelevant to his description of them. **102–104:** The statement is Epicurean; the "invalid" is Epicurus, who was popularly supposed to be afflicted with ill-health. **130, Caps head:** The cap was assumed by a freed slave to symbolize his new condition. Slaves were often freed by their master's testament. **144:** Orestes was the prototype of the madman.

Satire VI. **Line 2, Caesius Bassus:** a lyric poet and friend of Persius. **10–13:** The Gulf of Luna (now the Gulf of Spezia) is located at the eastern end of the Italian Riviera. The line is quoted from the prologue to the epic Annals, by Quintus Ennius, the first major poet of Rome (second century B.C.). In Ennius' time Luna marked the limits of Roman Italy. In the earlier part of the prologue, Ennius claimed a Pythagorean transmigration of souls from Homer to himself, including one incarnation as a peacock. **35, Bruttium:** the lands in the heel of Italy. **43:** It was the custom of shipwrecked sailors to carry a painting of their disaster through the streets, to make their begging more effective. Cf. Satire I, lines 113–114. **59–71:** Caligula celebrated a fake "triumph" over the German and Breton tribes. **80, Child of earth:** contemptuous term for a man who could not trace his ancestry. **108–114:** Translator's Note: — While these lines are not divided from the rest of the poem in the manuscripts and are obviously by Persius, I do not believe that they are part of the Sixth Satire. They have nothing to do with the theme of the poem, and may have been added from a draft for another satire to give the appearance of completion to a work which he left unfinished at his death. (All notes on Persius are by the translator.)

LUCAN. *Pages 257–258.*

The passage translated describes the pathetic return of Marcia to her first husband, Cato the Younger, after having been transferred by him to his friend Hortensius. This is one of the few quiet interludes in the tumultuous pages of Lucan's melodramatic epic; it is also an epitome of the Stoic way of life in its most austere form.

PETRONIUS. *Pages 259–263.*

For the texts see F. Buecheler's third edition, 1882; Buecheler-Heraeus, 6th edition, 1922; E. Baehrens, *Poetae Latini Minores,* rev. by W. Morel and F. Vollmer, 1911–35; or E. T. Sage, The Century Co., 1929. Some of the texts are also to be found in A. Riese, *Anthologia Latina,* II, thus: I, Riese, 2, 714; II, Riese, 2, 674; III, Buecheler, 39 B; IV, Baehrens, 4, 100, or Riese, 2, 702; V, Sage, 79, 8; VI, Baehrens 4, 99; VII, Sage, 123; VIII, Sage, 144. Edmund Wilson has a fine version of VIII in his book *Poets, Farewell!,* 1929.

MARTIAL. *Pages 264–274.*

All versions signed T. W. M., G. I. C., or W. F. Gosling are from the pages of *Greece and Rome,* I–IV (1931–35) and IX, X (1939–41). Robert Schnorr, the young German poet, wrote his versions while a student in my class in the University of Kansas. The selections by Robert Louis Stevenson are from his *Complete Poems,* published by Charles Scribner's Sons. My own two are from Hubert Creekmore, ed., *A Little Treasury of World Poetry* (Scribner's, 1952).

JUVENAL. *Pages 275–298.*

Satire I. **Line 12, Fronto:** a rich patron of the reciting poets who lent his house for their performances.   **17, advice to Sulla:** i.e., in his school themes and speeches.   **22, Lucilius:** the early Roman satirist, who set the tone for satire and wrote some of the best in Latin.   **46, Lyons:** where Caligula severely punished those who were defeated in an oratorical contest. **53, law suit:** against an extorting governor, whose conviction might bring no damages to the province which had him prosecuted at Rome — by a jury of his own class.   **54, Horace:** who also wrote satires.   **65, Automedon:** the charioteer of Achilles.   **86, Cluvienus:** an obscure and presumably bad poet.   **158, Mucius:** possibly part of a quotation from Lucilius in an attack against P. Mucius Scaevola.   **158, Tigellinus:** the vicious favorite and right-hand man of Nero.

Satire III. **Line 1, old friend:** Umbricius, who is introduced as the speaker.   **2, Cumae:** the home of the Sibyl, the famous witch and fortune-teller, in a cave near the bay of Naples.   **4, Baiae:** a summer resort near Cape Misenum, south of Cumae.   **5, Prochyta:** a desolate island near Cape Misenum;   **Subura:** the Forty-second Street of ancient Rome, crowded and noisy, running toward the Porta Tiburtina from the Argiletum near the Forum.   **11, dripping gate:** from the leaking of an aqueduct nearby.   **12, Numa:** the second king of Rome, whom Livy describes as establishing the Roman religion; he used to receive advice from the nymph Egeria at night.   **24, Daedalus:** After his flight from Crete, during which his son Icarus fell into the sea because the sun's heat melted the wings his father had made of wax and feathers, Daedalus dedicated his wings in the temple he built for Apollo at Cumae; see Vergil, *Aeneid* VI, 20–30.   **26, Lachesis:** the one of the three Fates who measured the thread of a man's life.   **28, Artorius, Catulus:** The names merely represent the Romans whom Umbricius is leaving behind.   **30, rivers, ports:** probably contracts to collect river and harbor tolls.   **35, thumbs of the mob:** Whether the crowd in the amphitheater turned their thumbs down or to their breasts as a signal for stabbing the fallen gladiator is debated by Mayor in his commentary on Juvenal I, 186, and by E. Post, *American Journal of Philology* 13 (1892), 213–225.   **52, Verres:** the grafting propraetor of Sicily prosecuted by Cicero, used here as an example of a corrupt governor.   **68, Sicyon, Amydon,** etc.: Greek cities or islands.   **70, willows:** the Viminal hill.   **73, Isaeus:** an Assyrian rhetorician.   **122, Albina, Modia:** rich, childless women preyed upon by fortune-hunters. **128, goddess of Ida:** the great mother goddess brought from Pessinus in Asia to Rome.   **129, Minerva:** Her image, the Palladium, was saved by Lucius Caecilius Metellus from the burning temple of Vesta in 241 B.C. **148, Otho:** Lucius Roscius Otho in 67 B.C. sponsored a law by which the first fourteen rows of seats in the theater next to the orchestra seats reserved for senators were reserved for knights; the law was obviously most unpopular and gradually fell into disuse.   **151, Aediles:** various city commissioners.   **187, Ucalegon:** a proverbial word for one's nearest neighbor; see Vergil, *Aeneid* II, 312, where Ucalegon's house burns in Troy.   **238, Corbulo:** some well-known strong man.   **300, Aquinum:** Juvenal's birthplace, on the Via Lata in southeastern Latium.

Satire VI. A selection from the famous satire on women.

Satire X. Line 32, **wise men:** one was Democritus of Abdera, the other Heraclitus of Ephesus.   **56, Meat Head Land:** Abdera, in Thrace, the home of Democritus, was known for its stupid people.   **82, Capri:** In his last years the emperor Tiberius retired here, where the ruins of his palace can be seen on the east end of the island.   **86, Sejanus:** the favorite of Tiberius, praetorian prefect, came of an equestrian family from Volsinii; when his plot against Tiberius was discovered in 31 B.C. he paid with his life for his treachery.   **97, Ajax:** stands for Tiberius.   **131, who led the conquered Romans:** Julius Caesar.   **134, Ceres' son-in-law:** Pluto.   **194, Prusias:** king of Bithynia, gave refuge to Hannibal after the battle of Zama.   **215, Sostratus:** some unknown poet.   **298, king of Pylos:** Nestor.   **306, Antilochus:** Nestor's son.   **311, Laertes:** father of Odysseus.   **314–315, Cassandra, Polyxena:** daughters of Priam.   **328, king of Pontus:** Mithridates;   **Croesus:** the proverbially rich king of Lydia.   **331, Marius:** the Roman general who fought Jugurtha and the German tribes.   **343, Lentulus, Cethegus:** associates of Catiline in his conspiracy.   **351, 353, Lucretia, Verginia:** noble Roman ladies who came to tragic ends, in earlier Roman history.   **385, Oppia, Catulla:** noble ladies of Juvenal's day.   **388–389, Hippolytus, Bellerophon:** famous Greek young men who sought to preserve their chastity from Phaedra and Stheneboea.   **395, him whom Caesar's wife:** C. Silius, loved by Messalina, wife of Claudius (Tacitus, *Annals* 11. 12 and 26 ff.)

SENECA.   *Pages 299–303.*

Thyestes. A chorus from the play of that name. The glyconic meter with four beats to the line is imitated in the translation.

Hercules Furens and *Medea.* Selections from the choruses of Elizabethan translations of these plays; see the *Tudor Translations,* with an introduction by T. S. Eliot, reprinted in his *Selected Essays, 1917–1932,* New York, 1932.

HADRIAN.   *Page 305.*

Text in J. W. and A. M. Duff, *Minor Latin Poets,* Loeb Classical Library, 1934.

AULUS GELLIUS.   *Page 306.*

The translation was published in *The Criterion* (London), Vol. 2 (1924) and also appears in the *Oxford Book of Medieval Latin Verse.*

SULPICIUS LUPERCUS SERVASIUS, JR.   *Page 307.*

Text in Duff, *Minor Latin Poets,* p. 576. Baehrens also prints a text in *Poetae Latini Minores,* IV (1882), 107–108, and shows (p. 39) that the language of Sulpicius is not indicative of African origin. Translation from Kenneth Rexroth, *The Phoenix and the Tortoise;* the translator condenses, and translates only the second and third stanzas of the poem.

THE VIGIL OF VENUS. *Pages 308–312.*

The text is elaborately printed by Cecil Clementi, 3d ed., Oxford, 1936. A useful short text is the Oxford Plain Text, 1911, with brief introduction. See D. S. Robertson, "The Date and Occasion of the Pervigilium Veneris," *Classical Review* 52 (1938), 109–112; E. K. Rand, "Spirit and Plan of the Pervigilium Veneris," *Trans. and Proc. of the Amer. Phil. Assoc.* 65 (1934), 1–12. The meter is trochaic octameter catalectic (one syllable is missing at the end of each line) and strictly quantitative; compare Tennyson, "Locksley Hall," for a parallel in accentual verse. The poem has been frequently translated: by Dr. Thomas Parnell (1679–1718); Thomas Stanley; J. W. Mackail; Sir Arthur Quiller-Couch; Miriam Allen deFord; Jack Lindsay (in *Song of a Falling World,* 1947); Richard Aldington (in John Arlott, *First Time in America,* 1948); and Allen Tate (first printed by The Cummington Press in 1943 and reprinted in *Collected Poems, 1922–1947,* 1948 — this printing has a prose note, pp. 175–183). The stanza-numbers in parentheses show the order followed by J. W. Mackail in his edition; Mr. Tate has occasionally shifted the order.

The refrain, "Cras amet qui numquam amavit quique amavit cras amet," has a haunting rhythm hard to translate; here are a few versions:

> Love he to-morrow, who loved never;
> To-morrow, who hath loved, persever. (Stanley)

> Let those love now, who never loved before;
> Let those who always loved now love the more. (Parnell)

> Who never loved shall love tomorrow, tomorrow lovers too shall love. (deFord)

> Love for loveless ones tomorrow, love for all the lovers too. (Jack Lindsay)

> Let the loveless love tomorrow, let the lovers love once more. (R. Aldington)

AUSONIUS. *Pages 313–317.*

Texts in Loeb Classical Library, by H. G. Evelyn-White, 1919–21. The epitaph on Hector is translated in G. Rostrevor Hamilton, *The Latin Portrait,* The Nonesuch Press, London, 1929.

PAULINUS OF NOLA. *Pages 318–319.*

Text in Helen Waddell, *Mediaeval Latin Lyrics,* 1929, or in Hartel *Corpus Scriptorum Ecclesiasticorum Latinorum* 30, Vienna, 1894.

AVIANUS. *Pages 320–321.*

Text in Duff, *Minor Latin Poets.*

FLAVIUS VOPISCUS. *Page 323.*

From the life of Aurelian. The translation is printed in *Four Beasts in One,* from *Tales of the Grotesque and the Arabesque: The Works,* ed. E. C. Stedman and G. E. Woodberry, IV (1927), 98. Text in David Magie, *The Scriptores Historiae Augustae,* III, Loeb Classical Library, 1932.

ST. AMBROSE. *Pages 324–325.*

Text in J. P. Migne, *Patrologia Latina* 16.1409–1412. See 17.1171–1222 for all of his hymns. An unsigned translation of the twelve most generally regarded as genuine, with the Latin text, appears in the *British Magazine* 18 (1840), 388–391; 19 (1841), 29–32, 141–143.

PRUDENTIUS. *Pages 326–328.*

Text: Cathemerinon, preface, lines 1–27, ed. Dressel, 1860. Blackett's translations are printed in *Translations from the Greek of Saint Gregory Nazianzen* etc., The Latin Press, London, 1937, by Guido Morris and his assistants. Mr. Blackett was the British controller of finance at the Treasury and finance member for India; he died in 1935.

BOETHIUS. *Pages 329–330.*

Text in Loeb Classical Library Boethius, 1926.

VENANTIUS FORTUNATUS. *Pages 331–332.*

Text in Leo, *Monumenta Germaniae auct. antiq.* IV, 1–270.

OCTAVIANUS. *Page 333.*

Text in E. Baehrens, *Poetae Latini Minores,* IV, 256.

PAUL THE DEACON. *Page 336.*

Text in Karl Neff, *Die Gedichte des Paulus Diaconus;* Quellen und Untersuchungen zur lateinische Philologie des Mittelalters, herausgegeben von Ludwig Traube; Munich, C. H. Beck, 1908.

ST. PETER DAMIAN. *Pages 337–339.*

Text in Migne, PL 145.980, carmen 226; translation in *Life and Letters* II (1934–35).

HILDEBERT OF LE MANS. *Pages 340–341.*

The translation of *Oratio ad Dominum* was done by the eccentric friend of Edgar Allan Poe; it was published in at least four magazines and newspapers in April and May, 1853. This text is from the *Waverley Magazine,* May 28, 1853, Vol. 6, p. 340. I am once more indebted to Prof. T. O. Mabbott, of Hunter College, New York City, for calling the poem to my attention, and to Prof. S. Foster Damon and Miss Marion Brown, of the Brown University Library, for supplying bibliographical material and a photostat. See Prof. Damon's biography of Thomas Holley Chivers, New York, Harper, 1930. Text in Migne, PL 171.1411. My translation of the epitaph of Seneca was first published in my edition of Reginald of Canterbury, *Vita Sancti Malchi,* University of Illinois Press, 1942, p. 201. Text in Migne, PL 171.1446, also in Haase, *L. Annaei Senecae opera quae supersunt,* III (1865).

ABELARD. *Pages 342–343.*

In attributing this poem to Abelard, I follow P. S. Allen, *Medieval Latin Lyrics,* 1931, and George F. Whicher, *The Goliard Poets,* 1949. The text is found in the Carmina Burana (Benediktbeuern manuscript).

BERNARD OF CLAIRVAUX. *Pages 344–345.*

The translation is printed by permission of the Very Rev. M. C. D'Arcy, S. J. The text is from a hymn of two hundred lines, *De nomine Iesu,* in eight-syllable iambic meter. See F. J. E. Raby, *A History of Christian-Latin Poetry,* 1927, p. 329, on this attribution.

ST. THOMAS AQUINAS. *Pages 346–347.*

The translation is printed in Hopkins, *Poems,* 2d ed. by Robert Bridges, Oxford University Press, 1930.

THOMAS OF CELANO. *Pages 348–349.*

The translation appears in *The University Review* 4 (1935), 22–23, and the text in Raby, *op. cit.,* p. 448, with full discussion, pp. 443–452, and bibliography. See another version in Swinburne's *Posthumous Poems,* ed. E. Gosse and T. J. Wise, London, Heinemann, 1917, pp. 89–91, and T. B. Macaulay's paraphrase in his *Collected Works, Poems.*

BERNARD OF MORLAS. *Pages 350–351.*

Text in T. Wright, *The Anglo-Latin Satirical Poets of the Twelfth Century* (Rolls Series, II, London, 1872), pp. 18–19; Swinburne's loose paraphrase is printed in *Personal Recollections by His Cousin, Mrs. Disney Leith,* New York, G. P. Putnam, 1917, pp. 36–37.

CARMINA BURANA. *Pages 352–367.*

This large and well-known collection of medieval Latin poems and songs in Codex Latinus 4660, Munich, of the end of the thirteenth century, was called *Carmina Burana* by its first editor, J. A. Schmeller, in 1847, from the Benedictine monastery of Benediktbeuern, where the manuscript originally lay. "Songs from Benediktbeuern" would be a suitable translation. Schmeller's text is now out of date, but the new critical edition by A. Hilka and O. Schumann (Vol. I, 1930; vol. II, 1941) contains thus far only the satirical and the love poems. George F. Whicher's *The Goliard Poets,* 1949, gives vivid accounts of the tribe of Golias together with brilliant translations of their poetry.

Potatores exquisiti. Translation in *Life and Letters,* II (1934–35), 287–288.

Nobilis, precor. Translation in *Life and Letters,* II, 286–287.

Juliana. Translation in *The Goliard Poets,* 1949, from which all of Whicher's versions are taken: the Latin text is printed on opposite pages.

Vidi viridi. This is a first version, later printed in *The Nation* 167, Aug. 7, 1948, with two changes — "country" for "summer," and "silverage" for "mediaeval." The text can be found in Helen Waddell, *The Wandering Scholars,* Boston, 1927, p. 215. Her versions are printed in her *Mediaeval Latin Lyrics.* See also Hilka-Schumann, Vol. I, Text (1941) 69 in poem 84.

Gaudeamus igitur. This famous student song is translated in Symonds, *Wine, Women, and Song,* New York, Putnam, No. 60.

HUGO PRIMAS OF ORLEANS. *Pages 368–370.*

The Latin text of Hugo was edited by Wilhelm Meyer in the Göttinger Nachrichten, 1907. For his life, see Raby, *A History of Secular Latin Poetry in the Middle Ages,* Oxford University Press, 1934, II, 171–180; and Whicher, *The Goliard Poets,* pp. 74–75.

THE ARCHPOET OF COLOGNE. *Pages 371–374.*

Text in M. Manitius, *Die Gedichte des Archipoeta,* Munich, 1913; 2d ed., 1929. For the life of the Archpoet, see Whicher's excellent brief sketch in *The Goliard Poets,* pp. 102–103, and Raby, *op. cit.,* pp. 180–189.

Omnia tempus habent. A clever use of the feminine-rhyming leonine hexameters, reproduced skillfully by the translator.

The Confession of Bishop Golias. This poem, in the much-used Goliardic measure — a trochaic seven-syllable verse combined with one of six syllables — has a number of sly parodies of religious poetry and hymns as well as of the Bible. The translator omits stanzas 4, 7, 17, 18, 23, and 25. Text in Whicher (with a full translation) and in C. H. Beeson, *A Primer of Medieval Latin,* Chicago, Scott, Foresman, 1925.

WALTER OF CHATILLON. *Pages 375–376.*

Text in Karl Strecker, *Die Gedichte Walters von Chatillon,* 1. Die Lieder der handschrift 351 von St. Omer; Berlin, Weidmann, 1925, pp. 34–35 (No. 21, a companion-piece to No. 18).

LATIN POETS OF THE RENAISSANCE. *Pages 378–383.*

Translated by Richard Aldington, *Medallions,* Chatto and Windus, 1930; see his foreword, pp. 89–90. This book contains sixty poems by the Italian humanists of the fifteenth and sixteenth centuries. Their influence on the Pléiade in France and upon the lyric poets of Elizabethan England was considerable. Aldington's note tells us that Ben Jonson's *Underwoods* contains another translation of Amaltheo's epigram on the hourglass. He lists the following by way of bibliography on these poets: J. A. Symonds, *The Renaissance in Italy;* Ezra Pound, *The Spirit of Romance* (which contains a number of translations of these poets which are omitted in the far-from-complete *The Translations of Ezra Pound,* introd. Hugh Kenner, New Directions, n.d.), and A. Bonaventura, *Poesia neolatina in Italia.* He adds the anthologies of Gherus and Toscanus, the eleven-volume anthology published in Florence in the early eighteenth century, and separate editions of Sannazaro, Navagero, Flaminio, the Amalthei, Buonamico, Calcagnini, Pontano, and Fracastoro. Short biographies of these humanists, with other selections from their writings in both prose and verse, can be found in Florence A. Gragg, *Latin Writings of the Italian Humanists,* New York, Scribner's, 1927, a book now unfortunately out of print; it should have more ample notes and introduction if it is ever republished.

IANUS VITALIS PANORMITANUS. *Page 384.*

For an instance of the influence of the Italian humanist poets on the Pléiade, compare this poem with Joachim du Bellay's "Rome," translated by Ezra Pound, *Personae,* New Directions, 1947. A Spanish parallel by Francisco de Quevedo y Villegas (1580–1645) called "A Roma sepultada en sus ruinas" may be read in J. M. Cohen, *The Penguin Book of Spanish Verse,* 1956, p. 282.

POLITIAN. *Pages 386–388.*

I have translated some of Politian's Italian poems in my anthology, *Lyric Poetry of the Italian Renaissance,* Yale University Press, 1954, pp. 234–

249, where a brief biographical note may be found. The Latin text used is the Paris *Opera* of 1519.

GEORGE HERBERT. *Pages 393–395.*

Text in F. E. Hutchinson, *The Works of George Herbert,* Oxford University Press, 1941.

RICHARD CRASHAW. *Pages 396–398.*

Text by L. C. Martin, Oxford University Press, 1927.
ii. In asinum. **The former one:** Balaami Asinus (Balaam's ass; Num. xxii.22–31).

O DEUS, EGO AMO TE. *Page 399.*

A Latin hymn dating from 1676, found for the first time at the end of P. Francisco García's biography of St. Francis Xavier. The Latin text is printed by R. Foulché-Delbosc, "Le sonnet a Cristo Crucificado," *Revue Hispanique* 2 (1895), 130. He says, p. 138: "La seconde poésie latine *O Deus ! ego amo te* figure pour la première fois en 1676 à la fin de la biographie de Saint Francois Xavier du P. Francisco García. Quel est l'auteur de cette poésie ? Je l'ignore; que ce soit García ou tout autre, peu importe: ce qui semble probable, c'est qu'elle fut faite d'après le texte portugais de la cantilena envoyée des Indes quelques années auparavant par Filipucci." Foulché-Delbosc discusses the relationship of the Latin and Portuguese versions to the famous Spanish sonnet sometimes attributed to Santa Teresa de Jesús and printed in the *Oxford Book of Spanish Verse,* 161, as "A Cristo Crucificado, Anónimo":

> No me mueve, mi Dios, para quererte,
> el cielo que me tienes prometido,
> ni me mueve el infierno tan temido
> para dejar por eso de ofenderte.
> Tú me mueves, Señor; muéveme el verte
> clavado en esa cruz, y escarnecido;
> muéveme el ver tu cuerpo tan herido;
> muévenme tus afrentas, y tu muerte.
> Muéveme, al fin, tu amor, y en tal manera
> que, aunque no hubiera cielo, yo te amara,

y, aunque no hubiera infierno, te temiera.
No me tienes que dar por que te quiera;
pues aunque lo que espero no esperara,
lo mismo que te quiero te quisiera.

See further remarks on this poem in Hurtado-Palencia, *Historia de la literatura española,* 2d ed., 1925, pp. 461–463, and in my article "Gerard Manley Hopkins: Poeta menor de la edad mediavictoriana," *Universidad de la Habana* 6 (1941), 48–55. Alberto María Carreño, in *Joyas literarias del siglo xvii encontradas en México,* Mexico City, 1915, declared that his investigations in Mexican archives showed that the author of the sonnet was an Augustinian named Miguel de Guevara, prior in 1638 of the convent of his order at Santiago de Athatzithaquaro; nothing is known of the man except his grammar of the Matlatzinga language; the sonnet is written at the beginning of the manuscript in the archives of the Sociedad Mexicana de Geografía y Estadística.

Bibliography

Aldington, Richard. Latin Poets of the Renaissance, in *Medallions*. 1930.

Allen, P. S. *Medieval Latin Lyrics*. 1931.

Allen, P. S., and H. M. Jones. *The Romanesque Lyric*. 1928.

Atkins, J. W. H. *Literary Criticism in Antiquity*, II: Graeco-Roman. 1934.

Bailey, Cyril. *The Legacy of Rome*. 1924.

Bieber, Margarete. *The History of the Greek and Roman Theater*. 1939.

Bradner, L. *Musae Anglicanae: a History of Anglo-Latin Poetry, 1500–1925*. 1940.

Butler, H. E. *Post-Augustan Poetry* (Seneca to Juvenal). 1909.

Butler, H. E., and E. A. Barber, *The Elegies of Propertius*. 1933.

Campbell, A. Y. *Horace, a New Interpretation*. 1924.

Curtius, E. R. *European Literature and the Latin Middle Ages*. 1953.

D'Alton, J. F. *Roman Literary Theory and Criticism*. 1931.

Duckett, E. S. *Studies in Ennius*. 1915.

Duckworth, G. E. *The Nature of Roman Comedy: a Study in Popular Entertainment*. 1952.

Duff, J. W. *A Literary History of Rome from the Origins to the Close of the Golden Age*. 1953.

——— *A Literary History of Rome in the Silver Age*. 1927.

——— *Roman Satire*. 1936.

Duff, J. W. and A. M. *Minor Latin Poets*. Loeb Classical Library, 1934.

Durant, Will. *Caesar and Christ*. 1944.

Farrar, C. P., and A. P. Evans. *Bibliography of English Translations from Medieval Sources*. 1946.

Fraenkel, Hermann. *Ovid, a Poet Between Two Worlds*. 1945.

Frank, Tenney. *Catullus and Horace*. 1928.

——— *Life and Literature in the Roman Republic*. 1930.

Garrod, H. W. *The Oxford Book of Latin Verse*. 1912.

Gaselee, Stephen. *The Oxford Book of Medieval Latin Verse*. 1928.

Glover, T. R. *Life and Letters in the Fourth Century A.D.* 1901.

——— *Virgil*. Sixth ed.; 1930.

Graves, Robert. *The Greek Myths*. Penguin Books, 1954–55.

Greene, William C. *The Achievement of Rome*. 1933.

Hadas, Moses. *A History of Latin Literature*. 1952.

Hamilton, Edith. *The Roman Way*. 1932.

Hamilton, G. Rostrevor. *The Latin Portrait*. The Nonesuch Press, 1929.

Harrington, K. P. *The Roman Elegiac Poets*. 1914.

Harsh, Philip W. *A Handbook of Classical Drama*. 1944.

Harvey, Sir Paul. *The Oxford Companion to Classical Literature.* 1937.

Highet, Gilbert. *The Classical Tradition.* 1949.

———— *Juvenal the Satirist.* 1954.

———— *Poets in a Landscape.* 1957.

Knight, W. F. J. *Roman Vergil.* 1944.

Lindsay, Jack. *The Complete Poems of Catullus.* 1948.

———— *Song of a Falling World:* Culture During the Break-up of the Roman Empire, 350–600 A.D. 1948.

Mackail, J. W. *Latin Literature.* 1900.

Masson, John. *Lucretius: Epicurean and Poet.* 1907–1909.

Nairn, J. A. *Classical Handlist.* Sec. ed.; Blackwell, Oxford, 1939.

Oxford Classical Dictionary. 1949.

Raby, F. J. E. *A History of Christian Latin Poetry from the Beginnings to the Close of the Middle Ages.* 1927.

———— *A History of Secular Latin Poetry in the Middle Ages.* 1934.

Rose, H. J. *A Handbook of Latin Literature.* Sec. ed.; 1950.

Sandys, J. E. *A Companion to Latin Studies.* Third ed.; 1929.

Sellar, W. Y. *The Roman Poets of the Republic.* 1889.

———— *The Roman Poets of the Augustan Age.* 1892.

Smith, Kirby Flower. *The Elegies of Albius Tibullus.* 1913.

———— *Martial the Epigrammatist and Other Essays.* 1920.

Smith, Stanley Barney, and W. E. Leonard. *Lucretius, De Rerum Natura* (edition). 1942.

Stevens, C. E. *Sidonius Apollinaris and His Age.* 1933.

Summers, W. C. *The Silver Age of Latin Literature.* 1920.

Waddell, Helen. *Medieval Latin Lyrics.* 1929 (now in Penguin Classics).

Warmington, E. *Remains of Old Latin,* 4 vols. Loeb Classical Library, 1935–1938.

Wheeler, A. L. *Catullus and the Traditions of Ancient Poetry.* 1934.

Whicher, George F. *The Goliard Poets.* 1949.

Wilkinson, L. P. *Horace and His Lyric Poetry.* 1945.

———— *Ovid Recalled.* 1955.

Wright, F. A. *Three Roman Poets* (Plautus, Catullus, Ovid). 1938.

———— *The Love Poems of Johannes Secundus.* 1930.

Index of Poets and Sources

Index of Translators

PB 3889-1